Campbeltown Whisky: An Encyclopaedia

Also by Angus Martin:

The Ring-Net Fishermen
Kintyre: The Hidden Past
Kintyre Country Life
Fishing and Whaling
Sixteen Walks in South Kintyre
The North Herring Fishing
Herring Fishermen of Kintyre and Ayrshire
Fish and Fisherfolk
Memories of the Inans, Largybaan and Craigaig, 1980-85
An Historical and Genealogical Tour of Kilkerran Graveyard
Kintyre Birds
The Place-Names of the Parish of Campbeltown (with Duncan Colville)
The Place-Names of the Parish of Southend (with Duncan Colville)
Kilkerran Graveyard Revisited
Kintyre Families
Kintyre Instructions: The 5th Duke of Argyll's Instructions to his Kintyre Chamberlain, 1785-1805 (with Eric R. Cregeen)
By Hill and Shore in South Kintyre
Kintyre Places and Place-Names
A Summer in Kintyre: Memories and Reflections
Place-Names of the Parish of Kilcalmonell
Place-Names of the Parish of Killean and Kilchenzie
Place-Names of the Parish of Saddell and Skipness
Another Summer in Kintyre
A Third Summer in Kintyre
South Kintyre Dialect
Tarbert Dialect

Poetry

The Larch Plantation
The Song of the Quern
The Silent Hollow
Rosemary Clooney Crossing the Minch
Laggan Days: In Memory of George Campbell Hay
Haunted Landscapes: Poems in memory of Benjie
Paper Archipelagos
Always Boats and Men (with Mark I'Anson)
A Night of Islands: Selected Poems
West

Campbeltown Whisky: An Encyclopaedia

Angus Martin

The Grimsay Press

Published by:

The Grimsay Press
An imprint of Zeticula Ltd
Unit 13
196 Rose Street
Edinburgh, EH2 4AT
Scotland

http://www.thegrimsaypress.co.uk

First published in 2020

Text © Angus Martin 2020
Cover photograph:Cask-filling from spirit vat (1,973 gallon capacity) at Loch-head Distillery, Campbeltown, in 1897. The photograph was taken by A.S. Miller, distillery manager (p 182), and is reproduced by permission of Mrs Jeanette Brodie, Campbeltown © Mrs Jeanette Brodie, 2020

ISBN 978-1-84530-166-8

All rights reserved. No reproduction, copy or transmission of any part of this publication may be made without prior written permission.

Introduction

This book is the offspring of *Glen Scotia Distillery: A History*, a booklet published in May 2019 for sale at the distillery. The original concept was to focus on Glen Scotia and to sketch other distilleries and whisky-related industries into the background, but I wasn't far into the research when I realised that one booklet wouldn't hold all the material. I then started a second, and that, too, was insufficient to hold the quantity of material. This became the final form: a secondary project which turned into the main project.

The primary sources for this and the Glen Scotia booklet have been local newspapers, which I examined exhaustively, starting with the *Campbeltown Journal* (1851-55), continuing with the *Argyllshire Herald* (1855-1918), and ending with the *Campbeltown Courier* (1873-). Other neglected sources have also been drawn on: Scottish Census records, 1841-1901, Campbeltown Old Parish Registers and the grave monuments in Kilkerran Cemetery, for examples, were the main sources of the genealogical information in the text.

There will doubtless be an excess of genealogy for many readers, but since beginning this work I have never doubted the importance of exploring the inter-relatedness of the Campbeltown distilling families and how these relationships powered the remarkable flourishing of the local whisky industry in the mid to late 19th century. 'Remarkable', indeed, may be too moderate an adjective; 'astonishing' might better describe the transformation of a small West Highland fishing town into a veritable industrial centre.

'West Highland' Campbeltown may have been, but the whisky industry was largely driven not by native families, but by descendants of Lowland families which came to

South Kintyre in the 17th century at the encouragement of the Campbells of Argyll. These numerous Lowland families appear and reappear throughout this work, intermarrying time and again, but the three most prominent were Greenlees, Colvill(e) and Mitchell, and, of these, the Greenlees family was far and away the most successful. That is not to say that the contribution of native families was negligible — far from it, as this compilation establishes. Nor was intermarriage between Lowland and Highland stock a perfect taboo. By the 19th century, 'mixed marriages' had increased in number. For examples, the Gaelic-speaking Stewart sisters, Agnes, Isabella and Jean, each married into Lowland distilling families — Mitchell, Gilkinson and Andrew, respectively — and Elizabeth, the wife of David Colville #1, was a daughter of Duncan McCorkindale and Catherine McIsaac.

In the estimation of a journalist who visited Campbeltown in 1908, the founding families of the whisky industry were 'practically all plain men of humble rank ... possessing neither capital nor outstanding ability, but lucky enough to catch the tide at its flood and be borne on its crest to success and affluence'. That judgement appears to me to be both simplistic and distorted. These founders were, indeed, of 'humble rank', if one accepts that label in the context of a class-conscious society yet to face the shattering impact of a European war, but the acute business acumen of the principal families, in their home town and across the world, cannot be doubted, and the claim that they achieved their 'success and affluence' by being 'lucky', does not merit consideration.

By the mid-19th century, these distillers certainly enjoyed enhanced social status and mixed with the leading men of Kintyre — the landed gentry and the professional classes — and they were certainly conscious of that new-found status. In general, they were, by modern standards, sexist, racist, militaristic and utterly convinced of British superiority and the necessity of 'civilising' and Christianising benighted 'savages'.

Against that, however, must be set their record in the social transformation of Campbeltown for the benefit of all its inhabitants. Many of these distillery-owners served on the Town Council and other civic bodies, and were instrumental in effecting the improvements which we now take for granted as our human rights — such as sewage disposal, universal water supply, and health and education provision — and also such major civic projects as land reclamation to create public parks. Council service was entirely unpaid, but there was undoubtedly social status attached to membership, especially when elected to the highest offices, as Provost, Dean of Guild and Senior Bailie. Many distillers were also philanthropists, and their wives and daughters might be prominent in the numerous charitable institutions which flourished in town to help the sick, the aged and the poor, at a time when a government-funded welfare state, in any form, was unimaginable. It is easy nowadays to sneer at 'do-gooders', but in the 19th and early 20th century, when poverty and destitution were rife, their efforts did matter.

Of the Campbeltown whisky magnates of the late 19th and early 20th century, few are now remembered, and the vast majority of townsfolk would struggle to identify more than a few sites where distilleries once stood, let alone name them. The scale and economic significance of an industry which dominated the life of the town for almost a century has been virtually effaced from the collective consciousness, and, among the thousands of visitors from all over world who come each year to Campbeltown to tour the three existing distilleries and sample their products, there will be some who know more about the history of distilling in town than the great majority of the people who live here.

The distillery-owners, both those who succeeded in business and those who failed, are interesting enough, but they didn't make the whisky: their employees did. I have gathered as much information as I could about these workers and their families, though the potted biographies offered here represent just a fraction of the workmen whose practical skills have kept Campbeltown distilleries in production for more than two centuries.

I hope that this book, with its emphasis on people and places, will kindle an interest among local readers in the history of whisky-making in their town. I hope, too, that it will enable future writers on the Campbeltown whisky industry to avoid the lazily recycled mythology and misinformation which has been passed off as history in earlier publications.

As for whisky itself, it is wonderful stuff, but I prefer to drink it than to describe its manufacturing processes or analyse its mysterious chemistries. In any case, there are more than enough 'guides' already available, and I gave up, long ago, trying to interpret the adjectival fluff which passes for descriptive analysis of individual malts.

It goes without saying — but I'll say it — that a work of this size and complexity will suffer from errors and omissions, in which connection I can be contacted at 13 Saddell Street, Campbeltown, Argyll PA28 6DN or e-mail: judymartin733@btinternet.com

Should there be a reissue of this work, proven errors will be corrected and omissions inserted, but my work on the Campbeltown whisky industry is now done.

A note on the text: in order to reduce the cluttering incidences of 'q.v.', where the abbreviation should occur against a name conjoined with '#1', '#2', etc, these numbers stand alone as cross-references.

Angus Martin,
Campbeltown,
28 October 2019.

Acknowledgements

For assistance, I have to thank the ever-helpful and friendly staff of Campbeltown Library, where the bulk of the research was done; Murdo MacDonald, retired archivist at Argyll & Bute Archive in Lochgilphead, now managed by Live Argyll; Ms Jackie Davenport, present archivist at Lochgilphead; Iain McAlister, manager of Glen Scotia Distillery, for access to his collection of legal documents and other acts of assistance too numerous to specify; Mrs Jeanette Brodie, Campbeltown, for loaning photographs and other assistance; Catherine Barbour (*née* Young), Southend (Templeton families); Alan Colvill, Beith (Colvill family); Maria McIntyre (*née* McSporran), Campbeltown (McSporran family); Mrs Margaret Thomson (*née* McIntyre), Campbeltown (McIntyre family); the late John Mactaggart, Campbeltown (Mactaggart family); David Mayo, Campbeltown (Colvill family); Sadie Galbraith, Warrington (Muir family); and, last but not least, my wife Judy for her patient internet research on Scotland's People and her usual assistance with computer matters.

The north end of Lochend Street before and after construction of the H. E. Clifford-designed Loch-head warehouse in 1899. Photographs by A. S. Miller, courtesy of Mrs Jeanette Brodie.

Sources, with abbreviations

AH: *Argyllshire Herald*, weekly newspaper (1855-1918).

AP: Argyll Papers, Inveraray Castle archive.

Barnard: Alfred Barnard, *The Whisky Distilleries of the United Kingdom*, London 1887.

CC: *Campbeltown Courier*, weekly newspaper (1873-).

CJ: *Campbeltown Journal*, newspaper (1851-55).

Colville (1923): Duncan Colville, 'The Origin and Romance of the Distilling Industry in Campbeltown', delivered as a lecture to the Kintyre Antiquarian Society on 10/1/1923, and published 20/1 — 17/3/1923 in the *Campbeltown Courier*, but with specific reference to Colville's 'List of Distilleries in Campbeltown, Erected Since 1817', in issue 24/2/1923.

DR/4/8: the generic reference for the miscellaneous distillery records collected by the late Duncan Colville and held in the Live Argyll archive, Lochgilphead.

Glen: Ann Glen, 'The Making of Whisky in Campbeltown', in *The Campbeltown Book*, Campbeltown 2003, pp. 122-57, with particular reference to 'Campbeltown Distilleries', pp. 153-56.

IMAP: Iain McAlister papers, a collection, chiefly legal in character, purchased on the internet.

KEL: Kintyre Estate Leases, extracted in 1958 by Duncan Colville from the originals, before their transfer to Inveraray.

KM: *The Kintyre Magazine*, 1977-, published bi-annually by the Kintyre Antiquarian & Natural History Society, Campbeltown.

Pigot: *Pigot & Co.'s Commercial Directory*, 1825 & 1837.

RP: Register of Poor, Campbeltown Parish, in Live Argyll Archives, Lochgilphead.

Stirk: David Stirk, *The Distilleries of Campbeltown: The Rise and Fall of the Whisky Capital of the World*, The Angels' Share 2005.

Wright (1963): Hedley G. Wright, 'A Note on Campbeltown and the Distilling Trade' and 'Scotch Whisky Distillers of To-day: Springbank Distillery, Campbeltown', *The Wine and Spirit Trade Record*, April 1963.

I gratefully acknowledge the assistance of *Kilkerran Graveyard Directory* — a compilation of gravestone inscriptions in the old section of Kilkerran Cemetery, now closed to the public — by David O. McEwan (Kintyre Civic Society, 2002) and the 'findagrave' website, though most of my research into the whisky families of Campbeltown was conducted on foot during multiple rambles in that beautiful graveyard, Kilkerran, at the foot of Ben Gullion.

Campbeltown Whisky: An Encyclopaedia

Albyn Distillery was built by William McKersie #1 in 1837 next to the town gas works at the Roading. His brother Alex (q.v.), who was born in 1826, joined the firm, William McKersie & Co., but emigrated to Australia in 1852, and William's sons ultimately took over. John (q.v.) managed Lochruan, assisted by William #2, but when their father retired, around 1876, William took charge of Albyn Distillery, and, when John died in 1904, William ran the whole business until his own death in 1916.

Archibald Keith (q.v.) was manager of Albyn for some 40 years, until his sudden death in 1914, and was succeeded by Campbeltown-born Archibald Fullarton #2. In 1923, three years before he died, Fullarton told a journalist visiting Albyn that as a young man he 'saw the mashing done with long wooden rakes, which were slowly moved round the mash-tun, a tedious process compared with the swift work of the revolving machinery in use today'.[1]

In 1920, a 'new company', Wm. McKersie & Co. Ltd. — subscribers: A. N. Murdoch and James McD. Crawford, wine and spirit brokers, 74 Wellington Street, Glasgow — was formed with capital of £15,000 in £1 shares. The company was to 'carry on the distilling business at Albyn',[2] but it may have been that the new firm was more interested in the liquid assets of Albyn than in any future production.

According to Glen (p 153), the distillery ceased production in 1920, but it was still operational in 1923 when its manager, Archibald Fullarton (above), was interviewed. And there is a published photograph of the Albyn workforce — 13 men, most of them holding malt shovels — taken in 1921 in the distillery yard. As was customary in such photographs, the centrepiece of the composition is a whisky barrel end-on and displaying stencilled data for posterity, in this case: 'Albyn Distillery/ W. M. Rennie Co. Ltd./ 1921/ Campbeltown.'[3] The company name, if correctly transcribed in the newspaper, is puzzling.

In May 1927, at a second extraordinary general meeting of William McKersie & Co. Ltd., two resolutions were passed: that the company be 'wound up voluntarily' and that Maurice Crichton, chartered accountant of Messrs. Wilson, Stirling & Co., Glasgow, be appointed liquidator. A year later, Crichton advertised the buildings, equipment and grounds for sale as 'suitable, and conveniently situated, for Garage or Store'. [4]

'Albyn' is presumably a form of *Alban*, from — to simplify the matter — *Alba*, Gaelic for 'Scotland'.

On 5 April 1955, a 'clothing factory' was opened by Andrew Douglas Ltd., Glasgow, manufacturers of men's suits, sports jackets and topcoats, in a 160-ft.-long warehouse, which had belonged to Albyn Distillery and had been bought by Campbeltown Town Council, as a store, in 1939. The ceremony was performed by the Earl of Home,[5] who would later, as Sir Alec Douglas-Home, become Prime Minister of the UK. In 1977, the business was taken over by Jaeger Tailoring, which closed the factory in 2001.

Anderson, David, was one of the founding partners of Glenside Distillery in 1835, and the firm bore his name. He was probably the David born to Allan Anderson and Susannah Armour in 1799. He was identified as a distiller in Campbeltown when he baptised three daughters between 1836 and 1839, on 10 October of which year he 'retired' from the business.[6] He named a further daughter 'Rebecca Clifford Anderson' in 1841, the year after Henry Clifford, 'Planter' in Port of Spain, Trinidad, married Rebecca Anderson, daughter of John Anderson, wool manufacturer at Lintmill, a union which produced the esteemed Scottish architect, Henry E. Clifford, designer of many of Campbeltown's finest buildings. David's wife, Ann, was also an Anderson, and a connection with Lintmill seems likely. When the 1841 census was taken, David, a 'merchant', Ann, and baby Rebecca — the earlier daughters are missing — were in Back Street, Campbeltown. He may have been the David Anderson in Campbeltown who took the farm of West Laggan, in Glenlussa, in 1841, and six years later assigned the remainder of the lease to Archibald Andrew (q.v.) and Andrew Montgomery[7] (q.v.), whose first wife Jean was an Anderson. In 1851, in an action for debt by William McKersie (see 'Glenside Distillery'), Anderson was described as a commission agent in Campbeltown, and thereafter seems to disappear from records.

Anderson, Janet, was a co-partner in the firm of David Anderson & Co., Glenside Distillery, from October 1839 — when David Anderson (above) withdrew from the business — until 10 August 1844,[8] the date of her death at the age of 62. She was a daughter of Hugh Ferguson, merchant, and Elizabeth Willison (Wilson), and her husband Allan Anderson's mother, Catherine, was also a Ferguson. Allan, son of James Anderson, was Inspector of Fisheries in Campbeltown and died in 1831, aged 66. A connection between him and the above David Anderson, whose father was evidently Allan, is likely; the then unusual forename 'Allan' goes back to the 17th century in the Lowland Plantation Andersons. Allan and Janet married in 1807 and had seven children, one of whom, Patrick Murray Anderson, died in Trinidad in 1845, aged 27.

Andrew, Archibald, built West Highland Distillery in 1830 with Andrew Montgomery (q.v.). Like Montgomery, he was born in Southend: in 1800, at Macharioch, to David Andrew and Betsy Mitchell. Distilling was just one of his business interests. When he married Jean Stewart in Campbeltown in 1833, he was described as a 'Malster'. By 1841, he was Treasurer of Campbeltown Town Council. In 1853, he took a 19-year lease of North and South Killocraw farms — on the west coast of Kintyre — at an annual rent of £240. Since the steadings were admitted to be 'not sufficiently commodious', the Duke of Argyll agreed to build an additional byre, cart-house and sheep fank (pen) and to improve the dwelling-house by plastering the inner walls and fitting new doors. Andrew was identified in the lease as 'Distiller, Campbeltown',[9] but it seems likely that this move signalled the end of West Highland Distillery, which Glen (p 156) reckoned closed between 1852 and 1860. As a guest at a dinner held after the trial trip of the Steam Packet's *Gael* in April 1867, he was referred to as 'Archibald Andrew, Killocraw'.[10] His gravestone, however, describes him as 'Farmer, Glencraigs', his address when he was enrolled in the Kintyre Club in 1862. He died on 12 January 1880, aged 79. 'Mr Andrew,' his obituary stated, 'in his earlier years engaged in the distilling business, but that trade then being in its infancy, and less remunerative than it has since become, he thought it more advantageous to turn his attention to agriculture, in which profession, by energy and perseverance, he achieved a large measure of success. His shrewdness, intelligence and common sense won general respect, and his genial and kind-hearted character made sincere friends.' [11]

His wife, who died in 1889, aged 76, was a daughter of Dugald Stewart and Isabella McMillan, and a sister of Agnes, who married Hugh Mitchell #1, and Isabella who married Peter Gilkison (q.v.). Their second daughter, Elizabeth, married Andrew McWilliam — see 'J. & J. McWilliam' — at Killocraw in 1864.

Andrew, Donald, was an early partner in Loch-head Distillery, built in 1824. When he sold his share in 1833 to James Taylor, he was a coppersmith,[12] and so he appears in *Pigot* 1837 (p 220). In Census 1841, he was living in Main Street with his wife and four children, two female servants and an apprentice coppersmith, John Gilchrist. When he died in 1867, aged 67, he was described as a 'hardware merchant ... much respected in town'.[13] His wife,

Margaret Campbell, with whom he had seven children, died at 317 Sauchiehall Street, Glasgow, in 1872, aged 67, and was buried in Greenock. His mother Mary was also a Campbell. His father James Andrew was a merchant, and two of Donald's sons, James and John, were also merchants, but in Calicut (Kozhikode), India. A third son, Duncan Campbell Andrew, 'a long-headed courteous Scot', had a successful career in shipping with the Union Castle Line in South Africa. He retired to Glasgow and died in December 1929, a year before Duncan MacCallum (q.v.), his old school friend and yachting companion. A faint echo of Donald Andrew's life is captured in his son Duncan's obituary: 'Deceased's father had a coppersmith's business in Main Street at one time, and was a prominent and greatly esteemed citizen, and an elder in Castlehill Church.'[14] His family's gravestones in Kilkerran stand beside that of Archibald Andrew, above.

Ardlussa Distillery. In December 1877, one of the local newspapers reported a rumour that 'another large distillery is about to be erected in the neighbourhood of the Gallowhill for a Glasgow firm'. The rumour proved correct: in April of the following year it was disclosed that James Ferguson & Sons, Cadogan Street, Glasgow — owners of Craighouse Distillery, Jura — had feud a piece of ground next to Glen Nevis Distillery. When built in 1879, the distillery was named 'Ardlussa' and was the 22nd operational distillery in Campbeltown[15] and the last one built.

The first grain was 'wet' in September 1879, and weekly output was estimated at 50,000 gallons. Two dwelling-houses were attached to the distillery, one for the manager and the other for a 'workman' (the mashman). Thanks to automation in the malt-barns, sacks of malt, and the manual labour required to handle them, were consigned to history. Additionally, there was only one pump in the entire distillery — for getting the worts up to the refrigerator — and 'everything else, which in many other distilleries in town

7

requires to be worked by means of pumping, is here carried on by gravitation'. The chimney-stack, at 85 feet high, provided 'a sufficient guarantee that the smoke emitted will not become a nuisance to the neighbourhood'.[16]

The Ardlussa stack was five feet higher than that of its neighbour, Glen Nevis, built two years earlier. Despite their height, or perhaps owing to their newness, neither stack was damaged by a gale which raged across Kintyre in December 1883. Albyn, Benmore, Dalaruan, Kintyre and Springbank all lost their stacks, and the Loch-head stack, though still standing, was visibly swaying. The Dalaruan and Kintyre stacks were blown clear of the distilleries, but the others fell on to buildings and caused additional damage. The Springbank stack collapsed through the roof of the malt-house, and the roof of the Albyn still-house was 'completely shattered'. Builders were to be brought from Glasgow to rebuild the chimneys.[17]

Ardlussa was acquired in 1919 by West Highland Malt Distilleries (q.v.), ceased production in 1923, and was advertised for sale by private bargain in January 1924. By then, it was being used mainly as a bonded store and malting area and was only partially equipped as a distillery. It was sold later that year for £1,500 and liquidated in 1926.[18]

Ardlussa is an estate on Jura and presumably lent its name to the Campbeltown distillery from its owners' association with the island. The place-name element 'Lussa', which also occurs in Kintyre, derives from Norse *laxa*, 'salmon river'. The site of the distillery is now the headquarters of McFadyen building and haulage contractors. The manager from c 1897 was James Murdoch (q.v.), who was succeeded by David G. Lorimer (q.v.), killed in 1917 on the Western Front.

Argyll Distillery, in its second manifestation — see 'MacKinnon's Distillery' for its first — was built in 1844 for Robert Colvill, Hugh Greenlees, maltster, and Robert Greenlees Jr., trading as Colvill, Greenlees & Co. When Colvill and Hugh Greenlees retired, the company was 'carried on by the junior partners', including Hugh's son, Robert Greenlees, who ultimately ran it himself.[19]

Following the retiral of Robert in 1887, the distillery was privately sold to Greenlees Brothers (q.v.), which already owned the neighbouring distillery, Hazelburn. The brothers, who retained the name Colvill, Greenlees & Co., intended to keep the distillery's 'sma' [small] stills', but would otherwise modernise the plant, dispensing with 'the old-fashioned mode of pumping and underground receivers' in favour of a gravitational system. A leasehold property on Lochend Street, extending back to the boundary of the distillery, had been acquired, and James Weir, architect, had drawn up plans for a new four-storey building on the site, to comprise 'spacious maltings', modern kilns, 'double drying floors' and 'hot air chambers'. The annual output of about 50,000 gallons was to be increased to about 180,000.[20] A fire in the 'kiln-head' of the distillery in 1892 destroyed seven tons of peat'.[21] Electric lighting was promised in 1887, but did not materialise until October 1896, when Mavor and Coulson, engineers and electricians, Glasgow, installed a steam-driven dynamo in both Argyll and Hazelburn, the first 'public works' in Campbeltown to receive electricity.[22] And a journalist who visited the distillery c 1922 remarked on its having the only 'upright Cochrane boiler' in Campbeltown.[23]

In 1919, Colvill, Greenlees & Co. appealed to Campbeltown Town Council against the £210 valuation of their large warehouse at Lochend (see above). It was 'only being used at present to a very small proportion of its capacity' and a valuation of £50 was requested, but the appeal was rejected.[24] In that same year, the 'Wee Argyll', as it was locally known, was sold to Macdonald, Greenlees & Williams (Distillers) Ltd. (q.v.), but by 1923 had passed to Ainslie & Heilbron (Distillers) Ltd., Glasgow.[25] According to Glen (p 153), the Argyll ceased production in 1923. In 1929, having been 'recently dismantled', it was sold by its owners, DCL, to Craig Brothers, motor engineers,

Longrow, for conversion into a garage and petrol-filling station,[26] and Campbeltown's main filling station, the County Garage, is still there. In 1936, the Craigs completed their business in the redundant distilleries market with the purchase of Benmore.

Armour, James #1, was one of the three founding partners of Glenside Distillery in 1835. Colville (1923) described him as a maltster and manager of the Campbeltown Gas Company. In Census 1841, he was a 34-year-old unmarried distiller in Longrow; in 1847, he was enrolled, as a distiller, in the Kintyre Club; in 1851, he married Anne Ballantine, widow of Roderick MacKenzie, inn-keeper, Campbeltown, who had died in 1842; in November 1860, he was elected to Campbeltown Town Council and at the post-election supper in the White Hart Inn was 'unanimously called to the chair'; in 1863, he was one of two Campbeltown agents for the North British and Mercantile Insurance Company.[27] He was born in Campbeltown in 1806 and died in 1865; his widow died in 1869 and is commemorated on the stone she raised in Kilkerran to her first husband. James's place of burial is unknown, but his parents, Edward Armour, merchant (died 1846, aged 87), and Florence or Flora MacDonald (died 1844, aged 75), are interred in Kilchousland with three sons who 'died young'.

Armour, James #2, was born in 1818 at Balliwilline, a farm north of Campbeltown, to Peter Armour, described as 'farmer and distillery workman', and Jean Huie. James himself was a distillery workman until 1890, when age and infirmity forced him on to Campbeltown poor roll at 2s 6d a week; his son John, maltster in Loch-head Distillery, was contributing a shilling a week to his father's upkeep. Another of James's seven surviving children, Margaret, was also involved in the spirit trade. She was married to John Grant, a publican and grocer from Granton-on-Spey, Inverness-shire (for his namesake in Campbeltown, see 'John Grant').

They sold a 'spirit shop' in Glasgow in October 1889 and set up again in Campbeltown, but the 'business is reported not what was expected'. James's wife Margaret, whom he married in 1843, was a daughter of John McQuistan and Mary Milloy. She died in the poor house in 1896, and James died in Saddell Street later that year.[28]

Armour, Robert & Sons, coppersmiths, was established in Longrow in 1811 and occupies a unique niche in whisky history through the survival of its 'Still Books', which record sales of stills to illicit distillers in Kintyre, Arran and Gigha between 1811 and 1817, which was also the year the first of the new licensed distilleries in Campbeltown was built. The firm gradually and necessarily shifted its customer-base from illegal to legal distillers: the equipment in the last distilleries built in Campbeltown, Glen Nevis and Ardlussa, was installed by Robert Armour & Sons.

Robert Armour, the founder of the business, died in May 1873 at the age of 86. The brief obituary published in the *Argyllshire Herald* (17/5/1873) omitted any mention of his trade, but made much of his having spent his entire life in Longrow, where the 'old houses' in which he was born had recently been replaced by 'a new tenement'. He was 'of a quiet and retiring disposition', took 'a deep interest in all local affairs' and was 'esteemed as one of our most able townsmen'. His parents were John Armour and Isabell Colvin (i.e. Colvill), and his wife, who survived him by 13 years, was a farmer's daughter, Mary Porter — three solid Lowland surnames.

His son Robert (1831-1918), who succeeded him in the business, married twice: to Mary Dunlop, who died in 1866, after less than four years of marriage, and to Agnes Snodgrass. A son by the first marriage, Archibald Dunlop Armour (1863-1938), whose wife, Esther Stuart, died aged 30 in 1903, next ran the business. He was succeeded by his son, Peter Stuart Armour, who had trained as a marine architect in Glasgow. He sold the business in 1948 and bought Campbeltown Picture House, in which his father had been one of the original directors, and, when he retired in 1983, its management passed to his son Peter. Peter Sr. died in 1988, aged 86,[29] and his wife, Muriel Joyce Mair, died in 1997.

When Robert Armour & Sons was sold in 1948, the business, which had become one of 'plumbers and engineers', was taken over by Hugh Thomson (q.v.). For an extended account of the firm, see I.A. Glen, 'A Maker of Illicit Stills', in *Scottish Studies*, v. 14 (1970), and the same author's 'The Making of Whisky in Campbeltown' in *The Campbeltown Book* (2003), pp. 127-30. For another prominent 19th century coppersmith, see 'Donald Andrew'.

The last coppersmith in Campbeltown, fittingly, was an Armour — William — who died aged 77 in 1955. He had 'served a lifetime in the trade' with Robert Armour & Sons and was 'particularly well-known in Islay',[30] presumably in connection with the distilling industry there.

ballman, an occupational name, recurs in notices in the *Argyllshire Herald*. In 1873, one such was wanted to 'take charge of Stills and assist at Mashing' at an unspecified location. Applicants were to apply, 'stating wages', to William Porteous & Co., advertising agents, Glasgow.[31] In 1875, a 'first class ballman' was wanted, 'in September or sooner', for Glenturret Distillery, Crieff.[32] During a trial in Campbeltown in 1926, involving alleged theft of whisky at Albyn Distillery, the responsibilities of the 'ballsman' were described simply as: 'to attend to the fires and look to the [spirit-]safe.'[33] As to the origin of the term, the on-line Dictionary of the Scots Language cites only one record, from West Lothian: 'The still man ... at the old Linlithgow distillery some 30 years ago ... was known as the "ball man", from his use of hollow glass balls or beads in testing the strength of the spirit.' Scottish novelist Iain Banks, in his whisky book *Raw Spirit* (p 71), offered a different explanation, noted on Jura: a wooden ball, on the end of a string, was swung at the still, and, by the sound it produced, the stillman could tell whether the 'liquid was simmering anaemically, frothing nicely or about to blow the place up', and then stoke or dampen the fire accordingly.

barley. The earliest whisky produced in Kintyre was distilled from 'bere', or 'bear', an older, distinct type of barley. Bere had four rows of grain on it, while barley had two, but the barley grains were tighter in the row, and bigger, which more than compensated. Until the mid-19th century, bere was probably the main grain crop in Kintyre, surpassing even oats. The traveller Thomas Pennant reported in 1772 that much bere was grown in Kintyre, yet there was 'often a sort of dearth, the inhabitants being mad enough to convert their bread into poison, distilling annually 6000 bolls of grain into whisky'. (A 'boll' was the equivalent of 140 lbs., or about 63 kg.) Two decades later, Dr John Smith, Gaelic minister in Campbeltown, complained at greater length about the 'enormous and increasing evil' of distilling, remarking: 'The great object of the farmer is to raise as much of this grain as he can, as it always finds a ready market for the use of the distiller.'[34] The quantity of barley consumed by the 20 distilleries in Campbeltown in the year August 1873 to August 1874 was 99,287 quarters, or 1,241 tons, which produced 1,588,593 gallons of proof whisky. [35]

By the mid-19th century, the time was long past when barley could be supplied to the Campbeltown distillers from local resources. The vital grain was imported from all over the British Isles and Europe, and occasionally from further afield.

In the space of a fortnight in spring 1859, Campbeltown Old Quay was 'the scene of great bustle and activity': 5,170 quarters of barley (a 'quarter' was a quarter of a hundredweight or 8 bushels) were discharged from six foreign ships, three Danish, two French and one Dutch.[36] In 1863, under 'Foreign Arrivals' and 'Foreign Grain', brief

13

but instructive reports on barley arrivals appeared in the *Argyllshire Herald*. In February, two vessels unloaded barley shipped at Nantes in France (or Brittany). In early April, two more cargoes from France were delivered to Campbeltown, but thereafter, from late April until June, all six consignments of foreign barley were from Stettin (or *Szczecin*), a Polish port on the Baltic Sea.[37] In May 1870, barley arrivals in Campbeltown included two cargoes from Malmo, Sweden, in the *Boline* and the *Kebe*.[38] In 1873, a total of 23 foreign ships discharged cargoes at Campbeltown: 15 from France, four from the 'North German Confederation' (a loose group of 39 states), two from Sweden and two from Denmark.[39]

In just one week in March 1879, the following cargoes of barley, from the East Coast of Scotland and Cornwall, were delivered to Campbeltown (there would be six more shipments in the following week):

Bloodhound, from Montrose, 85 tons for Greenlees & Colville.

Princess Beatrice, from Aberdeen, 81 tons, for various distilleries.

Penpoll, from Penzance, 92 tons, for McMurchy, Ralston & Co.

Emily, from Penzance, 46 tons, for David Colville & Co.

Grilse, from Montrose, 80 tons, for David Colville & Co.

Ossian, from Montrose, 90 tons, for Greenlees & Colville.

W.R.T., from Truro, 91 tons, for various distilleries.[40]

These quantities were relatively small, and were brought in by sailing vessels, but, as time went on, both ships and cargoes got bigger. In April 1885, a German steamer, the *Lithuania*, discharged 920 tons from Riga, then in Russia and now the capital of Latvia. The *Argyllshire Herald* commented that 'for some months back' Russian barley had been arriving in Campbeltown, but that 'owing to the war-like attitude of affairs in Afghanistan, the trade with Russia has been suddenly suspended'.[41] In 1894 the *Baines Hawkins* brought 826 tons from Riga, and the *Emma* 785 tons from

Danzig.[42] In 1897, a correspondent of the *Distillers' and Brewers' Magazine* remarked: 'The Campbeltown distillers are shrewd businessmen, and take advantage of every move to improve trade or increase profits. Barley for malting is shipped direct from the Danube. Large steamers of 3000 tons are familiar sights at our quays ...'[43]

In 1878, the smack *Osprey* of Glasgow was rammed and sunk at her moorings in Campbeltown harbour by the brigantine *Fanny P* with a cargo of barley from New York.[44] In 1892, owing to 'the high price for home and other foreign barleys', the steamer *John Redhand* discharged 1,800 tons of Canadian barley, 'the largest cargo ever shipped in one vessel to Campbeltown'. She left New York on 14 January and reached Campbeltown in 16 days.[45] In 1933, 92 tons of Australian barley were delivered to Scotia.[46]

The sourcing of barley, at acceptable prices, from markets all over the world was clearly a major concern of distillers, and grain merchants and ship-brokers had their parts to play. One of these brokers, J. C. Rennie, was a partner in the firm of J. J. McEachran & Co., and assumed sole ownership in 1898, when his brother-in-law, John J. McEachran, a coal and shipping agent in Cardiff, withdrew from the business. By then, Rennie, who had been running the business in McEachran's absence, had 'made himself pretty well indispensable' to the Campbeltown distillers: '... when a ship is required for a barley cargo, Mr Rennie generally can supply the want'.[47]

The names of two French seamen engaged in the barley trade are on record. In November 1864, Charles Gosson, mate of the brig *Marguerite Zelonide* [sic] of Nantes, forfeited a pledge of 10s on a charge of assault;[48] his ship had doubtless sailed by the time the case was heard in court. In March 1877, Stanislas Bequet, of the brig *Marie Aline* of St. Malo, fell from the rigging and fatally fractured his skull while stowing sails off Davaar Island. His burial in Kilkerran was attended by 'a number of shipmasters and others about the harbour'.[49]

The French brig, *Eugenie Desiree*, wrecked in a storm at Coledrain, Southend, on 3 March 1881, had discharged a cargo of barley in Campbeltown two weeks earlier and was returning to St. Malo with coal from Ardrossan.[50]

In January 1891, a 20-year-old Campbeltown man, Donald McLean, joined the crew of the steamer *Calliope* as 'mess room steward' while she was in port unloading barley. In the following month, in Newport, Wales, he and another seaman were burned to death after the ship's wooden forecastle caught fire. A cargo of iron-ore from Bilbao had been discharged from the ship, and the crew had gone on a 'spree' after being paid their wages. The assumption was that a lamp had been knocked over during the revelries.[51]

A London 'barley superintendent' died in his lodgings in Main Street on 23 October 1906. He was Alexander Henry Mavrocordato and had been overseeing the discharging of the steamer *Chicklade*. He was 44 years of age, unmarried, had been in 'indifferent health', and, having command of several languages, was 'well suited for his post'. His brother and sister arrived in Campbeltown on the day before his burial at Kilkerran,[52] and presumably erected the memorial to him there.

Mary Blair (*née* McGeachy), a Dalintober fisherman's daughter who was born in 1910, remembered watching, as a young girl, barley being unloaded from carts at Scotia Distillery. Sometimes a sack would burst as it was being hauled by pulley and chain to the hoisting door of the malt-loft, and grain would scatter on to the street. The workers never bothered to sweep up the spillage, and, when the carts left, Mary would gather the grain and sell it for a few pennies to neighbours in High Street who kept hens.[53] Three young Campbeltown boys were injured at Springbank Distillery in 1916 while 'picking up scattered grain'. One of the bags of barley slipped from the sling as it was being hoisted from a cart. It hit the cart before it landed on the boys, but, even so, the brothers Walter and

Malcolm McConachy each suffered a broken leg and Jim Cochrane was cut about the forehead.[54]

Some local distillers grew their own grain. By early August 1853, Reid & Colville, Dalintober Distillery, had cut half of a field of 'Chevalier' barley, but the other half, 'having a northern exposure, was not ready for the sickle'; and, in 1861, 'Bailie McKersie' — William, of Albyn and Lochruan distilleries — 'cut down a field of barley ... adjoining Argyll Distillery',[55] which was at the head of Longrow.

Early in September 1862, 'bere ... of excellent quality' and weighing 54 lbs. per bushel, was delivered to Hazelburn Distillery from Knockbay Farm. On 26 August 1863, Springbank Distillery received from a local farmer, James Huie in Dhurrie, an early 'parcel of new barley, of excellent quality', which weighed about 52 lbs. per bushel. In 1869, Campbeltown Distillery got about 80 quarters of barley from Robert Aitken, Drumore, '... and we may state that it was standing in stooks the day before'. Barley grown by Robert McLatchie at Glenramskill, in August 1876, had 'scarcely been an hour in the market before it was purchased by Mr Osborne for the Campbeltown Distillery Company'.[56]

In 1964, Springbank used Kintyre-grown barley for the first time since before the Second World War. Colonel James Taylor, Machrimore Farm, had offered part of a crop which he had grown for animal feed, and Hedley G. Wright, managing director of Springbank, was 'delighted' to accept, '... for not only was the barley of excellent quality, but also this meant the re-establishment of a link between two local industries which had been broken for many years'. Next winter, the emphasis would be on the purely native character of the thousand gallons of whisky to be distilled using Machrimore 'Ymer' barley: there was the Southend grain itself, malted in Campbeltown and dried using peat from Rhoin Moss; the water was from Crosshill Loch and the stills were heated using coal from Argyll Colliery at Machrihanish. As the *Campbeltown Courier* remarked, 'There could hardly be a more local whisky ...' In November

1965, the first steep of the season's Kintyre-grown 'Ymer' was on the malting floors of the distillery, but the supplier was now Peter McKerral, Brunerican Farm, Southend.[57]

Barnard, Alfred, stayed in Campbeltown for a fortnight in the summer of 1885 during his tour of the British Isles researching distilleries. His monumental survey, *The Whisky Distilleries of the United Kingdom*, published in 1887, has become the bible of whisky writers, but, like the Good Book itself, has been made to carry historical weight which its frame is ill-suited to support. It is strong on technical description, but Barnard, a Londoner, listened to too many pawky yarns, and his local history is unreliable, which may be excused, since reliable accounts of Kintyre history had yet to appear on the back of proper documentary research.

Beith, John #1, banker, was a pioneer of the legal branch of whisky-distilling in Campbeltown, but as an investor, not as a distiller. In 1817, he founded the first distillery in town, 'Campbeltown', with John Mactaggart (q.v.), a maltster; next came Longrow Distillery in 1824, built in partnership with another banker, John Colville Jr. (q.v. #1), and John Ross (q.v.), who was the active partner; finally, in about 1830, he established Kintyre Distillery as sole proprietor. He held, with his brother Alexander, the agency for the Renfrewshire Bank in Campbeltown and was Collector of Taxes for Argyll. In *Pigot's Directory* of 1837 (p 220), his name appears among the 'gentry and clergy' of the town. When he died in 1840, his nephew and namesake (below) succeeded him as tax collector, bank agent and partner in Kintyre and Longrow distilleries.

Beith, John #2, who died on 25 March 1879, was born in Lochgilphead, Mid Argyll, in 1800, but his family origins were in South Kintyre among the Lowland settler-stock: his parents were Gilbert Beith, distiller and farmer, and

Helen Keith Elder. At about the age of 16, he moved to Campbeltown to work for his uncles, Alexander and John Beith (above). After John's death, he succeeded him in the local agency for the Renfrewshire Bank. When the bank was 'stopped' in 1842, Beith had 'much to bear from angry depositors, and this he stood manfully, but wisely resolved never again to accept a bank agency'.

His obituarist described him erroneously as 'one of the first distillers in Campbeltown'. The error may have arisen from confusion with his uncle, after whose death, in 1840, John Jr. joined John Colville Jr. and John Ross in a new partnership, Beith, Ross & Co., to run Kintyre Distillery. Since his involvement in Longrow Distillery probably began about the same time, his entry into the distilling business dates to about 1840. By then, according to Colville (1923), 28 distilleries in his list of 33 had been built, so John Jr. could hardly have been 'one of the first distillers in Campbeltown'.

In 1876, Beith, Ross & Co. — partners now John Beith Jr., John Ross and John Galbraith — was dissolved, and Kintyre and Longrow distilleries were privately auctioned. Beith and Galbraith were bidding against Ross, who secured the distilleries for £8,010 and brought William Greenlees into the new firm, John Ross & Co., as a partner.[58] This split resulted in acrimony and litigation (see 'Longrow Distillery').

In 1843, when the 'Disruption' split the Established Church of Scotland — over the right of congregations to appoint their own minister — Beith 'came out' on the side of the break-away Free Church and was instrumental in securing the ground at Big Kiln on which two temporary churches were built, one for the Gaelic-speaking congregation and one for the English-speaking congregation. When the 'tasteful edifice', Lorne Street Church — now Campbeltown Heritage Centre — was erected in 1868, on the original site, 'the greater part of the expense ... was borne by himself'.[59] The redundant address, Beith Street, which leads from Castlehill to Lorne Street Church, was named after him.

Since Lorne Street served the Free Church Gaelic congregation, the question arises: was Beith a Gaelic speaker? There is no evidence that he was, but it is likely. His brother, Rev Dr Alexander Beith (1799-1891), wrote a book in the language, though he was a more prolific author in English.[60]

Beith was on the Town Council from 1832 until 1875. He was elected Provost in 1854 and served no fewer than five terms. Like his friend — and, ultimately, adversary — John Ross, he was remembered for his conviviality: 'He had a remarkable appreciation of the humorous side of events, and, as much as he was respected in his public capacity, it was in his private intercourse with his friends that the charms of his character were most conspicuous. Largely given to hospitality, the recollection of his rich store of anecdotes and brilliant mode of relating them, will be a valuable legacy to many who had the privilege of meeting him in private.'[61]

On 28 January 1859, 71 'gentlemen' attended a dinner in the Town Hall, Campbeltown, to celebrate the centenary of the birth of Robert Burns. Beith, who was in the chair, declared that in his youth he had 'paid court to the muses'. He had 'long ceased ... to invoke their favours', but none the less had composed a poem for the occasion. It ran to 72 lines of rhyming couplets and was a creditable effort, which concluded: 'Here end my lay. My mind to duty turns, / Drink to the memory of immortal Burns.'[62]

His wife Isabella Clark died in 1837 at the age of 31. They evidently had no children, and he never remarried. In 1861, having completed two terms as Provost and been presented with three silver salvers and a silver claret jug, suitably inscribed, he confessed touchingly in his response that '... at times a sense of loneliness creeps over me, when I think of my living by myself in a place where I have not now a single relation ...'[63]

He was the first person in Kintyre to communicate by telegraph when, in December 1864, he sent a message to Tarbert using the Universal Private Telegraph Co. Ltd.[64]

His death certificate described him not as a distiller, but as 'a collector of property and income tax' — he was assessor for Argyll in the Lands Valuation Office, Campbeltown — an office which, as his gravestone boasts, he and his uncle John occupied between them for 59 years. His legacy was divided among relatives and the clerks and domestic servants in his employment, and the remainder went to the Free Church, including his library; but his 'house property' in Campbeltown was left to the Duke of Argyll.[65]

Beith, William, was a retired distillery mashman, and, at the age of 91, the 'oldest resident in Campbeltown' when he died on 21 August 1899. Until two months before his death, he enjoyed 'the best of health' and took daily exercise 'along by the Poorhouse Road' (Witchburn).[66] He remembered 'the days of the press gang', witnessed the public flogging at Campbeltown Cross of two law-breaking brothers, and saw a woman drummed out of town for 'misbehaviour'. She was forced to walk up Longrow behind a cart, to which her hands were tied, with the town drummer 'beating vigorously' behind her, and the procession followed by 'a jeering crowd of townsfolk and weans [children]'. She was taken as far as Lagnagarach and 'literally cast out, and dared not enter the burgh again until her period of banishment had expired'.[67]

Lagnagarach, beside the road to Tarbert, was where Beith's wife, Margaret Fullarton, whom he married in 1841, was brought up. In the early 19th century, it consisted of two rows of little thatched houses, most of them occupied by hand-loom weavers, of which Margaret's father, John, was one. She, in her turn, was the oldest resident of the burgh when she died at Millknowe, aged 98, on 11 January 1913. She was of 'high intelligence', and, like her husband, was a fund of local knowledge; but she was a keen reader of newspapers and more interested in current affairs than in history. She clearly held a traditional view of women in society, and dismissed militant suffragettes — then very much in the news — as 'trash'. She was survived by two daughters, Janet and Isabella, who nursed her in her final illness following a fall.[68]

Benmore Distillery was one of just two distilleries in Campbeltown not built by local investors, and, significantly, they were among the last: Benmore in 1868 and Ardlussa in 1879. Benmore was built by Bulloch, Lade & Co., a major producer and exporter of Scotch whisky, on land in Saddell Street bought from Thomas Brown,[69] father of Thomas Lambert Brown (q.v.).

After the company was voluntarily liquidated in 1920, its stock and distilleries were purchased — reportedly for around £1.5 million — by J. & P. O'Brien & Co. Ltd., Liverpool, which declared that 'The business will continue to be carried on under the name of Bulloch, Lade'. Two months later, however, in April 1920, J. & P. O'Brien itself was reported to be in liquidation.[70] Benmore Distilleries Ltd. assumed control of the distillery and also bought Lochhead in Campbeltown, Lochindaal (Islay) and Dallas Dhu (Speyside).[71] Benmore Distilleries became part of DCL in 1929, by which time Benmore Distillery was redundant. In 1936, the distillery was bought by Messrs. Craig Brothers, of West Coast Motors Service, for use as a 'central bus garage',[72] and the premises remain the company's garage and administrative centre. The cul-de-sac beside the garage was named 'Benmore Street', after the distillery, at a Town Council meeting in 1953.[73] The name, which can still be seen engraved in the eroding stone arch of the original entrance, represents Gaelic *Beinn mòr*, 'Big hill'.

In 1871, John Carrick at Benmore Distillery — doubtless the manager – subscribed 10s to the local fund for a wedding present for Princess Louise[74] (p 97). In the census of that same year, he was a 38-year-old unmarried 'Distiller' in Saddell Street with his 23-year-old sister, Ellen, both of them born in Islay.

In April 1879, Bulloch, Lade & Co. published a notice stating that Dugald Mathieson, 'for some time employed as clerk and mashman at Benmore Distillery', was no longer employed by the company and had 'no power or authority to represent us in any way'.[75]

Later that year, a fire which broke out in the Benmore kiln was attended by the recently established town fire brigade with its 400-yard hose. Several tons of peats were damaged, but that was all. The following week, James Fullarton (p 75), who was in charge of the brigade, was instructed by the Town Council to employ 'a proper staff' at 1/- an hour during the day and 1/6d an hour at night, the wages to be recovered from insurance.[76]

In 1881, Campbeltown Town Council's Dean of Guild Court approved a petition from Bulloch, Lade & Co. to build a bonded warehouse within Benmore's premises.[77]

In 1886, a puncheon of whisky, containing 'upwards of 222 gallons', was too heavy for carting and had to be rolled manually from Benmore Distillery to the quay for shipment in the steamer *Davaar*.[78]

Bloch, Sir Maurice. On the day after Bloch's death, on 19 February 1964, the *Glasgow Herald* published an obituary headed 'Prominent Member of Glasgow Jewry'. If I had expected to uncover therein more information about his success as a businessman, I was disappointed. The lengthy anonymous account offered only this: 'He went to Glasgow while still a young man and founded the business which became the firm of Bloch Brothers (Distillers) Ltd. The shares of the company were acquired by Hiram-Walker-Gooderham and Worts, Ltd., in 1954.'

Of the success of his career, there can be no doubt. Following the sale of Bloch Brothers, Sir Maurice set up the Bloch Trust, a charitable foundation in which he placed more than £400,000 for 'the advancement of religion and education' and 'the cure and alleviation of sickness and disease'. Its first sizeable gift, of £35,000, was to the University of Glasgow, to endow an annual lecture on some aspect of medical science or practice and a medical research fellowship.

His brother Joseph, of whom no mention was made in the obituary, left a relatively small estate of £60,260, which was noted in the *Campbeltown Courier*; yet, in the same local newspaper there was nothing on the death of Maurice, his connection with Campbeltown having presumably been largely forgotten by then. The brothers lived together at 39 Newark Drive, Glasgow.

In February 1949, Sir Maurice ceased to be a lay magistrate, 28 years after his appointment as a Justice of the Peace. He was removed from the Commission of the Peace following criticism of his gifts of wine and spirits to a junior government minister, John Belcher. In 1948, during the Lynskey Tribunal into allegations of post-war corruption among British government ministers and civil servants, it emerged that Belcher had 'intervened' on Bloch's behalf to 'secure the granting of licences for the import of sherry casks'.

Bloch, who never married, was born in Dundee and educated at Harris Academy there. As quoted above, he moved to Glasgow 'while still a young man' and set up in business, with his brother, as a whisky blender and broker. His connection with Campbeltown began in 1933, with the purchase of Scotia Distillery, and lasted until 1954, when he retired from business and dedicated the remainder of his life to philanthropy, chastened perhaps by his Lynskey Tribunal ordeal.

He was treasurer and honorary president of the Jewish Board of Guardians for more than 50 years, and the other organisations which benefited from his 'practical sympathy' were the Jewish Consumptive Fund, the Home for Aged Needy, the Jewish Ex-Servicemen's Social Institute and the Glasgow Hebrew College. During the Second World War, he was chairman of the Jewish War Services Committee for Scotland and 'active in support of the cause of Jewish victims of the European crisis'. Politically, he was centre-right and thrice contested unsuccessfully the Gorbals constituency in Glasgow at general elections: in 1929, 1931 and 1935. He was knighted in 1937 for political and public services.[79]

Bonthrone, Alexander, who died in February 1969, had been a frequent visitor to Campbeltown in connection with Springbank Distillery. He had been a director of J. & A. Mitchell & Co. Ltd. since 1960 and had earlier acted as a consultant to the company. He was 'particularly noted' for his extensive knowledge of barley and malting, his family having been maltsters in Fife for centuries. Shortly after the sale of the family business to DCL, he moved from Freuchie, Fife, to Longmorn in Moray, where he died. An Alexander Bonthrone, who was doubtless a relative, appeared in Census 1861 as a boarder in the Roading, Campbeltown. A 45-year-old unmarried distillery maltman, he was born in Auchtermuchty, Fife. In 1853 the owner of Auchtermuchty Distillery was 'A. Bonthron'.[80]

Boyle, Hugh, was a partner in Caledonian Distillery from c 1840 until 1845. In March of that year, in a letter to Hugh Allan, merchant in Londonderry, Ireland, Boyle stated that he would have no more whisky for sale, as he did not intend to 'work the concern any more'. On the advice of 'Captain McGregor', he was seeking a 'Government situation', which would be 'infinitely better than Distilling here'.[81] His adviser was probably Captain John MacGregor, who had a distinguished career in the '1st Royals' and retired to Kintyre on half-pay c 1840. He died unmarried in 1861 at Kildonald Cottage, on the coast north of Campbeltown, and was buried at Kilmun in Cowal,[82] apparently his birthplace. In Census 1841, however, he was at Markland Cottage, Campbeltown, next door to Robert MacGregor, described as a Lieutenant in the Argyll Militia when Hugh Boyle married his daughter Jane in 1844. These two military MacGregors were just two years apart in age and are likely to have been related. In June 1845, Boyle was arrested for non-payment of £80 owed to the Londonderry merchant, Hugh Allan, and had to be bailed out by his father-in-law, Lieut MacGregor. That Boyle himself belonged to Londonderry is a possibility; a letter survives which he wrote in January 1845 to his mother, 'Mrs McBride', who lived at an address there.[83]

Lieut Robert and his Irish wife, Mary Mahon, had several children born in Campbeltown, the first, Mary Hislop, in 1816. A son Peter was born on 2 April 1822, but he must have died soon after, because a second son was named Peter, and he was born, remarkably, on 2 April 1823 — exactly one year later! In *Pigot's Directory* of 1837 (p 219), MacGregor is described as 'harbour master'. He died in 1847 and his gravestone in Kilkerran bears only his name.

In Census 1851, his widow — a 64-year-old 'lodging house keeper' — was still in Markland Cottage. With her were Jane Boyle, her daughter, aged 32, married, and born in England; her grand-daughter, Jane MacGregor Boyle, aged 4 and born in Helensburgh; and an 18-year-old female servant. Hugh Boyle was not there. In August 1864, 'Miss Boyle, Markland Cottage', aged about 17, attended a ball for the social elite of Campbeltown.[84] Mary MacGregor died at Markland Cottage on 3 August 1868, and on 10 March 1870 the contents of Markland Cottage, 'belonging to Mrs Boyle', were sold by public auction.[85] The MacGregors had been in Markland since at least 1825, when the Lieutenant was included with the 'gentry and clergy' of the town in *Pigot's Directory*.

brewers — see 'mashmen'. The earliest mention of a 'brewer' in the Campbeltown Old Parish Registers was evidently in 1787: Archibald Taylor. The term, which was synonymous with 'mashman', became more common from 1830 onward.

Broombrae Distillery will remain a phantom edifice unless proof of its existence emerges. In notes extracted from the 'Still Books' of Robert Armour & Sons (q.v.) by Archibald D. Armour, 'Broombrae Distillery' and 'Edward Watson' are joined beside the date 'July 1826'.[86] In Glen's list of Campbeltown distilleries, p 154, 'Broombrae' is followed by 'Edward Robertson 1833-4' ... and that's all. Stirk, p 169, attached 'Broombrae' to the nameless distillery in High Street (q.v.), in which an Edward Ralston was involved. Broombrae, however, is the upper part of Saddell Street, where it joins High Street, and it is unlikely that a distillery further along High Street would have been so named. So, three Edwards and no edification!

Brown, Thomas Lambert, T.D., J.P., died aged 70 at his home, Rockwood, on 20 April 1937. After 'early training in Glasgow', he 'became associated with Mr Duncan MacCallum in the Scotia and Glen Nevis distilleries', which must have been in 1891 — see 'Stewart, Galbraith & Co. Ltd.' He was then a 'clerk' living at the family home, Ardmore, but he later moved to Edinburgh and established himself as a whisky broker, at first with Alexander Edward, and, after his partner's retirement, on his own account. When enrolled in the Kintyre Club in 1903, his office was at 38 York Place, Edinburgh. He clearly maintained his association with MacCallum, for in 1919 he became a director of West Highland Malt Distilleries Ltd. (q.v.).

In 1913, a local newspaper speculated that some local distillery workers were 'likely to transfer their services from Campbeltown to Yoker'. T. L. Brown was behind the employment opportunities, Yoker Distillery having been bought for around £30,000 by A. Edward & Co. and about to re-open. (At least one Campbeltonian did move to Yoker, albeit briefly — see 'Neil McCallum'.)

Brown became wealthy and enjoyed a flamboyant lifestyle — he would travel around Edinburgh in a chauffeur-driven Rolls Royce — but, according to family tradition, he lost much of his fortune in the slump in the whisky business in the early 1930s and retired to Campbeltown to live, initially at Drumfin on Castlehill with his unmarried sister, Nellie, and his brother, Dr James P. Brown.

He had a lifelong interest in soldiering, which began in Glasgow when he enrolled as a private in the 1st Lanarkshire

Rifle Volunteers. When he returned home, he accepted a commission in the Argyllshire Volunteers, which became the 8th Argyll & Sutherland Highlanders. He commanded one of the local companies of the 8th, and, when the First World War broke out, went to France with the battalion as its second-in-command. After more than a year in France, he was promoted to Lieutenant-Colonel and returned to Britain to command a battalion of the Lancashire Fusiliers. After the war he was associated with the Territorial Army Association and was buried with military honours in Kilkerran.

His other interests included Freemasonry, golfing and shooting; he was a president of the Campbeltown Ornithological Society, president of the Kintyre Agricultural Society, honorary president of the Campbeltown Miniature Rifle Club, a trustee of the Victoria Hall and a manager of the Campbeltown and District Savings Bank.

He was a son of Thomas Brown, Ayrshire-born businessman in Campbeltown, who married Agnes Pearson, a daughter of James Pearson, Supervisor of Inland Revenue in Campbeltown, in 1866, and died in 1875.[87]

Burnside Distillery was described in 1905 by a visiting journalist as '... the most remote distillery from the town, being fully half-a-mile out on the road to Machrihanish — the famous golfing course on the shores of the Atlantic. This "work" has a unique appearance from the road, being planted on a grassy slope, with its white-washed range of buildings and peaked warehouses forming a bright contrast to the sombre hues of the heather-clad mountain called Bengullion, immediately behind.'[88]

The distillery was built in 1825 near the stream called Witchburn — hence its name, 'Burnside' — and beside Meadowburn Distillery, erected the previous year. The original firm was McMurchy, Ralston & Co., a partnership of Alexander and Hugh Greenlees, maltsters; James Ryburn, baker; John Colvill, saddler; and Robert McMurchy. In 1828, the distillery was sold by public auction to John

Colvill, who paid £1,950 on behalf of himself and the above-named partners, excepting McMurchy, who had withdrawn.[89] Alexander Greenlees (q.v.) was John Colvill's brother-in-law, through his marriage to John's sister Mary. James Ryburn, baker in Main Street, who belonged to an Ayrshire Plantation family, married Isabella McNair in 1816 and died in 1857, aged 66. There were Ryburn maltsters in Campbeltown in the 18th century.

Despite the firm's name, Colville (1923) was 'unable to find any trace' of a Ralston involvement; but, in the Argyll Estate archive in Inveraray, there is an unsigned letter, dated 3 January 1827, addressed to Robert Ralston, merchant, and David, his son, offering to buy their interest in McMurchy, Ralston & Co.[90] These were undoubtedly the Ralstons who took over Glenramskill Distillery (q.v.) in 1828 with their partner in Burnside, Robert McMurchy.

In 1840, the partners were Alexander, Hugh and Robert Greenlees,[91] the last-named of whom would be a founding partner in Argyll Distillery in 1844. Alexander #1 died in 1861, and with the death in 1864 of his son Robert #1, McMurchy, Ralston & Co. passed to Robert's sons Alexander #2 and James #1, after whose death in 1888 Burnside was put on the market.

The distillery was described as being 'in first-rate working order, has a good supply of water, and is capable of producing 120,000 gallons per annum'. The date of the sale was 31 October 1888, at the Faculty Hall, Glasgow. The reserve price was £6,500 and there were no bidders. On 14 November, a second attempt at selling the distillery was made, this time at the reduced price of £5,000, and, again, there were no bidders. After a third unsuccessful attempt, with the price down to £4,000, the distillery was sold privately, for an undisclosed sum, to Samuel Greenlees of Greenlees Brothers (q.v.),[92] which also owned Hazelburn and Argyll. Greenlees Brothers operated both Burnside and Argyll as Colvill, Greenlees & Co., and the managing director from at least 1899 until his death in 1915 was Arthur Hamilton Gardiner (q.v.).

In 1881, when James W. Greenlees appealed against the rateable valuation of Burnside, he complained that he had 'a steam-still which would cost £600', whereas certain other 'undervalued' distilleries used pot-stills, which would 'only cost £150'; furthermore, he had to 'malt outside his distillery', whereas the others 'could do all their work on their own premises'.[93]

Barnard, in 1887, remarked that one of the distillery's 'very spacious' malt-barns had served as a 'banqueting-hall and dance-floor when the present Duke of Argyll came of age'. The date of that event was 6 August 1866, when the Argyll Estate tenants were entertained there, and the civic 'rejoicings and festivities' were crowned by a huge bonfire on the summit of Ben Gullion.[94]

Burnside Distillery was purchased in 1919 for £400 by United Creameries Ltd. for cheese-making, and Meadowburn Distillery was also acquired to expand the site.[95] Campbeltown Creamery was still there, producing award-winning cheese, until its tragic closure in November 2019. Original buildings and walls of Burnside Distillery may still be viewed from the industrial estate road which passes along the south side of the creamery.

Cadenhead, William, Ltd., wine and spirit merchants, was founded in 1842 in Aberdeen and purchased in 1972 by J. & A. Mitchell and Co. Ltd. Cadenhead's whisky shop in Reform Square, Campbeltown, occupies the former premises of William Dickson & Co., wine merchants and grocers. When Dickson emigrated to Virginia in 1873, his partner Thomas Eaglesome became sole owner,[96] and the business operated in his name until 1972, by which time it was owned by J. & A. Mitchell. Cadenhead specialises in limited issues of choice malts, and, in addition to its local hub, has retail outlets across Europe.

Caledonian Distillery was built in 1832 and extended from the corner of Burnside Street, across the present

Glebe Street to the corner of Big Kiln Street.[97] The original firm was Peter Stewart & Co. — the brothers William, Edward and Peter Stewart (q.v.) — with Hugh Boyle (q.v.) added by 1840.[98] In 1845, the partners were named as Boyle, plus John Keys and James Johnston.[99] According to Glen (p 154), Johnston carried on the business, which was dissolved in 1842 and again in 1844. He was the brother of Robert and Charles Johnston, was described in Census 1841 as a distiller and died in 1853, aged 36: see 'Lochruan Distillery'.

When the company was finally liquidated in April 1851, the partners were, as in the beginning, William, Edward and Peter Stewart.[100] That same month, the redundant distillery, with 34 years of the lease remaining, was advertised for sale, 'as it presently stands, with two Malt Barns attached'. It was to be publicly auctioned, with a 'low' upset price of £600, if not previously sold by private bargain. Interested parties were to apply to Peter Stewart.[101] There were no bidders, even when the price was dropped to £400, and the distillery was finally bought for that sum by Stewart, Galbraith & Co.,[102] which owned Scotia Distillery and whose principal partner, James Stewart, was a brother of the three Stewarts; but there is no evidence that the company worked Caledonian.

There were two narrow entrances to this distillery. The more direct was the Warm Water Close, which took its name from the public custom of going to distilleries for supplies of free hot water. The manager of Kintyre Distillery, William Beith, remarked in 1870 that 'a great many women' came to his distillery, especially on Saturdays, and helped themselves to hot water from 'a small cock off the main pipe';[103] and see Appendix 2, 1888, for a scalding accident, involving a boy, at Glenside Distillery. It was in the Warm Water Close that the 1854 Campbeltown cholera epidemic broke out on 16 January.[104] The other close, further along Burnside Street, was the abbreviated 'Caley Close'.[105] An intact building which belonged to the distillery, and was acquired by CMC ship-chandlers *c* 2001, can still be seen at the bottom of Glebe Street. 'Caledonian' — from Latin *Caledonia*, the name the Romans gave to the unconquered lands north of *Britannia* — equates romantically with 'Scottish'.

Campbeltown, historically, was one of the four whisky-producing regions of Scotland, the others being Lowland, Islay and Highland (of which Speyside and Islands are now considered sub-divisions). When, in 1994, the Scotch Whisky Association produced a map of distilleries, the owners of the two surviving Campbeltown distilleries, Springbank and Glen Scotia, were astonished to discover that Campbeltown was no longer recognised — at least by the S.W.A. — as an independent region, but had been merged with Highland. When Springbank asked for a correction, the response from the S.W.A. was that, since Campbeltown had only two distilleries left, it could no longer be regarded as a region. Jim Murray, writing in 1997, stressed the continuing distinctiveness of the Campbeltown malts and vowed that '... in every map of every book on the subject I ever write, Campbeltown shall remain a region all its own ...'[106] Campbeltown now has three working distilleries and the S.W.A.'s revisionist map has been consigned to the waste-bin.

In 1901, Argyll — including the islands of Islay, Jura and Mull — made more whisky than any other county in Scotland. Of the 159 working distilleries in Scotland, 33 were in Argyll, followed by Banffshire with 24. Six years earlier, in 1895, the total for Argyll was 35 (the figure for Campbeltown, within that, was 22).[107]

Campbeltown & Glasgow Steam Packet Joint Stock Company (generally abbreviated in this work to 'Campbeltown Steam Packet') carried passengers, cargo and mail to and from Campbeltown for 110 years and was crucial to the expansion of the Campbeltown distillers' markets (see 'William Smith Junior').

The company's first vessel, the *Duke of Lancaster*, was bought at a public auction in Liverpool in 1826 for £3,800, but her first captain quickly condemned her as being unsuitable for the Clyde trade, because 'she drew too much water to reach the Broomielaw'. The fledgling company was thrown into turmoil, and the upshot was that, after several ineffectual attempts to sell her, she was taken over by a new company, consisting of a few of the original owners and additional local individuals and firms, and James Napier (q.v.) was appointed captain in 1827. Owing to the 'shallowness and windings' of the Clyde estuary, the earliest of the Campbeltown steamers often had to set out at three or four o' clock in the morning to catch flood tide, and a piper would march through the streets of the town to warn intending passengers that 'the steam was up and the boat about to start'.[108]

The first chairman of the revived company was Daniel Mactaggart (q.v.) and its board was subsequently dominated by distilling interests. The steward on the *Duke of Lancaster* was 'strictly prohibited from having any other whisky on board than the best Campbeltown'.[109] Vessels subsequent to the *Duke of Lancaster* were: *Saint Kiaran* (1835), *Duke of Cornwall* (1842), *Celt* (1848), *Druid* (1857), *Gael* (1867), *Kintyre* (1868), *Kinloch* (1878), *Davaar* (1885) and *Dalriada* (1926). The earlier steamers were not noted for speed, but the *Gael* and *Kintyre* in the 1860s could both reach Greenock from Campbeltown in four hours.[110]

The company throughout its history was registered in Campbeltown, managed from Campbeltown and largely owned in Campbeltown. Right to the end, when it was sold to Clyde Cargo Steamers Ltd. in 1937,[111] the bulk of the shares were held by descendants of the original shareholders or those who came in later when the capital of the company was increased.

Campbeltown Bonding Company was referred to in 1905 as owning a 'fine warehouse ... which holds about half-a-million gallons of whisky',[112] but no further information has emerged.

Campbeltown Distillers' Association was formed in 1848. Since none of its records appears to survive, the scope of its objects can only be surmised; but it clearly functioned as a consortium dedicated to the promotion and protection of its members' business interests.

In March 1862, for example, James Stewart and William McKersie travelled to London to represent the Campbeltown whisky industry in a delegation of Scottish, English and Irish distillers which met the Chancellor of the Exchequer at Downing Street to urge upon him 'the propriety of reducing the present high rate of duty of 10s per gallon on British spirits in order to protect the fair trader and prevent the increase of illicit distillation'. [113]

In 1860, the Association, through its chairman, Stewart, donated 100 guineas to help equip the Campbeltown company of Rifle Volunteers, which was then being formed.[114] This body of part-time soldiers became 3rd company Argyllshire Rifle Volunteers, with its headquarters in the Victoria Hall, built in 1887.

There was also, as might be expected, a social side to the organisation. In 1860, the distillers, accompanied by wives and 'sweethearts' and a 'very select party of friends', set off on a 'pleasure excursion' — destination undisclosed — on the morning of 31 August in the steamer *Celt*.[115] In July 1874, Association members and a few guests had lunch in the Argyll Inn, Southend, before walking to Keil 'to visit the mansion in course of erection by J. N. Fleming'.[116] James Nicol Fleming was a Glasgow merchant who married Elizabeth Galbraith, daughter of John Galbraith (q.v.), in 1859. As a director of the City of Glasgow Bank, which infamously crashed in 1878, he was subsequently jailed for eight months, having been found guilty of fraud, among other charges.[117] In 1875, the Association's annual summer outing was to Tayinloan, where, in the MacDonald Arms

Hotel, some 40 members and guests were served 'the choicest of viands' by the host, Mr Campbell. They arrived back in Campbeltown at 10 p.m. by the horse-drawn carriages in which they had set out at 9.30 a.m.[118]

The Association's first chairman was James Stewart, who resigned in 1872 after 25 years' service and was replaced by Charles C. Greenlees. Its first manager was Charles McEachran, who was succeeded in 1877 by Archibald Milloy, who, in turn, was succeeded by his son, also Archibald, in 1905. In 1908, the Association was described as having little commercial clout, its 'principal function being the carrying on of a dried grains factory'.[119]

Campbeltown Distillery, built in 1817 at the head of Longrow opposite Lochend Street, was the earliest of the distilleries established after a hiatus of 20 years in the legal trade.[120] The original firm, John Beith & Co., comprised John Mactaggart (q.v.) and John Beith #1. By 1835, Mactaggart's son Charles (q.v.) was proprietor of both Campbeltown Distillery and its neighbour, Union, and the tenant of each was Hector Henderson (q.v.), operating as H. & F. Henderson. The business later operated as Charles Kelly & Co., which became the Campbeltown Distillery Co. in 1853, when acquired by Captain James Melville (q.v.) and Duncan McMillan (q.v.), who died in 1873. Melville died the following year, but family papers show that his heirs were shareholders in the company until at least 1884.[121] The Glasgow-based industrialist Neil Macnish (q.v.) began his working life as a clerk in Campbeltown Distillery and by 1859, at the age of about 22, was manager. In 1877, Charles McEachran (q.v.) became managing partner, a position he held until his death in 1898.

In November 1869, a fire broke out in the engine room of the distillery. The ground-malt store was completely burned and 750 bushels of malt destroyed. The damage was estimated at about £400, which was covered by insurance, and the distillery would be inactive for about a month.[122]

In 1873, when a kiln and malt-floor were advertised to let in Queen Street, Dalintober, the premises had 'lately' been vacated by Campbeltown Distillery.[123]

Barnard in 1887 repeated a yarn that the quality of the Campbeltown Distillery 'brew' inspired Robert Burns to sing 'Willie brewed a peck o' maut' when he 'visited his Mary in Campbeltown'. She was 'Highland Mary' Campbell, who was brought up in Dalintober and was the poet's fiancée when she died in Greenock in 1786 at the age of 20; but there is no evidence that Burns was ever in Campbeltown; and, even had he been, Campbeltown Distillery would not have existed. (Mary Campbell is commemorated on a plaque at Glen Scotia — see my *Glen Scotia Distillery: A History*, p 9 — which is close to where she lived, and the wonder is that no Campbeltown distiller ever thought to capitalise on her worldwide celebrity by naming a brand after her.)

In 1888, whisky from Campbeltown Distillery joined that of 14 other Scottish malt distilleries in what was described as 'the largest blend of whisky ever made in Scotland — perhaps in the United Kingdom'. The blending, conducted by Robert Hillcoat & Sons, 39 Stockwell Street, Glasgow, was done in a huge vat — holding almost 12,000 bulk gallons and reckoned to be the largest in Scotland — at W. P. Lowrie & Co.'s bond in Dunlop Street, Glasgow. According to Messrs Hillcoat, the blending was 'partly an experiment and partly to meet a demand which has arisen for pure malt whisky'. The individual malts, which were three years old, had been blended by 'a patent steam mixer' and the result was said to be 'a spirit remarkably creamy and mild'. A 'company of gentlemen interested in the whisky trade' was present as the seal of the vat was removed by an Excise officer on 20 March and the whisky was run off into casks.

The 15 malt whiskies in the blend were from distilleries all over Scotland and included several now defunct: Auchtertool in Fife, Ben Wyvis in Cromarty, Dean in Edinburgh, Gleniffer in Renfrewshire, Tullymet in Perthshire and Glendarroch in Ardrishaig (Appendix 8).

Campbeltown Distillery was the sole representative of that region, but there were two Islay distilleries, Ardbeg and Bunnahabhainn. The others were from Speyside — Cragganmore, Glen Grant, Glenlivet and Glen Rothes — plus Ben Nevis in Fort William and 'Auchuagle',[124] which probably represents Auchnagie.

In 1905 Campbeltown Distillery was described as 'one of the smaller works' in town: 'It has a mash tun 15 feet in diameter, five wash-backs holding 3,000 gallons each, and two small pot stills containing 1,400 and 960 gallons each.'[125] Glen (p 154) has the distillery 'shut' c 1924.

Clarke, Robert, manager of Benmore Distillery, was 44 years old when he died suddenly of double pneumonia on Hogmanay 1923 at the distillery house. He was a fit man and keen on sports, and he frequently refereed local football matches. In games played immediately after his death, the players wore black armbands as a mark of respect. Clarke belonged to Aberdeen and had come to Campbeltown two years previously, having earlier managed Aberfeldy and Linlithgow distilleries. Loch-head Distillery had recently been added to his managerial responsibilities 'when it was acquired by his firm'. He had served in Egypt with the Royal Army Medical Corps during the First World War and was twice mentioned in despatches and awarded the Meritorious Service Medal. He was survived by his wife, Eliza Jane McLean (died 1956, aged 75), and a daughter Margaret, who married Archibald MacLeod, Campbeltown, 11 weeks after her father's death.[126] He is buried in Kilkerran Cemetery, where his stone describes him as 'Manager, Benmore Distilleries' — see 'Benmore Distillery' for explanation of the plural.

Club, The, was built in Main Street in 1898 for the town's business and professional classes, and, being a male-only and somewhat exclusive institution, was popularly known as 'The Gentlemen's Club'. To a legal debate, then current, on 'What is whisky?', the *Aberdeen Evening Express* contributed the observation that 'the manufacturers of whisky do not themselves patronise blended whisky, and yet it is to this blending process that all the present trouble is due'. The article alleged that in a 'club in Campbeltown', to which most of the local distillers belonged, these members kept their own malt whisky in a private locker and drank nothing else. It was the 'boast of the club that nobody ever took a headache out of it ... Distillers themselves, we are told, and those who are the best judges of whisky, will never drink a blended whisky if they can get a single one.'[127]

Coal. Although peat was the preferred fuel for malting, large quantities of coal were used in distilleries for general purposes, such as heating boilers, and much of it came from Ayrshire. In mid-October 1887, for example, four schooner-loads from Ayrshire ports were discharged in Campbeltown for distilleries alone.[128]

Early in the following year, newspaper reports of two accidents at coal-boats caught the carters — both, coincidentally, employed by Campbeltown Distillery — at work. In January, while waiting to load his cart from the S.S. *Glenhead*, Robert Kelly was blown into the sea by a blast of wind and injured his face when he fell between the quay and the boat. In February, while a cart was being backed towards the schooner *Wern*'s deck, it fell between boat and quay and took the horse with it. Fishermen, who witnessed the accident, hauled out the terrified horse using a rope and tackle.[129] In 1889, owing to a 'stoppage' at the local coal-mine, caused by subsidence, the Distillers' Association was forced to charter vessels to import coal.[130]

Local distillers, as noted, were far from dependent on local coal — they were far from dependent on local anything, apart from water and labour — but local coal, transported into town by rail from the pit at Drumlemble, was certainly extensively used and cheaper to buy.

A fatal accident enquiry, in 1896, graphically illustrated the loading procedures. John Taylor died on 23 March, at the coal depot in Argyll Street, when the wheel of a cart ran over him as he tried to control a runaway horse. He was aged 67 and had worked for 46 years with John Colvill & Co., Springside. He was with Daniel McTaggart, carter with the company, when the accident happened. Thomas Buchanan, who managed the depot for J. & L. Galloway, Argyll Colliery, told the court: 'I empty the hutches of coal into the customers' carts. These hutches come from the pit on waggons. They are rolled off the waggons on to a platform at the depot. They are emptied into a shoot which communicates with the cart ... The cart was backed in below the shoot ... McTaggart was in the cart to pack the coals with a shovel. The off-side rein was in the cart within reach of McTaggart. Taylor was holding the other on the near side of the horse's head. I called "Look out" and emptied the [first] hutch into the cart ... When the coals struck the cart the horse jumped, evidently at the noise, and then bolted at full gallop.'[131]

In 1905, *The Wine and Trade Record* reported that coal for the still furnaces in Campbeltown distilleries was 'obtained from the Campbeltown Coal Company'. In the malting furnaces, however, coke and anthracite were gradually replacing peat: 'In fact, under some kilns, peat finds no place except for initial kindling.' This change was attributed to 'the growing taste of the public for a more neutral spirit'. Londoners, in particular, 'are all the time asking for lighter tobacco, milder cheese and more neutral whisky'; and the 'hot countries', to which increasing quantities of whisky were being exported, were 'ill-adapted for the consumption of heavy, indigestible whiskies'.[132]

In 1962, Springbank Distillery installed a new boiler with an automatic 'coal-feed' system, on the initiative of its manager, D. R. Allan. It was described as 'one of the most up-to-date solid fuel distillery heating plants in Scotland', and, after a few weeks' use, a saving on fuel costs of 21 per cent was noted. Mr Allan and his fellow-directors were anxious to support the local coal-mine, Argyll Colliery at Machrihanish,[133] which, however, would close in 1967, delivering a massive blow to the local economy.

Colvill(e) families. The matter of the variant spellings 'Colvill' and 'Colville' may be disposed of here: they were used interchangeably and are insignificant. An earlier variant 'Colvin' has long been obsolete. The family was of Lowland Plantation stock and its presence in Kintyre dates from the mid-17th century. Four Colvilles were elected Provost of Campbeltown — John in 1842, David in 1848, Duncan in 1881 and John in 1919 — and all were in the distilling business.

Colvill, Archibald — see 'Hazelburn Distillery'.

Colvill, Charles, was a founding partner in Dalaruan Distillery in 1824. He married Janet Dunlop in 1798; was described as a merchant when his son Archibald was born in 1813; was a cartwright when Dalaruan Distillery was founded; in *Pigot's Directory* of 1825 — three years before his death at the age of 58 — was a 'ship owner and fish curer, Balgom st'; and is merchant on his gravestone in Kilkerran. His daughter Mary married Daniel Greenlees (q.v.) in 1824, and from her son, Charles Colville Greenlees (q.v.), came the much-recycled tale explaining how Colvill was inspired to invest in the whisky business. When in business as a cartwright, he travelled to sell his implements, and while staying in an Islay hotel he had to share a bed with an Excise supervisor, from whom he 'spent the whole night in gleaning information about the Islay distilleries'.[134]

Colville, David #1, 'writer', or lawyer, who died, aged 56, on 26 November 1858, at East Cliff, Kilkerran Road, founded Reid & Colville, Dalintober Distillery, in 1832, with his brother-in-law, Archibald McCorkindale (q.v.)

and Peter Reid (q.v.), when already a partner in Dalaruan Distillery. David's parents were John Colville, maltster, and Martha McMurchy, and his wife Elizabeth's were Duncan McCorkindale, merchant, and Catherine McIsaac.

At the age of 15, he started work in the office of John McLean, writer in Campbeltown, and, after about two years there, spent four-and-a-half years with Davidson & Turner, writers in Greenock, which he supplemented with a course in law at the University of Edinburgh in the winter of 1824/25. When he returned to Campbeltown in 1825, he was made a Notary Public and a Procurator. He was involved in the Campbeltown Steam Packet from its beginning and was six times its chairman. His many other business interests included a partnership in the Largie Farina Factory, a place on the committee of the Campbeltown and Tarbert Stage Coach Company, and three insurance agencies. He spent 26 years on Campbeltown Town Council and in 1848 was elected Provost, in which capacity he served two three-year terms. In about 1852, he was appointed agent for the Clydesdale Bank.[135] His wife, Elizabeth, who died in 1892, aged 85, at East Cliff, purchased the estate of Dalintober and Dalaruan in 1833. David and Elizabeth Colville had 11 children, of whom sons Duncan and David, below, bought Dalintober Distillery, and daughter Martha married a Fife distiller, William Haig (q.v.). Daughters Isabella (died 1894) and Elizabeth (died 1921) married ministers, Rev Neil MacMichael (in 1862) and Rev Donald MacCorquodale (in 1864), respectively.

Colville, David #2 and Duncan #1. These brothers died within four months of each other in 1916, Duncan on 4 March, aged 77, and David on 7 July, aged 71. Their headstones are separated in Kilkerran Cemetery by that of their parents (above). They married Syme sisters from Craigie, near Leuchars, in Fife: David to Margaret in 1870 and Duncan to Catherine in 1872. David met his future wife while they were both at St Andrews, he as a pupil at Madras College and she 'to complete her education'. In 1861, David won 12 first prizes at Madras College, including Greek and Latin.[136]

Duncan Colville was born, raised and educated in Campbeltown, and his formal education ended there. His 'early business training' was received in Glasgow and he returned to Campbeltown in 1863 as general manager, or agent, of the Campbeltown Steam Packet, a position which attracted more than 70 applicants. After two years, however, he resigned,[137] and in 1867 he and his brother bought Dalintober Distillery, with Duncan as senior partner. His public interests were extensive. When appointed Dean of Guild of Campbeltown Town Council in 1875, he was considered 'young' for the post, but, against that, he had 'varied business experience' and a reputation as an 'able financier'.[138] He was Provost of Campbeltown from 1881 until 1890, when he retired from the Council, and he served as chairman of the Campbeltown Distillers' Association, the Campbeltown Building Co. and the Campbeltown Steam Packet Co. He was 'known to be a generous giver to all deserving schemes'. He died unexpectedly in the night, at his house, Hazelbank.[139] His widow died in 1921 and left a moveable estate of £24,244.[140]

David Colville, too, died suddenly in the night, at The Hall, his house at the east end of High Street, Dalintober, which he bought in 1883 from another distiller, Samuel Greenlees, Hazelbank;[141] and Hazelbank was purchased by his brother Duncan in 1897 after the death of Samuel's widow. The Hall was later enlarged as an hotel and is now run as a bed and breakfast business. Unlike his brother, David took no part in public affairs. He took a 'deep interest' in the local horticultural society and was a frequent exhibitor and prize-winner at its shows, but latterly his preferred hobby was angling. He was 'genial', 'amiable' and 'highly respected', his obituarist judged. He left four sons, two daughters and his wife,[142] Margaret Gilloch Syme, who, in 1927, became the first 'full lady member' of the Kintyre Club,[143] which since 1883 had allowed women only 'associate' membership. She was from long-lived Fife farming stock and celebrated her hundredth birthday on 8 July 1939, and died the following year.[144]

Colville, Duncan #2. A son of David #2, Duncan became an authority on a diverse range of local subjects, including archaeology, genealogy, history, natural history and place-names. His contributions to the history of the Campbeltown whisky industry include the list of local distilleries, from the first built in 1817 to the last in 1879, which, if understandably incomplete, has been of singular value in elucidating the evolution of the industry and the complex changes in ownership; and the Live Argyll archive in Lochgilphead holds his large collection of distilling-related letter-books, account books, legal documents, letters, and newspaper cuttings, etc. He was almost 98 years old when he died in 1998.

A slight on his reputation as an historian requires to be redressed. Stirk, p 78, berates 'The Origin and Romance of the Distilling Industry in Campbeltown', without identifying the author as Duncan Colville, to whom his book was dedicated. He says that the paper was written in 1923 and criticises it for having 'failed to notice the dire state of the industry by 1923' and instead summarising 'the reasons behind the huge growth of the distilling industry in the burgh'. The paper was not written in 1923, but was delivered to a meeting of the Kintyre Antiquarian Society on 10 January 1923, by which date, according to Mr Stirk's own 'bleak statistics', precisely three distilleries had closed. In any case, it was not Colville's intention to write a full history of the industry, as the title of his paper explicitly stated and as he explained in the preamble to 'List of distilleries erected in Campbeltown since 1817': 'I am afraid, however, that to relate all about the progress of these distilleries and the corresponding growth and prosperity of our burgh, would involve so much time that I must defer from doing so ...'[145] Since he declined to address the growth of the industry in the 19th century, he was hardly going to address its decline in the 20th.

Colvill(e), John Jr. (#1), who died on 5 December 1851, was agent for the Clydesdale Bank in Campbeltown from 1839 until his death, and Provost of Campbeltown from 1842 until 1848. He was also an early investor in the distilling industry as a partner in Kinloch, Longrow, Kintyre and Scotia distilleries. His funeral at Kilkerran drew a large crowd — comprising clergymen of 'all denominations, the authorities of the burgh and private individuals of all ranks' — and shops and offices along the procession's route were closed.[146] He was succeeded at the Clydesdale Bank by another Colville, David #1, also a lawyer with distilling interests. His executors were John Colvill #2 and Robert Colvill (q.v.), his son-in-law, and his estate — including farm stock and crops — was valued at £12,917.[147]

His parents were Archibald Colville and Janet Clark, and he married Jean Galbraith, daughter of Archibald, merchant, in 1824. She died in 1864. Three of their daughters married into distilling families — Elizabeth to Robert Colvill (above, as executor), Jessie to Charles Greenlees (q.v.) and Martha to John Mactaggart Grant, son of John Grant (q.v.) — and in 1844 daughter Jean married Rev James Boyd, minister of Longrow Church. Their son, Andrew Galbraith Colville, born in Campbeltown on 17 December 1846, played rugby for Merchistonians and represented Scotland in the first ever rugby union international match, against England on 27 March 1871. He died on 19 April 1881 in Bournemouth, aged 34. There was no obituary in the *Argyllshire Herald*, but a death notice described him as 'of St Paul de Loanda, S.W. Africa, late of Campbeltown'.[148]

Colvill, John #2, of Muasdale and Machrihanish, died on 17 October 1883, aged 87. He was a saddler, but when Burnside Distillery was built in 1825, his name appeared among the partners. In 1830, he built Springside Distillery, which he ran as John Colvill & Co.; in 1858, he bought

Machrihanish estate for £12,300 and in 1860 Muasdale estate for £20,510, huge sums of money at the time. In 1862, he sued one of his tenants, William Armour, and Daniel McMurchy, cooper in Campbeltown, Armour's 'cautioner', for 'miscropping' on Mid Muasdale farm and was awarded the £14 damages he sought.[149]

His parents were Robert Colvill, cartwright and smith in Campbeltown, and Janet Mitchell. His wife, Margaret Colville, whom he married in 1823, was his third cousin. She was a daughter of John Colville, maltster, and Martha McMurchy. She died in 1847 at the age of 41, leaving four sons and three daughters, the youngest a year old. In Census 1851, he was a distiller employing six men and sharing his house at Burnside with sons Robert (aged 25), distiller; Archibald (21); John (23), a Divinity student (and later a well-known evangelist); and Mathew (14); his daughters were probably being cared for elsewhere by relatives.

He was a member of Campbeltown Town Council from 1833 until 1848, and in 1862 was one of the original members of the Campbeltown Bowling Green, which occupied the site of the present Victoria Hall from 1863 until 1879, and was revived as Stronvaar Bowling Club in 1906. He left an estate valued at £80,532. [150]

His son Archibald died on Madeira on 12 April 1858, aged 28. His place of death suggests that, like his brother, Mathew #1, Archibald had tuberculosis, and had gone to Madeira for the sake of his health. By a remarkable coincidence, there was a death notice in the same issue of the *Argyllshire Herald* (30 April) for Margaret Reid, who died on Madeira on 25 March, 19 days before Archibald. Her father was Peter Reid, 24 Burnbank Street, Glasgow, who can only have been the Campbeltown-born industrialist and partner of Archibald's maternal uncle, David Colville, in Dalintober Distillery.

Colvill, John #3. The local newspaper headline over the obituary of John 'Jack' Colvill was 'An Outstanding Public

Man'. He was so 'outstanding' that all his activities cannot be accommodated here. He was the eldest son of Robert Colvill (q.v.), and his mother, too, was a Colvill. He died, aged 69, at Bellgrove on High Askomil on 16 February 1926. The long obituary fails to mention the distilleries he owned — Argyll and Meadowburn — remarking only that 'although actively engaged in distillery management, the open claimed much of his time'. The 'open' was the outdoors, and he was evidently a man with much time for leisure.

He was of 'commanding stature and great physical strength' and was keen on both horse-breeding and -breaking. He had trained with a 'famous' horse-breaker, and, when a namely trotting horse, 'Jim Crow', was imported to Kintyre, Colvill was one of the few who could mount and master the 'spirited steed'. (Yet, for all his love of horses, he was one of the first motor-car owners in Kintyre.) In 1905, he sustained head injuries and a broken nose when a young horse he was breaking in at Bellgrove bucked and threw him.[151]

In common with many Campbeltown distillers, he honoured the family farming legacy and was a president of Kintyre Agricultural Society. Yachting was a favourite recreation and he owned a succession of small cruising cutters, notably the *Joppa*, *Roselea* and *Witch*, in which he 'made many adventurous voyages' through the Inner and Outer Hebrides. He enlisted in the 5th Voluntary Battalion, Argyll & Sutherland Highlanders, in 1887, was commissioned as second lieutenant in 1890, lieutenant in 1892 and resigned in 1895. Owing to his 'fine stature', he was a 'conspicuous figure in uniform', and also a 'good rifle shot', a skill which also served him on the hills. He was a Justice of the Peace; was in the Town Council from 1890 until 1925, and served as Dean of Guild from 1903 until 1919, when elected Provost for a three-year term. He was also a member of Argyll County Council until his death, and chairman of the Campbeltown Steam Packet. Needless to say, but his obituarist said it, 'He had a liking for public life, and few men in his day have held so many public offices at one time.'

The pall-bearers at his funeral were his brothers Archibald, Dunfermline; Robert, Hove, Sussex; and Matthew, Campbeltown; John Greenlees, nephew; Thomas Robertson, brother-in-law; R. Y. Maxtone; A. F. Huie; Tom Milroy, gardener, and Duncan Stewart, coachman.[152]

He was survived by two daughters, a son, and his wife Christina Gemmell Wallace, known as 'Teenie', whom he married in 1904. Twenty-three years younger than him, she was a daughter of Robert Wallace (q.v.) and died on 2 February 1965, aged 86.

Colvill, Mathew #1, a son of John #2, was 27 years old and unmarried when he died from tuberculosis on 26 February 1864 at Burnside Street. His death was registered by his brother, Robert (q.v.). He was doubtless the 'Matthew Colville, distiller' who bought a share in the Campbeltown & Glasgow Steam Packet Joint Stock Company at an auction in 1860, and two years later advertised for let a three-apartment house and 'half of a two-stalled stable, suitable for a farmer on the Sabbath'.[153]

Colvill, Matthew #2, died in 1946, aged 82, in the house in which he was born, Rockbank, Low Askomil. A son of Robert (below), he was 'for some time in his early life' connected with Meadowburn Distillery. Agriculture, however, captured him in the end. He managed the family estate of Muasdale, and also, for a time, a sheep farm near Bellochantuy. He had a very retentive memory and a 'great store of local knowledge', but was, by nature, 'very reticent and quiet'. He was widely travelled and had visited India, Australia, America and Canada, but he also enjoyed walking in his native Kintyre, and 'in his prime of life he thought nothing of taking a walk to Muasdale, fifteen miles away'. He never married.[154]

Colvill, Robert. When Robert Colvill died on 26 November 1891, at the age of 67, in Bellgrove, his mansion on

High Askomil, his obituarist described him as 'a confirmed invalid for the past two years'. His wife, Elizabeth, whom he married in 1854, shared his surname: her father was John Colville Jr. (q.v. #1). Robert's father was John Colvill #2 and his mother, Margaret, was also a Colville.

In 1844, Robert built Argyll Distillery in partnership with Hugh Greenlees and Robert Greenlees Jr., and in 1853 he purchased Meadowburn Distillery. By the time of his death, the business was being run by his eldest son, John #3. Robert inherited the estate of Muasdale, in Killean and Kilchenzie Parish, on the west side of Kintyre, to which he added the farm and inn at Drumore-na-bodach, Bellochantuy.

At the time of his death, he and his wife, who lived until 1916, had four sons and four daughters,[155] one of whom, Margaret, in 1889 married the Gaelic scholar Rev Donald John Macdonald, who was born in Benbecula and was minister of Killean and Kilchenzie parish from 1880 until his death in 1930. Rev Macdonald was one of three ministers who officiated at the wedding of Margaret's sister Jean, who also married a minister, Rev William Galbraith, Rothesay, in 1895.[156] Another of the sisters, Janet, born in 1869 and died in 1894, is commemorated on the family gravestone in Kilkerran, but was 'buried in the Indian Ocean'. 'Jenny' was on the *City of Cambridge* on passage to Calcutta with a sister, going out together to India as missionaries. News of her death was cabled home from Colombo, Sri Lanka.[157]

Colville wedding. 'Fashionable wedding' was used in turn-of-the-century local newspapers to headline marriages between 'toffs', and the union of Etta Colville and John Lindsay Anderson, in April 1903, was just that. She was a daughter of David Colville #2, and her husband was town clerk in Cupar, Fife. The sun shone, ships in the harbour were festooned with bunting, and Castlehill Church — decorated for the occasion with banks of flowers, pot plants and greenery — was packed. Three ministers officiated at the ceremony, two of whom, Rev Neil MacMichael and Rev Donald MacCorquodale, were uncles of the bride. Etta's attire was minutely described; this is how she appeared to the *Argyllshire Herald* reporter:

'The bride's dress was a beautiful one of soft ivory satin tucked all over. The skirt had a chiffon flounce roped at top with the same soft material. The hem was finished in front with a spray of orange blossom, and a large true lovers' knot with orange blossom caught in it adorned the edge of the long satin train. The bodice, which had a chemisette of rucked chiffon, was draped with a fichu [small triangular shawl] of chiffon with long stoles, the ends finished with silk tassels. Orange blossom also adorned the front of the bodice. A small handkerchief of Limerick point lace was fastened in the dress. The full sleeves were of chiffon. The bride's veil, which was worn off the face and fastened in front with orange blossom, was the same that had been worn by the bride's mother at her wedding. The bride was without gloves, and carried a bouquet of white roses and lily of the valley. Her ornaments were a pearl pendant, the gift of the bridegroom, and gold curb chain bracelet, presented by the town council of Cupar.'

The attire of 40-odd female guests was also described, albeit in much less detail. Among the 200-plus wedding presents was a 'handsome' dining-room clock, with inscription, presented to the bride by the employees of Dalintober Distillery.

The wedding reception, for around a hundred guests, was held in Hazelbank, home of the bride's uncle, Duncan Colville, and now the Ardshiel Hotel, with its award-winning malt whisky bar. Afterwards, the newly-weds left on the steamer *Kinloch* for Ardrossan, '*en route* for the Continent', their departure witnessed by a 'great assemblage of the townspeople'. The steamer was 'draped with bunting', and, as she steamed out of Campbeltown Loch, three shots were fired from her deck. 'The bride's going away dress, in which she looked exceedingly well, was of grey-green tweed with little coatee, trimmed with facings of duck's egg green spotted cloth and tassels. She wore a black hat.'[158]

An equally lavish report was conferred on Etta Colville's sister, Lizzie, when she married George Gow, factor to Lord Falmouth, the following year.[159]

Conley, Neil, Thornhill, Dalintober, died on 24 October 1908, aged 59. His only education was at the Free Church School, Lochend, where his teacher, Malcolm Campbell, persuaded him to become a pupil-teacher. He didn't stick that job for long, however, and found employment instead with the Campbeltown Steam Packet. His stay there was also brief, and he moved again, to David Colville & Co., Dalaruan Distillery, where he remained for 38 years as secretary. He was, his obituarist noted, 'held in high esteem' by the managing director of the firm, Charles C. Greenlees, 'who looked upon him more as a friend than a servant'. He was a deacon, elder and Sunday school teacher in Lochend Church, a collector for the Scottish National Bible Society, an officer in the 1st Campbeltown Company of the Boys' Brigade, and colour-sergeant in the local Rifle Volunteers. As a 'characteristic Scot', he sent, 'at great sacrifice', three of his four children to Glasgow University.[160] His parents were Dugald Conley, carter, and Margaret MacCallum. The surname Conley can be traced, in its 17th century Gaelic forms, to a farm on the Mull of Kintyre, Balimacilchonalie.[161] His widow, Jean Wallace, died in 1931, aged 80.

Coopering was once a thriving industry in Campbeltown. The Campbeltown Coopers' Society was founded in 1777 with 34 members, each of whom subscribed 10s to a fund for the benefit of 'reduced or ailing members of the Society or the widows of the members of the Society'. In the following year, the roll contained 61 journeymen coopers and several apprentices.[162]

Coopers at that time supplied containers to the entire Kintyre community, from capacious whisky and herring barrels to the little 'coags' from which children supped their porridge and soup. Staves for barrels were imported from Norway; wooden hoops, for binding the staves, came from Holland, until replaced by iron hoops in 1811; but the ends, or heads, of barrels were supplied locally from woodlands at Lossit, Carradale, Tarbert and Inveraray, in the form of 'rungs', 18 inches long and afterwards, as required, split into boards.[163]

In the 18th century, the main market was in the supply of barrels to the herring-curing industry, but by the late 19th century, in Campbeltown, that industry was being superseded by markets in fresh herring, and boxes were the required containers. By, then, however, the whisky industry was booming.

There were four categories of coopers, graded on specialisation. The most skilled, and highest-paid, were the 'wet coopers', who made barrels for beer and whisky. Initially, cooperages were independent family-run businesses, but by the time of Barnard's visit to Campbeltown in 1885, there were 11 operating in, and owned by, distilleries.

The choice of wood for the manufacture of casks was of prime importance. As Ann Glen explained: '... it must not flavour the contents, [must] be susceptible to bending when heated without cracking, and have a tight grain'. It must also have 'pores to allow the spirit to "breathe" ... yet be hard-wearing and durable'. The ideal wood was oak, which had to be imported, since timber in Kintyre was a scarce resource. Memel Oak from the Baltic and Red or White Oak from America were shipped to Campbeltown as staves, and local blacksmiths made the wrought-iron hoops for binding the casks. Increasingly, however, whisky distillers came to rely not on the import of wood for barrels, but on barrels themselves: used sherry casks, which impart from their wood both colour and additional flavour to the whisky stored in them, and used Bourbon whisky casks from America.[164]

In 1873, William Dickson & Co. — see 'William Cadenhead Ltd.' — was advertising a large stock of 'very OLD CAMPBELTOWN WHISKY Matured in Sherry Wine Casks'.[165]

The choice of casks in the whisky industry was addressed in an article, 'Whisky Enterprise in Campbeltown', published in 1897 in the first issue of the *Distillers' and Brewers' Magazine*, and reads as though the anonymous writer might have had a financial or other interest in Lowrie's wine-seasoned casks!

'The wine-seasoned casks, patented and supplied by Messrs. W. P. Lowrie & Co., of Glasgow, are extensively used in Campbeltown, and the results are most satisfactory. Whisky two years in these casks is equal to ordinary four-year-old, while if kept in wine-seasoned casks for three years, the whisky shows a quality which cannot be surpassed. Considering the difficulty there is in obtaining genuine sherry casks, distillers are pleased to obtain the excellent substitute provided by Messrs. W. P. Lowrie & Co., which is at the same time slightly cheaper than genuine sherry casks would be. Several of the Campbeltown distillers have this year imported sherry casks direct from Spain, which are expected to turn out a superior whisky.'[166] Superior to what — whisky aged in Lowrie's wine-seasoned casks?

See also 'Robert Ryburn McMurchy'.

Dalaruan Distillery, popularly known as 'The Brewaree', was built in 1825 on Broad Street, on the site of a brewery erected *c* 1770 for Orr, Ballantine & Co: Robert and John Orr, Daniel and James Ballantine, and John Campbell Sr., merchants in Campbeltown, and Archibald Fleming, merchant in London.[167]

Specifications, dated 20 January 1824, for the 'roofing and joisting' of a distillery by Nathaniel McNair, wright, have survived. The distillery was 'intended to be built by

Messrs Colvill Langlands',[168] but the name of the firm was ultimately David Colville & Co., being David Colville, lawyer and banker; his father, John Colville, maltster; Charles Colvill, cartwright; Ralph Langlands, merchant, and Daniel Greenlees.

Of these, David Colville would go on to build Dalintober Distillery in 1832 with two partners, and Daniel Greenlees would build Hazelburn in the same year that Dalaruan was built. One of Daniel's partners in Hazelburn was Archibald Colvill, son of Charles, a founding partner in Dalaruan.

Ralph Langlands was a son of George Langlands from Northumberland, agricultural improver and land-surveyor for John, 5th Duke of Argyll. From 1792 until 1833, Ralph managed a flax mill and bleachfield — for the bleaching and drying of the cloth — near Stewarton. That industrial settlement grew into a small village, known as Lintmill, of which almost nothing remains.[169] Langlands died in 1837 and his share in Dalaruan was bought by John McMurchy (q.v.), whose wife Jean's father was John Colville, one of the original partners.

In 1898, David Colville & Co. was registered under the Limited Liability Acts to 'purchase and carry on the business as maltsters and distillers now carried on by David Colville & Co. at Dalaruan Distillery'. The nominal capital was £31,500 in £1 shares.[170]

Charles Colville Greenlees, managing director of Dalaruan Distillery when he died in 1908, was a grandson of one of the founding partners, Charles Colvill. From C.C. Greenlees, evidently, came the tale explaining how Colvill was inspired to invest in the whisky business — see 'Charles Colvill'. From Greenlees also came an explanation of the origin of the distillery's name, but it is garbled;[171] suffice it to say that 'Dalaruan' was named after the village in which the distillery was built. The original Gaelic name may represent 'Field of the red place'.

In October 1864, it was reported that David Colville & Co. were 'now enlarging and remodelling their work', and

53

in October 1877 that a two-storey granary had been built for the distillery. In April 1875, during construction of a bonded warehouse at Dalaruan, one of the masons, 24-year-old John Smith, took ill, lay on the grass and died.[172]

In 1880, when the 1st Argyll Rifle Volunteers, under Colonel Malcolm of Poltalloch, arrived in Campbeltown from all over Argyll by the steamer *Gael* for their summer camp, the malt floors of the distillery were fitted up as a 'temporary barracks' and their tents were pitched in the field at the back of the building. Four hundred part-time soldiers, including members of the two local companies, assembled on Castleacres cattle show-ground for inspection.[173]

An outbreak of fire at the distillery in July 1896 caused about £800 worth of damage. The blaze was fought by the town fire-brigade, by around 60 men and boys from the naval training ship HMS *Northampton*, which was moored in the harbour, by workmen from Benmore Distillery, and by other volunteers. The safe, desks, books and papers in the office were removed outside, and about 200 casks of whisky transferred from No. 2 bonded warehouse to No. 6, at the back of the distillery. Malting houses 1 and 2, kiln No. 3 and the stable and hay-loft were gutted, and about 900 bushels of malt destroyed. The local firemen's hose was alleged to have had holes in it, and the 'bluejackets', or sailors, were credited with the containment of the fire. In August, a month after the distillery was 'destroyed', local masons, joiners, slaters and plumbers were contracted to restore the building and its plant.[174]

The distillery was demolished in 1931 — see 'Charles Stalker', who was killed during clearance operations — and in 1938, on its augmented site, Parliament Place, itself since demolished, was built.

Dalintober Distillery was founded in 1832 by Reid & Colville, comprising David Colville #1, Peter Reid (q.v.) and — the active distiller — Archibald McCorkindale (q.v.). In February 1867, when Dalintober was advertised for sale, the grounds extended to about three-quarters of an acre and the weekly output of the business was 1,300 gallons of whisky, which could be increased to 4,000 gallons. The malting premises were 'especially commodious' and in 'perfect working order', and operations could commence 'at once'. Applications were to be made to Peter Reid, 41 West George Street, Glasgow, or 'at the Works', where David Colville would 'exhibit the Title Deeds and shew the premises'.[175] The business was bought by David Colville's sons, Duncan and David Jr., who changed the company name, albeit minutely, from 'Reid & Colville' to 'Reid & Colvilles', and in the following year rebuilt the distillery on a site closer to the shore, on what is now John Street.

The distillery was destroyed by fire on Sunday, 17 December 1899. The blaze was discovered in the early hours of the morning by a police sergeant on his beat. By the time the fire-brigade arrived with its one hose, it was obvious that the distillery itself could not be saved, so efforts were concentrated on preventing the fire from spreading to the bonded warehouses and their stocks of flammable spirits. The flat, felted roofs of the warehouses kept threatening to ignite when showers of sparks fell on them, but the buildings were saved by an additional hose led from Scotia Distillery. A revealing point about the effect the many distilleries had on the town's water supply emerged in one report: 'Owing to the distilleries' having ceased operation for the Sunday, there was an abundance of water and good pressure, and with hoses attached to hydrants in John Street and Princes Street, a copious supply was kept playing on the burning building throughout the morning...' At the height of the emergency, it was feared that the blaze might spread to both Scotia and Lochruan distilleries, as well as to houses in John Street and Saddell Street, some of whose occupants were preparing to flee. The origin of the fire, which supposedly started in the tun-room, remained unexplained, but the damage — estimated at £4,000 — was covered by insurance[176] and the distillery was rebuilt.

Following the death, in July 1916, of David Colville, the surviving partner in Reid & Colvilles, his trustees appointed Peter Dewar to manage the affairs of the business, which he did until November 1919,[177] when Dalintober was bought by West Highland Malt Distilleries Ltd. Dewar would die at Caol Ila Distillery House, Islay, in 1935.

In 1923 the distillery was acquired by W. P. Lowrie & Co., owners of neighbouring Lochruan, for 'malting and warehousing purposes', and by 1926 600,000 gallons of whisky were stored there. In that year, Dalintober was said to be 'a big, empty shell' with 'no identity'.[178] The distillery was popularly known as the 'Tin Still', from its metal roofing, and the site is now occupied by public housing (see 'Lochruan Distillery').

The distillery took its name — Gaelic *Dail an Tobair*, 'Field of the Well' — from the fishing village in which it was located. The village was created by the landowner, John Campbell of Glensaddell, in the mid-18th century.[179]

In 1984, a bottle of Dalintober whisky distilled in 1868 was reported to be in the possession of a teetotal whisky-broker in Dunkeld, Bill MacKenzie, 'who stores 104 bottles of malt in his airing cupboard'. This was presumably the bottle which fetched £2,530 at auction in 1990.[180]

Distilleries, maximum number working simultaneously. The question of the highest number of distilleries operating simultaneously in Campbeltown is one which is often debated. In *Pigot*, 1837, the list of distilleries and owners totals 27, which would appear to be that maximum. Rev Danicl Kelly, who compiled the *Second Statistical Account* for Campbeltown, recorded 25 distilleries in 1842. The figure in 1851, as stated by John Murdoch (q.v. & Appendix 5), was 23, and in 1856 there were 17 distilleries working and five 'silent'.[181] John Beith #2 in 1859 testified before a public enquiry into the operation of the 'Forbes Mackenzie Act' — introduced six years earlier to enforce the closure of public houses on

Sundays and at 10 p.m. on week-days — that there were 16 distilleries operational, each employing, on average, eight men. There were 53 public houses in the burgh, which had a population of about 6,000, and a police force numbering three.[182] When Barnard visited all the working distilleries in Campbeltown in 1885, there were 21. Samuel Thomson (q.v.), whose lifelong involvement with the whisky industry in Campbeltown began in 1897, could recall, when he retired 60 years later, 'twenty-two distilleries working at one time in the town'.[183]

Rev Dr. John Smith, who wrote the *First Statistical Account* of the burgh, reported 22 licensed distilleries in 1791, but these were tiny and produced just 19,000 gallons a year, which may be compared with the peak year, 1897, in which 1,810,226 gallons of whisky were made in Campbeltown. The 22 distilleries in 1791 were, however, merely the licensed producers; illicit distillers all over Kintyre would have exceeded their meagre output many times over, but, in the nature of their business, no records were kept! The true expansion of the industry can be dated to 1823, when the government drastically reduced the duty on whisky to 2s 4d a gallon in an attempt to combat illicit producers, who paid no duty at all. The last few 'smugglers', who lingered in the wilder parts of north Kintyre, appear to have retired or been suppressed by the 1860s.

Draff. The great quantities of barley required in distilling generated great quantities of waste, in the form of the spent grain after the mashing process, known as draff, and the fermented wash, or pot-ale (q.v.).

Draff was marketable as animal fodder, and is still in demand among local cattle farmers. In the 1830s, most of the draff was sold cheaply to the poor of the town who kept pigs — 'this filthy infliction' — and little of it went to dairy farmers.[184] In 1862, three women spent 30 days in jail for the theft of draff from Albyn Distillery, and two years later a distillery workman, John Stevenson, was jailed for 30 days on the same charge; he had been 'caught in the act by the police at twelve o' clock at night'.[185]

In October 1859, Archibald Fullarton, master of the *Maid of Campbeltown*, died in the schooner's cabin. She was at the Old Quay, laden with draff and 'waiting the night tide'. When a boy in the crew went below to stoke the fire, his captain was snoring heavily. The boy went 'up to town' for some matches, and, when he returned, 'the heavy breathing had ceased and all was still'. A doctor was summoned, but Fullarton, who had a wife, Margaret McPherson, and six children, was already dead, having been overcome, in the unventilated cabin, by 'the noxious vapour arising from the draff'.[186]

In December 1876, draff fumes from a ship's hold claimed another victim in Campbeltown harbour, in identical circumstances. A young deck-hand, Murdoch Matheson, had gone to sleep in the forecastle of the loaded *Northumbrian Maid* and died in the night. The 'noxious gas' was so powerful that two men almost died attempting to remove his body, which was eventually pulled on deck on the end of a rope which a local boy, Smollett McNaughton, had attached at 'great risk' to himself. (In January 1894, while master of the ketch *Oimara*, McNaughton disappeared, presumed drowned, at Larne Lough, County Antrim.)[187]

As whisky production increased, so too did the quantities of draff which required disposing of, and markets were created. As early as 1850, the local distillers formed themselves into a company, the Draff Association, and appointed an agent, and by 1853 cargoes were being shipped to the Ayrshire ports of Ayr, Girvan and Irvine, to Belfast, Glasgow and Rothesay, and even to Dundee. One large farm in Ayrshire was using draff as fertiliser. In 1852, between 8,000 and 10,000 tons were exported from Campbeltown, and a 'monster' storage pit — 160 feet long by 6 feet deep, surrounded by a stone wall and its floor lined with stone — had been constructed near the gas works at the Roading.[188]

The demand for draff in Northern Ireland was particularly keen. In 1885, John McKersie — see 'McKersies in Ulster'

— was appointed agent for the sale of draff at Belfast, in place of John Fleming, who had died. The trade was mainly with Belfast, and at times the demand in that market could not be met. At other times, there was a surplus, and in 1887 the Draff Association appointed agents at Carrickfergus, Larne and Drogheda[189] to shift more draff.

The export business appears to have been consistently brisk — at least when distilling was brisk — from the early 1850s on. In November 1884, the *Bengullion*, *Campbeltown*, *Exit*, *Kandy*, *Jessie Ann* and *James* were all wind-bound for a fortnight in Campbeltown with cargoes, but eventually sailed with the *Northumbrian Maid*, *Mary Colville* and *Scotia*, also bound for Belfast with draff.[190] In April 1885, the demand in Belfast was 'exceedingly good', owing to 'the backwardness of the grass' and the 'cold and withering weather', and 90 tons of draff a day were being shipped out. In that month, unusually, 60 tons went to Stranraer in the schooner *Mary Ann*.[191] In December of that year, the Distillers' Association delegated Duncan MacCallum (q.v.) to travel to Belfast and 'smooth' some 'difficulties' which had arisen among the draff carters there.[192] In November 1886, the *Exit* and *Bengullion* encountered 'very severe weather' and sustained damage on passage to Belfast.[193] In November 1889, the Draff Association appointed Hugh Littlejohn to manage a new agency in Ayr, and in the following month the smack *Carskey* loaded the first shipment for that port.[194] By then, however, the bulk of the exports would have been in dried draff, for which see 'Dried grain'.

Dramming. In 1899, the custom of giving distillery workers free, and duty-free, 'drams' of whisky each working day was ended. The men could still get their whisky, but duty had to be paid on it. 'Dramming' was akin to the Royal Navy custom of issuing sailors with a 'tot' (one-eighth of a pint) of rum daily at mid-day. The origin of the custom is uncertain, but it was believed that it discouraged employees from stealing whisky.

Until August 1899, managers of distilleries were allowed to keep a cask of spirits in a locked warehouse or store on the premises for the dispensing of drams. Under that system, however, a gallon of untaxed whisky cost the proprietor only half-a-crown (2s 6d), while the Revenue Service lost about half-a-guinea (10s 6d). Under the new regulations, distillers could, if they liked, pay duty on a cask of spirits and store it anywhere on the premises,[195] and that alternative was generally adopted. The custom of 'dramming' in distilleries appears to have ended, as did the naval 'tot', around 1970.

At the trial, in 1871, of a workman in Lochruan Distillery accused of stealing whisky, the mashman, Archibald McPherson (q.v.), said in evidence that 'the men get an allowance of about two or three glasses in twelve hours, sometimes more, not often'. He added that 'it was not usual to get whisky when racking'.[196]

Dried grain was processed draff, to which refer. Duncan Colville #2 in 1950 alluded to this local industry, but his account is rather vague. He refers to 'the draff refinery or grain-drying factory which was run by the whole of the distillers in combination'. The business, he said, was started by the Scottish Grains Company Ltd. and taken over by the Campbeltown Distillers' Association when the original company 'went into liquidation round about 1892'; but the take-over appears to have happened in late 1894. The unprocessed draff, or 'wet grains', was sold locally at 4d a bushel and shipped to Belfast, he said, while the dried product was frequently sent to Rotterdam 'for the horses of the German army'.[197]

It appears, ironically perhaps, that the marketing of dried draff was pioneered in Germany before an industrial process was developed in Britain. That process — perfected and patented c 1889 by an engineer, George Johnstone, and a starch manufacturer, Joseph Brown — led to the formation of the Scottish Grains Feeding Exports Co. Ltd.

in Glasgow, with Johnstone as its managing director. By 1894, the company had factories for the compression and drying of draff at Alloa, Campbeltown, Port Dundas (Glasgow) and Tobermory, and expansion was planned at Port Askaig, Islay, and Burton-on-Trent, England.

The Campbeltown factory was built in 1891, but was destroyed by fire in 1893. By the following year, a new, bigger — and 'fire-proof!' — factory had been built, on a half-acre site at the Roading, opposite the town gas works, employing 20 men. About 280 tons of wet draff were processed weekly, yielding 70 tons of dry. The company had entered into a contract with the Distillers' Association to take half its members' weekly output of wet draff, which was emptied into a pit and conveyed from there to the factory on a 'self-feeding' elevator. A large store, nearing completion, would be capable of holding 600 tons of dried grain.[198]

The construction of the new factory was supervised by John B. Watson, the company's general works manager, who, in January 1894, was a guest of the Distillers' Association at a 'smoking concert' in the Town Hall.[199] In March, Watson gave the *Campbeltown Courier* reporter a conducted tour of the plant. The account is unavoidably heavy on descriptive detail, but, on the assumption that it might interest the more technically-minded reader, it appears in an edited form as Appendix 6.

(Another Watson, Archibald, who was born in Campbeltown, appeared in Census 1881 in Millknowe as 'Draff Storekeeper and Gaelic Precentor' — in the absence of instrumental music in Presbyterian churches at that time, the precentor's job was to lead the singing by delivering the lines for the congregation to repeat.)

On 21 April 1894, a consignment of 30 tons of dried draff was shipped out on the S.S. *Davaar*, the first from the 'new premises'. By then, the store was almost completed, the machinery was 'giving entire satisfaction', and the men were working day and night in shifts.[200] By May 1897, the factory was processing imported draff; cargoes had arrived from Islay distilleries for what was now referred to only as the 'Grains Company'. Local farmers, however, preferred wet draff, and, 'consequently, the dried material has to be shipped to distant centres'.[201]

In September 1903, improvements were planned for the Distillers' Association factory: the buildings would be extended and four new, improved drying machines installed. Local masons, slaters, joiners and plumbers had already been contracted.[202] Two years later, a visiting journalist reported in detail on the factory, a photograph of which — in a snowy landscape — accompanied the piece. It was from that account that Colville (above) took his information on the export of dried draff to Rotterdam, omitting the quantities: '… as much as 120 tons per month …' [203]

The business was still operational in 1924 — in March of that year, an employee, Hugh Newlands, was elected secretary of the local branch of the Transport & General Workers' Union[204] — but its demise was imminent, as the local distilleries, one after another, went out of business, leaving only three by 1929. By 1922, however, two local distilleries — Lochruan and Hazelburn — had installed their own draff-drying machinery.[205]

Towards the end of the 1920s, the redundant factory was converted into a textile workshop, but that attempt to 'revive trade and industry' in the town, which was largely financed by Duncan MacCallum (q.v.), failed in 1930.[206]

Drumore Distillery (Gaelic *Drum mòr*, 'Big ridge') was built in 1834 for Templeton, Fulton & Co: Robert Templeton, farmer, West Drumore; his brother William, distiller; Mary Mitchell or Fulton; and John McMillan.

One of the four founding partners, Mary Mitchell — widow of Robert Fulton, merchant — was a daughter of Archibald Mitchell, maltster, and Isabella Ferguson, and a sister of the four Mitchell distilling brothers, Archibald, William, John and Hugh. In *Pigot* of 1825, Robert Fulton appeared as a grocer and hardware dealer in Longrow, and in *Pigot* of 1837 his widow, Mary, was among the grocers and spirit-dealers listed. In Census 1851, she was a 71-year-old grocer in Longrow, living with son Archibald — described as a 44-year-old retired distiller — and an unmarried daughter Mary, aged 37 and a 'servant' ... presumably in her own mother's household. She died on 22 January 1867, the day her brother John's daughter, Isabella, married Robert Dickie.[207] She erected a gravestone in Kilchousland churchyard for her husband, Robert, who died in 1825, and three children who 'died young', but she herself is not commemorated on it.

There were Mitchell links to two other founding partners in Drumore. When William Templeton married his first wife, Jean Mitchell, in 1835, he was described as a 'malster'. When he remarried in 1851, his second wife, Elizabeth, was, like himself, a Templeton. He was a 'grocer' when he died at Drumore in 1868. Robert Templeton, farmer in West Drumore, and a brother of William, married Margaret Mitchell, who died in 1855, aged 79. Her parents are known: James Mitchell, wheelwright, and Mary McNair. The fourth partner, John McMillan, was described in 1849 as 'sometime Saddler in Campbeltown, thereafter farmer and Distiller at Drumore'.[208]

The distillery was built by the side of the A83 on the outskirts of the burgh, where the present Drumore Farm stands, on land leased by Robert Templeton. When the 1841 census was taken, there was a small community of workers around the distillery. William Templeton (aged 40) was 'Distiller', and there was a maltman, James McIvor (20), living with him and his wife. Archibald Reid, mashman, was in another house with his wife and family, and Fred 'Howle', the English Excise officer attached to the distillery, was nearby with his family. Finally, there was Hugh Templeton, described as a maltster, and his wife Catherine Galbraith.

The first known Templeton in Kintyre was Robert (see 'Peter Reid'). His grandson, Thomas Templeton, in

Drumgarve farm, at the head of Glenlussa, was married twice, to Janet Armour and Agnes Colville, and had a total of 21 children;[209] yet the name has entirely disappeared from Kintyre.

On 22 April 1847, when Archibald Johnston's wife, Janet — a daughter of Robert Fulton and Janet Mitchell — gave birth to Robert, Archibald (q.v.) was 'Mashman in Drumore'; but the firm was soon afterwards sequestrated, and its assets — including 'Several Pews in the Relief [Longrow] Church, Campbeltown' — were advertised for auction on 29 May 1847. The firm's trustee was William Taylor, Loch-head Distillery, who was still acting in that capacity two years later.[210] After 1849, no more was heard of the distillery, but in 1851 a house, with garden, was advertised for let at Drumore Distillery. Applications were to be made to 'Mr Taylor, Lochend'.[211] Drumore was one of the shortest-lived of all the Campbeltown distilleries.

Dunlop, James #1, who died at Longrow, Campbeltown, in 1871, aged 77, was one of the three founding partners of Lamb, Colvill & Co., Kinloch Distillery, and the active partner: the others were lawyers. When, in 1825, the year after the distillery was built, Dugald Campbell, laird of Kildalloig, alleged that carters employed by Lamb, Colvill & Co. had 'carried away stones from Kildalloig Point or Island Davaar' without permission, and demanded damages and a fine, James was said to be manager of 'the new distillery'.[212] He was a trustee of Burnside Independent Chapel in Campbeltown — built in 1805 and affiliated to the Congregational Union in 1823 — and its books and papers were discovered in the property of his son James after his death in 1901.[213] James Sr. lived, according to his obituarist, a life characterised by 'quiet, unobstructive manners' and took no part in public affairs; his mind, rather, was preoccupied with 'the progress of the Redeemer's cause in the world ... and the cause of the Christian missions'.[214] On his gravestone in Kilkerran he is described as a 'merchant'. His parents were Alexander Dunlop and Margaret McNair. His wife Margaret, whom he married in 1828, was a daughter of Archibald Harvey, cooper, and Agnes Corbet, and died in 1846, aged 36. For his distiller sons James and Robert see below. The name 'Dunlop' derives from an estate in North Ayrshire.

Dunlop, James #2. At the time of his death, on 5 November 1901, aged 66, James Dunlop was said to have been 'sole partner' in the firm of Lamb, Colvill & Co., but see 'Kinloch Distillery'. He was 'a good all-round scholar' and 'expert arithmetician', and his first job, after leaving school, was in the office of the Campbeltown Steam Packet, which he left to join the Glasgow and South Western Railway Co. as a clerk. A further move took him to London with the Royal Mail Co., and there he met with an accident which left him partially but permanently disabled. After he had recovered sufficiently to work again, he returned home to assist his father James (above) in Lamb, Colvill & Co., and there he remained until his death.

He was clearly a respected figure in the distilling industry, for in 1891 he travelled to London to represent not only the Campbeltown distillers, but also the Highland distillers, at the 'Whisky Enquiry' (q.v.). When asked if he was satisfied with 'the present official designation of malt whisky', he replied that he would prefer that it were called 'malt whisky' instead of 'plain British spirits'. Asked if he approved of blending German spirits with fine malt whiskies, he replied dismissively: 'I know very little about German spirits; [they] may be made with rotten beet or diseased potatoes for all I know.'[215]

He was elected to the Town Council in 1878, held the post of Burgh Treasurer from 1881 until 1893, and repeatedly turned down the offer of Provostship. He served on various other local bodies, including the Burgh School Board, the Parochial Board and its successor the Parish Council, the Campbeltown and District Savings Bank, was manager of Lochend Church and for many years was a director of the Campbeltown Steam Packet, in which he had begun his career.

His obituarist described him as 'a man of few words', adding: '... but these were of the golden type and always commanded respect'. A man of 'very high mental ability and attainment', who 'always acted on his own initiative', he was 'a gentleman in every sense of the term ...'[216]

Dunlop, Robert. The body of 'quiet and retiring' 61-year-old Robert Ralston Dunlop — he was almost certainly named after his father's partner in Lamb, Colvill & Co., Robert Ralston — was discovered in Campbeltown harbour on 9 August 1903, two days after he disappeared. He was last seen at about 10 p.m., when he disembarked from the last Glasgow steamer. He was short-sighted, and the assumption was that he had walked over the edge of the quay in the darkness without anyone noticing the accident. He had worked away from Campbeltown, but had returned some years earlier to assist his older brother James (above) in the management of Kinloch Distillery.[217] In the 1891 census, James was described as 'distiller' and Robert as 'clerk'. They lived in Askomil Cottage with their unmarried sisters, Agnes and Jessie, and a servant, Margaret McEwing. His sister Margaret married Rev John McCallum, Free Church minister in Kincardine, in 1859, and brother Archibald, a sheep farmer at Forbes, New South Wales, Australia, died in 1894, aged 62.[218]

Excisemen. Eighteen-thirty-four was the year Joseph Pacy came to Campbeltown from England 'on promotion'. He was an Inland Revenue or Excise officer, colloquially known as a 'gauger' — locally pronounced 'gadger' — from the gauging-rod used to calculate capacity or content of casks. Excisemen in general were not exactly popular, particularly among illicit distillers, some of whom did not hesitate to assault and even murder their persecutors. The widespread refusal to pay duty on whisky stemmed in great measure from the belief that revenues went straight to England.

Pacy's dealings were with legal distillers in the town, and he made himself very unpopular by his role in a large seizure of barley on which full duty had not been paid; a native variety, 'bere' (p 13), was taxable at about one-fifth of ordinary imported barley, which invited fraud. He had to endure 'a good deal of petty persecution' in the aftermath of the prosecutions, which resulted in fines and forfeitures, but he remained unrepentant: 'I had no personal desire of a conflict with what I knew to be a powerful interest; but when I was convinced the law was being evaded and the revenue defrauded, I could not rest satisfied without joining, in all the vigour I could command, to break down the system. The more powerful the interest I had to combat, the more gratifying to my nature. I was delighted in meeting a formidable foe, for in such a case defeat is not ignoble, whilst victory is glorious.'[219]

The birth of Thomas Bird, to Joseph Pacy, 'Officer of Excise', and his wife, Frances Bird, was recorded in January 1836 in Campbeltown. The first specific reference to an Excise officer in Campbeltown in the Old Parish Registers was in 1725: John Fulton, the baptism of a child.

A book could be written about the numerous Excise officers and their families in Campbeltown in the 19th century. In general, they appear to have integrated well. The highest-ranking officers mingled with the social elite of the town, including, of course, the distillery-owners. Many officers, from all levels, married local women, and a few left 'illegitimate' children, such as John George Bain Dow, to whom Mary Keith had a son, James George, in 1842. Marriages within the service were not uncommon. For example, on the same day, 28 November 1843, Grace and Marion, daughters of the late William Cairns, 'Revenue Service', each married an Excise officer, Edward Welstad and Henry Wicks, respectively, and Cairns was 'Mate of the Earl Moira Excise Cutter' when he married Isobell Ferguson, daughter of the late John Ferguson, 'Excise officer at Campbeltown', on 20 April 1816.

In '"Camalton" Folks are Sayin'', a feature in the *Argyllshire Herald*, the following jocular observations on the social impact of the Excisemen were offered in 1874: 'That Ireland has devoted a great number of her sons to the Excise. That a great number have been sent to Campbeltown. That they don't find objection to the manners and good looks of the Scotch girls. That Campbeltown would be rather dull were there no Excise.'[220]

Twenty-five members of the Inland Revenue, 'including some English and Scotch friends', attended a Saint Patrick's Day celebration in Campbeltown in 1879. Mr G. L. O'Callaghan gave a talk on the origin of the celebration, and the remainder of the evening was devoted to toasts, recitations and songs, which latter included 'The Shamrock', 'Ould Ireland, you're my darlin'' and 'Let Erin remember'. Of Home Rule sentiment, however, there was no hint, and the first toast proposed was to 'The Queen and Royal Family'.[221]

At the second annual Inland Revenue dinner, in January 1887, in the Argyll Arms Hotel, Campbeltown, one of the officers, W. Elliot, proposed a toast to 'The Town and Trade of Campbeltown' and appealed to his fellow-officers to identify more with the locality in which they served — 'place-love', he called it — and indulge less in 'cosmopolitanism', which, though 'in itself not evil', was 'apt to be over-developed in members of the Revenue department'.[222]

Some Inland Revenue officers identified with Campbeltown to the extent of serving on public bodies. In 1881, the flamboyantly named duo, Vipond Clementson and Simeon Lord, were, respectively, a Town Councillor and a member of the Parochial Board.

Excise officers were occasionally injured in the course of their duties, and in 1876 William Court died from scalding after falling into a large 'copper' of boiling water in Kintyre Distillery, while avoiding 'cockroaches crawling about'. He left, in England, a young widow who had yet to join him at his new posting, and never would.[223]

Each distillery would have an office for accommodating the Excise officers, of which there might be as many as three in the largest of the establishments. In 1832, the Inland Revenue staff in Campbeltown consisted of the Collector, two Supervisors and 22 officers, 'all strangers',[224] an increase in staff of 14 since 1825.[225] In 1837, the total was 31,[226] in 1859, 68,[227] and, in 1866, 46, plus three 'preventative' men, stationed in Muasdale,[228] whose job was to suppress illicit distilling. In 1884, there were 56 officers 'of all grades' in Campbeltown.[229] Two years later, with the distilling industry 'very depressed', the Inland Revenue proposed to reduce staff by one member at every distillery.[230] In the 1901 census, I identified a total of 45 officers — there may have been more — from lowest to highest grade, from all over the British Isles, but mostly from England and Ireland, and the majority of them young, unmarried and in lodgings.

Membership of the Roman Catholic Church in Campbeltown undoubtedly benefited by the presence of Excise officers, but greater numbers belonged to the Episcopalian Church. Such families were instrumental in the founding, in 1848, of Saint Kiaran's Episcopal Church in Campbeltown, which had its own cemetery at Narrowfield, long disused, but still known as 'The English Graveyard'. Excise officers also brought cricket to Campbeltown before football arrived: Campbeltown Civil Service Cricket Club was formed in 1859 and played its first game in August, and two years later a cricket ground was laid out at Limecraigs.[231] That football was also introduced to Campbeltown by Inland Revenue officers, in 1879, is a probability. [232]

The Inland Revenue Literary Association, formed in 1869, was a forerunner of the plethora of educational groups in Kintyre later in the century. In November 1869, W. D. Hewitt lectured on the chemical properties of alcohol and conducted 'several beautiful experiments, all of which were most successful'.[233] Alexander Innes, I. R. Supervisor in Campbeltown, delivered a lecture on 'Intoxicating Liquors

— Their History and Early Uses', to the Kintyre Scientific Association in May 1891. He referred to Campbeltown as '"Whiskyopolis" of the British Empire'.[234]

The promotion of 'smoking concerts' was attributed to Inland Revenue officials. By 1894, these 'entertainments' had 'caught on', and 'deservedly so, as there is no form of social intercourse between such a recognised able body of men which tends more to increase the *esprit de corps*'.[235]

Acting on a motion by Dean of Guild James Stewart (q.v.), the Town Council in 1867 unanimously agreed to petition the Government in support of raising the salaries of Inland Revenue officers. Many of the councillors were aware of the officers' 'onerous and responsible duties' and of the 'inadequacy of their present salaries to enable them to support that status in society to which, as responsible officers of the Crown, they are entitled and expected to hold'.[236]

In 1876, the oldest distiller in Campbeltown, John Ross (q.v.), reminisced on the Inland Revenue Service at a gathering to mark the retiral of Archibald Lyle, after 20 years as Supervisor in Campbeltown. In 51 years as a distiller, Ross claimed, he had not met with more than two 'bad' Excise officers; and, as for supervisors, he 'never met with a bad one at all'.[237]

In May 1903, the Campbeltown Customs office in Kinloch Road moved to the ground flat of the Inland Revenue building at Lochend,[238] which was built in 1870 for Alexander MacKelvie (q.v.). The building still stands, converted back into flats, with the Tesco supermarket car-park — the site of Lochend United Free Church until its demolition in 1990 — on one side, and, on the other, the roofless shell of a bonded warehouse, the faded letters 'Hazelburn' now barely visible on the sandstone blocks forming the arch of the entrance. In 1909, the two separate bodies, Customs and Excise, were merged under the same management, as the Department of Customs and Excise,[239] and in 1922 Campbeltown District (which included Islay) ceased to be a Customs and Excise Collection Centre and was added to the Greenock Collection Centre.[240]

Some Excisemen were stationed for only a few years in Campbeltown, while others spent the greater part of their career there, and some retired and died there. Even after Excise families had left Kintyre, their movements, and the major events in their lives, are traceable in the births, marriages and deaths columns of the Campbeltown newspapers. These notices would reach three figures, were they to be counted; here are five examples:

1857: Huie Wilson, wife of William Campbell of the Inland Revenue, died on 4 September, aged 48, at Elgin.[241]

1872: Robert McQueen, I.R. — 'for many years a respected officer at Rieclachan distillery here' — died at Kirkgate, Dunfermline, on 7 January.[242]

1874: At Derwent Villa, Belper, Derbyshire, the wife of James Dunbar, I.R., gave birth to a son on 7 July.[243]

1908: At St. Peter's Episcopal Church, Glasgow, on 8 January, George Edward Wood, I. R., married Henrietta Burge, eldest daughter of the late Henry Ettwel, Campbeltown, and grand-daughter of the late William Burge, Supervisor of Inland Revenue.[244]

1921: At 18 West Claremont Street, Edinburgh, on 20 February, Violet Cordelia McRodden died at the age of 16. Her father Charles was with H.M. Customs and Excise in Edinburgh, but had earlier been in Campbeltown. 'Kind, kind, and gentle was she.'[245]

The Excisemen left two minor place-names which are now almost forgotten. Tangy Place, the high tenement at the east end of High Street, was known as The Gadgers' Berracks (Gaugers' Barracks) from the number of Excise families which once occupied it; and on the shore past Trench Point there is a tidal rock, at which an Exciseman habitually bathed, which was called The Gadger's Rock.[246]

The saddest legacy, however, is the Excise officers' children who died in Campbeltown and were left behind, under the smallest of headstones, when their families moved on. These poignant 19th century infant burials in Kilkerran include Mary and Margaret Forrester, Willie and George Gordon Ross, Maggie May Moore, Lizzie McGoldrick and George Ellis Grantham. I researched the Grantham family, and George's story was all too brief. He was born in Campbeltown and died there, on 24 September 1885, aged 18 months. He contracted measles, followed by bronchitis and, finally, convulsions. His stone bears the words: 'A Parting Token.'[247]

Generations of 'gaugers', were they restored to life, would be amazed to discover that there is no permanent H.M. Revenue and Customs presence in Campbeltown. Distillers are effectively self-regulating when stock is re-warehoused or, indeed, bottled; and a form, detailing grain delivered against whisky produced, is submitted quarterly to H.M.R.C.

Ferguson maltsters and distillers, once numerous, had faded from prominence by the mid-19th century. In accounts discovered c 1930 in an old mahogany bureau which once belonged to John Armour, cooper and merchant in Campbeltown, the name 'Hugh Ferguson' recurs ('Hugh' was very common among the Ferguson families of Lowland origin). For 1794, e.g., there is an account of 'Bear' received from various sources and 'distilled by Hugh Ferguson & Co'.[248] The only significant post-1817 Ferguson distiller was James (q.v.), but the surname appears in the genealogies of such distilling families as Anderson, Greenlees, Harvey, Mitchell and Wylie.

Ferguson, Duncan. In January 1920, Duncan 'Fergie' Ferguson's colleagues in Springbank Distillery presented him with a silver cigarette-case before his emigration to Detroit, USA, to join members of his family there. He was a well-known local piper and played in the pipe-band of the 1/8th Argyll & Sutherland Highlanders in France during the Great War. Nine years later, the local newspaper reported that he had won the William Hendrie Gold Medal for Piobaireachd at Hamilton, Ontario. The report added:

'He was quite a promising young piper before he crossed the Atlantic, and old comrades will be pleased to learn that he is still fingering the chanter to some purpose.'[249]

Ferguson, Hector, a clerk in Hazelburn Distillery office, was presented with a purse of sovereigns and a fountain pen from the distillery staff, and a pipe, tobacco pouch and tobacco, from the 'traveller' for Messrs. Greenlees, Glasgow, before his departure for London, on 3 May 1901, to work for the parent firm, Greenlees Brothers.[250] In the census taken a few weeks before he left Campbeltown, he was 21 years old and living at Lagnagarach with his parents and siblings. His father was Neil Ferguson, head of a prominent firm of builders, and in 1880, at Wimbledon, Hector's marksman brother Alexander, a private in the 1st Argyllshire Rifle Volunteers, won the Queen's Prize, which was the National Rifle Association's most prestigious award.[251]

Ferguson, James, was a founding partner in Rieclachan Distillery in 1825. His father, also James, died in 1838, aged 83, and his mother, Mary, who was also a Ferguson, died in 1841, aged 70. Both father and son were identified as maltsters in Longrow in *Pigot's Commercial Directory* of 1837. In Census 1841, he was living in Longrow with a 25-year-old servant, Martha Ferguson (perhaps his sister, below); as a 'Distiller', he was enrolled in the Kintyre Club in 1845; he died in 1848, aged 43. His one-fifth share in Wylie, Mitchell & Co. went to his brothers and sisters, who were: Hugh, baker; Jean, widow of John Harvie, distiller; Archibald; Mary, wife of Robert Maxwell, farmer; Agnes, wife of William Johnston, farmer, all in Campbeltown; and William and Martha, wife of Peter Greenlees, both in Willow Creek, Illinois. In 1850, when the whole business was valued at £1,058, they sold the inherited share to Archibald Mitchell #2, though Agnes, through her late husband's shareholding, continued in the new co-partnery.[252] James's brother Hugh, identified above as a baker, later took the tenancy of Kilmaho Farm and was a partner in Glenside Distillery Co. until 1865. He died in 1876, aged 70, and his wife, Martha Huie, in 1901, aged 84.

Ferguson, Peter. His death announcement in a local newspaper recorded that he was a distillery manager for 20 years, first at Loch-head, Campbeltown, and later at Lochindaal, Islay. He was likely the Peter Ferguson named as the contact in the sale of Highland Distillery (q.v.) in 1859. He died in Port Charlotte, Islay, on 10 June 1878, aged 54.[253] He was twice married, to Jane Morrison and then Mary MacLean, and his parents, who married in Glasgow in 1822, were Peter Ferguson, joiner, and Julia Macdougall. The cause of death was hepatitis followed by jaundice.

Ferguson, William, was manager of Benmore when Barnard visited the distillery in 1885, and he gave the journalist a tour of the premises, starting at 'the three large Granaries'. Ferguson was born in Glasgow, but his wife Martha Kelly belonged to Campbeltown. He is pictured in an undated published photograph of the Benmore staff, which numbered 14, including himself and his son George William.[254] He died in 1924 and Martha died in 1938, aged 83, at Dunalaister, Kilkerran Road. George William was awarded the Military Cross in 1918 while serving with the 1/4th King's Own Royal Regiment (Lancaster). Thirty years later, in March 1948, he left Dunalaister in a rainstorm and was never seen again. He had laid his watch, pocket-book, keys, identity card, driving licence, cigarettes and matches on a table, and taken away his coat, hat and walking-stick. When declared dead in the Court of Session in 1956, he was described as a 'retired businessman' whose worries — 'things were piling up on him' — were not, however, financial.[255]

Fraser, George Greig, who died in Campbeltown in 1920, came to the town as engineer of the Dried Grain (q.v.)

factory when it opened, and remained with the business when it was taken over by the Campbeltown Distillers' Association. He was manager for eight years until he retired in 1902. At a farewell party, he was presented with a 'handsome gold albert' (a watch-chain), and 'the evening reached its climax with a rendering of the burlesque song "Tommy MacIndoodle" by R. O'May'. He was 57 when he died, and 'by his long residence in the place, he had become quite a Campbeltonian'.[256] He was survived by his wife, Mary McMullin, who, like him, was born in Glasgow. She died in 1947, aged 84.

Fullarton, Archibald 1#, foreman mashman at Scotia Distillery, was oiling machinery in November 1863 when his cravat caught in a revolving wheel and was drawn so tightly around his throat that he was 'within a hair breath [sic] of being strangled'. Fortunately for him, a workman close by was able to stop the machine, and, assisted by James Stewart (q.v.), extricate him. His father was John Fullarton, weaver at Craigs, and his mother, Margaret, was also a Fullarton. He died in March 1867, aged 57. His wife, Margaret, whom he married in 1839, was a daughter of Archibald Sillars, Southend, and survived him by almost 35 years.

They named their younger son James Stewart Fullarton, presumably as a tribute to Archibald's boss in the distillery. James, who died in 1918, aged 63, served an apprenticeship as a plumber with Robert Armour & Sons (q.v.) and was for 35 years Campbeltown burgh master of works, in charge of building and engineering projects in town. He was twice married and twice widowed and, at the time of his death, his only son, James, was on active service in France with the Siege Artillery.[257] As late as 1900, when possession of clocks and watches was by no means general, it was James's duty to ring the Town Hall bell at 10 p.m. to encourage local tradesmen to retire to bed. At an earlier period, the bell was rung at 6 a.m. to signal that tradesmen should begin work and at 6. p.m. for them to stop work.[258]

Fullarton, Archibald 2#, a son of Archibald, above, was born in 1851 in Campbeltown and worked there as an Inland Revenue officer from 1873 until 1911, when promoted to Greenock. In Census 1891, he was living in Lochend Place — the Customs and Excise headquarters — and was described as 'Principal Clerk of Inland Revenue, Excise Branch'. With him were his wife and three daughters, the eldest of whom, 18-year-old Sarah, was an 'Arts Student'. He retired in 1912, but was recalled to service in 1914, after the outbreak of war. He later took on the management of Albyn Distillery, to which refer. In earlier life, he was a keen volunteer soldier and bowler and a director of the Campbeltown Steam Packet. He married Agnes Gemmell Wylie — a daughter of James Wylie, Campbeltown — in Kilmarnock in 1879. He died on 8 December 1926, of pneumonia, leaving Agnes, two daughters and a son.[259]

Fulton, Mary (*née* Mitchell) — see 'Drumore Distillery'.

Galbraith, John, of North Park, Kilkerran Road, died suddenly on 12 September 1881 in Manchester. He was 71 years old, in poor health and had gone the previous week to the Peak District spa town of Buxton 'for a change'. He was a founding partner in Stewart, Galbraith & Co., Scotia Distillery, and a partner in Beith, Ross & Co. until the company was dissolved in 1876 — see 'Longrow Distillery'.

He recalled, in a speech in 1873 at the Kintyre Club annual dinner, that, when a clerk in the office of the Campbeltown Steam Packet — his first job, at the age of 16 — there was only 'one small vessel', the *Duke of Lancaster*, trading between Campbeltown and Glasgow, and that her first cargo from her home port was 'one cask of whisky and a lot of old bones'.[260]

Galbraith was 'one of the most extensive farmers in Kintyre', and farming occupied most of his time, though doubtless his involvement was more proprietorial than practical. Nonetheless, he took 'a special interest' in the rearing of sheep and Highland cattle, and at local markets was a well-known figure, around whom 'clustered many friends attracted no less by his genial and hospitable manner, than by the sound advice and knowledge he was ever ready to impart on whatever related to the quality or management of stock'.

Like James Stewart, his friend and partner in Scotia, he had a long involvement with the Campbeltown Steam Packet — some 40 years, as a director and periodically as chairman — and was an active member both of the United Presbyterian Church and of Campbeltown Town Council. He was elected to the Council in 1846 and served two terms as Provost, the highest office in local government.

His Galbraith family was not of native Kintyre stock, but descended from 17th century Lowland settlers. John's parents were Archibald Galbraith, merchant, and Jean Corbet. His grandfather, Archibald Galbraith, was a merchant in Campbeltown, and his great-grandfather, William, was a maltster. Each of these, like his father, married into a Plantation family: Langwill and Dunlop, respectively. John's brother William, a merchant in Campbeltown, was a partner in Stewart, Galbraith & Co. from its foundation until his death in 1883. His other brothers, Archibald and Andrew, who left Kintyre, were cotton-spinners and merchants, and Andrew was Lord Provost of Glasgow from 1857 until 1860.

Galbraith's body arrived in Campbeltown by steamer on 16 September and was buried in Kilkerran the following day.[261] His widow, Mary Colville McEwing, was aged 82 when she died in 1900. Her parents were John Townley McEwing, R.N., and Elizabeth Colville. For daughter Elizabeth, who married disgraced bank director James Nicol Fleming in 1859, see p 34.

Gardiner, Arthur Hamilton, who died on 10 July 1915, aged 51, after 'a long and trying illness', was the fourth son of James Gardiner, W.S. — Sheriff-substitute at Campbeltown until his death in 1879 — and Charlotte Ferrier, youngest daughter of Louis Henry Ferrier of Belsyde and widow of Sir John Eyton Campbell of Auchinbreck, who married in 1855,[262] almost two years after Auchinbreck's death. In 1891, Arthur married Tindie Beatson Mactaggart, a daughter of Charles Mactaggart — procurator-fiscal of Kintyre, town clerk and local agent of the Commercial Bank of Scotland — and Margaret Stewart Beatson. They had two daughters, Margaret and Charlotte, and built Redholme on Kilkerran Road. From at least 1899 until his death, he was managing director of Colvill, Greenlees & Co. Ltd., Argyll and Burnside distilleries. His hobbies were shooting, fishing and golfing.[263]

Gardiner, Robert, who was evidently no relation of Arthur, above, was born in 1821 in Campbeltown. He began his career in the office of C. & D. Mactaggart, solicitors, after which he was taken on by Lochruan Distillery as a clerk. He ultimately became manager of the distillery and 'a well-known figure in distilling circles throughout Scotland'. As 'Mr Gardiner', he is referred to repeatedly in the wartime letters of Peter Dewar, manager of neighbouring distillery, Dalintober, and he was still managing Lochruan when a staff photograph was taken c 1921. He was a 'keen Territorial' and a veteran of the — for those who were there — unforgettable 'Wet Review', staged in Edinburgh on 25 August 1881, when Queen Victoria reviewed some 40,000 Volunteer soldiers (926 of them from Argyll) in unrelenting torrential rain. He died at his home, Falkland Lodge, on 27 April 1940, and was survived by his wife, Annie Parker,[264] who was born in Irvine, Ayrshire. There were three Robert Gardiners in succession. 'Our' Robert (3) was the son of a shoemaker (2) and cooper's daughter, Janet Wilson, who married in 1844. Robert (2) was born in 1811 at Corputachan, in Kilchenzie Parish, to Robert (1) and Kate Sinclair. In 1823, at Corputachan, Robert (1) was arrested as an illicit distiller and taken to Campbeltown jail in a cart.[265]

Gilkison, Peter, was a founding partner in Lochside Distillery in 1830 with William Hunter (q.v.) and William McKersie #1. When Gilkison married Isabella Stewart in 1837, he was described as a merchant. His parents were John Gilkison and Martha Langwill, and his sister Mary Ann married Thomas Train (q.v.) in 1845. He was enrolled in the Kintyre Club as a distiller in 1835 and died in 1842, aged 34. His widow must have assumed his partnership, for in Census 1851 she described herself as a distiller, 'one of 3 [in] firm'. She was then in Longrow with three children, John, Dugald and Martha (Langwill), and a domestic servant, 17-year-old Isabella McGeachy. Daughter Martha would marry Duncan Love, merchant, in Melbourne in 1875.[266] In Census 1891, Isabella was in Argyll Street and was described as an 86-year-old widow, bi-lingual in Gaelic and English and 'living on own means'. Son John (aged 62) was also living on his 'own means' and Dugald (61) was an 'East India Tea Planter'. Isabella's parents were Dugald Stewart, farmer in Tonrioch, and Isabella McMillan, and two sisters married distillers: Agnes to Hugh Mitchell #1 and Jean to Archibald Andrew.

Girvan, James Hunter, draff manager for the Campbeltown Distillers' Association, in 1901 had two ribs and a shoulder-blade broken at the draff store when a restive horse he was holding knocked him over.[267] His next accident at work, in January 1906, proved fatal. While walking up the Old Quay after supervising the loading of a draff vessel, he fell into the harbour in darkness. Some fishermen at the Weigh-house — a popular gathering place at the quay-head — heard the splash and hurried to investigate, guided to the spot by the barking of his dog. Owing to his stout build, he could not be gaffed from the water, and by the time the fishermen commandeered a small skiff and reached him, he was unconscious and died soon after. He was 62 years old and left a wife — Christina McCallum, who died the year after, in 1907 — four daughters and three sons.[268] He was

'Garvan' when his birth was registered in 1844, and both his parents — John Garvan, shoemaker, and Jane Hunter — were born in Ireland. When they married in 1841, her father, James, was described as 'of Derrydarroch, Ireland'.

Glen, Robert. The death in Glasgow, in 1905, of Robert Glen, of Bulloch, Lade & Co., which built Benmore Distillery in 1868, was noted in the *Argyllshire Herald* of 23 September. That he was 'well-known in Campbeltown', which he visited 'once or twice a year', is confirmed by his enrolment in the Kintyre Club in 1890. He had started in the business as a junior clerk in 1876 and rose steadily to become a partner. In 1896, when the firm became a limited liability company, he was one of two managing directors. He left a personal estate of £162, 662,[269] fabulous wealth at the time.

Glengyle Distillery was built by William Mitchell a year after he parted company with his brother John in Springbank. Neil Ferguson was contracted in January 1873 to build the new distillery at 'the west end of the Roading', and by November of that same year malting had begun in Glengyle.[270] The main entrance to Glengyle was on what is now Glengyle Road, which took its name from the distillery. The mashman's house was at the entrance, with the distillery and Excise offices behind it, facing the courtyard. The stills were of the 'Common Furnace' type and were capable of producing 210,000 gallons of whisky a year.[271] Two other Mitchell distilleries, Springbank and Rieclachan, stood in close proximity to Glengyle, and Springbank, of course, still does.

In July 1873, while a nine-ton boiler was being unloaded at Campbeltown from the steamer *Kintyre*, for Mitchell's 'new distillery', a link on the hoisting chain broke and the boiler fell 'with great force' against the gangway and gunwale of the vessel; but none of the bystanders was injured.[272]

William Mitchell successfully sued the Campbeltown Steam Packet for £52 2s 5d, the value of 70 gallons of whisky 'allowed to leak' from a puncheon while being shipped from Campbeltown to Glasgow on 5 March 1875.[273]

William Mitchell & Co. was acquired in 1919 by West Highland Malt Distilleries. In January 1924, Glengyle, Glen Nevis and Ardlussa distilleries were advertised for sale 'by private bargain'. Glen Nevis and Glengyle were each described as being 'fully equipped as a Distillery', whereas Ardlussa was used mainly as a bonded store and malting area and was only 'partially equipped as a Distillery'. There were no takers, and, three months later, Glengyle and Glen Nevis were again advertised, this time by public auction, and the notice carried more detail. Glengyle had a distilling capacity of 2,800 proof gallons per week, a malting capacity of 1,000 bushels of barley and a bonding capacity of around 250,000 gallons. The auction was to be held in Glasgow on 9 April. Glengyle sold for £350 and Glen Nevis for £500.[274] In 1925 Glengyle closed, and its and Dalaruan Distillery's whisky stocks — 22,500 gallons combined — were auctioned off.[275] In the following year, Craig Brothers, 95 and 97 Longrow, converted one of the warehouses of the 'defunct and dismantled' distillery into a garage for car-owners. Named 'Glengyle Garage', it provided a 'washing stance' and 'gas lighting for night work' and was opened in September 1926.[276]

In 1940, the distillery was bought by Bloch Brothers, the owners of Glen Scotia, whose intentions at that stage were vague; no decision had been taken as to whether Glengyle would work as a distillery, but the building would 'most certainly be reconstructed'.[277] The cessation of whisky production in 1942, as a consequence of wartime barley scarcity, put an end to whatever plans Bloch Brothers may have had for Glengyle.

In July 1957, Campbell Henderson, wholesale wine and spirit merchants, submitted to Campbeltown Town Council a plan — costed at £250,000 — to reopen Glengyle as 'a modern distillery, which would be a model of its kind'. In September, Argyll County Council agreed to use its powers of compulsory purchase — under the Town & Country Planning (Scotland) Act, 1947 — to 'carry through the proposed rehabilitation of Glengyle Distillery'. In December, however, it was reported that 'The District Valuer has failed to reach agreement with the proprietors of Glengyle Distillery for the acquisition of the property', and the proposal foundered. In 1960, the buildings were acquired by Kintyre Farmers, a local agricultural co-operative.[278]

The premises returned to the Mitchell fold in 2000, when purchased by Mitchell's Glengyle Ltd., headed by Hedley G. Wright (q.v.), a great-great-nephew of William Mitchell. The buildings were painstakingly re-fitted as a distillery and impeccably restored, and the first whisky was produced in 2004. It is not, however, marketed as 'Glengyle', for that trade name — acquired, along with the distillery, by Bloch Brothers — was passed on through a succession of companies and now belongs to Loch Lomond Group, owners of Glen Scotia.

The malt whisky now produced at Glengyle is marketed as 'Kilkerran', a name which, remarkably, had not been taken by any early distiller in Campbeltown. It represents Gaelic *Cill Chiaran*, 'Ciaran's Cell or Church', the earlier name for the settlement which became 'Campbeltown'. The full form is *Ceann Loch Chille Chiarain*, 'Head of the Loch of the Church of [Saint] Ciaran', and the initial two elements were taken by two distilleries, Kinloch and Lochhead, the latter a translated form.

Glengyle, the place, is at the head of Loch Katrine, and was likely chosen as the name for the distillery from its romantic associations with Rob Roy MacGregor, the Highland outlaw who was born there, in 1671, to Lieutenant-Colonel Donald MacGregor of Glengyle and his wife Margaret Campbell.

Glen Nevis Distillery. In 1875, Campbeltown Town Council considered plans for a new distillery to be built on land acquired from Gallowhill farm.[279] When built on Glebe Street two years later, Glen Nevis was the 21st distillery in town. The owners were D. MacCallum & Co., headed by Duncan MacCallum (q.v.). The first stone in the construction was laid on 15 March 1877, and seven months later, on 16 October, a start was made on barley-steeping. The contractors were Neil Ferguson (mason), Charles Martin (joiner, and MacCallum's uncle), Robert Armour & Sons (coppersmiths), R. McNair & Sons (engineers) and Andrew Giffen (smith). The buildings' dimensions and equipment were detailed in the *Argyllshire Herald*, and of the chimney-stack it was remarked that it 'reaches an altitude of 80 feet, so that the smoke from it will not be likely to become a nuisance'.[280] In the following year, a warehouse built at Glen Nevis was, at 120 by 110 feet, the largest yet erected in Campbeltown.[281]

Glen Nevis was sold to Scotch Whisky Distillers Ltd. in 1887, but 'held on lease' by MacCallum and bought back by him in 1890.[282] Stirk, p 172, remarks that the distillery 'somehow found its way into the hands of Stewart, Galbraith & Co. Ltd who also owned Scotia Distillery'; but Scotia had been sold to Duncan MacCallum by James Stewart of Stewart, Galbraith & Co. in 1891 and the company name was simply carried on by the consortium formed to operate both Scotia and Glen Nevis. Stirk adds that 'They sold out to West Highland Malt Distilleries Ltd in 1919'; but that company was a second consortium, which, again, was effectively headed by MacCallum.[283] In 1924, Glen Nevis — weekly distilling capacity 4,000 proof gallons, malting capacity 1,800 bushels of barley and bonding capacity 500,000 gallons — was sold for £500.[284] See 'Glengyle Distillery' for more details.

In March 1896, local masons, joiners, slaters, and plumbers were contracted to build a 'drying kiln and maltings' at Glen Nevis.[285] In 1905, a visiting journalist remarked on the four malting floors and described a 'novelty' which he noticed: '... an apparatus for regulating the draught of the kiln furnace. It is worked automatically by means of two brass rods which expand and contract according to the heat, and so open or close a swing-door in front of the fire. The result is an equable temperature produced without any attention on the part of the stoker. Messrs. H. & J. King, Nailsworth, are the makers of this ingenious apparatus.'[286]

In June 1915, the local Red Cross branch made Glen Nevis Distillery its store for sphagnum moss,[287] which, from its antiseptic properties, was widely collected by volunteers for use as wound dressings in the First World War.

In 1949, an 11-year-old Campbeltown boy, Robert Morrison, was trapped for almost 24 hours inside a warehouse vent at Glen Nevis. He and a friend had been 'looking for pigeons on the distillery roof' when Robert fell into the 40-ft. shaft of the 'granny' — or granary — which 'allows the fumes from the drying malt to escape'. He was rescued when his companion in the pigeon hunt finally confessed the accident to the police. When discovered, Robert was bruised and shocked, but conscious. 'I want a piece [sandwich] — I'm hungry,' he implored.[288]

MacCallum's choice of name for the distillery remains enigmatic, but may have been influenced by Ben Nevis Distillery at Fort William, founded in 1825. Two small Glen Nevis warehouses, with distinctive barred windows, still stand against the pavement near the top of Glebe Street.

Glen Nevis and Ardlussa Warehouses Ltd. In September 1936, the formation of a private company was announced in the *Campbeltown Courier* under the headline 'Important Distillery Development in Campbeltown'. The subscribers to Glen Nevis and Ardlussa Warehouses Ltd. were Samuel Thomson, distillery manager, Glen Nevis, Campbeltown, and Alexander Wright Gow, 200 Glencroft Road, Cathcart, Glasgow. The share capital of the company was £5,000, issued in £1 shares, and the stated object of the venture was to 'carry on the business of bonded warehouse-keepers, blenders and bottlers'. A 'considerable quantity' of whisky had already been brought in and further consignments were due from Islay and 'the North'.[289]

The active partner in the business was clearly to be Samuel Thomson (q.v.), at that time manager of Glen Scotia Distillery, a position to which his son Hugh would succeed in the following year, presumably allowing him to concentrate on the new venture. There is no indication as to how he acquired the use of two redundant distilleries and their warehouses, but presumably they came from his employers at Glen Scotia, Bloch Brothers, who got them when they bought the residue of West Highland Malt Distilleries three years earlier.

Stirk, p 94, remarks that 'this venture was short-lived', but the business, acquired in 1955 by A. Gillies & Co., along with Glen Scotia, was certainly fully functional when a youthful Richard Paterson — later a whisky-blender — was sent to Campbeltown c 1967 by his first employer, A. Gillies & Co., to 'learn something about what we're doing down there'. That 'something' was blending, and there was a staff of nine employed in the operation.[290]

Glenramskill Distillery. In a storm of 'almost unprecedented violence', in February 1856, the roof of Campbeltown Distillery was 'completely blown off' and the chimney-stack of Rieclachan Distillery 'laid in ruins'. At Glenramskill Distillery, which had closed and would never re-open, the sluice, supported by substantial stone pillars, was 'overturned and broken'.[291] That sluice carried the water from Glenramskill Burn to a large wheel which powered the distillery machinery, as Smith noted in 1835 in his *Views of Campbelton and Neighbourhood*. He described the distillery as 'the largest work of the kind in or near Campbelton', and the accompanying lithograph, 'View near Kilkerran', does show a substantial building; but Glenramskill was dismissed in 1856 as 'generally classed in the catalogue of "Wee Stills"'.[292]

The year Glenramskill Distillery was built is unknown, but it obviously pre-dated 1828, when the distillery was sold. A year later, a contract of co-partnery was signed in the name of McMurchy & Ralstons,[293] which appears to equate with McMurchy, Ralston & Co., Burnside Distillery, to which refer. In 1835 the business was advertised for sale in *Kay's Argyllshire Magazine*. Colville (1923) found references, up until 1840, to Robert and William McMurchy and David, Alexander and Robert Ralston as partners. In 1837, in *Pigot*, the distillery owner is identified as Robert Ralston. See also 'Kinloch Distillery'

Robert, described on his gravestone as a 'merchant', died on 17 May 1840, aged 60. His widow, Margaret Dunlop, was at Glenramskill with her sons in Census 1851 and died the year after.

Alexander Ralston married Amelia McNeill in 1830 and was dead by 1841. His widow married Archibald Walker, accountant in the Clydesdale Bank, Campbeltown, in 1843, when she was described as a daughter of the 'late Malcom McNeill of Corran Esquire', and her obituary connects her to the McNeill Campbells of Kintarbert and Saddell. That same obituary, under the heading 'Death of a Nonegenarian', describes her as 'a wonderful wiry old lady' with a retentive memory and the ability to 'converse with more than average intelligence'. In Census 1871 her birthplace was given as Glasgow; she died at Millknowe in 1903, aged 91.[294]

There was a small community at Glenramskill Distillery when the 1841 census was taken. The head of the Ralston household was the widowed Amelia (29); David (34), Archibald (25) and James (16) Ralston — her brothers-in-law — were all described as distillers. There were also three 'Distillery Labourers' — James McEacharn, Archibald Johnston and Duncan McCallum — and their families, and an English Excise officer, John Davis, and his family.

On 15 August 1843, David Ralston, 'Distiller', married another Ralston, Jackie, whose parents were John Ralston, merchant, and Agnes McNair. In Census 1851, David was at Glenramskill with Jackie, four children and a servant, Janet McNaughton. He was a distiller 'employing 5 men' and was clearly managing the business. In another house nearby were his brothers Archibald (37), Robert (29), who was mashman, and James (26), along with their widowed mother, Margaret (69), sister Isabella (23) and a servant, Catherine Watson. There were two additional workers, Duncan McCallum and William Mitchell, each with wife and four children, and an Inland Revenue officer, William Lindsay, with his wife, six children and a teenaged servant, Mary McMillan.

The brothers Archibald, James and Robert Ralston, above, almost certainly sailed to Australia from Greenock in the clipper *Glenroy* in March 1854. These three names appear together among other local individuals – Alex Kirkwood, John Wylie, John McKersie, John Muir and Daniel McMillan – described as 'just the pick of emigrants and certain to succeed'.[295]

The distillery seems to have operated until 1854, the year the trio of Ralston brothers emigrated. In October 1853, the fishing boat *Eliza*, which had been driven on to rocks at Kildalloig, was 'conveyed in a cart to the New Quay Head ... through the kindness of Mr David Ralston, distiller, Glenramskill', and in April 1854 a bizarre story was published in the local newspaper involving a gull and Skye terrier pup 'belonging to the distillery at Glenramskill'.[296] In May 1857, a four-apartment house, with garden, was advertised to let at Glenramskill, applications to James Dunlop, distiller, or Mrs David Ralston, Glenramskill. When the property was advertised again the following year, with 'beautifully situated' added to the description, Mrs Ralston was in Longrow.[297] David Ralston died in July 1858 and his widow in December 1891.

There is little of the distillery left, apart from the remains of the sluice. The distillery itself was situated where Glenramskill House stands today, and, had it survived, would have afforded a splendid scenic location for a visitor centre!

Glen Scotia Distillery. The most intriguing question in the history of Glen Scotia is how it managed to survive. Springbank — the one other Campbeltown distillery which emerged intact from the catastrophic post-war collapse of the industry — has been in the continuous ownership of one family since 1837 and has therefore enjoyed a degree of stability. By contrast, Glen Scotia changed hands many times and was more often out of production. It should have failed several times, but it survived and is now arguably in its healthiest state since its foundation.

The oldest surviving distillery in Campbeltown, it was founded as plain 'Scotia' by Stewart, Galbraith & Co. in 1832, though its distilling licence was not received until 1835. The premises were subsequently restructured and modernised, most radically during the period 1896-98, when the present fortress-like building on High Street was erected. The original partners were James Stewart (q.v.); John Galbraith (q.v.); his brother, William; James Napier (q.v.); and John Colville Jr. (q.v. #1). In 1864, a year after the death of William Galbraith, Alexander MacKelvie (q.v.) became a partner.

In 1891, Scotia was sold by James Stewart to a consortium, headed by Duncan MacCallum (q.v.), operating as Stewart, Galbraith & Co. Ltd., and incorporating Glen Nevis Distillery. In 1919, Scotia became part of a new company, West Highland Malt Distilleries Ltd. (q.v.), again with MacCallum at its head. In 1933, following MacCallum's suicide, the company was sold by his trustees to Bloch Brothers Ltd. of Glasgow, which two years later, for unknown reasons, changed the distillery's name to 'Glen Scotia'.

When Sir Maurice Bloch (q.v.) sold Glen Scotia in 1954, there followed decades of recurrent uncertainty about its survival. Hiram Walker & Sons (Scotland) bought Glen Scotia in 1954 and almost immediately afterwards sold it to A. Gillies & Co., which in 1970 became Amalgamated Distilled Products; in 1983, A.D.P. merged with the Argyll Group, headed by Campbeltown-born James Gulliver (q.v.);

in 1986, having made no whisky at Glen Scotia, the Argyll Group sold the distillery to Gibson International Ltd. and a French brandy company; in 1994, the business was acquired by Loch Lomond Distillery Co., which in 2014 mutated into the Loch Lomond Group, the present owners.[298]

In 1938, local historian James H. Mackenzie reported that a locally manufactured steam engine in Scotia Distillery had been 'going since 1832' — an exaggeration — and was 'still in perfect working order'.[299] Had the engine been preserved, it could have formed a unique and fascinating display in the distillery.

Glenside Distillery was established, according to Colville (1923), in 1835 by David Anderson & Co., original partners David Anderson, merchant (q.v.), Jessie Miller (q.v.) and James Armour (q.v.). In 1836, Joseph Hancock (q.v.) became a partner, and the partners from October 1839, until the dissolution of the company in August 1844, were said to have been Hancock, Armour, Mrs Isabella MacNair and Janet Anderson (q.v.), whose death caused the dissolution. In 1844, one T. Wilkie, about whom nothing is known, joined the partnership.[300]

In 1851, William McKersie #1 brought an action for debt against the dissolved co-partnery of David Anderson & Co., being Mrs Margaret MacAlister or Hancock; her sister Mrs Isabella MacAlister or MacNair; James Armour, distiller in Campbeltown; and John Anderson, grocer in Campbeltown. Depositions were taken from James Armour, above, Alexander Greenlees, distiller, James Grant, merchant, and David Anderson, commission agent, all in Campbeltown.[301] For another debt action in 1851, see 'John Grant'.

In the meantime, a new firm, the Glenside Distillery Co., had taken over, partners: James Armour, above, Hugh Ferguson, baker (later 'Farmer Kilmaho'), and John Kerr Orr, described as a commission agent in Glasgow.[302] Orr had a half-share in the business and the others a quarter.[303]

Upon Armour's death on 10 January 1865, Ferguson agreed to retire and the company was dissolved.[304] On 24 September 1866, J. K. Orr, then described as distiller in Campbeltown and Jura and merchant in Glasgow, signed a contract of co-partnery with his brother Daniel, distiller in Jura and merchant in Glasgow, to carry on the Glenside Distillery Co.[305] Just 10 days after the contract was signed, J. K. Orr died, and in 1870 the contract became the subject of a Scottish Court of Session action, Orrs Trustees v Orrs, in which Dugald Campbell Macintyre was identified as the manager of Glenside, on an annual salary of £100, and, from 1867, a partner in the Glenside and Jura firms. In 1878, a feu contract was signed by John MacIntosh Orr, Margaret Kerr Orr, William Jarvie Orr and Robert Louis Orr.[306] See 'Orr family'.

In 1908, a new firm, Glenside Distillery Co. Ltd., was formed, with capital of £10,000 in £1 shares and registered at the distillery. The subscribers were Duncan MacCallum (q.v.) and J. Duff, distiller, Glasgow, who were also directors, along with J. Robertson and Thomas W. Dewar.[307] Duff and Dewar would become directors of West Highland Malt Distilleries Ltd. (q.v.), the consortium MacCallum formed in 1919.

By 1921, the 'controlling agents' of Glenside were Robertson & Baxter, and in 1926 production ceased.[308] By the end of 1930, Glenside Distillery was in voluntary liquidation, and a meeting of creditors was advertised for 18 December in Glasgow. In September of the following year, the liquidator offered Campbeltown Town Council, as a 'gift to the town', the sites of Glenside and nearby Highland Distillery, both 'dismantled'.[309] The offer was ultimately accepted, and these sites, combined with that of Kintyre Distillery and other cleared ground on Lady Mary Row and Broad Street, resulted in the building of 46 variously sized tenements by the end of 1935.

When my maternal great-great-great-grandfather, John McKerral, registered the birth of his daughter Barbara, on 5 August 1839, instead of being described as a 'distillery worker', the designation was, unusually, 'Glenside Distillery'. In 1842, he and his wife, Amelia McKay, named a further daughter Agnes Hancock McKerral. The woman so honoured, and from whom a token of appreciation was doubtless expected, was surely a relative of Joseph Hancock (q.v.) — a partner in Glenside Distillery at the time — and probably the 'Mrs Handcock' who died on 13 August 1853 in Cross Street.[310]

In January 1873, Robert Crawford, a workman at Glenside, was sent to the Steamboat Company office with a 'box of samples' — presumably of whisky — but the box was never delivered; he had drowned in the harbour.[311]

Glenside was evidently the first Campbeltown whisky to be advertised in a local newspaper, and that at the beginning of the slump. In December 1921, Don Campbell, trading from 'The Glenside House', 40 Main Street, was offering 'Glenside Pure Malt (Over 6 Years)' at 12s 6d a bottle and 'Special Glenside (82% proof)' at 14s 6d. Later that month, Eaglesome's (p 30) had 'Fine Old Glenside Whisky' at 12s 6d a bottle. Ten years on, and five years after Glenside Distillery ceased production, its product was being imaginatively marketed by Campbell. First on offer was a cut-glass decanter containing a full bottle of Glenside, priced at 12s 6d. Next came 'Glenside Pure Malt Whisky', which Campbell claimed did not 'become cloudy or opaque by the addition of water'. Then came 'decorated miniature jars' of Glenside 'pure malt' in three sizes, quantities unspecified. The large size was priced at 5s 9d (postage 9d), medium at 3s 3d (6d) and small at 2s (6d). The labels bore the Royal Burgh of Campbeltown coat of arms and motto, *Ignavis precibus fortuna repugnat*, 'Fortune helps those who help themselves'.[312]

Graham, Daniel/Donald — see 'MacKinnon's Distillery'.

Grangemouth Bonding Company. In November 1971, the company was issued with a compulsory closing order, under the Buildings (Scotland) Act 1959, applying to bonded warehouse No. 4a in Glebe Street. The company stated its intention to reinforce the building, which held thousands of gallons of whisky.[313]

Grant, A. B. & Co. Ltd., a blending, bottling and distilling company, was incorporated in 1951 and bought Bladnoch Distillery in Galloway in 1956. In the following year, the company contacted Campbeltown Town Council's Development Committee to state that it had considered building a distillery in Campbeltown, but 'decided to rebuild Bladnoch first'. The letter, as reported, ended on an optimistic — or perhaps enigmatic — note: 'Nevertheless, if the production of a lighter malt was shown to be successful in Campbeltown, the company would be interested in acquiring a site in the town.'[314] No more was heard of a new distillery in Campbeltown, and, in the event, the company bought Bruichladdich Distillery, Islay, in 1960.

Grant, John, was proprietor of both the Highland and the Union distilleries, each of them founded by members of the Mactaggart family, into which he married. In 1825, when he married Isabella Mactaggart, he was a sergeant in the Argyll Militia; in 1827, when he baptised his daughter Ann MacDonald, he was a merchant; and in 1832, when his son John Mactaggart was baptised, he was a distiller. He died on 13 January 1849, of typhus, and Isabella died in 1851, aged 62. They erected two headstones in Kilkerran, one to three children who died young — Ann, Isabella and Lewis — and the other which commemorates only them.

Grant's origins are slightly hazy, since no birth record has been found for him and he died six years before registration of deaths began, but his gravestone gives his date of birth as 22 October 1796, and from other evidence — chiefly relating to his brother James, who was born in 1792 and died in 1858 — it can be stated with reasonable certainty that he was born in Cromdale, Strathspey, to

Lewis Grant, 'Sergeant', and Ann MacDonald. His rise as a businessman and public figure would have been assisted by his marriage into a prominent local family. In 1847, he was chairman of the Campbeltown Steam Packet,[315] a prestigious appointment.

His daughter, Helen Kennedy, married Alexander Ross, rector of Campbeltown Grammar School, in 1849, the year Ross was dismissed from his post in a dispute over his membership of 'the Secession called the Free Church'.[316] Grant, in 1843, the year of the Secession, or 'Disruption', allowed the break-away Gaelic congregation, led by Rev Duncan MacNab, to erect a large wooden shelter, as its place of worship, in the courtyard of his Union Distillery,[317] and he was an original trustee of the Free Church and one of the three earliest 'ruling elders' in the Free Presbytery of Kintyre.[318] At the Provost's Dinner of 1867, Ross, then headmaster of the Free Church Grammar School, in proposing a toast to 'The Distilling Trade of Campbeltown', remarked that his wife's grandfather, John Mactaggart, and her father, John Grant, were 'the first distillers in Campbeltown',[319] a claim which may have raised a few eyebrows, since Grant was no pioneer in the business.

By c 1833, Grant's partner in Highland Distillery was one George McLennan. The firm's name was McLennan & Grant, which also owned Lochindaal Distillery in Islay around that time.

In 1849, the year of Grant's death, his widow, Isabella, sold her share in Union Distillery, to which refer, and in 1851 she brought an action against Margaret MacAlister, widow of Joseph Hancock (q.v.), Margaret's sister Isabella MacNair, James Armour #1 and the young sons of the late Jessie Miller (q.v.), alleging that her late husband had not been paid for auditing the books of Glenside Distillery in 1844. She claimed that he had incurred expenses in going to Liverpool to investigate the affairs of Robertson, Alexander & Co., debtors to David Anderson & Co., and asked for £30 19s 3d, with interest, in settlement. Liability was strenuously denied, and the outcome of the action is unknown.[320] A few months before her death, she appeared in the 1851 Census in Back Street as a 'Proprietor of houses'; there were no family members with her, only an elderly servant, Catherine Loynachan.

Grant's son, John Mactaggart Grant, married Martha, daughter of John Colville Jr. (q.v. #1), in 1858. She died in Willesden, London, in 1910, aged 79, and he died in 1924, aged 92.

Greenlees, Alexander #1, was 80 years old when he died on 22 August 1861. A partner in Burnside Distillery, he was described as 'a respectable and persevering man of business', who, although retired from public life, 'continued to take an interest in all that related to the welfare of the burgh'.[321] In Census 1851, he was in Back Street with his wife, Mary Colville, and three daughters, Ann (31), Janet (24) and Mary (19), who would marry Hugh Goold, Customs officer in Liverpool, later that year. Alexander's widow died in 1874, aged 83, at St Clair Terrace, Low Askomil.[322] His parents were Mathew Greenlees, cooper, and Margaret Ryburn. Hers were Robert Colville, merchant, and Janet Mitchell, and she was a sister of John Colvill #2. Alexander's son Robert #1 was also a distiller, and the Mathew Greenlees, distiller, whose daughter Mary Colville was born on 14 October 1849 in Campbeltown, was probably another son, but he and his wife Elizabeth Jack have so far eluded elucidation.

In 1888, it was remarked that, although many Greenlees distillers were active in Campbeltown, the actual name occurred in just two of the 22 company titles — Greenlees & Colvill Ltd. and Colvill, Greenlees & Co. — compared with Colvill(e) in seven firms and Mitchell in three.[323]

Greenlees, Alexander #2, ran Burnside Distillery with his brother James #1, in succession to his father Robert #1 and grandfather Alexander #1. His election to Campbeltown

Town Council in 1874 — he came fifth out of eight candidates — prompted a sniffy editorial in the *Argyllshire Herald*, which accused his supporters of excessive campaigning and tasteless celebration. It was, on the evening after an election, 'somewhat unusual' to see 'a tar barrel blazing gloriously before one's residence, accompanied by a motely crowd cheering and shouting vociferously and giving vent to enthusiastic cries of "Three cheers for Provost Greenlees!"' In the history of the Royal Burgh of Campbeltown, two members of the Greenlees family were elected Provost, but Alexander wasn't one of them: three years later, when he sought re-election, he lost his seat by three votes.[324] He died of pneumonia, aged 39 and unmarried, on 20 May 1882 at Seafield, Kilkerran Road.

Greenlees Brothers. Eighteen-seventy-one was the year in which the brothers James and Samuel Greenlees moved to London and established the firm of Greenlees Brothers, the greatest success story in the history of the Campbeltown whisky industry. They were the sons of a Campbeltown distiller, Samuel Greenlees #1, by his marriage to his cousin Agnes Greenlees, which must account for the unusual repetition in the name of Samuel Jr.'s son, Weir Loudon Greenlees Greenlees, who was born in 1882 in London and died there in 1975, and is commemorated in Kilkerran on the immense family memorial, on which two out of the three large stone tablets are quite blank.

In 1893, 'Master Loudon Greenlees' appeared as a prince in 'Tableaux Vivants' at a Machrihanish Ladies' Golf Club fete,[325] but more prestigious stage appearances lay in the future. In 1937 the local newspaper reported that Major Loudon Greenlees 'has been building up for himself a high reputation as a vocalist in Canada'. His talent was first recognised at Harrow public school, and thereafter his vocal studies took him to France and Germany. During the First World War, in which, with the Scots Guards, he received his military rank, he fought at Gallipoli in 1915 and in Egypt in 1916, and was later badly wounded. Opera was his 'great musical love' and he had been broadcast on radio from Paris, London, Oslo and Vienna.[326] He was also a notable cricketer, and in 1904, when in his third year at Magdalen College, Oxford, he played in the London County team with the veteran W. G. Grace, who afterwards reported to the *Daily Mail* that Greenlees, with a score of 39 not out, had 'played very pluckily and made quite a number of fine shots to the off'.[327]

Samuel Jr.'s wife, Jessie Eliza, or 'Daisy', whom he married in 1881, predeceased him by more than 30 years. She belonged to the tragic family of the Rev Walter Weir, minister of the Lowland Church in Campbeltown from 1854 to 1864. In December 1863, the year before her father's death, four of her five siblings died from diphtheria.[328] Her mother, Elizabeth Lamb, married again, in 1872, to Captain James Loudon, Pollokshields, and Jessie assumed the surname 'Weir Loudon'. Her sole surviving sibling, David N. Weir-Loudon (q.v.), married her husband's sister, Isabel.

When Samuel left school in Campbeltown, he entered the family business, Hazelburn Distillery. His elder brother, James, had already gone to Glasgow to work for the iron and coal merchants William Baird & Co., one of the partners in which was super-rich Alexander Fleming, born of Lowland Plantation stock at Balevain farm, Kintyre, in 1824.[329] In 1871, when Samuel was just 20 years old, he and James moved to London to explore the potential of the English whisky market. Having concluded that single malt whisky — 'then practically the only Scottish product' — was not popular in England, they decided to establish the firm of Greenlees Brothers, whisky blenders and bottlers, at Gresham Buildings in London.

Their gamble paid off. The verdict, in Samuel's obituary in the *Campbeltown Courier*, was that Greenlees Brothers could be 'regarded as the pioneers of whisky-blending as well as the pioneers in popularising Scotch whisky throughout the world'. That assessment had already been delivered in less biased publications, for example *Wyman's*

Commercial Encyclopaedia in 1890: 'To Messrs Greenlees Brothers belongs the credit of having made the trade in Scotch whisky, and of having introduced that beverage to the British public in a wholesome and agreeable form, blended with the utmost nicety and judgement, so that delicacy of flavour and absolute purity are, as far as possible, combined.'

Greenlees Brothers marketed hundreds of blends over the years, but their first was 'Lorne Highland Whisky' in 1871, the foundation year of the company and also the year of the hopeless marriage of the 8th Duke of Argyll's son, John, Marquis of Lorne, to Princess Louise, the artistic daughter of Queen Victoria. The *National Guardian* in 1895 recounted: 'As a matter of history, at a large and representative banquet, held by the Trade on the day of the Royal wedding, Messrs Greenlees' firm introduced a blend of Scotch whisky, known as "Lorne", which took the company by storm. Suddenly, Scotch whisky caught on and soon found as many friends there as in the land of its birthplace.' The first advertisement for 'Lorne' in the local newspaper appeared during the week, in September 1871, that the newly-weds arrived in Campbeltown, on the Duke of Argyll's yacht, to a civic reception.[330]

Three later blends were named after places in the brothers' native Kintyre: 'Davaar Scotch Whisky' (1885), 'Dew of Bengullion' (1885) and 'Glenlussa' (1875): an island, a hill and a valley (Glenlussa was where their ancestors farmed). There was also 'Hazelburn' (1872), a single malt from the family distillery. In 1896, *London Society* calculated the number of brands marketed by the firm, up until that year, as a remarkable 554, and its current price list contained 77 brands.[331] The last notable blend was 'Old Parr', introduced to the market in 1909, shortly before the break-up of the brothers' company, and now, after a succession of mergers, owned by Diageo.

The business innovations and successes of the Greenlees brothers were eagerly reported in the local newspapers.

The following are examples.

In 1879, copied from the *Glasgow News*, a cabinet of massive proportions, carved in walnut 'in the Scotch baronial style', was shipped to Australia on the steamer *Garonne* 'for the great exhibitions at Sydney and Melbourne'. Resembling 'a fairy temple', it had been made for Greenlees Brothers to showcase the firm's 'Lorne Highland Whisky'.332

In 1880, from the London *Morning Advertiser*: Greenlees Brothers had opened 'new and extensive stores' at 31 Commercial Street, London. The four-storey building, with basement, was still being fitted out with 'machinery and appliances', after four months' adaptation. The new premises attested to 'the rapid growth of their home and their export trade, and the large measure of popularity which their "Lorne Whisky" has gained itself'.333

In 1885, from the *Glasgow Mail*: Greenlees Brothers had 'just made very large purchases of north country [i.e., Highland] whiskies for their home and export trade'. The Caledonian Railway Company had to run a special train to Glasgow, and about 50 'lorries' were required to carry the whisky from Buchanan Street Station to the bonded stores in Osborne Street.334

In 1889, Greenlees Brothers was awarded the exclusive contract for the supply of whisky at 'Messrs Barnum's great show' at the Olympia, London.335

In 1891, copied from the *Surrey Leader*: Greenlees Brothers had 'hit upon a very ingenious and novel method of advertising their celebrated "Lorne" whisky'. During the Naval Exhibition at Chelsea, they arranged for 'aeronauts' to distribute advertising circulars from balloons; anyone finding a circular bearing a special coupon could claim a bottle of the whisky.336

In 1910, Samuel was interviewed by a journalist from the London *Globe* about a recent business trip he made to New York, his first time there for 30 years. What struck him most were 'the huge commercial buildings which have sprung up and the immense growth of the city northwards'. He remarked on the 'tremendous flow of traffic morning and night to and from the city', but the hotels were 'sumptuous' and each room now had a telephone instead of a bell. Even better, whisky was 'becoming more popular with Americans'.[337]

Following their father's death in 1886, the brothers took over Hazelburn Distillery, which they operated as Greenlees & Colvill, Ltd.; in 1887 they bought Argyll Distillery and in 1888 Burnside Distillery, both of which were operated as Colvill, Greenlees & Co. By 1888, Samuel had returned to Campbeltown, bought Glenadale House, Kilkerran Road, and was running the Campbeltown operation, while James remained in London.[338] In Census 1891, at Glenadale, there was a servant for each member of the family.

James retired from the business in 1910 and died in a nursing home in London on 1 September 1916, aged 68. For many years, he was a 'regular annual visitor to his native place' and enjoyed shooting, fishing, golfing and yachting. In 1894, he was the subject of *Yachting World*'s 'Yachting Celebrities' feature, with his yacht *Amethea*.[339] He left Jessie Maclean Malcolm, whom he married in 1878, and two sons, Weir Loudon and J. Walter.

Samuel had evidently moved back to London by 1908 — his wife died there, at 92 Portland Place, in that year — and he, too, died there, on 24 January 1939. He was prominent in the London Argyllshire Association and was an enthusiastic yachtsman and golfer. He was also a keen theatre-goer and claimed to have 'attended every production at Drury Lane' for almost 50 years. In 1923, he sensationally sank £1,000 — a fortune at the time — into *Ned Kean*, a romantic play which he admired. His money kept the production running for a fortnight after audiences at Drury Lane Theatre had given it an emphatic thumbs' down.[340] His nephew, Norman Loudon, was a film producer who founded Shepperton Studios — see 'David Nisbet Weir-Loudon'.

Greenlees, Charles Colville. In his name is displayed not one, but two of the leading distilling families in Campbeltown: his parents were Daniel Greenlees, merchant, and Mary Colville, and his wife Jessie — whom he married in London in 1868 and who died in 1930, aged 89 — was also a Colville, a daughter of John Colville Jr. (q.v. #1) and sister of Archibald Colville, who succeeded to the Glasgow cotton-spinning business, A. & A. Galbraith, founded by his uncles, Andrew and Archibald. He died unmarried in 1905 and his cremated remains were the first to be interred in Kilkerran cemetery.[341]

When Charles died at Dunara, High Askomil, on 12 May 1908, aged 77, he was managing director of David Colville & Co., Dalaruan Distillery, which he joined after early 'business training' in Glasgow.

He was very much a public man and his commitments are almost tedious to relate: elected to the Town Council in 1867 and Provost from 1875 until his retiral in 1881; chairman of the Parochial Board; chairman of the School Board from 1899 until 1900; Justice of the Peace and Honorary Sheriff-substitute; chairman of the Campbeltown & District Savings Bank; a trustee of Campbeltown & District Cottage Hospital; chairman of the Campbeltown & Glasgow Steamboat Co. Ltd.; a founder and, for a time, president of the Campbeltown Liberal Club; senior elder of the Longrow Church congregation; president of the local Bible Society branch; retired in 1888 from the local Rifle Volunteers with the rank of Major and Honorary Lieutenant-Colonel.[342]

He was described in 1905 by a visiting journalist as 'one of the most interesting personalities in the town ... and replete with the history of the district'. In a photograph of him, taken outside his distillery and captioned 'Campbeltown's Oldest Distiller', he is white-bearded and dressed in a black coat and bowler hat.[343]

He was survived by his wife and one son, Daniel Colville Greenlees, who was 'on a trip to Australia' when his father died. In 1896, D. C. Greenlees had married into the local gentry. His wife was Mary Henrietta Macneal, only daughter of Captain Hector Macneal of Ugadale. The marriage service was held in St. Kiaran's Episcopal Church, Campbeltown, on 12 February, after which ex-Provost Greenlees and Mrs Greenlees entertained the Dalaruan Distillery staff, with their wives and friends, to a supper in the Masonic Hall, while Captain and Mrs Macneal did the same for their 'tenantry' in the Pans Hotel, Machrihanish.[344] D.C. Greenlees died at Dunara in 1931, aged 62; his wife Henrietta died in 1916 at Parkstone, Dorset.

Greenlees, Daniel, 'better known by his civic title of "Bailie Greenlees"', was 96 years old when he died at Dalintober House in June 1892. He wed Mary Colvill — daughter of Charles, merchant, and Janet Dunlop — in 1824, and they were in the 65th year of marriage when she died at the age of 87 in 1888. He was actively involved in the running of Hazelburn Distillery until 1881, when he was about 85 years old. His partner in the business of Greenlees & Colvill was Samuel Greenlees (q.v.), who was both his cousin and his brother-in-law. They also owned Argyll Distillery. In 1838, Daniel acquired the nameless distillery in High Street (q.v.), but evidently did not work it. His only surviving son, Charles C. (q.v.), was a partner in the firm of David Colville & Co., Dalaruan Distillery. Three of Daniel's five daughters married merchants — Margaret to Robert Greenlees, London, in 1850; Agnes to James Blackwood, London and Port Natal, in 1859; and Mary to Archibald Greenlees, London, in 1863 — and in 1864 Kate married Alex L. Bruce, brewer, London and Edinburgh.[345]

His father, William Greenlees, was a 'shipmaster', or captain, in Campbeltown. His mother, who also belonged to a family of 17th century Lowland origin, was Agnes Andrew, '... a woman of strong character, universally respected and distinguished for her godliness. The spiritual training of her family was very much the mission to which she felt she was called, especially in the absence [at sea] of her husband'.[346]

Daniel was one of the founding partners of the Campbeltown Steam Packet in 1826; served as a Town Councillor for 26 years; was a member of the United Presbyterian Church (Longrow), of which he was an elder for 60 years; was reckoned to be the oldest Freemason in Scotland, having enrolled at St. John's Lodge, Campbeltown, on 17 May 1819; politically, he was an 'advanced Liberal' and supported both the 1832 Reform Bill and Gladstone's Irish home rule policy.

On the day of his funeral, the bells of Longrow Church and the Town Hall were 'tolled at intervals' and the ships in Campbeltown harbour flew their ensigns at half-mast.[347]

Greenlees, Hugh, was a partner in Burnside and Argyll distilleries. His father was Thomas, maltster, and his mother, Helen, was also a Greenlees. His wife Jean, whom he married in 1822, was a daughter of Robert Colvill, cartwright, and died in 1879, aged 79. When Hugh died in Bolgam Street, on 14 February 1855, aged 57, he left four children: Helen (31), Robert (28), Thomas (24) and Janet (18). Son Robert #2, a distiller, registered Hugh's death, and five days later registered the death of his own son, Archibald, at three years old. Younger son Thomas was a sheriff clerk in Census 1851 and a distiller in 1861 and in 1871, when in Kirk Street with an aunt, Janet Colvill, and a house servant; he died in 1873, aged 43. Daughter Helen married William Mitchell #1 in 1845 and daughter Janet married the Rev John Burns Smith, Greenock, in 1867.[348] On Hugh's death certificate it was noted that he had been in Campbeltown 'all his life'.

Greenlees, James #1. When he died, aged 44, at Seafield House, Campbeltown, on 29 August 1888, James Watson Greenlees was 'sole partner' in McMurchy, Ralston & Co., Burnside Distillery, and was also a director of Highland

Distillers Co. — incorporated in 1882 as Islay Distillery Co. Ltd. — which built and operated Bunnahabhainn Distillery.

He had an earlier connection with Islay, having leased the island farm Finlaggan with his brother Alexander #2. In 1870, 'Mr Greenlees, Burnside Distillery', advertised in the Campbeltown newspaper for two shepherds and a ploughman 'for a Farm in Islay', and in 1876 'Messrs. Greenlees, Finlaggan' took first prize for a two-year-old colt at Islay Cattle Show. In 1885, it was reported that he had let a part of the farm.[349] The Greenlees brothers' schooner *Finlaggan*, launched in 1877, was named after that farm (see 'Shipping').

After leaving Glasgow Academy, he 'received an excellent business training' in the Glasgow office of Messrs J. &. R. Young & Co., shipping agents and brokers. After a spell in the Glasgow office of his father Robert #1, he returned home, in 1864, to run the family business with brother Alexander, who predeceased him in 1882. He was a past chairman of the local Distillers' Association and a director of the Campbeltown Steam Packet.[350]

Seafield House — now an hotel — where both he and Alexander died, was later owned by another distiller, Hugh Mitchell #2. Among the beneficiaries of his legacy were the Royal Infirmary and Western Infirmary, Glasgow, which each received £500, 'payable free from legacy duty'.[351]

Greenlees, James #2, died 1916 — see 'Greenlees Brothers'.

Greenlees, James #3, who died, aged 66, at his home, Davaar, in Uddingston, on 1 August 1926, was a son of John Greenlees, merchant, and a brother of William (q.v.), with whom, in the earliest years of his business career, he was a partner in the firm of John Ross & Co., Longrow and Kintyre Distilleries. He moved to Glasgow when he became a partner in Bennett & Co., wine merchants there. He was a president of the Kintyre Club, and recognised the

Club's centenary in 1925 by donating £500 to its funds, and was captain of both Machrihanish and Southend golf clubs.[352] He was survived by four sons, two of whom, John and Wallace, were involved in the whisky business. For the family of his wife, Agnes Galbraith Wallace, whom he married in 1889 and who died in a nursing home in Glasgow in 1923, see 'Robert Wallace'. James's estate was valued at £23,084.[353]

Greenlees, John, who died on 17 February 1956, aged 65, was associated for many years with Bennett & Co., wholesale wine merchants in Glasgow, through his father, James #3. He later went into business on his own account as a whisky-broker and agent for Macdonald & Muir, Leith, and, until his death, was a director of J. & A. Mitchell & Co. Ltd., Springbank Distillery. In line with family tradition, he was a 'noted golfer' and followed his father as captain and club champion of St. Mungo Golf Club, Irvine. He belonged to Uddingston, as did his wife, Mabel Hird. They lived at Helensburgh, and, at the time of his death, had one daughter, an 'orthopaedist' in Carlisle.[354] His brother Wallace (q.v.) spent the greater part of his life in Campbeltown.

Greenlees, Mathew, was connected with Meadowburn and Hazelburn distilleries, but is described on his gravestone in Kilkerran as a merchant, and in Census 1851 as a 'Farmer and Distiller' at Hillside Farm, on the outskirts of Campbeltown. He married his first wife Isabella — a daughter of Hugh Ferguson, merchant in 1820. She died in 1825, aged 34, and three years later he married Janet Breakenridge, widow of William Armour, merchant in Campbeltown, and daughter of Andrew Breakenridge, farmer at Killeonan. Mathew's parents were William Greenlees and Agnes Andrew, for whom see the entry on Daniel Greenlees, his brother. See also Samuel Greenlees #1, who married their sister Agnes. Mathew died on 28

November 1853, aged 50, and two years later Hillside Farm was given up by his widow, and the livestock, crops, agricultural equipment and household furniture fetched 'most lucrative' prices at public auction.[355] Janet died in 1858 in Longrow, and his son Hugh, who had been with them on the farm, died at Dumfries in 1868.[356]

Greenlees, Robert #1, a son of Alexander #1 and Mary Colville, was a partner in Burnside Distillery, with his father and Hugh Greenlees, in 1840. In that same year, he married Ellen, or Helen, daughter of James Watson, brewer in Ayr. The family gravestone in Kilkerran commemorates six sons, all of whom predeceased their mother. A notice in the *Argyllshire Herald* gave his place of death, on 16 August 1864, at the age of 51, as 12 St James' Place, Glasgow. There was no obituary, but later that year, when his estate was wound up, he was described as 'sole Partner' in McMurchy, Ralston & Co., the executors and trustees of which were William McKersie; Archibald McKersie, son-in-law; David Colville Jr.; John Alexander; and son Alex #2.[357] For another son, see James #1. Robert's widow, like him, died in Glasgow: at 17 Wilton Mansions, Kelvinside, in 1899, aged 79.[358]

Greenlees, Robert #2, who died, aged 71, on 5 January 1897 at Burnbank, Campbeltown, was, for the greater part of his working life, associated with Argyll Distillery. When he left Campbeltown Grammar School, he was apprenticed to David Colville #1 as a clerk in his law office. He was later taken into Colvill, Greenlees & Co., of which his father, Hugh (q.v.) — a 'maltster' in 1825, when Robert was baptised — was a founding partner, and, according to his obituarist, he ultimately ran Argyll Distillery himself until his retirement in 1887. He was active in Longrow U.P. Church; was on the Parochial Board, until it was reformed in 1895; was a director of the Campbeltown and District Savings Bank and also of the Campbeltown Steamboat Company.[359]

His mother, Jean, was a daughter of Robert Colville, cartwright; his wife, Janet, whom he married in 1856 and who predeceased him in 1893, was also a Colvill, a daughter of Archibald, cartwright, and Catherine Harvey; and in 1887 the eldest of his three daughters, Kate Harvey, married a Colville, David Jr., of the Motherwell iron and steel manufacturers. These Colvilles, unlike their whisky-distilling relatives in Campbeltown, were advocates of total abstinence. David Sr. was tee-total for 60 years, and his son John, who was Member of Parliament for North-East Lanarkshire and died from cholera in 1901, was described as 'perhaps the most strenuous, earnest and untiring advocate in Scotland of total abstinence'.[360] For the steel-making Colvilles, see A. Martin, *Kilkerran Graveyard Revisited*, p 69.

Greenlees, Samuel #1, who died on 11 May 1886, served on the Town Council for 19 years; was a director, and several times chairman, of the Campbeltown Steam Packet; a member of the Parochial Board; was instrumental, in 1887, in the formation of the Campbeltown Building Company, which aimed to provide comfortable accommodation for the working classes at 'reasonable' rents and 'under strict sanitary regulations'; joined the Kintyre Club (in 1860); was active in church affairs; and there was more, including a formative role in the raising of the 6th Argyllshire Artillery Volunteers, of which he was commissioned Captain in 1861. In May 1862, the new artillery battery at Kilkerran was ceremoniously named 'Fort Greenlees' by the firing of its 32-pound guns across the Loch. His daughter Catherine 'applied the fuse' to the first of the guns, which went off with a reverberating boom. He resigned his commission in 1874.[361]

In common with most of the prominent distilling families in Campbeltown, Samuel's background was solidly Lowland. The Greenlees family is believed to have come to Kintyre from Lochwinnoch, Renfrewshire, in the mid-17th century. Samuel emerged into the world in 1812 at Smerby, a coastal farm three miles north of Campbeltown. He was one of 11 children born to James Greenlees, farmer, and Catherine Galbraith. There were native, Gaelic-speaking Galbraiths in Kintyre, but Catherine belonged to a Lowland family which also left its mark in distilling history.

When Samuel married in 1840, his wife Agnes, daughter of William Greenlees, shipmaster, was both his cousin and a sister of his business partner, Daniel. He and Agnes had two daughters and two sons — James and Samuel, who founded Greenlees Brothers — before her death in 1853, aged 42. In 1861, at Renfrew, he married into another prominent family of Lowland origin: his second wife, Isabel or Isabella, with whom he had four daughters, was a daughter of Robert Ralston, for whom see 'Glenramskill Distillery'.

Like many distillers in the 19th century, his family background was in farming, and he never lost his interest in the land, though his involvement would have been more proprietorial than practical. In 1858, Samuel and his partner, Daniel, bought the 300-acre arable farm of Moy, near Campbeltown. When the company had a schooner built at Campbeltown Shipyard in 1878, she was named the *Moy* (see 'Shipping'). In the year the *Moy* was launched, Samuel's mother Catherine — 'relict of James Greenlees, farmer, Peninver' — died at Moy, at, for that time, the grand old age of 90.[362]

In 1881, when Daniel retired, the farm became Samuel's sole property, along with the two distilleries, Dalaruan and Argyll, and he became increasingly interested in farm improvements and in the rearing of sheep and cattle, 'which were eagerly picked up ... and the best prices readily obtained'.

In politics, Greenlees was 'always a robust Liberal', though he disagreed with Prime Minister Gladstone's Irish Home Rule Bill, and his 'last public action', in the week before his death, was to sign a local petition opposing it.

He was given a military funeral, attended by the officers and men of the local Artillery Volunteers and the staff of the 6th Brigade, Scottish Division, Royal Artillery, and the ships in harbour flew their flags at half-mast.[363]

Samuel's second wife, Isabella Ralston, died on 14 January 1897, aged 69, at the family house, Hazelbank, which, seven weeks later, was advertised for sale by public auction at the upset price of £2,000[364] and bought by Duncan Colville #1.

Samuel's daughter Margaret, who was married to Colonel George P. Rome of the firm of Glasgow plasterers George Rome & Co. Ltd., died in 1927.[365]

Greenlees, Samuel #2 — see 'Greenlees Brothers'.

Greenlees, Thomas — see 'Hugh Greenlees'.

Greenlees, Wallace. According to his obituarist, Robert Wallace Greenlees, J.P., came from Uddingston just after the First World War to 'assist his uncle, John Greenlees, in the management of the family distillery'. When he joined the Kintyre Club in 1909, however, his address was Redcliff, Campbeltown, the home of his uncle, William Greenlees (q.v.), a partner in John Ross & Co. from 1876 until Ross's death in 1886, and thereafter sole owner until his own death in 1922. John Ross & Co.'s Longrow Distillery had closed in 1896, and Wallace offered the remaining distillery, Kintyre (q.v.), to Campbeltown Town Council in 1926. In 1933, he bought East Cliff,[366] which had belonged to Duncan MacCallum (q.v.).

His parents were James Greenlees #3 and Agnes Galbraith Wallace, who was a sister of Christina, the wife of John Colvill #3. Wallace himself married into a distilling family in 1925: his wife was (Victoria) Isobel McKersie.

During the First World War he was in the Ross & Cromarty Battery, attained the rank of Major and was awarded an M.B.E. in 1919 for military services. From 1930 until 1962, he was in business as a stockbroker, but was also active in civic affairs. When he stood for Campbeltown Town

Council in 1949, he topped the poll, and in 1953 gained 'the highest number of votes by any candidate at any election in Campbeltown'. He was Provost in 1950 — a busy year, in which Campbeltown celebrated its 250th anniversary as a royal burgh — and served two terms.[367] He died on 23 March 1964 and his wife died the following year.

Greenlees, William, who died, aged 72, at Redcliff, Kilkerran Road, on 1 November 1922, was the eldest son of John Greenlees — merchant at Lintmill and then Stewarton — and Jean Mitchell. When William left school, he started work in the Campbeltown branch of the Royal Bank; having completed his apprenticeship, he was transferred to the head office in Glasgow, and from there returned to the local branch. He left banking to become a partner in the firm of John Ross & Co., formed in 1876, and, when Ross died in 1886, he became sole owner of the firm's distilleries, Longrow and Kintyre. He served one term as a Town Councillor, but 'had no bent towards public life'. Like his father before him, he was a keen golfer and was captain of both Machrihanish and Southend golf clubs. His pall-bearers were his brothers John, James and Archibald Greenlees, nephews John, Wallace, William and James Greenlees, and cousin James Weir. He was unmarried.[368] His gross estate amounted to £23,878, which went to his relatives, apart from £500 to his long-serving housekeeper, Maggie McKendrick, and £300 to his 'servant', Kate Galbraith.[369] He was buried in Kilkerran with his parents, brother John, who died in 1935, and brother James, who died in infancy at Lintmill in 1857 and was the first interment in the first extension of the cemetery beyond the medieval churchyard.

Gulliver, James. Campbeltown-born 'Jimmy' Gulliver was described in 1987 as 'amongst the most successful businessmen Britain has ever produced'. From 1983 until 1986, when Glen Scotia was owned by Gulliver's Argyll Group, the distillery became a tiny stalled cog in a huge fast-revolving commercial machine. In 1986, Argyll Group expressed interest in building a supermarket in Campbeltown, but the project was dropped a year later, after planning permission had been granted, another nod at his roots which bore no fruit.

James Gerald Gulliver was born in 1930, the son of a grocer, William Frederick Gulliver, of Bermondsey, London, and Mary Martha Lafferty, daughter of a Donegal-born carter in Campbeltown, who married in 1915. He attended St. Kieran's R.C. School in Campbeltown and then Campbeltown Grammar School, of which, in 1949, he was Dux Medallist — the top academic distinction there — and received the James Greenlees Bursary of £25 from the Kintyre Club. At Glasgow University, his success continued: in 1952, he was awarded a bronze medal in Philosophy, and in the following year received a B.Sc., with first class honours, in Civil Engineering.

After graduation, he studied for a year at the Georgia Institute of Technology in Atlanta. This was reported in Gulliver's home town newspaper in 1954 under the headline, 'American Degree for Law Student James G. Gulliver'. In that same newspaper, 31 years later, under the headline 'A look at the work of Gulliver, Campbletown [sic] born businessman', the U.S. degree was said to have been awarded by the more prestigious Harvard Business School, a claim which Gulliver had allowed to proliferate and on which he was eventually challenged.

Gulliver's business exploits are too numerous to list here, so just two landmarks in his career may be mentioned. His first notable success was as chairman of Fine Fare, which, during his seven years there, he transformed from an ailing business into one of the UK's top three supermarket chains. In 1972, the year he parted company with Fine Fare, he received *The Guardian* Young Businessman of the Year award, 'the accolade of which he was most proud'.

In 1985, as chairman of the hugely successful Argyll Group, Gulliver launched a bid for Distillers Co. Ltd., at £1.9

billion the highest ever in British history. Argyll ultimately lost DCL to rival bidders Guinness, an episode which was described as 'one of the darkest in the annals of the City', and which culminated, in 1990, in the jailing of Ernest Saunders, former chairman of Guinness, and two other City figures. The thwarted DCL bid was Gulliver's last big business gamble, and in May 1988 he resigned from Argyll.

Later that year, the *Campbeltown Courier* reported, somewhat feebly, that Gulliver was 'front-page news again with his takeover of the ailing carpet giant, Harris Queensway'; but the meat in the item was that Gulliver was to 'speak publicly in Campbeltown for the first time', as a guest of the Campbeltown Conservative Committee, at a ticket-only cheese and wine evening in the Royal Hotel on 23 September. No report of the event appeared; nor, strangely enough, was there an obituary in the *Campbeltown Courier* following his death on 12 September 1996. Gulliver, who was married four times, was buried with his parents in Kilkerran, his home town graveyard.[370]

Haig, William, belonged to the famous whisky-distilling family of that name. The Colville papers in the Live Argyll archive, Lochgilphead, contain the whisky production book of Seggie Distillery, Guardbridge, Fife, for 1852-54.[371] How it came to be in Duncan Colville's possession has, until recently, been a puzzle, but the answer lay in a family tree Colville drew up. William Haig, a widower, married Martha Colville on Christmas Day 1861 at East Cliff, Kilkerran Road. Born in 1833, she was a daughter of David Colville #1, whose grandson, Duncan, in his genealogical notes, described Haig as a corn factor, maltster and distiller in Kincaple, Guardbridge. The Haig-Colville marriage explains several otherwise mysterious notices in the Campbeltown newspapers, e.g. the death in 1867 at Star Bank, Cupar, of Frances Alicia Moodie, aged 55, 'relict of Robert Haig, Esq., late of Seggie Distillery'[372] — she was William's mother. Martha Colville Haig died a widow at

Crieff in January 1900.[373] Her nephews David and Duncan Colville (q.v.) married Syme sisters from Craigie, a couple of miles from Guardbridge.

Hancock, Joseph, in 1836 became a partner in David Anderson & Co., Glenside Distillery, and in March 1844 he and one T. Wilkie, by then a co-partner, appointed John Grant (q.v.) to audit the company's books.[374] Hancock, 'formerly of Chelsea', was living on Askomil Walk, Campbeltown, when the 1841 census was taken, and died in September 1844. He was described in 1841 as a 70-year-old distiller, born in England. In Census 1851, his widow Margaret MacAlister was still in Askomil Walk, aged 71 and born in Port Glasgow, but the head of the household was now her sister Isabella MacNair, a 62-year-old widow and retired innkeeper. Both women were named in the action for debt brought by William McKersie, distiller, against the dissolved co-partnery of David Anderson & Co., Glenside Distillery, to which refer, and in a separate action brought by the widow of John Grant, to whose entry refer. Daughter Margaret, supposedly 15 years old in 1841 and born in England, married John Glass, Excise officer in Campbeltown, in 1842. The 'Mrs Hancock' who died in Dalintober on 9 April 1852[375] was doubtless Margaret MacAlister.

Harvey, **Harvie**, **Hervey** family — see 'Mountain Dew Distillery'.

Harvey, James. When he died in his sleep on 21 October 1880, aged 51, James Harvey was managing partner of Rieclachan Distillery and unmarried. His father John (below) was one of the original partners in the distillery.

After receiving 'as good an education as the burgh schools then provided', James went to Glasgow for legal training with the city police. He was back in Campbeltown and in charge of Rieclachan by 1857, when he advertised two houses to let in Burnside Street.[376] After his return, life as a distiller assumed a familiar pattern: in 1866, he purchased a front pew in Longrow Church for £10 5s,[377] and in that same year was elected to the Town Council; in 1871, he became Junior Bailie, in which office he remained until he retired from the council in 1875; he was a member of the parochial board and a director of the Campbeltown Steam Packet Co. 'Socially, he was an agreeable companion, apt at retort, had a good fund of ready wit and was well-informed on all the topics of the day.'[378]

At a 'complimentary dinner' held in the Town Hall in July 1865, for the re-elected Member of Parliament, James was called upon to propose a toast to 'The Ladies'. His response, unremarkable at the time, would provoke an outcry nowadays: 'They are a class that I am deeply interested in — (cheers and laughter) — whether you look at them as single, married or widows.'[379]

When Harvey was offered the post of Junior Bailie in 1871, fellow-councillor, Donald MacDonald, objected and proposed instead William McNair. MacDonald 'did not think it proper' that any distiller or spirit dealer should be involved in the granting of alcohol licences, an opinion which perplexed Dean of Guild Thomas Brown: 'It is surely a new light that has come upon us that a distiller can't be a Bailie.' Harvey professed a 'great respect for Mr McNair', but insisted that he would never respect 'the spirit of the opposition from whence the proposal came'. The dispute was put to a vote and Harvey was duly elected.[380]

After his death, his property in Saddell Street was auctioned along with his shares in the Campbeltown Steam Packet, Campbeltown Bread & Flour Co., Commercial Bank of Scotland and India Jute Company.[381]

Harvey/Harvie, John, was one of the original partners in Rieclachan Distillery, built in 1825. His wife Jean, whom he married in 1823, was a daughter of James Ferguson, maltster, and Mary Ferguson, and a sister of James Ferguson (q.v.), who was also in the original partnership — indeed, all four partners had a Ferguson connection. It was said of Harvey that, prior to his becoming a 'distiller and maltman', he captained one of the mail packets which sailed between Campbeltown and the Clyde and 'were not infrequently six weeks on their homeward passage, being obliged to stay in the Kyles of Bute, waiting for a fair wind'[382] — see 'Shipping'. He died on 6 February 1842, aged 62, and his wife Jean on 9 December 1854, aged 75. They are buried in Kilchousland with their infant children, Andrew and Margaret. In Census 1851, Jean was a 'Proprietor of Houses' living in Saddell Street with daughter, Mary, and sons James (above) and John, who was described as an accountant.

Hazelburn Distillery was built for Greenlees & Colvill in 1825 in Longrow. To meet the demands of increasing business, however, in 1845 the distillery was relocated to Millknowe, where the main building still stands as a 'business park'. During the summer closure of 1863, the distillery was 'considerably enlarged' to produce 'a greatly increased quantity' of whisky.[383] Its capacity would ultimately exceed that of all the other Campbeltown distilleries.

The original partners were the brothers Mathew (q.v.) and Daniel Greenlees (q.v.), and Archibald Colvill (1813-94), a son of Charles Colvill, Dalaruan Distillery, and doubtless the distiller who became a shareholder in the Campbeltown Steam Packet c 1835[384] and retired from Greenlees & Colvill c 1845. Shortly after Archibald left the firm, the Greenlees brothers' cousin Samuel Greenlees (q.v.) joined. On 1 July 1881, he bought Daniel's interest in Greenlees & Colvill, including Moy Estate, and became sole owner. Following his death in 1886, Hazelburn was taken over by his two sons, of Greenlees Brothers (q.v.), who turned the business into a limited liability company, with capital of £25,000, and traded as Greenlees & Colvill Ltd. The distillery was acquired in 1919 by Mackie & Co., Distillers — which became White Horse Distillers Ltd. in

1924 — and ceased production in 1925.³⁸⁵

In 1864, employees at Hazelburn each received, 'according to usual custom', a New Year bonus of a sovereign, a gold coin worth £1. Its value may be understood when compared with the weekly wage of £1 5s offered, two years earlier, to journeymen slaters by a Glasgow firm advertising in the local newspaper.³⁸⁶

In 1867, when the Campbeltown Steam Packet's new steamer, the *Gael*, was launched by Miss Minnie Galbraith, daughter of Andrew Galbraith (p 77), a bottle of 'fine old Hazelburn whisky' was broken against her bow.³⁸⁷

In March 1904, local building contractors Robert Weir & Sons were instructed by Greenlees & Colvill to 'build a large addition to their duty-free warehouses at Hazelburn'.³⁸⁸

In 1905, a visiting journalist described the distillery offices as 'fine ones, equipped with electric light and telephones', which would 'do no discredit to either Glasgow or London'. In one of the offices hung the original 'Highland Distillery Licence No. 133', granted to James Armour in Campbeltown in 1796, which the writer transcribed and published in full.³⁸⁹ Later that year, a new steam boiler was shipped into Campbeltown for Dalaruan. Made by Penman & Co., Glasgow, at 18 tons it was the largest ever landed.³⁹⁰

By 1922 Hazelburn had a storage capacity of 1,300,000 gallons of whisky in six bonded warehouses and in its general warehouse, which had recently received a consignment of 124,000 gallons of whisky from Mackie & Co.'s Craigellachie Distillery in Banffshire.³⁹¹ See also 'Whisky, theft of'.

Springbank Distillery in 1997 revived the 'Hazelburn' name in a triple-distilled product bottled at 10 and 12 years old.

Henderson, Hector, is perhaps best known as the founder of Caol Ila Distillery, Islay, in 1846, but he had earlier acquired Littlemill Distillery in Dunbartonshire and, still earlier, was involved with Campbeltown and Union distilleries in Campbeltown. That the Mactaggart family had interests in both of these distilleries cannot be coincidental. By 1835, according to Colville (1923), Henderson had the tenancy of Campbeltown Distillery and was operating as H. & F. Henderson; and in that same year Mactaggart & Henderson's Union Distillery was sold. Henderson probably quit Campbeltown soon after. His son John was born in England in 1837; he took over Littlemill Distillery c 1840, and in Census 1841 he was a merchant in Rhu, Dunbartonshire. In 1851, he was a distiller living in 24 Marwick Street, Gorbals, Glasgow, with wife Mary Ann, two schoolboy sons — John Baillie and Hector Charles — and a 65-year-old widow, Ann Norris, who was presumably his mother-in-law. Henderson was born in Urray, Inverness-shire, c 1803, and in 1832, in Gorbals, married Mary Ann Norris, born in Kilmarnock, Ayrshire.

Highland Distillery was built in 1827 in Broad Street, Dalaruan, on a site feu on 8 January of that year by Daniel Mactaggart (q.v.).[392] Daniel Mactaggart & Co. was dissolved in 1831, taken over by John Grant (q.v.) — who had married into the Mactaggart family and also bought Union Distillery — and shortly afterwards became McLennan & Grant, the new partner being George McLennan. Thereafter, the succession of ownership becomes muddled. In 1839, McLennan was identified as owner and reported to be 'residing in Glasgow',[393] though Glen, p 155, has the firm sequestrated in 1835, and *Pigot's Directory* in 1837 named Duncan 'McCullock' as the owner. Duncan Colville cites a note in the Dalintober Distillery letter-books, dated 8 September 1846: 'John Honeyman buys Highland Distillery.'[394] In 1848, the owners were Dawson & Baird, Glasgow, according to a note on a Campbeltown Distillers' Association document dated 1 November.[395] According to Glen (p 155), Highland was managed from 1837 until 1844 by Duncan McCulloch (above). He was recorded in Broad Street in the 1841 census, aged 39 and a 'Distiller' living on his own.

In 1859, Highland's sale by private bargain, 'with or without utensils', was advertised; Peter Ferguson would 'show the premises and give such information as may be wanted'.[396] In 1861, when its rateable assessment was appealed against, it was described by John Kerr Orr, Glenside Distillery, as an 'old work ... in a state of great dilapidation' and lacking a still, worm and steam boiler. Only the malt-barns were still in use,[397] a claim confirmed in 1862, when a fire broke out in the barns and was extinguished by 'workmen ... on the premises'.[398] In 1869, a daughter was born to William Armour at 'the Highland Distillery',[399] but he was probably just living in the distillery house. When the liquidators of Glenside Distillery and nearby Highland offered the Town Council the sites of these 'dismantled' distilleries as 'a gift to the town' for the provision of public housing — see 'Glenside Distillery' — there was a caveat: a former Glenside employee, Donald MacCallum, was housed in the 'old Highland Distillery', and the Council would have to provide him with somewhere else to live.[400]

High Street (name unknown). This distillery, probably founded in 1828, was located, Colville says, 'opposite Woodland Place'. Since that property was demolished c 1950, the location may be revised to: across the road from Glen Scotia Distillery on the site of the tenement which neighbours the modern high flats. The site was feud in 1826 and 1827 to John Campbell, Lieutenant John Macfarlane, Royal Marines, and William Harvey, but sold three years later to Edward Ralston of E. Ralston & Co. In 1838 Ralston made over the distillery and malt-kiln to Daniel Greenlees (q.v.) for £378 14s 6d; but there was no reference to this distillery in *Pigot* of 1837. In 1857, Greenlees advertised for sale a property with a garden on the north-east side of High Street, 'formerly used as Malt Barns'.[401] These were clearly the remains of the defunct distillery, which the High Street Census enumerator in 1851 had noted as 'Uninhabited house (Malt Kiln)'.

John Macfarlane's wife, Joanna, whom he married in Glasgow in 1830, was a daughter of the Rev John Macfarlane, minister of Kilbrandon Parish, Argyll. She was in Dalintober in 1851, when described in the census as a widow and 'Annuitant'. With her were son John (19), daughter Margaret (18) and a 19-year-old servant, Flora Brown. She died in Dalintober House in 1890 at the age of 84.[402]

Hunter, Peter, became a partner in Lochside Distillery with his father William (below) and Peter Gilkison (q.v.) in 1837. His father was from Cumbrae, and when Peter married in 1837, his wife, Jean, was a daughter of another Hunter from Cumbrae, Alexander, a merchant. Jean must have died early in the marriage, because in 1848 Peter married Janet Smith, daughter of Andrew Smith, farmer in Moy. In Census 1851, he was in Argyll Street with his wife, daughter Janet, aged seven, by his first marriage, daughter Elizabeth, aged one, by his second, and a 19-year-old servant from Gigha, Catherine McNeill. He described himself as 'Manager of Distillery'. In 1854, he was treasurer of the Campbeltown 'ragged school', which was founded in 1851 to provide free education for poor children, and of which his brother William was director until its closure.[403] In 1856, he was one of six retiring Town Councillors,[404] and he evidently did not seek re-election. In October 1863, he resigned from his 'situation' in the Steam Packet Company, and in May of the following year the public auction of the contents of his house on Kilkerran Road was advertised.[405] He and his family emigrated to the U.S., where he died on 13 February 1888, aged 78, in Winnebago County, Illinois,[406] a popular destination for Kintyre settlers: the Argyll Settlement was founded there in 1836 by Southend-born George Greenlees.[407]

Hunter, Robert, was named in a newspaper advertisement in 1854 as the contact at Lochruan Distillery (q.v.). Three years earlier, in Census 1851, he was in lodgings in Back Street and was described as 18 years old, single, born in Shettleston, Lanarkshire, and 'Manager of a Distillery'. In 1861, he was a distiller employing nine men, which suggests proprietorial status, a case strengthened by his enrolment in the Kintyre Club in 1860. He moved to Campbeltown at a young age, but whether he had any local connections is unknown. He himself said that he had arrived in Campbeltown 'as a stranger and comparatively a juvenile'. In January 1862, before he emigrated to Otago, New Zealand, a farewell dinner was held for him by 'a number of respectable townsmen'. James Stewart (q.v.) was in the chair and delivered the encomium. Hunter's reply was clearly an emotional one. Here is part of it: 'But, gentlemen, although I am not only about to leave this place, but the hearth of my home and childhood, and those I revere and love, for a foreign land, I trust it is not for ever ...'[408]

Hunter, William, who was from the Isle of Cumbrae, established a watch-making and jewellery business in Campbeltown in 1803 and four years later married a local merchant's daughter, Isabella Langwill. He died in 1855 and Isabella died two years later. He was a founding partner in Lochside and Mossfield distilleries, and was joined in the former by his son Peter (q.v.). His other son, William Jr., who died in 1886, carried on the watch-making business and was no friend of the distilling industry; on the contrary, he was a public advocate of total abstinence and a prominent Good Templar. His daughter Isabella, who married Archibald McTaggart, an Inland Revenue officer and brother of the great Kintyre-born landscape painter, William McTaggart (1836-1910),[409] was prominent in the Campbeltown branch of the British Women's Temperance Association — see 'Total Abstinence'. Of William Sr.'s six children commemorated on the family gravestone, the last was Mary, who died in 1882, aged 73, and whose inscription includes the enigmatic tribute: '... by her loving service lives in the grateful memory of a wide circle who knew her as "Aunt Mary"'.

Industrial accidents. In January 1903, while descending a ladder from a warehouse loft at Kinloch Distillery, William McAllister, a 70-year-old brewer, fell to the ground floor and died the following day from head injuries. He was in the loft helping lower casks of whisky by winch and chain to the ground floor. Duncan Reid was below, and, after the casks had been removed on the instruction of the Inland Revenue officer, Thomas Pike, he saw McAllister leave the loft with his back to the ladder and a lamp in his right hand. 'He was just about the top when he fell. He fell to the left over the wall which divides the ground floor of the warehouse ... There is an opening in the wall. When he fell, I went through there and found him lying on his back at the end of a cask.'[410] See Appendix 2 for a chronological catalogue of distillery-related accidents compiled largely from local newspapers.

Accidents — many of them fatal — were frequent in all industries throughout the 19th century and into the 20th, and financial compensation virtually unknown. 'Health and safety' regulations in the present time are widely perceived to have become excessive to the point of ridicule, but, historically, the necessity of introducing measures to protect workers in their work places cannot be disputed. Accidents in the distilling industry were certainly less frequent and less catastrophic than in, say, the coal-mining or fishing industries, but they occurred from time to time and invariably involved only one worker.

In 1892, in the Court of Session, Glasgow, an appeal was heard from Glasgow Sheriff Court. The widow of a distillery worker had sued Bulloch, Lade & Co., Loch Katrine Distillery, for damages: £400 for herself and £150 for each of her four children, or £195 under the Employers' Liability Act. William Robb was crushed in the machinery of a mash-tun and died the same day. Mrs Mary McKechnie or Robb claimed that the machinery, which revolved on top of the tun, should have been fenced (Factory and Workshop

Act, 1878), but the company argued that the dead man had known the risks, and the appeal was dismissed.[411] Bulloch, Lade & Co. also owned Benmore Distillery (q.v.).

Industrial unrest. Distillery workers in Campbeltown notified their employers in December 1871 that they 'required a further rise in wages'. The demand was rebuffed by the distillers, who argued that 'the wages they pay their workers are as high or higher than the same class of men obtain elsewhere'.[412] No more was reported on the dispute.

In October 1913, the Campbeltown distilling industry was briefly plunged into turmoil. The workmen had been offered a wage increase of two shillings, but demanded four. The local newspapers' coverage of the dispute was scant, and contained nothing on the 'several meetings' the workmen organised, but the upshot was that the organisers contacted 'Mr Houghton' of the Dockers' Union, who came to Campbeltown to negotiate with the distillers. After meeting them, he addressed a well-attended gathering of workmen in the Town Hall and recommended acceptance of the distillers' offers. The terms of the deal were not reported, but presumably a compromise had been reached. Agreement was unanimous, and the workers formed a branch of the Dockers' Union, which 'practically all' the men joined.[413]

'Mr Houghton', above, was Joe Houghton, and the 'Dockers' Union' was the Glasgow-based Scottish Union of Dock Labourers, formed in 1911 and led by Houghton until 1922, when assimilated into the Transport & General Workers' Union. In the immediate future, wage negotiations would be conducted by Houghton, whose visits to Campbeltown were documented by Peter Dewar, manager of Dalintober Distillery (q.v.) between 1916 and 1919.

On 29 March 1918, the Distillers' Association met to consider a workers' demand for a weekly wage increase of 7s a man. Duncan MacCallum proposed 5s a week, which Houghton 'accepted on behalf of the men'. In January 1919, at a distillery workers' meeting, the resolution was passed that, if the distilleries resumed work, a wage increase of £1 should be asked for, giving a weekly minimum of £2 18s, with 4s extra for Sunday work. Next month, after negotiations with Houghton, a minimum wage of £2 12s 6d, with extra for maltmen and mashmen and for Sunday attendance, was offered and accepted. The deal included all 'workers in silent distilleries'.414

There was another wages dispute in 1923, when the Campbeltown whisky industry was entering its near-terminal decline. This time negotiations with the local distillers were conducted by the Transport & General Workers' Union, whose Scottish organiser, 'Bro.' Peter Gillespie, addressed the men at an evening meeting in August in the Christian Institute.415 The outcome of the dispute is unknown.

Innes, Peter M. In 1923, two years before Hazelburn Distillery ceased production, the manager, Peter M. Innes, was 'promoted' to the managership of Cragganmore Distillery on Speyside, and a presentation, attended by employees and friends, was held in the distillery. Speeches were delivered by E. Wright, Customs and Excise, A. D. Armour, N. Morrison and A. Stewart, who praised the 'nobility of character and high social qualities' of Mr Innes: '... his sympathy for the poor and bottom-dog of society was boundless, he was generous and warm-hearted ... ever ready to lend a helping hand to those who could not help themselves'. Innes received a gold watch, chain and pendant and his wife a gold wristlet watch.416 Innes, who was manager of Hazelburn in 1919, when Masataka Taketsura (q.v.) had a spell at the distillery learning the craft, was succeeded as manager by Murdo McEwan.417

Johnston, Archibald, who died in his sleep on 13 April 1897, aged 82, at Broombrae Place, the home of his son-in-law, Alexander Campbell, painter, was employed as a mashman in Glenside Distillery for almost 40 years. He started 'under the late James Armour' and worked there 'till the day of his death'. On his last afternoon of life, he 'exercised himself by taking a walk into the country', and, in the evening, sat up reading until about 11 o' clock. 'Of a quiet and unassuming nature, he did not seek to lead a public life, but he took an intelligent interest in all that passed around him and was a worthy member of the community.'[418] His wife, Janet Fulton, whom he married in 1838, died in 1872, aged 59. She was a daughter of Robert Fulton, merchant, and Mary Mitchell, who was one of the founders of Drumore Distillery (q.v.), where Archibald was mashman in 1847, the year it closed.

Johnston, John, was for 50 years head maltman with Bulloch, Lade & Co., first at Benmore Distillery and then at Loch Katrine. He died in Glasgow, aged 75, on 8 May 1918, and was buried in Kilkerran three days later.[419] He was born in Islay to Archibald Johnston, maltman, and Mary Livingstone, and was twice married, to Agnes Brown and then to Margaret Campbell or McAffer, both of whom predeceased him. In Census 1851, he was a 'maltman' living in Saddell Street with first wife, Agnes, born in Kilmun, and six young children.

Johnston, Robert and Charles Rowatt — see 'Lochruan Distillery'.

Johnston, Thomas. In November 1920, Thomas Johnston and his wife, Margaret McInnes, celebrated their golden wedding anniversary. He came to Campbeltown from Greenock in 1887 to work as a cooper in Hazelburn Distillery and retired in 1916. He was a cornetist of 'recognised merit' and played with the band of the Argyll Highland Rifles until it 'went wholly for the bagpipes'.[420] In Census 1891, they had 10 children, all of them born in Greenock, except the last two, Mary (aged 2) and Walter

123

(4 months), who were born in Campbeltown. Thomas, who died in 1922, was born in Largs, Ayrshire, and Margaret, died in 1942, was born in Glasgow.

Johnston, William, was a son of Thomas, above. There were clearly no hard feelings when, in 1893, at the age of 17, he left Greenlees Brothers in Campbeltown — also his father's employers — to join the clerical staff at Springbank Distillery. At a staff gathering in September, he was presented with a silver albert — a type of watch-chain — a gold scarf-pin and a knife.[421] In Census 1891 he was described as a 15-year-old distillery clerk, and 10 years later as a distillery manager.

Keith, Archibald, who had been suffering from 'an affection of the heart', died suddenly on 18 April 1914 at the age of 61. He had been about 40 years manager of Albyn Distillery, and on the day of his death he drove by pony and trap from his house, Marchwood Cottage, on Kilkerran Road, to his office, 'intending not to stay long'. He had hardly settled behind his desk when he took ill. The doctor who was summoned advised that he should be taken home, and his employer, William McKersie, put him into his motor car and set off down Glebe Street; but just as the car passed from Glebe Street into Lorne Street, he died.

Though born in Campbeltown, he was buried at Paitean Cemetery near Bellochantuy, the family burial-ground. His father, a spirit dealer, was also Archibald Keith, and his mother was Margaret McSporran. The cause of death was identified as 'fatty disease of the heart' and his death was registered by his employer, McKersie. In the 1891 census he was in Marchwood with his sisters Margaret and Julia, both retired dressmakers. All three spoke both Gaelic and English. In 1896, he married Mary Findlay, who survived him.

He was an elder in Castlehill Church, and the minister, Rev G. W. Strang, in a tribute from the pulpit, recounted that, 'knowing the weak state of his health, and how dangerous all physical exertion was to him', he called on him the day before his death and offered to relieve him of the duty of delivering communion cards to members of the congregation in his neighbourhood; but Keith insisted on fulfilling his obligation. He kept a stock of sheep on High Glenramskill farm, the lease of which was taken over, six weeks after his death, by William Russell, Ballymeanach Farm, who also took the stock 'at valuation'.[422]

Kelly, Charles, was a partner in both Campbeltown and Union distilleries, to which refer. He was described in the 1851 census as a 50-year-old 'Distiller and House Proprietor' in High Street. Both he and his wife, Agnes Turner, were from the Largieside and married in Barr in 1823. Her father David, described on her death certificate as 'farmer', was presumably the David Turner recorded in the Armour 'Still Books' as innkeeper at Barr in the year of her marriage. Her mother, Margaret, belonged to the Langlands family which came to Kintyre c 1773 from England (see 'Dalaruan Distillery'). 'Charles Kelly, distiller, Campbeltown', erected the stone in Paitean graveyard for his parents John Kelly, farmer in Upper Barr (died in 1830), and Susan Munro (died in 1816). Kelly himself died in October 1857, aged 69, and his wife in April 1880, aged 82. The family gravestone in Kilkerran commemorates four unnamed children who 'died young', a son, David, died in Queensland, Australia, in 1882, and a daughter, Susan, died at Durham in 1899. Of his three daughters known to have wed, Margaret married an Inland Revenue officer, James Donnahey, in 1859 in Campbeltown.

The inventory of Kelly's personal estate refers to a 'discharge' by Archibald Kelly to Charles Kelly and John Ross in 1853. Archibald was described as a son of William Kelly, 'mashman' in Campbeltown,[423] who would have been the 'brewer' who died in 1844, two years after his wife Janet Galbreath, as recorded in the Campbeltown Old Parish Records.

The surname Kelly in Kintyre is generally not of 19th century Irish immigrant origin, but is found, in various Gaelic forms, as far back as the 17th century.

Kelly, Neil Munro, the most colourful of all the Kintyre-born 'gaugers' of which there is record, spent the earlier part of his working life at sea, first in the merchant service and then in the Royal Navy. His service with the Inland Revenue was spent not indoors, supervising the affairs of the legal distillers, but outdoors, in the hills and glens, hunting 'smugglers'. He was promoted to the rank of Ride Officer and, as such, was stationed for several years at Cullen, in North-East Scotland, before being transferred to his native Kintyre.

A report, published in 1851 in the earliest of the local newspapers, the *Campbeltown Journal*, described 'Monroe Kelly' in action at 'Killin', which was Killean, in the Largieside, a hotbed of illicit whisky distilling and lawlessness. He and an assistant noticed a moorland track, which seemed newly tramped, and decided to follow it. The track ended abruptly at a stream, but they continued searching and eventually picked it up again. When they followed it around a hill, they found themselves almost back at where they had started, but in a secluded hollow. There they discovered the site of an illicit still, built of stone and with most of the equipment in place. The smugglers had 'fled', and Kelly and his assistant had nothing to do but carry away the 'whole apparatus'. The report, which Kelly himself may have sent to the newspaper, concluded by praising him for his 'activity and vigilance', and noting that it was his fourth seizure of an illicit still within three months.[424]

The Largieside, at that time, was Gaelic-speaking; indeed, there would have many men and women who spoke only Gaelic and understood no English. Kelly himself, necessarily, was a Gaelic speaker, but spoke — and wrote — English as well. He was born in 1823 at Southend Manse, a son of the eccentric Rev Daniel (or Donald) Kelly, minister there and later in Campbeltown, until suspended in 1836 for 'irregularities'.

Kelly retired in 1857, at the remarkably early age of 34, which suggests that he had private means to supplement his pensions. In 1870, he had a house built at Baraskomil, two miles north of Campbeltown on the Carradale road, and lived there until his death in 1906. The roofless ruin still stands, behind a smaller, roadside cottage. It was known as 'The House of Lude', and he styled himself 'Neil Munro Kelly of Lude', from the name of a Robertson estate in Perthshire. His mother was Louisa A. Robertson and through her he claimed descent from King Henry VIIth of England and kinship with several families of the Scottish nobility. His ancestry — whether real or fabricated — was his 'absorbing pride'. He adopted the surname 'Robertson' late in life, but was generally known as 'Munro Kelly'.

In 1868 Kelly stood for Campbeltown Town Council, as one of 12 candidates contesting two seats. He came second-bottom with 19 votes, compared with the 186 votes cast for David McEachran, blacksmith, who topped the poll.[425]

In 1888, unusually for the time, he divorced his wife, Ann Stewart, who had gone to New Zealand and refused to return to him.[426] They had a son and a daughter, both of whom died in infancy. His brother, Arthur Hill Kelly, was a surgeon in the Royal Navy, and, after his death in 1864, aged 28, Munro lovingly preserved his uniform, cutlass and other effects.

He had a great stock of smuggling tales, which, as his obituarist noted dryly, 'he was seldom loath to recount', and was knowledgeable on the genealogies of local families. Yet, he was also a rather remote figure, owing to his 'somewhat hermit mode of life' and his 'many peculiarities'. Many years before his death, he had his name and date of birth carved on a gravestone in Kilkerran, with a blank for the date of his death, and specified that he was to be 'laid as near the surface of the ground as possible'.[427]

Kinloch Distillery was situated at the junction of Longrow and Lochend Street. A journalist in 1923 claimed that 'as far back as 1792' the premises were used only as malting houses until converted into a distillery.[428] Colville (1923) dates its construction to 1823, but that is improbable, because, on 29 November of that year, Alexander Dunlop, maltster, applied to the Duke of Argyll's chamberlain for an extension of his father James's lease of ground in the Longrow in order to build a distillery.[429] The true date is probably 1824.

The distillery was built for Lamb, Colvill(e) & Co., original partners James Dunlop #1, John Colville Jr. (q.v. #1), and Robert Lamb, 'writer' (or lawyer) and also town clerk of Campbeltown. Lamb, whose wife was Janet Black, retired from the business in 1825, the year his son, James Augustus Lamb, who was also a lawyer, died at the age of 30. Robert died aged 53 in 1826. There must have been a significant connection between Lamb and Charles Rowatt Mactaggart (q.v.), because the Lamb and Mactaggart gravestones stand together in the old section of Kilkerran and Mactaggart named two sons 'Robert Lamb'.

Following Lamb's death, Robert Ralston, of Glenramskill Distillery, joined the firm. He died in 1840 and his one-third share in Lamb, Colvill & Co. passed to his family. In 1852, the year after John Colville Jr.'s death, Robert's son, David Ralston, offered Colville's trustees £700 for his interest in Kinloch.[430] In 1875, a William Ralston at Kinloch Distillery was dealing with claims against the late Daniel McMurchy, cooper.[431] He was presumably the William, 'distillery manager', whose wife had given birth to a daughter at Lochend in 1868.[432]

James Dunlop #2 was said by his obituarist to have been 'sole partner' of Lamb, Colvill & Co. when he died in 1901. He became a partner after the death of his father in 1871, and was described as 'managing partner' by Barnard in 1887. When Isabella Ralston, widow of Samuel Greenlees #1, died in 1897, she held a quarter-share in the business.[433]

After Dunlop's death, David Colville, who was born in Strathmiglo, Fife, was appointed manager for the trustees of Lamb, Colvill & Co. His experience of the distilling business included employment at Cameron Bridge Distillery, Fife, and Liverpool Grain Distillery. He was in Springfield Terrace, Dalintober, in 1912, and died in 1918. His son, John Harrower Colville, a lawyer, survived Buchenwald concentration camp and in May 1945 was 'in an American hospital'.[434]

In 1919, the firm was bought by Thomas L. Brown (q.v.), acting for West Highland Malt Distilleries Ltd., and in 1924 became the property of Duncan MacCallum (q.v.), who gifted it in 1928 to Campbeltown Town Council,[435] which later built Park Square public housing on the cleared site. The last filling of new whisky at Kinloch was dated to 6 April 1926.[436] The distillery's name is an Anglicised form of *Ceann loch*, 'Head of the loch', as Campbeltown is known in Gaelic.

1875: A dilapidated building belonging to Kinloch Distillery caught fire in April and was fought using buckets of water relayed by hand. The building, which had been used as a hay store and stable, was totally destroyed, but not before all the horses were rescued.[437]

1877: In April, a new warehouse for Messrs Lamb & Colville & Co. was reported to be 'in course of erection'.[438]

1879: In April, at Kinloch Distillery, 16 tons of 'damaged barley ... suitable for feeding purposes', was offered at a public auction.[439]

Kintyre Club — see Appendix 1.

Kintyre Distillery. In April 1926, the site of the 'recently dismantled' Kintyre Distillery in Broad Street was offered to Campbeltown Town Council for £100, which sum was to be 'handed in its entirety' to Campbeltown and District Cottage Hospital. The offer, which was made by R. Wallace Greenlees, on behalf of John Ross & Co., was remitted to the housing committee.[440] Wallace Greenlees (q.v.) was a nephew of William Greenlees (q.v.), a partner in John Ross & Co. from 1876 until Ross died in 1886, and thereafter sole owner until his own death in 1922.

Kintyre was probably erected in 1830. According to Colville (1923), gas pipes were laid to it in 1831 from the newly built gas works at the Roading. The original owner was John Beith Sr. (q.v. #1), upon whose death, in 1840, a partnership was formed in the name of Beith, Ross & Co., being John Beith Jr., merchant, John Colville Jr., banker, and John Ross, distiller. In 1876, the name of the company, which also owned Longrow Distillery, became John Ross & Co: see 'Longrow Distillery' for changes in ownership. Kintyre ceased production around 1920.

In 1870, Gavin Ralston was scalded in an empty tun when a fellow-workman in Kintyre Distillery, Donald McPhail, turned on a hot water cock. He later died and McPhail, after trial, was jailed for three months for culpable homicide. The distillery's manager at that time was William Beith.[441]

In 1875, a fire in the distillery malt-kiln caused £225 worth of damage, including the loss of 190 bushels of malt. The fire was supposed to have been caused by embers from the kiln furnaces having 'got among the peats that were stored around'.[442]

Kirkwood, Alexander, merchant in Campbeltown, was one of the earliest investors in the legal distilling industry in town, as a founding partner of Kirkwood, Taylor & Co., which built Meadowburn Distillery in 1824. He was born in Campbeltown in 1795 to Alexander Kirkwood and Elizabeth McKechnie. His first wife, Jean, whom he married in 1820, and who died two years later, having given birth to two children, was a daughter of James Hogg, manager of the Campbeltown Coalwork. In 1825, in Glasgow, he married a minister's daughter, Magdalene Cochran MacFarlane, born in Kilbarchan, Renfrewshire, with whom he had 10 more children. The family, with a domestic servant, 17-year-old Eliza McMichael, was recorded in Askomil Walk,

Campbeltown, in Census 1841. He died in Glasgow in 1848, and Magdalene died in Helensburgh in 1879, aged 77. His son, Alex, by his first marriage, emigrated to Australia in 1854 and died in Brighton, Melbourne, in 1902, aged 79 (see 'Glenramskill Distillery').

Lamb, Robert — see 'Kinloch Distillery'.

Loch-head Distillery, which stood on the corner of Lochend Street and Lady Mary Row, on the site of the present Tesco supermarket, was built in 1824 for A. & R. McMurchy & Co., being Archibald, lawyer in Campbeltown, and Robert, who died in 1833. The partners were subsequently Archibald McMurchy, Donald Andrew (q.v.), coppersmith, and James Taylor, mason. In 1833, ownership changed to William Taylor & Co., comprising father and son James and William Taylor, the latter being the active partner. James died in 1847 and William in 1851, leaving William's brother, Archibald — see 'Taylor family' — in charge of the business, which he advertised for sale, by private bargain, in 1854.

The package included: 1. The distillery itself, 'now in full operation', comprising still-house, two malt-barns, two bonding warehouses, malt-mill house, 'counting house', stable, and an 'extensive stock' of casks. The distilling capacity was estimated at from 1,300 to 1,400 gallons a week. The property was bounded on one side by a stream, which provided power for grinding malt and pumping, etc, and there was a 'copious stream' within the premises which supplied water for the distillery, as well as water-pipes which had been 'recently fitted up' and could be 'continued or not as the owner may incline'. 2. A dwelling-house of two stories, with attics. 3. A piece of vacant ground, with a frontage of 86 feet and extending for 160 feet to the sea. That site contained a 'commodious bonded warehouse', a garden and a stock of empty casks, but would be 'a very eligible stance for building purposes'.[443]

Three years later, in December 1857, a public notice announced that the distillery was under new (undisclosed) ownership, but with the name of the firm retained: William Taylor & Co., distillers in Campbeltown, declared that William and Archibald Taylor, distillers in Campbeltown, deceased, who had operated as William Taylor & Co., 'had no connection with us', and since 14 January 1857 'they and their representatives ceased to have any interest in, or connection with, the Loch-head Distillery'.[444]

The distillery traded as William Taylor & Co. until 1895, when it was sold to J. B. Sherriff & Co. Ltd. (q.v.), which, in 1899, demolished the 'congested' old buildings ranged from Lady Mary Row to Parliament Lane. The malt-kilns were rebuilt in the courtyard of the distillery, and the 'artistic' new structure facing Lochend — four stories high with turreted corners and built with Ballochmyle (Ayrshire) and Kilkivan (local) sandstone — was designed by leading architect, H. E. Clifford (p 4).[445] The distillery later boasted a 'private locomotive' for transporting barley and other supplies to the maltings, which comprised two large barley lofts and two germinating floors.[446]

In 1920, Loch-head and J. B. Sherriff's other distillery, Lochindaal in Islay, were briefly owned by J. & P. O'Brien & Co. Ltd., Liverpool, but were later acquired by Benmore Distilleries Co. — owners of Benmore Distillery in Campbeltown — which became part of DCL in 1929, by which time Loch-head was redundant.

In February 1871, Campbeltown Town Council refused William Taylor & Co. permission to put a felt roof on a bonded warehouse being built on Lochend Street, and instructed the Dean of Guild 'to see that the roof is made of incombustible material' (see 'Dalintober Distillery' for the effect of fire on felt). In the following year, the Council refused the company permission to close off Parliament Lane — deemed a 'right of way' — which ran between its premises and Lochend Free Church.[447]

In March 1873, the furniture belonging to 'Mr Carmichael, late manager in Lochhead Distillery', was sold by public auction at his house 'near Lochend Bridge'. In August of that year, a young boy, whose brick-layer father was building a chimney-stalk at Loch-head, fell through the water-wheel which drove the chains of the wash still, and was extricated with just a few bruises.[448]

In 1881, a two-storied bonded warehouse, 'extending from Broombrae to Scotia Distillery', was built for William Taylor & Co.[449]

The distillery's name is another Anglicised form of *Ceann loch* — 'Head of the loch' — as Campbeltown is known in Gaelic.

Robert 'Bobby' Colby was the last occupant of the former brewer's house at Loch-head Distillery. An employee of Scottish Malt Distillers (q.v.), which managed warehouses in various parts of town, he and his family lived in Loch-head House from 1972 until about 1982. The building was situated off Parliament Lane, which linked Lochend Street with Parliament Place. He recalled uncovering in its garden — more resembling waste ground, before it was brought under control — a well which had been covered with two large stone slabs.[450] By 1990, the house was demolished, along with the church and the Clifford-designed warehouse. In 1993, a William Low supermarket — now owned by Tesco — was built on the site of the warehouse, and the site of the church became its car-park.[451]

Lochruan Distillery, on Princes Street/High Street, Dalintober, was built in 1833 for Johnstons & Co., comprising Robert Johnston and Charles Rowatt Johnston. These brothers are buried in Kilchousland, the churchyard on the coast three miles north of Campbeltown, along with siblings and parents, who were James Johnston, merchant in Campbeltown, and Janet Colvill.

Robert, described as 'distiller Dalintober' on one of two family gravestones, was also a shipmaster, or captain. His share in the smack *Lavinia*, which he owned with the partners in David Colville & Co., Dalaruan Distillery, was sold to the partnership in 1848,[452] the year after his death. He was enrolled in the Kintyre Club in 1837.

When Charles was born in 1810, his father James was described as a hosier, or stocking-maker, and was still a hosier — one of two in town — in 1825.[453] In 1841 Charles married Agnes Boyd, daughter of a Paisley merchant, and in Census 1851 was described as a distiller employing 10 workers. With him and his wife in High Street, Dalintober, were three young children and a servant, Margaret McNeillage. He died in 1886, aged 75, but had given up Lochruan long before then.

In 1847, after the death of Robert, a third brother, James, was taken into the family firm.[454] He died in 1853, aged 36 — see 'Caledonian Distillery'. Also in 1847, Johnstons & Co. signed an agreement with Buchanan, Wilson & Co. — the Glasgow whisky agents which had acquired Ardbeg Distillery, Islay, in 1838 — granting the firm exclusive rights to all whisky produced in Lochruan, and, by 1 November 1848, Lochruan had been 'converted over in security to Buchanan, Wilson & Co.'[455] Robert Hunter (q.v.) later took over Lochruan, though in 1856, when the distillery was said to be the biggest in town, it was still referred to as belonging to 'Messrs. Johnstone & Co.'[456]

Lochruan was bought in 1865 by William McKersie #1 and immediately renovated and modernised, circumstances which led to the jail sentences with hard labour served by Daniel Mitchell (six months) and Daniel Robertson (four months) for the theft of copper and other metals from the site during the renovations.[457] In the following year, Lochruan Distillery Co. appealed against the rateable valuation of £112 on the basis that 'the distillery had only recently been put in a working state'; the assessment was reduced to £77 for that year.[458] In 1879, plans for a new bonded warehouse at Lochruan, to be built on High Street, were passed by the Council's Dean of Guild Court.[459]

Glen, p 155, gave the 20th century owners as James Buchanan & Co. (1919) and DCL (1925). In all local newspaper reports, the earlier owner was identified as W.

P. Lowrie & Co. Ltd., from 1906 a subsidiary of Buchanan & Co. In 1920, Lowrie announced that, in the year ended 31 March 1920, it had 'acquired an interest' in Port Ellen Distillery, Islay, and had bought Lochruan.[460]

In 1921, the firm made 'additions and alterations' to the distillery, including a grain-drying loft, an elevator, and draff-drying machinery, and two years later acquired the neighbouring distillery, Dalintober. Lochruan ceased production early in 1925, and in the following year the company appealed unsuccessfully for a reduction in the rateable valuation of the property (Appendix 7). The manager for many years was Robert Gardiner (q.v.), whose successor John Stephen died at the distillery in March 1927, aged 54.[461]

The site, as with that of Dalintober Distillery, is largely occupied by public housing, completed in 1939, but taken over by HMS *Nimrod* as accommodation for naval personnel during the war. However, a small warehouse, which was part of the original premises, abuts on the end of Glen Scotia Distillery in High Street and is used as a furniture store by a local business. Around 1980, an employee of Glen Scotia, Jim Grogan, witnessed the tipping into a drain of the contents of a barrel of Loch Ruan which had been stored in that warehouse. The whisky belonged to a minister of religion who had died, and, as there were no known relatives, it was poured away under the supervision of a Customs and Excise officer. Had that whisky survived, its commercial value now would defy imagination!

The name 'Loch Ruan' derives from a reservoir north of Campbeltown, which took its name from the adjacent hill, Knock Ruan: Gaelic *ruadhan* = 'red land'. A journalist who visited the distillery in 1923 was treated to a 'romantic legend' — actually, nonsense conjured from who knows where — that 'in ancient times Lochruan was said to be haunted by beautiful spirits who cast spells over its moonlit waters, and so freed from disease the first mortal thereafter drinking from the loch'.[462]

Lochside Distillery. From 27 June until 14 November 1856, the *Argyllshire Herald* advertised the private sale of 'Distillery Utensils' at Lochside Distillery. The notice advised interested parties to apply at the distillery, which had clearly closed and was disposing of its equipment.

Colville (1923) described the location of the distillery as 'behind the present shop of Robert Armour & Sons, Longrow', but, since that shop no longer exists, a better description would be: across from the bus terminus on Kinloch Road. When the distillery was built in 1830, its name would have been apposite, but, by the creation of Kinloch public park in the late 19th century, the original extent of Campbeltown Loch was pushed back. With a span of just 25 years, or less, Lochside was among the shortest-lived distilleries in Campbeltown.

The original partners were Peter Gilkison (q.v.), distiller, William Hunter (q.v.), watch-maker, and William McKersie #1, trading as Gilkison, McKersie & Co. (Two of the partners were probably connected: Gilkison's mother was Martha Langwill and Hunter's wife was Isabella Langwill.) After McKersie withdrew from the business to set up Albyn Distillery in 1837, the firm became Gilkison & Hunter, with Peter Hunter (q.v.), son of William, taken on as a partner.

In 1971, a signboard for 'Gilkison & Hunter, licensed maltsters', was found in the rafters of one of two Longrow Distillery malt-barns purchased by J. & A. Mitchell. The discovery was made during a survey of the buildings, which were adjacent to Springbank Distillery and had previously been occupied by a builder.[463]

Longrow Distillery. When Barnard visited Longrow Distillery in 1885, it was probably little changed from its origins in 1824. 'It covers two acres of ground, and is so built in by the houses and shops in Longrow that it would be difficult for a stranger to find it,' he wrote. 'To reach it we entered a covered archway under the houses, which opened up into a courtyard, round which the Distillery buildings are ranged. They are old-fashioned and of various styles of architecture.'

The original owners were John Colville Jr. (q.v. #1), John Beith Sr. (q.v. #1) and John Ross (q.v.), trading as Colville, Beith & Co. In 1852, after the death of Colville, the firm became Beith, Ross & Co., partners John Beith Jr. (q.v. #2), John Ross and John Galbraith (q.v.), who replaced Colville.[464] In 1876, the partnership was dissolved and its distilleries, Kintyre and Longrow, sold by private auction. Beith and Galbraith were bidding against Ross, who secured the distilleries for £8,010 and brought another partner, William Greenlees (q.v.), into the new firm, John Ross & Co.[465] This split resulted in acrimony and litigation at the end of the year: see *Argyllshire Herald* 25/11 and 2/12/1876, John Galbraith v John Ross, and subsequent issues of the newspaper. When Ross died in 1886, ownership of Longrow and Kintyre passed to the surviving partner, Greenlees. According to Glen, p 156, Longrow closed in 1896, but a report in 1888 referred to the distillery as having 'shut up within the past few years',[466] though that closure may have been temporary.

The surviving distillery buildings, formerly maltings but latterly 'a building yard', were bought in 1971 by J. & A. Mitchell & Co. Ltd.,[467] which uses one as a warehouse and the other as its bottling plant at Springbank. In 1973, the company attached the name 'Longrow' to a heavily peated product in three distinct bottlings.

In 1861, Beith, Ross & Co. offered a reward of £10 — approaching £1,000 in present value — for information leading to the conviction of the culprits who bored 'certain small holes' in the spirit receiver of Longrow Distillery.[468]

Longrow is the main road into and out of Campbeltown and originally described a long row of houses. Many distillers and their families lived there until, in the final decades of the 19th century, increasing prosperity gave them the means to buy or build big houses on the outskirts of town.

Lorimer, David G. (Bombardier), died on 6 June 1917 of a head wound received at Wytschaete on the Western Front. He succeeded James Murdoch (q.v.) as manager of Ardlussa Distillery and 'made many friends in Campbeltown' before moving to Glentauchers Distillery in Banffshire. In Campbeltown, he was a deacon in the Highland Parish Church and a member of Stronvaar Bowling Club. He left a widow and three young children.[469]

Lowrie, William Phaup, was born in 1831 in Dalkeith, Midlothian. He began his career as a commission agent in a bonded warehouse, and, as the business grew, he founded W. P. Lowrie & Co., which became a limited liability company in 1898. His death in July 1916 was reported in the *Campbeltown Courier*, which referred to him as 'a great authority on whisky blending' and one who had 'large dealings with the trade in Campbeltown, by the members of which he was held in high esteem'. When his net estate — £297,889 — was declared later in the year, that too was reported, under the heading 'Bequests to Charitable Institutions'.[470] Lowrie also had 'sporting' interests in Kintyre. As 'Mr W. P. Lowrie of Glasgow', he 'secured many fine sea trout of considerable size' in Kintyre in September 1874, after heavy rain put the rivers 'in first rate order for rod fishing'.[471] W. P. Lowrie & Co., a subsidiary of Buchanan & Co. from 1906, acquired Lochruan and Dalintober distilleries, to which refer, after his death. See also 'Coopering' and Appendix 7.

Loynachan, Duncan, appears to have been accident-prone. In 1865, at Campbeltown Distillery, one of his feet was caught in the fly-wheel of an engine he was oiling and 'severely bruised and mangled', and in 1869, while sweeping the underside of the mash-house roof, he fell 19 feet to the floor when a rafter 'suddenly snapped'. He was reported to have 'sustained severe internal injuries' and to be 'in a dangerous state',[472] but he survived for 27 more years.

He was born c 1808 on the farm of Balnatuine, in the hills south of Campbeltown and facing the Ayrshire coast. His parents were Lachlan Loynachan and Agnes MacPherson, and his sister Catherine famously observed a 'mermaid' while herding cattle on the shore below the farm in 1811. His wife was Flora Reid, who was born at Carskey, Southend, in 1819. He was admitted to the poor roll in 1889, suffering from 'age, etc.', and given 2s 6d a week. He died in 1896, by which time the surname 'Loynachan' — originally *O Loinachan* — was well on the way to mutating into the less culturally challenging 'Lang'. By Census 1901, there were no Loynachans in Kintyre, only Langs; but the older form survives in the U.S.A., through the emigration in 1836 to Washington County, Ohio, of David Loynachan, Eden, Southend.[473]

MacCallum, Donald, who died at the age of 79, on 14 August 1933, at his home in Albyn Road, had been 'out and about daily' until the day of his death. He reportedly spent his working life in Albyn Distillery as an employee of William McKersie & Co., and 'retired with the passing of the firm'. Even in retirement, he maintained his association with the McKersie family as 'a faithful retainer' and 'great favourite', and every morning, until his death, he could be seen walking to Craigard, the McKersie mansion on Low Askomil. That relationship was unusual, for distillers and their workers generally never mingled outside the work place, and, even there, social distinctions would have been observed. Old Donald, however, had 'sporting' credentials.

'During the silent season [i.e., summer] in the distillery, deceased was principally engaged accompanying members of the family on their sporting expeditions to hill and loch. He had a rare knowledge of the wild and was an expert adviser and sure guide with either rod or gun. This occupation was very congenial to himself, and there was no happier day in his life than when he was out on the heather with dogs and gun. Like most men of his craft, he

139

was almost tireless on the hill, and even at a good old age his physical vigour and endurance often surprised much younger men. The passing of a fine type of Highlander like "Old Donald", even at the good old age which he attained, is much to be regretted.'[474]

MacCallum's obituary was probably supplied to the local newspaper by a member of the McKersie family, for other than his length of service in Albyn Distillery and his field craft in the wilds of Kintyre, it contains little about the man's background. He was born in Killean Parish, in the west of Kintyre, and spoke both Gaelic and English. Many of the distillery workmen in 19th century Campbeltown who had migrated from Killean Parish — the Largieside — had a background in the illicit whisky trade and gravitated to the legal branch of the industry as a safer environment for the practice of their skills, but Donald was probably born too late to have been one of them. And his father, James, was described as a fisherman on Donald's death certificate, which delivered two more MacCallums: the death was registered by a son-in-law, Morris MacCallum, and the doctor who signed the cause of death — heart disease — was Duncan MacCallum. Donald's mother was Janet McMurchy, and his wife was Marion Smart, who, in common with all his children who were living with him in 1901 at 3 Albyn Road, had no Gaelic.

On 4th February 1921, at about 5 p.m., two men entered Albyn Distillery 'in search of liquor'. One of them, James McMillan, asked Donald MacCallum if there was anyone in the tun-room, and to discourage McMillan from going in there, MacCallum replied, 'Yes, the mashman and the exciseman'. An altercation then ensued, with McMillan pushing MacCallum over, so that he fell to the floor among the malt; or, the opposite testimony, with MacCallum first shoving McMillan. The intruder then struck MacCallum twice on the head with a stick — he had lost a leg in the recent war and used the stick, which was of 'exceptional thickness and weight', to help him walk — whereupon MacCallum grabbed a malt-graip (used for spreading malt) and struck McMillan so hard with it that the head of the graip 'was split in two'. McMillan then left with his companion, and MacCallum, with 'blood streaming down his face', reported the incident to the mashman, Alex McIntyre (q.v.), and then to the police. He was treated by Dr James Brown, who testified in court to the severity of the first blow.

Sheriff J. Macmaster Campbell assured the accused that 'nobody ... appealed to him more than an ex-serviceman, especially a disabled ex-serviceman', but that 'this assault committed on a man of Mr McCallum's years might have had the most serious consequences, and might, indeed, have resulted in the gravest charge of all'. If he imposed a fine, the punishment would 'fall not upon the accused but upon his household'. The accused 'would probably benefit by being sent away and getting time for reflection', and when he emerged from prison 'he should be a wiser and better man'. The sentence was 40 days in jail.[475]

A journalist who visited Albyn Distillery in 1923, noted that Donald — 'a sturdy old Scot and a well-known local character' — remembered 'the days when the whole of the distilling machinery was worked by horses'. The article was accompanied by a photograph of the distillery, with Donald, hands in pockets and pipe in mouth, standing under the sign-board: 'Albyn Distillery/ Wm. McKersie & Co. Ltd./ Licensed Distillers.'[476]

MacCallum, Duncan, drowned himself in Crosshill Loch between 10 a.m. and noon on 23 December 1930. Two men who were walking around the reservoir found 'evidences at the loch side which pointed to tragedy' — clothes, presumably — and informed the police, who recovered the body close to the jetty at the dam.[477]

MacCallum was 83 years old, unmarried, lived at East Cliff on Kilkerran Road and was fabulously wealthy. That he killed himself after going bankrupt is a myth — his estate exceeded £284,000, which would make him nowadays a multi-millionaire — and that his ghost haunts Glen Scotia Distillery is another myth (though employees on night shift at the distillery have been known to reserve judgement!) His suicide would have caused a sensation at the time, for he was public-spirited and popular, but no persuasive explanation for his final act has yet emerged.

On the morning of 4 June 2019, seeing a party of whisky tourists on the opposite side of the street from Tesco supermarket, I slowed my pace as I passed the group, and overheard the 'guide' deliver the following nonsense about MacCallum: 'He walked out the door one morning and disappeared, never to be seen again, and it's said his ghost haunts the Tesco supermarket there.'

His house, which comprised four public rooms, four bedrooms, two bathrooms, and a billiards room, was slow to sell, perhaps owing to the circumstances of his death. It was advertised for sale by public auction in April 1932 at the incredibly low upset price of £200, but there were no offers. East Cliff was finally bought in 1933 by Wallace Greenlees (q.v.).[478]

MacCallum's grandfather moved from Inveraray to Campbeltown, where his father, Peter, was brought up. Peter MacCallum, who married Mary Martin in Campbeltown, invested first in fishing boats and later shifted his capital into other investments, including distilling with Duncan.

Duncan MacCallum began his working life in the drapery trade with his brother James; their business, J. & D. MacCallum, was established in 1863 in Reform Square. In 1877, with the distilling industry flourishing, Duncan bought farm land beside upper Glebe Street, and, as D. MacCallum & Co., built Glen Nevis Distillery. In 1891, as head of the consortium Stewart, Galbraith & Co., Ltd. (q.v.), he added Scotia Distillery to Glen Nevis. In 1905, a visiting journalist noted that MacCallum held 'the controlling influence in Benromach, Glen Albyn and Glendronach Distilleries'. In 1908, he and 'some trade friends' bought Glenside Distillery, and in 1919 he set up West Highland Malt Distilleries Ltd. (q.v.) to run Scotia, Glen Nevis,

Glengyle, Kinloch, Dalintober and Ardlussa distilleries; but the collapse of the whisky industry in Campbeltown was just around the corner.

MacCallum led a very full life. He travelled widely, both for business and for pleasure: his obituary mentions Canada, the U.S., the West Indies, South America, Australia, New Zealand, South Africa, India, and 'the East generally'. His last trip was a cruise in the summer of 1930 to Norway and the Soviet Union. One of his fellow-passengers wrote for a 'leading' London newspaper, and this is how MacCallum, in his last year, appeared to its readership: '... he was the life of the ship, and ... it was the surprise of all on board to learn that he was 83 years of age. To convince them that he was not a man of sixty or thereabouts, he had, indeed, to exhibit his passport.'

His greatest joy was in yachting, and 'the sea had a great attraction to him'. His cruising yacht, the *Armide*, was followed by the motor auxiliary yawl *Snowfleck*, which he co-owned with a friend and former school-mate, Duncan Campbell Andrew (see 'Donald Andrew').

We'll leave MacCallum at sea, perhaps the environment which gave him most contentment. Barnard in 1887 recalled an invitation from MacCallum to 'join him in a sail': 'It was just the morning for a cruise; a brisk breeze was blowing off the land and the white crests of the billows were gleaming and dancing in the sunbeams. Off we started, and were soon scudding through the water at a great rate, the white wings of the yacht skimming the rippling waves, and all of us enjoying the delightful sensation of rapid movement through the air without the slightest bodily exertion. We made almost straight for the bluff Isle of Devarr [*sic*], and the view of Campbeltown we got from that point was very beautiful. Our friend landed us close to [Dalintober] distillery, whither we proceeded.'[479]

MacCallum, Edward. The obituary of Edward 'Iver' MacCallum, who died on 25 September 1880, aged 84, celebrated, for the most part, his Christian principles and his 'love to [sic] the Free Church and its early struggles and ultimate victory in Campbeltown'. Of more interest here is the information that he came to Campbeltown (from Killean Parish) in 1823 and 'joined the distillery of the late John Mactaggart, at the head of the Longrow ... with whom he remained for twenty years'. This refers to Campbeltown Distillery. In 1827, when he registered the birth of daughter Margaret, he was described as a 'Brewer'. Iver, who 'would have towered head and shoulders above the average of the present day', left the distillery in 1843 and joined the Campbeltown Steam Packet as watchman, a job from which he retired in 1877 with a pension.

'Iver's Bible', his anonymous obituarist recalled, 'was a well-thumbed book, and our first lessons in Gaelic were learned from its pages; and though still a foreign tongue, the first chapter of John, learned, we may say, at his knee, in the still hours of the night, after our active day's work was done, will continue with us as long as we live.'[480]

His wife, Agnes MacKeich, lived to the age of a hundred. On the family gravestone in Kilkerran, Edward is described as a 'Spirit Merchant', but Agnes it was who ran the family public house, near the junction of Longrow and the Roading. She spent the greater part of her life in that house, and died in it on 11 December 1893; by 1922 it was the last thatched house in Campbeltown. She was born on the farm of Arnicle in Barr Glen and, when she came to Campbeltown as a young girl, spoke only Gaelic; and, until within months of her death, she had been in the habit of rising early and sitting at the fireside, 'where she enjoyed a talk in her native language'. She was survived by three sons and three daughters, 23 grandchildren and 18 great-grandchildren.[481]

Her Campbeltown-born grand-daughter, Maggie MacCallum, was a nationally recognised singer in Gaelic and English during the closing decades of the 19th century. Maggie first married Archibald Sinclair, a policeman, in

1878, but he died of tuberculosis in 1883. Ed Sinclair, the husband of Oscar-winning actress Olivia Colman, is a descendant of that marriage. In 1883, Maggie married again, to a boat-builder, John Macaffer, and afterwards used the stage-name, 'Madame Macaffer'.[482]

McCallum, Neil, spent the earlier part of his working life at sea. When he came ashore, around 1870, he worked in Longrow Distillery; there followed 26 years in Campbeltown Distillery; seven years in Burnside; then back to Campbeltown for seven more years; and, finally, in 1913, a year in Yoker Distillery, Glasgow. From 1914, he was club master of the Campbeltown Conservative Club until it closed in 1931. He was a 'vocalist of great repute' and in great demand at local concerts, and he sang in the Highland Parish Church choir for 60 years and was a member of the Campbeltown Musical Association. His vocal contributions to a Campbeltown Distillers' Association 'smoking concert' in 1894 included 'The White Squall' and 'After the Ball'.[483] Three years before his death on 18 November 1936 at the age of 80, he suffered a serious head injury from which he never fully recovered. Two sons and two sons-in-law were pall-bearers at his funeral.[484] His wife, Jane, who was born in Moffat, Dumfries-shire, was the daughter of Andrew Tweedie, who came to Kintyre as a shepherd c 1870. Son Malcolm was injured in a fall at Hazelburn Distillery in 1923 (Appendix 2).

MacCallum, Ronald McAlister, who worked at Dalaruan Distillery — in Census 1901 he was described as 'Foreman Maltman' — belonged to the Campbeltown family which produced a succession of pre-eminent bagpipers and champion Highland dancers. A piper himself, he was taught by John MacDonald of Inverness and was pipe major in the local Rifle Volunteers.[485] He died from tuberculosis on 26 December 1904, aged 50. His parents were William MacCallum, mason, and Mary McAlister, and his wife, who predeceased him, was Mary McArthur. His grandson, Pipe Major Ronnie MacCallum, was piper to the 11th Duke of Argyll and head gardener at Inveraray Castle. For the MacCallum piping family see my *An Historical and Genealogical Tour of Kilkerran Graveyard*, p 54, and the late Bridget Mackenzie's *Piping Traditions of Argyll* (the Kintyre historical and genealogical content of which is not, however, entirely reliable).

McCorkindale, Archibald, was one of the three founding partners in Reid & Colville, Dalintober Distillery, and the manager. When the contract of partnership was drawn up in 1832, he was obliged, at his own expense, to learn clerical and book-keeping skills and also the processes of mashing, fermenting and distilling, over which he would exercise 'active superintendence', for an annual wage of £50.[486]

He was a son of Bailie Duncan McCorkindale, merchant, and Catherine McIsaac, and a brother-in-law of David Colville, a partner in Dalintober. When Archibald and his wife, Isabella, had a daughter in 1851, they baptised her 'Davina Colville McCorkindale', probably after that partner. Archibald and Isabella married in Campbeltown in 1842, when her father was recorded as Daniel McKillop, 'Blacksmith, Liverpool'.

At a 'Dancing-School Ball' in the Town Hall in the summer of 1853, one of Archibald's young daughters performed two solo dances 'in such a manner as to elicit great praise'.[487] In 1862, Archibald was unanimously elected chairman of the Campbeltown Steam Packet; in 1864, when daughter Margaret Isabella married a Glasgow merchant, Alfred Brown, Archibald invited the distillery workers and their wives to a Saturday evening supper, after which 'a number of very capital songs were sung'; in that same year, he retired as a member of Campbeltown Town Council after a three-year term.[488]

Some time between the end of 1864 and his death on 29 March 1867, he and his family emigrated to the U.S. He died at Tremont, New York, aged 55; in 1871 his eldest son Duncan died in Brooklyn, aged 25; in 1872 second daughter Catherine married Adolphus B. Cornwall in Brooklyn; later that year, in Brooklyn, Archibald's widow, Isabella, who was born in Greenock, died at the age of 51; and in 1882, in Yonkers, New York, his youngest daughter, Lizzie Colville, married William H. Dety.[489]

McDiarmid, Dugald Stewart, was employed from youth until death by Greenlees Brothers (q.v.) and for many years represented the firm in London, where he died, from an abscess of the liver, on 18 March 1920, aged 48. He was born in Campbeltown to James McDiarmid, labourer, and Agnes McCorvie, and his paternal grandparents were Donald McDiarmid, farm servant, and Mary Stewart. His mother died in 1909 and the following year his father was admitted to the poor roll, suffering from sciatica, and would die in the poorhouse hospital in 1915.[490]

Dugald visited his home town 'as often as occasion served'. His 'genial manner made him many friends', his obituarist noted, and the large number of mourners who attended his funeral at Old Southgate Cemetery, London, included his widow and son, brother and sister — James and Agnes — and the following, most of whom are now obscure: 'Samual [sic] Greenlees, Messrs John McMillan, A. McMurchy, W. Campbell Galbraith, Peter Clapham, David Orchadson [sic], Dolorey, Hicks, Pratt, Mackay, Edmunds, and representatives from his old Employers and the London Scottish.'[491]

MacDonald, David, born in 1848, was in Kintyre terms a 'half-breed'. His father, John MacDonald, farmer at Pennygown, was of Gaelic stock and his mother, Elizabeth, of Lowland: she was a Kildavie Reid, as was Peter Reid (q.v.). The same combination applied in the previous generation: John MacDonald's father John (1771-1845) married Mary Reid (1785-1865). John Jr. and his wife,

147

who married in 1838, were both long-lived and celebrated their golden wedding anniversary. They had 11 children, of whom seven were still alive when Elizabeth died at South Carrine farm in 1915, at the age of 94 the oldest person in Southend Parish.[492]

David left Kintyre at the age of 15 for an office job with a wholesale wine and spirit merchant in Glasgow, Thomas Train (q.v.), who was also born in Kintyre. Train took a special interest in MacDonald, who was steadily promoted until, upon Train's death in 1883, he was made a partner in the business, Thomas Train & Co. Under the management of MacDonald and his partner, John M. Ross, the company ran a whisky-blending business and held agencies for, among other distilleries, Dailuaine-Glenlivet, of which MacDonald was a director, Talisker, and Kinloch in Campbeltown.

In 1898, when a feature on MacDonald was published in *The Celtic Monthly*, the company had just merged with 'another old and reputable house', John McIntyre & Co., to become Train & McIntyre Ltd. In that same year, MacDonald was serving his second term as president of the Kintyre Club. He was also a member of the Celtic Society, the Argyllshire Society, honorary president of the Glasgow Cowal Shinty Club, and a past captain of Dunaverty Golf Club. He was married with four sons and two daughters and 'never failed to visit Kintyre at least once a year'.[493]

Macdonald, Greenlees & Williams, Leith, was floated in 1919 when Alexander & Macdonald Ltd., Leith, was amalgamated with a company formed in 1918 after William Williams & Sons Ltd. acquired the business of Greenlees Brothers (q.v.). Macdonald, Greenlees & Williams owned the Glendullan-Glenlivet, Auchinblae and Stronachie distilleries, and controlled, jointly with other companies, distilleries in Islay, Speyside and Campbeltown (see 'Argyll Distillery'). In 1926 the greater part of the business was sold to the Distillers Company Ltd.[494]

McEachran, Charles, was a Gaelic-speaking grandson of the last laird of Killellan, Neil McEachran, who, in the mid-18th century, 'kept race-horses and indulged in horse-racing and lost the property'. Neil's numerous children were thrown into hardship — Charles's father, also Charles, was variously described as 'carter', 'labourer' and 'cow herder' — but with the next generation the family bounced back to prosperity. The surname MacEachran, which represents Gaelic *Mac Each-thighearna*, 'Son of the Horse-lord', is among the oldest in Kintyre.

Charles McEachran, who died, aged 74, on 19 January 1898, at Belmont, Low Askomil, served his apprenticeship as a draper in Campbeltown with Alexander Love, whose employment he left to set up on his own as a coal merchant and commission agent. When the Campbeltown Distillers' Association was formed in 1848, McEachran was its first secretary, a post which he successfully combined with his own business interests until he resigned in 1877 to become managing partner in Campbeltown Distillery, a position he held until his death.

He served on Campbeltown Town Council from 1857 until 1885, becoming a Junior Bailie in 1867, Senior Bailie in the following year and Treasurer in 1879. His other involvements included the School Board, the Parochial Board, the Campbeltown Steam Packet, the Campbeltown Savings Bank, the Campbeltown Building Company and the Artillery Volunteers, in which he was a Lieutenant. He was, his obituarist remarked, 'nothing if not a businessman' and 'was able to meet adverses in the proper spirit', as when he suffered heavy losses in the crash of the City of Glasgow Bank in 1878.[495]

His father Charles was married thrice and had 14 children by his first two wives, Grizzel (Grace) Campbell and Helen McCoag, who was a daughter of Donald McCoag, maltster in Campbeltown, and Charles Jr.'s mother.

Even at a time when the spectre of death was ever-present, Charles McEachran had a lot of grieving to get through.

He and his wife, Jane Johnston, lost two sons in infancy; in 1865, Jane died, aged 35; in 1866, daughter Jane died, aged 7; daughter Helen died at Cannes in 1881, aged 35; daughter Lizzie died in 1896, aged 34; a grandson, James Rennie McEachran, who died in 1885, aged 18 months, appears on the gravestone in Kilkerran above Charles's own inscription. His other grandson, Lieutenant Charles McEachran, Devonshire Regiment, was killed in 1917 while 'leading his men' at Kut Al Amara in Mesopotamia (Iraq). On the other side of the wall from Charles's monument, his daughter Rebecca is buried. She married Samuel Armour, an ironmonger in Campbeltown, and died at the age of 28 in 1885, having been predeceased by three infants, Margaret, Edward and Jeanie.

When Charles McEachran died in 1898, only two of his children remained alive, Jessie Colville, who lived until 1924, and John Johnston, a coal and shipping agent in Cardiff. A month after Charles's death, John retired from the firm his father had founded, which was by then known as J. J. McEachran & Co., and the business was continued by his partner and brother-in-law, J. C. Rennie, who had been running it in his absence and, as a ship broker, had made himself 'pretty well indispensable' to the Campbeltown distillers.[496]

McEwing, William, was 59 years old when he died unexpectedly on 11 October 1907 at Hazelburn. He joined Greenlees & Colvill as a 'lad' and was with the firm for more than 40 years. When Hazelburn was taken over by Greenlees Brothers in 1886, McEwing was appointed secretary, and, in that capacity, 'superintended and looked after the whole of the organisation and supervised the rebuilding of the distillery, which is one of the most perfect works of the kind in Scotland'. He was made a director of Greenlees & Colvill in 1902 and was effectively also in charge of Greenlees Brothers' sister company in Campbeltown, Colvill, Greenlees & Co. He was described as having been of a 'scientific and mechanical turn' and 'fully conversant with every branch of the distilling industry'. He was also chairman of the family business, A. MacEwing & Co. Ltd., printers and publishers. His church was the Lochend United Free, and, as a 'musician of some note', he was also a member of local musical associations.

He was the youngest son of Alexander MacEwing (died 1876, aged 67), printer, stationer, and the founder, in 1854, of the *Argyllshire Herald* newspaper, on the micro-filmed files of which this book heavily depends. His mother, Ann, who died in 1903, aged 90, was a daughter of a Campbeltown cooper, James Harvey. A brother, James (1841-1928), was a printer with the *Chicago Tribune* and 'lost all he possessed' in the great fire which devastated the city in 1871.[497] William was survived by his second wife, Nessie Williamson — whom he married only the year before he died — four daughters and two sons. [498]

His first wife, Hester Jane Bull, who was born in Queensferry, Linlithgow, died in 1889, aged 40, five weeks after the death of their year-old twin daughter, Barbara. In Census 1891, William was in Millknowe with seven children, aged between 14 and three, and Isabella McKellar, a middle-aged domestic servant. Hester Jane was a daughter of Edward Bull (died 1876, aged 79), an Inland Revenue officer in Campbeltown. Her brother Richard (died 1908, aged 63) also became an I.R. officer and retired in 1906 after 42 years in the service; another brother, John Edward (died 1899, aged 44), was drowned at Chinde-bar, South-East Africa, while chief engineer on the S.S. *Muttra* of the British India Steam Navigation Company.[499]

McIntyre, Alexander. In January 1920, a golden wedding celebration was held in Albyn Road for Alex McIntyre and his wife, Margaret Merrilees, who were married on 13 January 1870. Alex, who belonged to the Largieside, had been employed at Albyn Distillery for more than 52 years and was 'still doing a full day's work'.[500] He died at Millknowe in 1930, aged 86, and his wife died, later that year, in Edinburgh. On his gravestone in Kilkerran he is described as 'retired mashman', one of the very few distilling specifics in the graveyard.

McIntyre, Malcolm, was the fifth son of Alexander, above. He began his working life as a clerk in the Argyll Estate office in Campbeltown and was under-manager at Port Ellen Distillery, Islay, for about eight years before the Great War claimed him. A 2nd Lieutenant in the 6th Battalion Cameron Highlanders, he died from battle wounds at Le Touquet, France, on 21 August 1916, at the age of 26, and was buried at Etaples Military Cemetery. He was a talented golfer and had been secretary of Machrie Golf Club, Islay. Before the war, he knew of Le Touquet as a 'noted golfing centre' and had expressed the desire to visit the town, '... little dreaming, as did anyone else, that for him the light of life was to go out there'.[501]

MacKelvie, Alexander, became a partner in Stewart, Galbraith & Co., Scotia Distillery, in 1864 — a year after the death of founding partner William Galbraith — and in the same year married Jeanie Maxwell McMurchy, a daughter of John McMurchy (q.v.). She predeceased him by five years, aged 41, and when he died on 10 July 1883, aged 48, at his home, 'Jeaniefield' — presumably named after his wife — he left six children.

MacKelvie's obituarist described him as a gifted businessman: 'His faculties of perception and power of analysis were keen and thorough, and to his ability for the practical exercise of these qualities is greatly due his success in life. As a friend, he easily won and ever after kept the confidence of those who knew him. He was calm, quiet, consistent, patient, and gentle, ever ready to lend a helping hand to those in less fortunate outward circumstances than himself ...'

He was born in Campbeltown in 1835 to Thomas MacKelvie, seaman, and Marion, or 'Mysie', Watson, from

Killean Parish. At the age of 13, he started work in the office of John Beith Jr. (q.v. #2), with whom he remained for 16 years, latterly serving also as clerk to the Commissioners of Income Tax, of which Beith was assessor for Argyll. In common with James Stewart and John Galbraith, fellow-directors in Stewart, Galbraith & Co., he served on the Town Council, was involved in the Campbeltown Steam Packet, as auditor, and was a member of the Kintyre Club, which he joined in 1860. With Stewart, he also played an active role in the management of the local savings bank. For the last seven years of his life, he was consumptive and suffered precarious health, but he attended to the business of Scotia Distillery, with 'few interruptions', until six weeks before his death.[502]

For his sons Colonel Maxwell and Colonel Thomas, and his daughter Marion Watson MacKelvie, see my *Glen Scotia Distillery: A History*, pp. 18-19.

McKersie, Alexander, was the youngest son of John McKersie, mason, and a brother of William #1, whom Alex joined in the firm of William McKersie & Co., Albyn Distillery. In October 1852, however, he emigrated to Melbourne, Australia, where he set up the warehousing firm of McKersie, Love & Co., with a fellow-Campbeltonian, Alex Love. On 29 October 1859, McKersie, Love and three friends went out from Brighton, near Melbourne, in a small boat to fish. One of the friends, a heavy man, put his foot through the boat's planking and sank her, and Love was one of the three who drowned.[503] In 1858, at Brighton, McKersie had married Susannah, daughter of a Melbourne merchant, James Webby. McKersie also had interests in horse-trading: in 1866, he and his partner in Messrs. McKersie & Learmouth shipped 120 horses from Hobsons Bay, Melbourne, to Calcutta on the clipper *Marpesia*.[504]

An article in the *Campbeltown Journal* on 18 March 1854, 'Intelligence from Australia', lauded the 'success' of Campbeltonians in Melbourne and associated the names

Ferguson, Taylor, Love and McKersie with 'everything that is praiseworthy, affluent and respectable'. (The displacement and slaughter of an indigenous population was naturally omitted from the account, but 'scarcity of women' in Melbourne merited notice.)

McKersie returned to Scotland with his wife and son in 1871 and set up in business in Glasgow. On 12 May 1874, he took a train to Wemyss Bay, on the Firth of Clyde, and booked into an hotel there. At about six o' clock the following morning, he left the hotel and was seen undressing behind rocks and then entering the sea. Shortly after, workmen at Castle Wemyss heard 'cries of distress' and saw him 'floating away to the south-west ...' They immediately launched a boat and went to his assistance, but by the time they reached him he was dead. He was buried in Kilkerran,[505] but appears to have no memorial.

McKersie, Archibald, died at Portmore House, Ballinderry, County Antrim, on 22 July 1875, aged 38. He was a son of William #1, and his wife, Rose Andrew, was a daughter of Robert Greenlees #1. There was no obituary in the local newspaper and little is known about him. Early in 1862, the brigantine *Helena* was built for him and a partner: see 'Shipping'. In June of that year, to celebrate his marriage in Glasgow, the Albyn workers and their families were 'entertained to a sumptuous dinner on the Distillery premises' and danced 'with great spirit until an early hour'.[506] In 1866, the sloop *Albyn* was launched for him: again, see 'Shipping'. Between 1866 and his death in 1875, he must have moved to Ireland, perhaps as a distiller, but his wife returned to Campbeltown and died there in 1915, aged 74, and they are buried together in Kilkerran.

McKersie, John, who died on 7 November 1904, at the age of 62, was a son of William #1, who established the firm of William McKersie & Co., Albyn and Lochruan distilleries, of which John and his brother William became joint-owners. He was doubly connected to the Mitchell distilling family: his mother Jane was a daughter of Archibald #1 and his wife Helen a daughter of William #1. When Helen died in 1932, at the age of 77, her obituarist remarked, indisputably, that 'she was intimately connected with a long and interesting period in the industrial and commercial life of Campbeltown'.[507]

Each McKersie brother built a mansion-house on Askomil, facing south across Campbeltown Loch, and each house was designed by the esteemed Scottish architect, H. E. Clifford (1852-1932), whose mother, Rebecca Anderson, and wife, Margaret Alice Gibson, both belonged to Campbeltown.[508] Craigard was built for William McKersie in 1882, and Auchinlee followed in 1886 for John, who, such was the rivalry between the brothers, instructed Clifford to build it 'bigger and grander'![509] In July 1952, Auchinlee was opened as an eventide home by John's daughter-in-law, Mrs E. C. L. McKersie, who had gifted it to the Church of Scotland.[510] The Church controversially closed Auchinlee in 2018 and put the property up for sale.

John McKersie was a member of Campbeltown Town Council for 21 years: elected in 1875, Dean of Guild from 1880 to 1890, when elected Provost, a position he held for six years. As an indication of the influence of the distilling class in town, his predecessor as Provost was Duncan Colville #1 and his successor his brother-in-law Hugh Mitchell #2. Politically, he was a Unionist, and, in religion, he belonged to Longrow United Free Church. According to his obituarist, he 'had all the faculties of a successful businessman; and alike in public and in private life he was regarded with the utmost veneration'.[511] His personal estate in the United Kingdom amounted to £79,544 and, abroad, to £3,223.[512]

He was survived by his wife, two sons and a daughter, Edith Kate, who would die, aged 23, in 1913, while visiting friends in Dundee. Son Archibald, a Captain in the 7th Highland Light Infantry, was wounded at the age of 23 during the Dardanelles campaign in 1915, died on board the hospital ship *Asturius* and was buried in Alexandria, Egypt. The final child, William Mitchell McKersie, married Elizabeth Cochran Loudon Motherwell in 1914 and lived until 1940. He was a chartered accountant in Glasgow and held directorships in several manufacturing companies. In the First World War, he served as a Captain with the Glasgow Highlanders and was awarded a Military Cross.[513]

Most unusually, a golden wedding notice, presumably inserted by John's widow, appeared in the local newspaper in 1929, a quarter of a century after his death, recording their marriage on 10 September 1879, at Drumore, by the Rev J. B. Smith of Greenock, an uncle of the bride.[514]

McKersie, William #1. The McKersie family was one of the most prominent in the history of Campbeltown distilling, and William was the first in the line. Superficially, the name appears to represent a break in the latter-day domination of the industry by Lowland Plantation families, but, in fact, McKersie is not a native Kintyre surname. The first McKersie, John, was a mason from Greenock, who first appears on record in 1810 in Dalintober. His wife was Catherine McCalla (McAulay), who was born in Glasgow and died in Campbeltown in 1859, aged 73. See also my *Kilkerran Graveyard Revisited*, pp. 14-15.

William McKersie, who was born in Greenock, died on 2 December 1878, aged 72. His wife, who died two years later, was Jane or Jean Mitchell, whom he married in 1834, and the McKersie gravestone in Kilkerran stands at one end of a line of Mitchell monuments to her distiller brothers William, John and Archibald. William started out as a distiller at Lochside in 1830, but left the business to build Albyn in 1837, and later bought Lochruan. His sons, William and John, later took over the business.

In the estimation of his obituarist, 'Perhaps among all the businessmen of Campbeltown, who, by their own exertions, have risen to a position of opulence, there is no more striking example than that of the deceased ... As a businessman, he possessed invaluable qualities, being shrewd and persevering, and had withal that spirit of commercial enterprise by which so many Scotchmen are distinguished'. Like many of his fellow-distillers in the 19th century, he 'took a deep interest in town affairs', and he was a member of the Town Council for about 30 years and served as a Bailie. He was a member of the United Presbyterian Church and 'a liberal contributor towards its support', and also 'aided generally those philanthropic schemes of which he approved'.[515]

The family gravestone also commemorates son James, who died in 1873, aged 23, and daughter Isabella, died in 1916, aged 69, at Norwood, High Askomil.

McKersie, William #2. Unlike his brother John, William took 'no direct part in public affairs', but 'gave liberally to all good and worthy causes, while no suppliant for assistance was turned away unaided'. A private individual, his leisure was devoted to shooting and fishing. When he died, on 3 August 1916, at his villa, Craigard — a maternity hospital from 1940 and now an hotel — he was aged 72 and had been in failing health for two or three years.

Like many another distiller, he received his business training in a Glasgow office. The narrative of William McKersie's career, after his return from Glasgow, was, according to his obituarist, as follows: '[He ...] became associated with his brother, the late ex-Provost John McKersie, in the management of Lochruan Distillery. On the retiral of his father from business, about 40 years ago, Mr McKersie took charge at the Albyn Distillery, and since the death of his brother he has been managing partner in connection with the Albyn and Lochruan Distilleries. His business aptitude and ability were beyond question ...'[516]

Singularly for a distillery-owner, William was involved in an industrial accident. In 1866, at Albyn, while 'examining a large vessel filled with hot water', the plank he was

157

standing on slipped and he fell in. A foot and part of an arm were 'severely scalded'.[517]

His wife, Marion McCall, whom he married in 1881, belonged to Ayr and died at Craigard in 1940. A woman of 'upright and noble character', she devoted the greater part of her life to charities and in 1918 received the Order of the British Empire for her voluntary work in the Red Cross Society during the First World War.[518] Her daughter, Jean Mitchell, who died in 1946, was in an ambulance unit attached to the Italian army during that war and was thrice decorated. She afterwards emigrated to California, where she and a sister ran an 'orange ranch' before returning to Campbeltown prior to the Second World War.[519]

McKersie, William #3, Norwood, High Askomil, who died on 15 April 1952, aged 68, in an Edinburgh nursing home, was the elder son of William #2. He was educated at Fettes College, Edinburgh, and, after 'commercial training' in Glasgow, joined the family firm, William McKersie & Co., from which he retired after its distilleries, Albyn and Lochruan, were sold. During the First World War, he was badly injured on active service in France with the 5th Camerons and was invalided home. In 1921, he married Margaret Stewart Beatson Mactaggart, eldest daughter of John Norman Mactaggart, solicitor in Campbeltown, and had three children, William Norman (born 1923), Ian Stewart (1925) and Margaret Jean (1933), who achieved some success as a singer. On the day of McKersie's funeral, flags were flown at half-mast at The Club, Main Street, and at Campbeltown Bowling Club.[520]

McKersies in Ulster. See Archibald McKersie, who died at Ballinderry, County Antrim, in 1875.

James McKersie was buried in Ballinderry Presbyterian Churchyard with his wife, Mary Lyle, and four of their children. They both died in Belfast, he in 1887, aged 68, and she in 1899, aged 77. They married in Campbeltown in

1842, when he was described as a mason — his father John's occupation — and she as a daughter of Alexander Lyle, farmer at Knockrioch, near Stewarton, Kintyre. Lyle died in 1873 on a farm at Lisloonen, Saintfield, near Belfast.[521]

Their son John McKersie, who was born in Campbeltown in 1849, is also buried at Ballinderry. In 1885, when he was appointed by the Campbeltown Distillers' Association as its Belfast draff agent, he was in Glasgow, but was reported as having been 'brought up near Belfast'.[522] By 1911, he was a distillery manager in Belfast. He died in 1920, aged 71, and his wife, Lizzie, in 1923, aged 68.[523]

Their daughter Elizabeth Lyle, wife of William Graham, solicitor, died in Belfast on 25 April 1890, eight days after her sister Mary Jane Mitchell McKersie married William Lyle Hay, Clonbrock, County Galway, in the same city. The only son of that marriage, Second-Lieutenant J. L. Hay, Northumberland Fusiliers, was killed in action in July 1916.[524]

Mackie, Sir Peter Jeffrey, who died on 22 September 1924, was a distiller, but not a Campbeltown distiller, though the firm he headed, Mackie & Co. (Distillers), purchased Hazelburn Distillery in 1919 and he owned an estate in North Kintyre. He was, almost inevitably, a member of the Kintyre Club, enrolled in 1921.

He was born at St Ninians, Stirling, in 1855, son of a distiller, Alexander Mackie. In 1878, he joined an uncle's firm, James L. Mackie & Co., which ran Lagavulin Distillery on Islay, and a decade later he became a founding partner in Mackie & Co., which was formed to market Lagavulin and other whiskies in London. In 1890, the two firms amalgamated as Mackie & Co. (Distillers) and began to blend 'White Horse' whisky, which became a leading brand. Mackie & Co. in 1924 became White Horse Distillers Ltd. and in 1927 was absorbed by the Distillers Company Limited.

His connection with Kintyre appears to have begun in 1903 with the purchase of Glenreasdell, where, two years later, he built a mansion.[525] His other 'estates' were

Lagavulin in Islay and Corraith in Ayrshire. He travelled extensively and was interested in exploration (he funded the Mackie Anthropological Expedition to East Africa in 1919); he wrote on political and 'sporting' subjects, and his *The Keeper's Book* went through 14 editions between 1904 and 1924; he was a collector of antique furniture, silver, china and paintings.

In 1920, Mackie & Co. bought the William McTaggart painting, 'Rainy day, Carradale harbour' (1883), for 1,700 guineas and donated it to the National Gallery in Sydney, Australia.[526] The choice was rather apt, albeit unconsciously so, because the artist's father, Dugald McTaggart, was both an illicit distiller at Aros, in the Laggan of Kintyre, and a peat-carter to Campbeltown distilleries.

In 1920, four years before his death, a baronetcy was conferred upon Mackie, but there was no heir, his son, Captain J. Logan Mackie, Ayrshire Yeomanry, having been killed in Palestine in the last year of the Great War. In 1921, Isobel, one of his two daughters, married Captain Geordie O. L. Campbell, M.C., of Stonefield, Tarbert.[527] Campbell was enrolled in the Kintyre Club in 1927 as 'G. Mackie Campbell', distiller, Monkton, Ayrshire, having changed his name two years earlier.

MacKinnon's Distillery. Colville (1923) locates MacKinnon's Distillery, also known as 'Argyll Distillery', at the Big Kiln, Lorne Street, and adds that the malt-barn was in Longrow. It was built 'not later than 1828' and named after a Duncan MacKinnon. Identifying the partners in this distillery has proved difficult.

In Kilkerran graveyard there is a Duncan MacKinnon who died in 1835, aged 58. He is described as 'Distiller' on the headstone, which was raised to his parents, John MacKinnon and Catharine McCallum, by 'affectionate relatives'.

Beneath his name is that of Donald Graham, 'teacher in Campbeltown', who died in 1844; and the last name, with no date attached, is Elizabeth MacKinnon. Donald Graham, 'Teacher or Schoolmaster in Campbeltown', in 1811 married an Elizabeth MacKinnon, whose father was John MacKinnon, sailor in Campbeltown, so she would appear to have been a sister of Duncan. In the year after the marriage, a daughter, Catharine, was born, and, in that entry, Donald has become 'Daniel' (the names were used interchangeably: p 171). Was he the Daniel Graham, distiller, who was MacKinnon's partner? It seems probable.

Duncan Colville's candidate was Duncan MacKinnon, 'formerly of the Excise'. This Duncan, who died in 1836, aged 70, was described as an 'Excise Constable' in 1823, when his wife, Isabella Currie, gave birth to son William. That son became Sir William MacKinnon Bart, C.I.E., of Loup and Balinakill, founder of the British India Steam Navigation Company and the Imperial British East Africa Company, and a statue of whom — originally erected in Mombasa, Kenya — stands outside the Aqualibrium leisure-centre on Kinloch Road. That the two Duncans were related is likely, because their headstones are together. One of them — more likely the former — was enrolled in the Kintyre Club as a distiller in 1828.

According to Colville, the distillery was defunct by 1844, when the second Argyll (q.v.) was built near the head of the Longrow by a new firm.

McKinven, John, died at the age of 80 at Tangy Place, Dalintober, on 8 July 1922, and was buried at Kilchenzie. That he had worked at Glen Nevis Distillery is known from his death notice in the local newspaper, for his obituary dealt entirely with his religious life. Rev Norman MacKenzie: 'He served the Highland Parish Church well, for he loved it well. He loved the Church, for he loved the great Head of the Church.' At the time of his death, he was the oldest member of Campbeltown Kirk Session. In 1900, he took the lease of Campbeltown Meal Mill and its grounds at Millknowe, but whether he intended to work the mill himself or to employ a miller is uncertain. His wife, Elizabeth McLauchlan, had died at Glen Nevis Distillery in 1894 'after a long and severe illness'.[528]

Their son Donald was a pupil and then pupil-teacher at the school in Dalintober which stood on ground now forming part of Glen Scotia Distillery. He graduated M.A. with distinction at the University of Glasgow and had a career in education in the Highland whisky region. He retired in October 1927 after 24 years as headmaster at Mortlach Secondary School, having gone there from Fettercairn.[529]

McLachlan, Lachlan. On 6 February 1873, while oiling moving machinery at Dalaruan Distillery, McLachlan got his cravat caught in a roller. One of his ears was split and, in raising a hand to free himself, his thumb was severed. He was able to walk home, but died shortly afterwards, leaving a widow, a son and a daughter.[530] His widow, Elizabeth Campbell, was born in Killean Parish in 1823, a daughter of Duncan Campbell, roadman, and Barbara MacLean (great-great-great-grandparents of the author). She married McLachlan in 1849, when he was described as a 'maltman', and married again in 1880. Her second husband, John McLean, a plasterer, abandoned her on 17 February 1884 and 'left town soon after'. By 1891, when she was admitted to the poor roll, she had been 'bedfast' for two or three years. Daughter Barbara and children were living at Lochend, and son Alex, a cooper, was 'supposed to be about Glasgow'. She was awarded 2s 6d[531] and died in 1896.

McLennan, George, distiller — see 'John Grant' and 'Highland Distillery'.

McMillan, Alexander, who belonged to Campbeltown, retired in 1924 after 17 years as manager of Lochindaal Distillery, Islay. He was transferred there from Loch-head

— J. B. Sherriff & Co. owned both distilleries at that time — where, at the time of the 1901 census, he was mashman and living in the distillery house with his wife, Annie Muir — born in Auchinleck, Ayrshire — and nine children.

Four of his sons served in the First World War, and two of them — Duncan (1/7th Argyll & Sutherland Highlanders) and Alexander (6th King's Own Scottish Borderers) — were killed in action on the Western Front. Alexander had his own wartime experiences, involving Islay shipwrecks. He led the rescuers of the crew of the naval tug-boat *Flying Falcon*, driven ashore in Machrie Bay in June 1917, and 'rendered yeoman service' when the *Tuscania* and *Otranto* troopships sank in 1918, with a combined death-toll of more than 600 U.S. servicemen.

McMillan 'took an active interest in the social and religious life' of his adopted community and 'treated his employees with great consideration and absolute fairness'. Before his return to Campbeltown, he was presented with a 'wallet of Treasury notes' by the oldest employee in the distillery, Alexander Turner. McMillan remarked that it was an 'acute wrench' to part from his staff and the good friends he had made on Islay, and that his time on 'green, grassy Islay' would 'always remain green in his memory'.[532]

Fourth son, Allan, drowned at Port Charlotte in 1908 at the age of 14, and second daughter, Elizabeth, married Samuel Thomson (q.v.) in Lochindaal Distillery in 1910.[533]

McMillan, Daniel. When he retired as mashman at Campbeltown Distillery in 1890, McMillan had worked there for 37 years. He died the following year, on 22 February. He was predeceased, in 1879, by his wife, Isabella Gillies. 'Above the average in intelligence' and politically 'an ardent Liberal', he 'lived to see his family occupying respected positions in life'.[534] He was born at East Kilmichael farm in 1815, a son of William McMillan and Jean Breakenridge, but the year after he was born his father signed over the lease to Alexander Dunlop, maltster, and Alexander Colville, merchant.[535] In 1865, his 80-year-old widowed mother, Jean, was admitted to Campbeltown poor roll on a shilling a week, but she was removed three years later, with the explanation: 'Supported by son Daniel.'[536]

McMillan, Duncan, was born on 3 June 1821 on Auchaleek farm, near Campbeltown, and died on 7 February 1873 at Polmont, near Falkirk. In Census 1871, he was at Whyteside, Polmont, and was described as a distiller, brewer and landowner. When enrolled in the Kintyre Club in 1851, his designation was 'of Polmont'; but in his death notice in the Campbeltown newspaper he was 'of Whyteside'.[537] He was unmarried, and in Census 1871 was with two unmarried sisters, Barbara (aged 47) and Mary (35), a servant Margaret Blackstock and a nurse Jane Clark, whose presence suggests that the invalid was Duncan: the cause of his death, two years later, was epilepsy. The entire household was born in Campbeltown Parish.

Duncan's parents both had the surname McMillan: Duncan Sr. was a farmer in Kilmichael — where Daniel McMillan, above, was born — when, in 1809, he married Isabella, daughter of Archibald McMillan, farmer in Balliemenach.

Little is known about Duncan McMillan's career, other than that in 1853, when described as a commission agent in Glasgow, he became co-partner in Campbeltown Distillery with James Melville (q.v.). In 1874, the year after his death, his trustees requested the release of the balance due from the Campbeltown Distillery Co., which was a substantial sum, the first of three instalments having been £1,601 13s 11d. The one trustee who was identified was a nephew, D. McLean, 45 Dunlop Street, Glasgow,[538] who was almost certainly David McLean, of W. & D. McLean, commission agents at that address, which was also the address from which McMillan had operated.

McMurchy, John, bought shares in 1838 in Dalaruan Distillery, which was founded by David Colville & Co. His wife, Jean, whom he married in 1834, was a daughter of John Colville, maltster, and a sister of David Colville #1; her mother Martha was a McMurchy. John's parents were John McMurchy, cooper, and Jean Maxwell. John — described on his gravestone in Kilkerran as 'distiller' — died, at Lochend, on 18 November 1870, aged 64, and Jean on 26 August 1872, also aged 64. The only other name on the stone is that of their daughter Martha, who died at Cannes on 5 January 1892, aged 56, and was 'interred in [the] English Cemetery' there. Cannes was then a popular health resort, the French Riviera's winter sunshine being considered conducive to recovery from tuberculosis. Daughter Jeanie married Alexander MacKelvie (q.v.) and died aged 41 in 1878.

The only other distillers in Campbeltown with the name McMurchy were Archibald and Robert of A. & R. McMurchy Ltd., which built Loch-head Distillery in 1824; Robert, who was connected with Burnside and Glenramskill distilleries; and William, Glenramskill. Since the first Robert died in 1833, and the second had a connection with Glenramskill until 1840, the two appear to be distinct. A Robert McMurchy, maltster, in 1813 married Jean, daughter of Alexander Watson, maltster.

In 1864, a maltster in Campbeltown, John McMurchy — one of that name married Jean Colvill in 1834 and another, 'brewer', married Helen Howie (or Huie) in 1856 — was found guilty of falsehood, fraud and wilful imposition and jailed for 20 days for having passed off a 'tradesman's token' as a sovereign in the shop of John Stalker, grocer.[539] A Donald McMurchy in Melbourne, Australia, was enrolled in the Kintyre Club as a distiller in 1861.

MacMurchy is one of the old native names in Kintyre and is linked to the distinguished *MacMhuirich* hereditary bardic family, for which see my *Kintyre: The Hidden Past*, pp. 6-10. In Kintyre in the 19th century, the generality of

MacMurchy families would have been Gaelic-speaking, but in Campbeltown itself there were families — or perhaps just one family — of McMurchys which consistently intermarried and identified with Lowland Plantation stock (see also the following entry).

McMurchy, Robert Ryburn, who died in a Glasgow nursing home on 27 February 1931, at the age of 68, was not a distiller, but a cooper. When he began his apprenticeship, he represented the sixth unbroken generation in the trade, for the family business, his obituary claimed, 'was founded in the Longrow ... when George the third was King'.

The McMurchy property, 36 Longrow, was built on the site of one of the last thatched houses in the street, from which the family moved, across to the Kirk Close — see 'Mossfield Distillery' — while the new tenement was going up. The entrance to the property is still known as Cooper's Close, and the last purpose-built cooperage in Campbeltown still stands in the lane, though its slated roof has been replaced by steel and its windows blocked.

Despite the decline in the distilling business, McMurchy worked at his trade 'practically up to the end'. His business 'maintained many of the characteristics that were common in old time industrial concerns in Campbeltown. The master worked day in, day out, along with the men: he was a feuar with his dwelling-house fronting the street and the workshop and yard behind'.

McMurchy was a keen gardener, bee-keeper and poultry-breeder, an elder in Longrow Church, and he qualified for a Volunteer Long Service Medal with the local detachment of the Argyll & Sutherland Highlanders, in which he was a corporal. He never married and lived with a sister.[540] His parents were Daniel McMurchy and Martha Armour.

Macnish, Neil, died on 16 February 1905, aged 68. His parents were Donald Macnish, a shoemaker born in Whitehouse, North Kintyre, and Margaret McMichael. He began his working life as a clerk in Campbeltown Distillery, was manager by 1859, at the age of about 22, and, on the strength of his experience of the whisky business, in 1891 was made a director of Stewart, Galbraith & Co. Ltd. (q.v.), which position he held until his death.

In 1860, he moved to Glasgow — the *Argyllshire Herald* of 3 February reported a 'complimentary supper' for him in the Argyll Arms Inn, on the eve of his departure 'to fill an important mercantile appointment' — and his main business interests were in that city. He joined the firm of J. J. Cochrane & Co., muslin manufacturers of Wellington Mills, Glasgow, and ultimately became principal partner. Until he left Campbeltown in 1860, he was secretary of the Young Men's Association and 'won the approbation and esteem of those who attended the lectures under the superintendence of that society'; he was a member of the Glasgow-based Kintyre Literary Association, founded in 1868, and captain of Machrihanish Golf Club in 1896.[541]

He left a personal estate in the U.K. valued at £37,976 3s 9d, and his share in J. J. Cochrane & Co. was valued for probate at £36,885. Duncan MacCallum was among those granted probate, as was Neil's brother Hugh, a tea-planter in Assam, India, who was born in 1841 in the vanished village of Lintmill (p 53). Neil's wife, Agnes Garroway, whom he married in Cumbernauld in 1867, died in childbirth the following year, aged 32, and she and her premature son lie in Janefield Cemetery, Glasgow. He never remarried and, since he had no issue, his substantial property holdings in Glasgow were inherited by his brother Hugh's four daughters.[542]

MacPherson, Archibald, is described as 'distillery manager' on his gravestone, but elsewhere as 'brewer, Albyn Distillery'.[543] He died in 1876, aged 69; his wife, Mary Martin, died in 1885, aged 76. Son Alexander was manager of Lochruan Distillery when he married Catherine Smith in July 1866 in Dalintober;[544] but he died in February of the following year, aged 27, and she died a year after him, also at 27. Eldest son John, engineer on the SS *Mohratta*, was aged 29 when he died off the coast of Burma, on 7 June 1867, three months after Alexander.[545] Son Archibald was a distillery manager when he married Jane MacPherson, a domestic servant from Appin, in 1870, and died in 1912, aged 66.

The Archibald McPherson, 'mashman, Lochruan Distillery', who was praised for his 'cool courage and daring' on the night the engine house of Campbeltown Distillery (q.v.) caught fire in 1869, was probably Archibald Jr. 'It was feared that owing to the flames having enveloped the boiler, the steam would increase to such an extent as to render the danger of a disastrous explosion exceedingly probable; and Mr McPherson, with great intrepidity, ventured, at imminent danger to himself, to inspect the safety valve and see that it was open.'[546]

McSporran, Donald and Charles. These brothers became distillery managers in Campbeltown despite a poor start in life. When their father, Archibald, died in 1885, aged 39, their mother, Margaret Curdie, who had five sons — Archibald (17), Charles (15), Donald (11), Duncan (9) and Neil (5) — was admitted to the poor roll on three shillings a week.[547] In the 1891 Census, Donald was a distillery workman, Charles a distillery clerk, and the oldest brother, Archibald, a distillery workman.

Donald, who died on 28 December 1944, aged 72, spent 48 years in the distilling business, about half of that period with the Kintyre and Longrow distilleries and the latter half with Argyll, Burnside and Hazelburn. When he retired in 1936 as manager of Scottish Malt Distillers' bonded warehouses in Campbeltown, he was 'entertained to tea' in the Hazelburn offices and presented with a solid silver cigarette-case by Miss Minnie MacKenzie, his clerk. He remarked in his response that he 'had tried to be human in all his dealings with the men in his employ, and if he had erred in any instance, it was not done intentionally'.[548] He was a director of the *Campbeltown Courier* newspaper, in which he 'took more than an executive interest': during the Second World War, when the newspaper was very short-staffed, Donald regularly assisted in the printing department. His obituarist on the *Courier* remarked of him that 'the simple things in life pleased him most'. In his early life, he enjoyed walking the hills of Kintyre 'to spend an afternoon quietly fishing', and latterly he devoted his time to cultivating flowers in his garden at Greanan, Dalintober.[549] His wife Flora McNeill, whom he married in 1903, died in 1953 at Greanan, aged 78.

Charles Curdie McSporran died at his home Otira — named after a small town in New Zealand — on 28 August 1946, aged 76. He spent some 45 years with Springbank Distillery and was steadily promoted: 'After a fine record of service to his firm, he was appointed manager and secretary, and made a director.' In the year before his death, he retired as manager, but continued as secretary and director. Like many other Campbeltonians of his generation, he witnessed the decline of his home town from 'a famous whisky distilling centre' to 'a town industrially decadent, with only two distilleries working'. In 1897, he was secretary and treasurer of the Campbeltown Cycling Club, but he later took up motor cycling and in 1921 broke a leg in a collision with a cart on the Southend road.[550] Golf, however, was his 'life-long recreation', to which he added bowling at Stronvaar Club. He was enrolled in the Kintyre Club in 1922. His wife Mary was a daughter of John MacKenzie, cooper, who died in 1894, and their wedding in 1901 took place at 'The Cooperage, Glebe Street'. She predeceased him in 1937 and he was survived by an only child, Archibald, an officer in the Merchant Navy.[551]

The last surviving McSporran brother, Duncan, lived in Edinburgh. His wife, Penelope Mitchell, was a gamekeeper's daughter from Killean in Kintyre, and their daughter Margaret was the mother of the famous Scottish mountaineer, Dugald Haston (1940-77), whose real name was Duncan Curdy McSporran Haston. His main successes were in the Himalayas, where, in 1970, he and Don Whillans were the first to climb the south face of Annapurna, and five years later he and Doug Scott were the first Britons to reach the summit of Mount Everest by the previously unclimbed south-west face.

(Remarkably, there was another eminent climber with local connections, Alex MacIntyre, who died, aged 28, in 1982, when struck by a falling stone as he set up a new route on the south face of Annapurna. He was born in Cottingham, Yorkshire, but his parents, Hamish MacIntyre — a member of the same family as Alexander McIntyre (q.v.) — and Jean Parker, were from Campbeltown. A biography, *One Day as a Tiger*, by John Porter, was published in 2014.)

McSporran, Morris, mashman, who died at the age of 82 on 4 March 1919, was employed at Loch-head for more than 50 years and had retired only a few years earlier. He was survived by four daughters, two sons, 32 grandchildren and 31 great-grandchildren. His wife, Jean McIntyre, had died in December 1917, but not before they celebrated their diamond wedding anniversary on 17 May (they married on 5 May 1857). He was an elder in the Highland Church and 'had much of the old Highland dignity and address in his ways'.[552] He and his wife, unusually for Gaelic speakers settled in town, passed on the language to their children. In Census 1891, two sons, a daughter and two grandchildren, living with them in Dalaruan, were all recorded as having both Gaelic and English. Morris's father was Daniel McSporran, and his mother Marion was also a McSporran.

Mactaggart, Charles Rowatt, was born on 18 June 1809 to John Mactaggart (q.v.) and Helen Kennedy. He was a 'surgeon', or doctor, in Campbeltown, and, as such, was caught up in the fearsome cholera epidemic of 1832;[553] but he also had a financial interest in distilling and by 1834 was a partner in Union Distillery with Hector Henderson (q.v.). The 'Charles McTaggart, Surgeon', who fathered an illegitimate daughter with Agnes Love — truly a 'Love child'! — must have been him. Baby Agnes was born on 10 July 1829 and baptised on 7 January 1830. In the following year, he married not Agnes Love, but Mary Watson. In Census 1841, they were in Longrow with four children — Robert (9 years old), John (7), Charles (3) and Helen (1) — and a 25-year-old servant, Isabella Sinclair. Charles died in 1846 and his wife in 1852. The only other name on the gravestone is that of a son, Robert Lamb Mactaggart, who died as an infant in 1832 and was succeeded by Robert Lamb Watson Mactaggart, born in November of the same year — see 'Kinloch Distillery' for Robert Lamb, after whom the boys were named. Charles himself bore a tribute-name, that of Charles Rowatt (q.v.), who, like Charles himself, was a doctor with distilling interests. (There was another Charles Rowatt McTaggart, born in 1814 to Donald, blacksmith at Kilkivan, and Margaret Arnot.) In *Pigot* of 1837, Charles was one of nine 'surgeons' listed in Campbeltown Parish and was practising in Main Street. His brother Daniel, below, was born almost 23 years before him.

Mactaggart, Daniel, of Kilkivan. 'Dan', the form he preferred, was born on 26 July 1786 and died on 31 May 1859. When his birth was registered, the name was written as 'Donald', but this was scored out and replaced with 'Daniel', which was widely used, both in Gaelic Ireland and Gaelic Scotland, as an Anglicised form of Gaelic *Domhnall*, 'Donald'. The change may appear insignificant, but I suggest that it indicates a shift from a rural Gaelic identity to an alignment with the town-based merchant class which was of predominantly Lowland origin and Scots-speaking. The surname 'Mactaggart', which was common throughout Kintyre, represents Gaelic *Mac an t-sagairt*, 'Son of the priest'.

Dan was a 'writer', or lawyer, and the law firm he established in 1810 continues to this day as C. & D. Mactaggart. He was also procurator fiscal of Kintyre from

1815 until his retirement, when his son Charles succeeded him. Dan was the eldest son of John Mactaggart (below) of Campbeltown Distillery and himself founded a distillery, the Highland.

Father and son were both evidently involved in the illicit whisky trade (Appendix 4) before Dan became procurator fiscal and his father became a founding partner in the first legal distillery of the 19th century; but, as local historian Fr. James Webb observed in 1960 of the trade in illicit whisky, 'nearly everybody in the town and district was implicated in it, from the Provost and Magistrates down'. Dr Norman Macleod was fond of telling the story of an old woman who appeared before Sheriff Duncan Campbell on a charge of illicit distilling. The sheriff seemed a bit uneasy, but eventually addressed the accused: 'No doubt, my good woman, it is not often you have been guilty of this fault.' — 'Na, na, Shirra,' she replied, 'I hae'na made a drop since yon wee keg I sent yoursel'.'[554]

In 1811, the Mactaggarts, who together owned a packet, or mail-boat, the *Caledonia*, which sailed between Campbeltown and Greenock, were in bother with the Customs service over allegations that passengers boarding the vessel at Campbeltown were smuggling whisky. The detention in port of the *Caledonia* was a real threat, which, Dan protested, would hurt him considerably. The temptation to conceal even small quantities of whisky becomes apparent when the value of Campbeltown whisky at that time is compared with spirits distilled in Glasgow: 17s to 25s a gallon against about 9s a gallon. Fr. Webb's summary of the cases against John and Dan Mactaggart, which cover some 30 pages in the Campbeltown Customs Letter Books, appears as Appendix 4.

With the coming of steam ships, travel conditions improved enormously, not least in the greatly shortened times spent at sea, and Dan Mactaggart was the first chairman of the revitalised Campbeltown & Glasgow Steam Packet Joint-Stock Co. Ltd. (q.v.), which began its first financial year in February 1827.

Dan was elected to Campbeltown Town Council in 1852. His obituarist described him as 'Conservative in bias' in matters of religion and politics, but 'completely above narrow bigotry and intolerance', and remarked tantalisingly: 'His knowledge of local and district history was most minute and accurate, and it is a subject of regret that it should not have been preserved in some lasting form.'[555] As 'Daniel McTaggart of Kilkevan', he was enrolled as a member of the Kintyre Club in 1827, two years after its foundation. His wife, whom he married in Edinburgh in 1811, was Christian Hamilton Campbell, a daughter of Lieutenant Scipio Duroure Campbell, of the 100th Regiment of Foot, and Gilles (Julia) Campbell.

The Mactaggart family had faded from the distilling scene by the mid-19th century, but in 1891 two of Dan's descendants, John Norman and Daniel Mactaggart, both solicitors, became share-holders in Stewart, Galbraith & Co. Ltd. (q.v.).

Mactaggart, John, was, at various times in his life, a sheriff's officer — one who carried out the warrants of a sheriff and served writs, etc — merchant, ship-owner, maltster and distiller, but his gravestone in Kilkerran defines him as 'Merchant in Campbeltown'. He was born on 19 August 1762 to Archibald 'MacIntaggart' and Ann (or Agnes) Morrison, who married in 1759. Archibald is commemorated on the earliest of the Mactaggart stones in the old section of Kilkerran, along with his father, Malcolm McIntagart, who died in 1738 and is described as a farmer at 'Craigag', which is now a huddle of well-preserved ruins on the Atlantic coast south of Machrihanish. John, who died on 12 October 1832, was a founding partner in Campbeltown Distillery, built in 1817, and his sons Daniel (q.v.) and Charles (q.v.) followed him into the whisky business, as an adjunct to their main professional interests. His wife, Helen Kennedy, died in 1830, aged 62.

Colonel Charles Mactaggart (p 233) showed Duncan Colville #2 a George III crown piece stamped 'J McT. 1822'.

The initials represented 'John McTaggart', the Colonel's great-grandfather, and 1822 was said to have been the year Campbeltown Distillery paid its first dividend, of which the crown was a part.[556]

Andrew McKerral in *Kintyre in the Seventeenth Century* included MacTaggart in his appendix of 'Lowland Names', cautioning that 'some of them may have been Highland'; but all evidence points to the absolute reverse. That Malcolm (above) was a Gaelic speaker is certain, given where and when he lived, and it is likely that his son Archibald, too, had Gaelic, and perhaps also John himself.

McWilliam, J. & J., wine and spirit merchants and distillers' agents in Glasgow, was founded in 1850 by the brothers John and James McWilliam. One of the firm's products was a popular blended whisky named 'Strathduie', which must be the Kintyre Gaelic place-name *Srath dubhaidh*, 'Gloomy strath', a wide valley at the upper reaches of the River Lussa: their father, Alexander, farmed Kilkeddan, at the lower end of the Lussa, until 1833.[557] The Glasgow public house 'Strathduie' was built in 1893 for J. & J. McWilliam, and by 1899 the family had 10 pubs in the city.[558]

Alexander McWilliam died at Clochkeil farm in 1854, aged 81, and his wife Agnes, also a McWilliam, died in 1864, aged 87, at Uigle, a farm in the hills south of Campbeltown. The McWilliam family was connected for generations with Uigle. Alexander's son Donald was farmer there in 1860 when John Dewar, a collector of Gaelic oral tradition, enlisted by J. F. Campbell of Islay, visited him seeking historical tales in the language. Donald died there in 1875, aged 74. His death was registered by his brother James, who owned Uigle and was there when the 1881 and 1891 censuses were taken. In both, he described himself as an unmarried 'spirit merchant and farmer', bi-lingual in Gaelic and English. He died in Glasgow in 1901, aged 81, and his gravestone in Kilkivan — one of a group of McWilliam memorials spanning three centuries — describes him as 'of Uigle'.

James, the leading partner in J. & J. McWilliam, was credited with having revolutionised the spirit trade's protectionist body, the Scottish Licensed Trade Defence Association. He perceived that the Association should embrace 'all sections of the licensed industry', rather than retailers only, and extended its membership to brewers, distillers and wholesale traders. He left £500 to each of three Glasgow hospitals, the Royal Infirmary, Western Infirmary and Victoria Infirmary. Aside from a number of smaller charitable bequests to institutions, and £210 to his 'shopman' James Jeffreys, the estate was divided among relatives.[559]

The Kintyre Club membership roll contains 10 McWilliams, including — in addition to John and James — Andrew, a wine and spirit merchant in Glasgow (enrolled in 1857, died in 1878) and Archibald, brewer in Londonderry (enrolled in 1865, died in 1869). The name McWilliam — sometimes Anglicised as 'Williamson' — was recorded in Kintyre from the 17th century, but disappeared in the 20th.

maltsters/malsters could also be distillers — i.e. making malt for their own use as well as the use of others — but primarily they turned barley into malt and sold it to distillers, legal or otherwise. (Illicit distillers could and did malt their own barley, but that could lead to just as much trouble with the Excise service as the distilling of the whisky itself.) In early 19th century records, the terms 'maltster' and 'distiller' were interchangeable, and not until towards mid-century did 'distiller' come to signify 'distillery-owner'.

In the 16th and 17th centuries, malt was manufactured on many farms in Kintyre for the brewing of ale, which, before the introduction of tea, was the usual drink with meals. Ale then was flavoured with locally gathered herbs or with imported additives, such as liquorice and ginger, and was only mildly alcoholic. 'Aquavitae', the forerunner of whisky, was a distilled spirit which was likewise flavoured with herbs and on which duty was not required to be paid.[560]

In the 18th and the 19th centuries, maltsters formed a sizeable industrial class, as the Old Parish Registers and other records amply demonstrate. *Pigot & Co.'s Commercial Directory* for 1825 records 22 in the town alone: William Breakinridge, William Brolachan, Archibald Colvill, John Colvill, Duncan Currie, James Dunlop, James Ferguson, Matthew Fleming, Archibald Galbraith, Alex Greenlees, Ann Greenlees, Daniel Greenlees, Thomas Greenlees, John Harvey, James McLachlan, James McNair, John McNair, John McTaggart, Archibald Mitchell, David Smith, Robert Thomson and Alex Wylie. Of these 22, 18 are of recognisably Lowland descent. *Pigot* of 1837 records 21 maltsters, including two who operated outside of town.

Four account books kept by John Colvill(e), maltster in Campbeltown, who died in the cholera epidemic of 1832, are preserved in the Live Argyll archive. Two of them — 1814-19 and 1823-26 — record transactions with illicit distillers. For a summary of these dealings, see this writer's *Kintyre Country Life*, p 105.

In October 1818, four Campbeltown maltsters, with the familiar names Archibald Mitchell, John and Alexander Greenlees and James Ferguson, complained to the Justices of the Peace Court that Donald McCorkindale, Barr Glen, and James Armour, Balloch, had bought malt from them and paid duty, but were stopped near Kilchenzie by John McNaughton, gunner of the Revenue Cutter *Maria*, who demanded to see their certificates and then destroyed them. When four other Largieside men who had bought malt refused to hand over their certificates, McNaughton seized the seven horses and carts and 9½ bushels of malt. The *Maria*'s captain, Joseph Wright, subsequently renounced his claim to the seizure.[561] That they were all intending to distil whisky illicitly is a near-certainty, hence McNaughton's rash actions.

On 8 April 1852, the *Argyllshire Herald* reported that 'the band of Revenue detective officers now in Kintyre' had searched Glen Braid in the Largieside and destroyed two sacks of 'concealed ... dry malt'.

In 1819, John Greenlees received a complaint about his malt. The letter was penned by Donald MacCallum at Auchinbreck in Carradale Glen. MacCallum's first language would have been Gaelic, and his literacy in English, albeit very imperfect, would have been unusual at that time and in that place. This is the first part: 'you Be will Be plesed to send me 2 Bolls of your Malt as soon as this com to pass and Be Sure and Sended it better is [as = than] the Last for it is the wors that ever I got of you for I got only 12 gallon of Spirit out the two Bolls that you send me Last and you may Lern yourself that it was very Bad.'[562]

In 1822, Ann Ferguson, widow of John Greenlees, had two customers in Barr Glen, Adam McCorkindale, 'Baruachrach', and John McCaull, 'Killagruier', arrested for a debt of £5 each. Her business dealings with the legal branch of the industry could be no less frustrating. In 1843 she pursued A. & R. McMurchy & Co. — James Taylor, Archibald McMurchy and Donald Andrew — for £83 5s 9d owed to her for malt delivered to Loch-head Distillery between 19 April 1832 and 18 August 1835.[563] (The distillery, by the time of her action, was under the management of William Taylor & Co.)

In the latter half of the 19th century, maltsters effectively disappeared and were replaced by 'maltmen', who manufactured malt in the distilleries in which they were employed. Springbank Distillery, continuing traditional practice, malts its own barley, but Glen Scotia has, for the past half-century or more, imported malt from other parts of Scotland. See also 'Barley'.

mashmen. The frequency in local newspapers of 'wanted' notices for mashmen, or brewers, suggests that the mashing, or brewing, process in whisky-distilling was considered the most vital; and for not a few mashmen in local distilleries the next career step was into management.

In 1855, an experienced mashman was wanted immediately by a Campbeltown distillery. He had to be 'capable of taking the Pumpings and attending to the Cellar', and 'None need apply whose character will not stand the strictest investigation as to honesty and sobriety'. In 1889, 'must be thoroughly sober and industrious' were stated conditions of employment.[564] In 1866, an Edinburgh advertising agency, Robertson & Sons, inserted a notice in the local newspaper seeking a brewer for a malt distillery in an undisclosed location. The applicant would have to 'thoroughly understand distilling in all its branches' and, if successful, would receive a 'liberal salary'.[565]

If there was a dwelling-house attached to a distillery, it was generally occupied by the mashman. For example, a local distillery advertising in 1873 for a mashman 'competent to take full charge of Mashing and Distilling', offered a house 'at the work'. An advertisement in 1881 offered 'free house and coal'.[566] Ardlussa Distillery had a house for both manager and mashman; in Census 1901, James Murdoch (q.v.) was in the former and his son George in the latter. A distillery's resident mashman also acted as caretaker, a role which emerges in evidence given at criminal trials for theft of whisky.

Archibald Sillars, mashman at Rieclachan, testified in 1878 that on a Saturday at 11 p.m. he finished his shift by checking every part of the distillery and then locking up, and that even on the day after, a Sunday, he 'went to the work to see if everything was all right'.[567] In a report of the trial of John Stalker, charged with attempting to break into an Albyn bonded warehouse in 1927, one of the witnesses, John McPhee, was described as 'mashman, Albyn Distillery', though the distillery was by then 'silent'. He said that he was in charge of the premises and attended to 'the removal of whisky, etc'. His house was in Albyn Road, beside the distillery, and every night, before retiring to bed, he would go to the back door 'to see if everything was all right'.[568]

Mason, William, fell 10 or 12 feet while hosing a wall in the tun-room of Benmore Distillery in July 1905. He landed on his head and was taken home, 'badly stunned' and bleeding.[569] On 7 December 1908, he was admitted to Campbeltown register of poor having been 'hurt at Distillery'. He was awarded 8s a week, to supplement the 7s 6d a week he was receiving from his employers, Bulloch Lade & Co. Mason, 50 years old, was born in Glasgow and was married to Jeanie Brown, daughter of a Campbeltown butcher. At the time of his accident, they had nine children, ranging in age from Maggie (27), herself married with three children, to Robert (5). Another of their sons, William (23), was a distillery workman, married with two children.[570] In 1927, by which time he had nine children, William Jr. was forced on to the unemployment register — successor to the register of poor — as a 'distillery workman unemployed', a fate shared by many other casualties of the whisky crash in Campbeltown in that decade.

Meadowburn Distillery was among the earliest of the Campbeltown distilleries. According to Colville (1923), it was built in 1824 by Kirkwood, Taylor & Co., which comprised Alexander Kirkwood, merchant, James Taylor, mason, William Armour, and Mathew Greenlees, who was later connected with Hazelburn. In correspondence relating to Meadowburn, there is a site plan of the distillery by Lewis D. Robertson, surveyor, dated 1825.[571] In 1837, John McNair, maltster, sold his quarter-share in the distillery for £450 to James Taylor, Mathew Greenlees and James Paterson.[572]

The partners in 1840 were James Taylor — see 'Taylor family' — James Paterson and Mathew and William Greenlees. Taylor's daughter Mary married James Paterson, 'Distiller', in 1840. In Census 1851 they were in Kirk Street with two children, and Paterson was described as a distiller employing eight men. He had a one-third share in the distillery, which was valued at £550 when his estate was sequestrated in 1852.[573] He died on 23 April 1862.

When the census of 1851 was taken on the night of 3 March, the enumerator found Hector MacEachran and Peter MacLellan at work in Meadowburn.

In 1853, it was reported that Meadowburn, 'which was long in the market', had been bought by 'new firm', Robert 'Colville' & Co.[574] — see 'Robert Colvill'. Duncan Colville, however, has it sold in 1855 for £1,200.[575]

In 1865, Campbeltown Town Council dealt with a complaint about a 'potale hole' at Meadowburn Distillery by referring it to 'the Inspector of Nuisances'.[576] Meadowburn Distillery stood beside Burnside Distillery at Witchburn — so many burns! — but Meadowburn and Witchburn were the same water-course. In 1866, 'Meadow Burn' — 'so long an offence and a nuisance to the olfactory nerves of those in the neighbourhood' — was to be 'arched over and hid from sight'.[577]

Meadowburn Distillery is missing from Barnard's book and must have closed before his visit to Campbeltown in 1885. The site is occupied by Campbeltown Creamery: see 'Burnside Distillery'.

Melville, Captain George, appeared in Census 1861, at Beach Hill, Low Askomil, as a 'Distiller employing 9 men', and was still a distiller 10 years later. As he is absent from any history of Campbeltown distilling, the entry was puzzling, until a reference in 1855 to Melville's being a partner in Campbeltown Distillery turned up.[578] There afterwards emerged a contract of co-partnery in the Campbeltown Distillery Company, dated 24 May 1853, between Melville and Duncan McMillan (q.v.), commission agent in Glasgow.[579]

Melville was born in Kinghorn, Fife, and his earlier career was as a ship-owner and captain. His wife was Jane McNeill, who was a natural child of Donald McNeill, laird of Canna, and was born on the island. Two of their sons died in Calcutta: Donald in 1859, aged 18, and James in 1883, aged 41, the latter while commanding a ship of the British India Steam Navigation Company, which was founded in 1847 in Calcutta by William MacKinnon (see 'MacKinnon's Distillery') and Robert MacKenzie, and employed a succession of Kintyre men as officers and engineers. Eldest daughter Jane McNeill married Campbeltown-born Duncan Macfadyen, whose business was in India, and died in 1929, aged 82; daughter Margaret Stewart married bank agent Alexander Duncan — see 'Stewart, Galbraith & Co. Ltd.' — and died in 1884, aged 34.

The seafaring Melville family was closely connected with the fleet of fast, armed Revenue Cutters stationed at Campbeltown to intercept smuggling traffic. George's father, Captain James Melville, who died in 1850, commanded Her Majesty's Revenue Cruiser *Wellington*, as his gravestone declares; and George's brother, also James, was captain of H.M.R.C. *Moira* in 1822, when he married Margaret, daughter of Captain Henry Beatson of the same service.

Melville was a member of Campbeltown Town Council and in 1865 was elected Junior Bailie, a post from which he hastily withdrew, prompting an anonymous contributor to the local newspaper to speculate mischievously that his reasons were to avoid the 'dirty work' of the police courts and the consequent 'imprecations and threats of vengeance'.[580] In the following year, he retired from public life and was replaced on the Council by another distiller, James Harvey (q.v.).[581]

Melville was predeceased by his wife in 1869, and died on 8 May 1874, aged 71. Remarkably, neither of the local newspapers published an obituary of him.

Mile-End Distillery. A sale of distillery utensils at Mile-End Distillery, Glasgow, advertised in the *Campbeltown Journal* in 1854, must have been aimed at Campbeltown distillers or would-be distillers. The distillery, at Provanmill, was presumably undergoing modernisation. The equipment, which was 'suitable for small distilleries', included a low-wine still, capacity 430 gallons; worm tubs; a worm engine of 12 horse power; copper pumps with brass boxes; malt rollers and framing; and pipes. The local contact was Robert Hunter (q.v.).[582]

Miller, Alexander Smart, the last manager of Loch-head Distillery, died on 10 September 1954 at the age of 91 at Seaside Cottage, Low Askomil. He was born in Kirkcaldy, Fife, and was a man of many and varied interests, yet there was no obituary in the local newspaper. One of those interests was photography, and two fine images of his accompanied Ann Glen's article, 'The Making of Whisky in Campbeltown', in the *Campbeltown Book* (2003): Lochhead warehouse in Lochend Street and cask-filling at Lochhead Distillery in 1897.

His parents were Alexander Miller, grocer in Campbeltown, and Margaret Smart, who married in Dysart, Fife, in 1857. In Census 1891, he was a 'Malt Distillery Manager' living at Lochend with his widowed mother, who was born in Dysart. Later that year, on 5 August, he was married at Darlochan farm, in the Laggan of Kintyre. His wife Jessie Mackinlay's father was described as 'the late Archibald Mackinlay, Cincinnati',[583] and Jessie herself was born in the U.S.

Miller was evidently of a disputatious nature. In 1913, he was feuding with a neighbour on Low Askomil, Dugald Robertson, a fisherman and boat-owner. Miller objected to Robertson's net-drying poles' being in front of Seaside Cottage and to the disturbance he and his crews made 'at all times of the night when they return from the fishing'.[584]

In 1929, following Duncan MacCallum's gift of the site of Kinloch Distillery to the town, Miller wrote to the local newspaper criticising the destruction of a building which would have been 'a valuable asset to any company who may yet desire to start an industry in Campbeltown'. Several of the distilleries already demolished had been 'twice bought and sold at a good profit to the owners', and he knew that two of them would still be working 'but for the astuteness of these individuals'. He appears to have had personal designs on Kinloch, for he claimed that in November 1928 he had been 'given an option of purchase in the Kinloch to run for six months'; but, on seeking confirmation, he was told that 'it had been offered to the town'.[585]

Fifteen years later, in 1944, the destruction of distilleries continued to vex him: 'The ruthless and shortsighted policy of demolishing the distilleries has debarred seekers from obtaining premises for industry ... Some years ago, a councillor said that if all the distilleries in the town were wiped out it would make no difference to Campbeltown. I did not agree with him.'[586]

Mrs Jeanette Brodie, the present owner of Seaside Cottage, found, in the attic of the house, labels from a parcel which had been posted in 1943 from the U.S.A. to Madge Miller, Alexander's daughter. At that time, of course, wartime rationing was in force, and the Millers would doubtless have been grateful to receive 6 lbs. sugar, 2 lbs. coffee, 1 lb. bacon and '2 plugs gelatine', estimated value $3 20c. The sender was Virginia Drysdale, Lynnfield, Massachusetts.[587]

Miller, David Smith, born in Kirkcaldy in 1858, was a brother of Alexander, above. He was manager of Lochindaal Distillery, Islay, when he died in the Western Infirmary, Glasgow, on 20 August 1896, aged 38, but was a distillery clerk when he married Jessie Macintyre in 1883 at Kilchenzie, the home of her parents, Dugald Macintyre and Janet McKinlay. The Macintyre family descended from *Ailean nan Sionnach*, 'Allan of the Foxes', who was Allan Macintyre (1745-1840), Gaelic bard and fox-hunter. Jessie's brother, Dugald Macintyre (1870-1957), was, like his father, a gamekeeper, but retired at the age of 55 and turned himself into a writer of popular sporting and natural history books.[588] Jessie Macintyre Miller lived until 1937. Three of her sons, all officers, survived active service in the First World War, and two of them — Captain David (Argyll & Sutherland Highlanders) and Lieutenant Alexander (Royal Scots) — were awarded the Military Cross for conspicuous gallantry.[589]

Miller, Jessie, was one of the three founding partners of Glenside Distillery in 1835. As a female investor in a male-dominated industry, she is of undoubted significance in the history of Campbeltown distilling, but she is also one of the most mysterious figures in that history. I found no trace of her in the 1841 census of Campbeltown, and when she married John Stewart, Excise officer, in 1844, her father's first name was missing from the register. She gave birth to a son, James MacNair Stewart, on 2 November 1845, and to a second son, Archibald Stewart, on 6 January 1847, six months before she died. In Census 1851, the motherless boys were living on Askomil Walk with Isabella MacNair, their grand-aunt (see 'Joseph Hancock'). Their father's whereabouts had been unknown until, in January 1851, he was declared to be in Lochgilphead. Jessie was said to have 'retired' from the business on 10 October 1836,[590] so her involvement with Glenside was very brief. She alone is commemorated on the gravestone erected in Kilkerran by John 'Stuart'.

Milloy, Archibald. His first employer was Charles McEachran (q.v.), whom he succeeded as secretary and manager of the Campbeltown Distillers' Association in 1877 on a weekly wage of £2.[591] When he retired in 1905 through ill health, he was said to have discharged his duties with 'the greatest acceptance, efficiency and satisfaction to all concerned'. He was 'a gentleman who is very highly respected and esteemed in the community ... his business relations with all [with] whom he came in contact were always of the most pleasant and harmonious order'.[592] The praise, one senses, given his length of employment, was probably merited. His retirement, which brought with it a pension, was cut short three months later: he died on 13 March 1906, at the age of 63, and his wife, Janet Owler, died in 1909.

He was succeeded as manager of the Distillers' Association by his son Archibald, who since 1889 had been employed in the County Assessor's Office, where he had received 'a good training' for his new post. In May 1917, he left the

Association to become manager of Saltoun (Glenkinchie) Distillery in East Lothian.[593] In that same year — the fourth of the Great War — his brother Stewart, a Second Lieutenant in the Northumberland Fusiliers (Tyneside Scottish), was awarded the Military Cross.[594] The family gravestone in Kilkerran records his death in 1943 at Chipanga, Southern Rhodesia (now Zimbabwe).

The surname Milloy in Kintyre replaced *MacGille Moluaig*, 'Son of the Servant of [Saint] Moluag'.[595]

Mitchell, Alexander, was the younger son of John (q.v.) and a brother of Archibald #3. He managed J. &. A. Mitchell & Co. with his father and ultimately became its managing director. In 1873, when about 20 years old, he appeared as a witness at the trial of two men accused of breaking into No. 3 duty-free warehouse at Springbank.[596] A few years after his father's death in 1892, Alexander moved to Glasgow and ran the business from there, 'only making very occasional visits to his native place'. He was described as 'a genial and kindly gentleman' and 'an active and alert business man'. He died at his home, 1 Loudon Terrace, Glasgow, on 9 December 1912, aged 59, leaving a wife and no children.[597] He was buried in Kilkerran with his parents, but his wife's name is missing from the stone.

Mitchell, Archibald #1, maltster in Campbeltown, was born in 1766 and died in 1835. His father, also Archibald, was a farmer in Craigs and died in 1818, aged 84; his mother, Mary Ferguson, died in 1787, aged 45. His wife Isabella, whom he married in 1798, and who died in 1849, aged 75, was also a Ferguson and was his cousin through her mother Mary Mitchell, who married Hugh Ferguson, maltster, in 1763.

In 1818, Archibald was involved, with three other maltsters, in a legal action, for which see 'Maltsters'. *Pigot's Directory* of 1825 (p 209) records him as a maltster in Longrow. Wright (1963) claimed that Springbank

Distillery was built on the site of an illicit still operated by Archibald, who is remembered as the father of the four Mitchell distillers, Archibald, Hugh, John and William.

There was another, contemporaneous, Archibald Mitchell, maltster, whose wife was Agnes Greenlees. When the birth of their son James was registered in December 1804, 'Campbeltown' was scored out and replaced with 'Dalintober'. The same parish register contains at least two more Mitchell maltsters in the opening decade of the 19th century: David, wife Janet McMillan, and Hugh, wife Janet McNair.

Lowland Plantation Mitchells were involved in malting in Campbeltown since the late 17th century, or soon after the family settled in South Kintyre. Thomas Mitchell was a 'maltman' in town in 1679; in 1725, John Mitchell, maltster, eldest son of the late James, maltster, went to court claiming he was owed money from the estate of Jean Moor or Maxwell. The 'bond of cautionary' (or security) was signed by Archibald Wylie, maltster in Campbeltown.[598]

By the 18th century, there were Gaelic-speaking Mitchell families in North Kintyre, but whether these were Lowland Mitchells 'gone native' or natives whose surname had mutated from a Gaelic original remains unclear.

Mitchell, Archibald #2. At about 8.30 in the evening of 2 March 1863, at home in Longrow, Archibald Mitchell, distiller, 'fell off a chair on which he had been sitting and immediately expired'.[599] His death certificate gave the cause of death as sudden apoplexy. He was aged 59, unmarried, and a son of Archibald #1. In Census 1851, he was living next door to his brother, John, with an elderly house servant, Jane Giffen. A founding partner of Rieclachan Distillery, he was one of the four Mitchell brothers who were distillers. His sister Isabella, who died in 1892, aged 77, is buried with him in Kilkerran She married James Campbell, baker, in 1836, but Campbell deserted her c 1858, took a job as a ship's steward on a steamer running between Glasgow and Liverpool, and by 1865 was in New Zealand 'or elsewhere furth of Scotland'.[600]

Mitchell, Archibald #3. Before setting off for town from the Laggan farm of Clochkeil on the morning of 5 July 1903, the tenant, Archibald Mitchell, climbed on to a stack in the hay shed to fix the tarpaulin covering and fell to the ground. There was no one about when the accident happened and he lay unnoticed throughout the day. He died 11 days later, aged 58, paralysed by a spinal injury. His death was registered by his son John, who had recently taken the tenancy of Killinochonoch farm, Kilmartin, and would marry a Kintyre farmer's daughter, Maggie Mitchell Young, in 1906. Archibald's wife was Jeanie Wylie Hunter, and he was a son of John Mitchell (q.v.), but he preferred farming to distilling, and at the age of 21 took the tenancy of Lagloskin farm on Largie Estate. Nonetheless, his obituarist stated, after his father's death he 'became local director of Springbank Distillery',[601] though the business was effectively run from Glasgow by his brother Alexander (q.v.).

Mitchell, Helen Greenlees, B.Sc., J.P., was, in 1934, the last manager of her father Hugh's distillery, Rieclachan, and 'probably the only woman in Scotland to hold such a position'. She graduated in chemistry from the University of Glasgow in 1921, and it is tempting to speculate whether she applied her scientific education to whisky production at Rieclachan. When she stood for Campbeltown Town Council in 1946 for the Citizens' Association, she was secretary of Springbank Distillery, in which her grandfather, William Mitchell, was an original partner. Both he and Hugh, his son, were Town Councillors, and Hugh served 12 years as Provost. With 1,291 votes, Helen topped the poll in the election and became only the second woman to be elected. In her election address, she had stated that 'women should take their share in civic responsibility'. In July 1954, as Bailie Mitchell, she was the first woman to sit 'on the bench' in a burgh court; she despatched one drunk and disorderly and two breach of the peace cases with a £1 fine each. She resigned from the Council in 1959, explaining that she was unable to 'devote enough time' to her civic duties.⁶⁰² 'Ellie' Mitchell, Springbank House, Low Askomil, died in the Cottage Hospital, Campbeltown, on 10 July 1986, aged 88. The local newspaper, curiously, carried no obituary.

Mitchell, Hugh #1, a son of Archibald #1, died on 22 July 1835, aged 34. Owing to his early death, he is the least documented of the four Mitchell brothers, but he was a partner in Rieclachan Distillery with Archibald #2. Much more is known about Agnes Stewart, who married him in 1830 and inherited his share in the distillery five years later. In Census 1851, she was living alone in Longrow and described herself as 'Distiller'; in October 1859 she announced that she was 'now in America' and had 'ceased to be a partner' in Wylie, Mitchell & Co., Rieclachan; ⁶⁰³ but by Census 1861 she was back in Longrow, a 'Distiller's Widow' and 'Fund Holder'. She would die in Longrow on 22 November 1889, aged 82. She belonged to a local Gaelic family — her parents were Dugald Stewart, farmer at Tonrioch, and Isabella McMillan — and her sisters Isabella and Jane also married into Lowland families (see 'Peter Gilkison' and 'Archibald Andrew'). Her death was notified by Charles Martin, joiner in High Street, who undertook her funeral. A stone was raised to Hugh and Agnes in the old section of Kilkerran cemetery by their son, Archibald, who died in Glasgow in 1911, aged 79, and is commemorated on the same monument.

Mitchell, Hugh #2, who died at Seafield on 10 February 1935, was 82 years old and had seen the distilling industry expand, peak in the 1890s, decline, and almost perish in the 1920s. A son of William #1 and Helen Greenlees, he was schooled locally and in Edinburgh and received his business training in the office of James Watson & Co., iron merchants, Glasgow, whose employment he left to run Glengyle and Rieclachan distilleries with his father, who died in 1887, and brother William, whose death at the age of 42, in 1899, left him in sole charge. Glengyle was sold in 1919 to West Highland Malt Distilleries Ltd. and closed in 1925, to Mitchell's great regret; but he kept Rieclachan going until the year before his death — 'principally in the interests of employment in the town he loved so well' — under the management of his daughter, Helen.

Hugh Mitchell's public commitments were many and varied. He was elected to the Town Council in 1885 'by the largest number of votes ever polled by any candidate in Campbeltown', and after six years as Dean of Guild was elected Provost in 1896. (At the end of that year, he was profiled in the *Dundee Weekly News*, and, in the following year, was the subject in the 'Men You Know' feature in *The Bailie*, a weekly Glasgow magazine.) He was a Justice of the Peace; an Honorary Sheriff-substitute for Argyll; chairman of the Parish Council; chairman of the Campbeltown & Glasgow Steamboat Co.; chairman of the Campbeltown Distillers' Association; Captain in the Argyll & Bute Artillery Volunteers; trustee of Longrow Church; active in the Campbeltown and District Trustees Savings Bank and Royal National Lifeboat Association; associated with Machrihanish and Dunaverty golf clubs and the Horticultural Society, which was defunct by the time of his death. When the bowling green at Stronvaar was opened on 8 June 1906, he was the club's president, and his wife 'threw the first jack'.[604]

His obituarist, who was doubtless Alick J. MacLeod, owner and editor of the *Campbeltown Courier*, remarked, in an unusually personal testimony, that in his long journalistic career he had never met anyone keener to 'sacrifice in the interests of Campbeltown's prosperity' or readier to 'defend its honour'. Nothing, he added, grieved Mitchell more than 'the depression which has touched his native place so sorely'.

He lost his only son, Willie, in the First World War — Second-Lieutenant Mitchell, R.A.F., was shot down and died of pneumonia in 1918 at the age of 19, as a prisoner-of-war in Leuze, Belgium — and was survived by his wife and two daughters, Helen (q.v.) and Marjory, M.B., Ch.B., who married a Shettleston dentist, Alexander Lucas, in 1923. His funeral was private, 'in accordance with his own wishes'.[605]

On 8 November 1946, in Campbeltown Council Chamber, 50 years to the day that Hugh Mitchell was invested with his chain of office as Provost, his widow, Barbara Jane, whom he married in 1895, was made an Honorary Burgess, until then only the sixth person, and the only woman, to receive the freedom of the burgh, which recognised her 'unselfish labours to the community'. The ceremony, at her own request, was private.[606] She was a daughter of Lachlan Clark, Tangy, a prominent farmer of Gaelic stock, and Marjory McFarlane, and died in 1952.

Mitchell, John, when he died on 11 May 1892 at Lochend, was described as 'the last of a large family, the members of which were well known, and occupied positions of influence in Kintyre'.[607] A son of Archibald #1, he was associated for the greater part of his life with Springbank Distillery, to which in 1851 he added Toberanrigh, but he also farmed extensively.

His involvement in farming began in earnest in 1844, when he took the lease of Low Balliemenach farm — three miles north of Campbeltown — to which, in 1861, he and his brother William added the adjacent farms of High Smerby and High Balliemenach, and, in 1863, High Crossibeg, all rented from Argyll Estates until 1874, when the leases were taken by Alexander Campbell.[608] John also rented the farms of Arnicle, Garvalt, Blarie and Ronadale, further north, and parts of other farms for grazing purposes. In Census 1861, he described himself not only as a distiller employing 10 men, but as a farmer of 17,660 acres! In October 1864, the Mitchell brothers shipped from Campbeltown 40 head of cattle in the *Celt* and 'a large cargo of sheep' in the *Albion*, and in the following October sent more than 900 sheep away on the *Druid*, all bound for the famous Falkirk Tryst. In May 1874, the sale of the brothers' Balliemenach horses was reported to be the 'most successful … ever known in Kintyre', and one filly, 'rising three years', fetched £111.[609] These reports of the brothers' livestock dealings could be multiplied *ad nauseum*.

Mitchell built Lochend House shortly before 1870, when a visiting journalist described his 'very substantial and handsome range of houses', which had replaced the 'humble erections which not so long ago skirted the head of the bay'.[610]

Mitchell's estate was valued at almost £40,000 and confirmation was granted on 27 July 1892 to his widow Mary, a daughter of Alexander Wylie (q.v.); his sons Archibald and Alexander; his sons-in-law, Robert Dickie, farmer, Killeonan, Kintyre, and John Bennett Wright, 18 Royal Terrace, Glasgow; and his daughters, Agnes, Annie, Helen and Janet.

At Lochend House in 1874, daughter Jane married William Watson, merchant in Glasgow. In 1881, at Lochend House, she died, aged 34,[611] and is commemorated on a gravestone in Kilkerran with son John, who died in infancy. In the year after Mitchell's death, daughter Helen married a wine merchant, Timothy Warren,[612] who traded as Timothy Warren Jun. & Co. at 39 Scotia Street, Glasgow.

When Mitchell's widow, Mary, died in 1913 at the age of 95, she was the second-oldest person in Campbeltown Burgh and had been cared for by two of her six surviving daughters.[613]

Mitchell, Robert, is the only one in this name group who was not a member of the distilling family … unless, of course, in remoter history. He was a carter at Lochhead Distillery and in March 1907 was presented with '£15 odds' by 'friends and well-wishers' before he sailed on the Anchor liner *Columbia* for Boston, Massachusetts. The presentation was made by Alexander McMillan (q.v.)

and 'a few words of good fellowship' were added by Morris McSporran (q.v.). In December 1901, while driving his horse and cart up the Old Quay with a load of barley, the horse took fright at a steam-roller and bolted. Robert fell off the cart, which ran over him, and he suffered 'severe bruising' to one of his shoulders.[614] In Census 1891, he was in Lady Mary Row, aged 25, with his parents Malcolm Mitchell and 'Mirron' (Marion) Barr and three siblings.

Mitchell, William #1, was 68 years old when he died at Drumore House on 24 August 1887, after a protracted illness. He was a son of Archibald #1, and, according to his obituarist, he started out in the distilling business at the age of 18. He and his brother John (q.v.) bought Springbank Distillery in 1837, but in 1872 they parted and in the following year William built Glengyle Distillery, to which he added Rieclachan in 1881. He was also involved in farming with John, but that partnership dissolved when they 'quarrelled violently ... about sheep', an estrangement which also ended their partnership in Springbank (q.v.). In 1875, he bought the mansion of Drumore, Campbeltown, with its four acres of ground and 'beautiful little glen'.[615]

He was a Town Councillor for 12 years; was a Liberal, 'but never intolerant or extreme in his political views'; and a member of the United Presbyterian Church. Above all, however, his obituarist stressed, his 'chief characteristic was that of an eminently practical business man, endowed with more than the ordinary share of good sense and acumen'.[616]

He left an estate valued at £15,803 19s 10d. His executors were Hugh #2, son; Helen, widow; William #2, son; James Russell, bank agent, Airdrie (son-in-law: he married Jane Mitchell in 1869); and John McKersie (q.v., son-in-law). His widow Helen, a daughter of Hugh Greenlees (q.v.) and Jean Colville, died aged 79 in 1901.

Mitchell, William #2, was 42 years old when, on 22 December 1899, he was discovered dead on his bedroom floor in Drumore House by a nephew. He had been seriously ill with pleurisy in 1892 and suffered recurrent bouts of the illness. He was a son of William #1 and was connected with Glengyle Distillery from its opening in 1873. Following his father's death in 1887, he was a partner, with his brother Hugh #2, in both Glengyle and Rieclachan. His favourite pastimes were fishing, shooting — he was for several years tenant of Ardnacross shootings — and bowling at the Argyll Club. He 'possessed a powerful bass voice' and was a member of the Campbeltown Choral Union and Musical Association and of Longrow Church choir. Like his father, he was interested in farming and reared a 'very valuable' sheep stock at Drumore.[617]

Montgomery, Andrew, built West Highland Distillery (q.v.) in 1830 with Archibald Andrew (q.v.). He was born in Southend in 1805, a son of Robert Montgomery, farmer in Christlach. In 1839 he married Jean Anderson, a daughter of William Anderson, shipmaster in Campbeltown, and Agnes Mitchell. Andrew and Ann had four children, the last born in 1849. In the 1851 Census of Campbeltown, he was in Longrow and gave his occupation as 'Distiller and Farmer'. In 1847, he and Archibald Andrew had taken over the lease of West Laggan farm, in Glenlussa, when David Anderson gave it up.[618] In 1857, after Jane's death, he married Ann Templeton. They emigrated c 1867 and in the 1870 U.S. Census he appears as a farmer in Owen, Winnebago, Illinois, with Ann (aged 50) and son James (21), the last-born of the children of his earlier marriage.

When he died in 1892, aged 86, his local newspaper, the *Rockford Register-Gazette*, recorded that he had farmed at Owen for 29 years and spent his final 10 years in retirement at Rockford. He was survived by his wife, son James, 'of Burritt', and daughter, Mrs James Langwell, Owen. 'At no place in the city,' his obituarist remarked, 'will the honest face of the deceased old man be missed more than in the *Register-Gazette* office. Ever since his removal to

Rockford, he has been a constant reader ... and twice each week he wended his way down the stairs to the office to get his copy, preferring the walk for exercise than to have it delivered to his door ... He always insisted that every reader should pay his subscription a year ahead, and thus enable the publishers to give them a better paper.'

That published tribute made its way to Campbeltown from the U.S. and 17 days later was reproduced in the *Argyllshire Herald*, which added only that Andrew was 'a native of Campbeltown' — which he wasn't — and that he was an 'uncle of the late John Montgomery, grocer, Main Street'.[619]

His brother James had emigrated as a farmer to the Argyll Settlement in Illinois in 1842. He, too, died in Rockford, in 1871, and his obituarist remarked that he had brought with him 'that firm, strict, zealous belief of the Scotch Presbyterian faith'.[620]

The name 'Montgomery' belonged predominantly to Southend Parish and represents both 17th century Lowland Plantation stock and native stock, 'Montgomery' being the final form of a Gaelic *Mac-* surname with debatable origins. The family of Canadian novelist Lucy Maud Montgomery (1874-1942), whose *Anne of Green Gables* was published in 1908, has been traced to Hugh Montgomery and Mary McShannon, Southend, who sailed in 1771 in the *Edinburgh* from Campbeltown to Prince Edward Island.[621]

Mossfield Distillery was built in either 1834 (Glen, p 156) or 1835 (Colville 1923). Colville recorded only one reference to it: 'William Hunter, joint tenant of Mossfield Distillery in Longrow Street, being part of the premises held in lease by the heirs of Matthew Fleming.' Fleming would have been the maltster recorded in Longrow in *Pigot* of 1823, and Hunter (q.v.) was a watch-maker and an original partner in Lochside Distillery.

The other partner in 'Harvey & Hunter, Mossfield distillery' in 1837[622] may have been William Harvey, who, with two others, built the distillery — name unknown — in High Street in 1828; or Mathew Hervey, who was a partner in Mountain Dew Distillery (q.v.); or he may have been John Harvey (q.v.).

Mossfield was sold by public auction for £1,950 on 5 October 1838 to John Colvill, who was bidding on behalf of himself, Alex Greenlees, Hugh Greenlees and James Ryburn[623] — the partners in Burnside Distillery — but there is no evidence that they revived distilling operations.

Mossfield was situated in the Kirk Close, Longrow, so named because the 'close', or entry, led to Longrow Church. The close was created in 1767, the year the church was built, by the demolition of buildings belonging to Edward Orr, merchant; in 1952, the buildings through which the close passed were, in turn, demolished to create a wider entrance to the church,[624] presumably for the convenience of motor vehicles.

Colville (1923) remarks rather obscurely that 'it was from this distillery that the Longrow Church was preached vacant by the Rev. Dr Harvey when the Rev. James Smith was deposed in 1835'. The dispute, simply put, arose from an attempt by the Rev Smith to take the congregation and all the church property back into the Established Church; but, following legal action, the congregation regained possession of the church and reasserted its 'Relief' — or secessionist — status. On the first Sunday of the congregation's exclusion, a 'cold, snowy day', Harvey preached from the door of a grain loft in Mossfield Distillery. The women and children were gathered in the loft and the men were crowded outside, in the Kirk Close.[625]

The distillery's name suggests that it could have been built in a boggy field, which is validated by a newspaper report in 1870 describing the workmen who were digging the foundations of the new Longrow Church coming on a 'bank of moss' (i.e. peat) and casting blocks of it to dry for fuel.[626]

Mountain Dew Distillery. Colville (1923) had no record of this distillery, but Glen (p 156) suggested correctly that it could have been built as Thistle Distillery in 1834. An earlier date may, however, be proposed, unless the firm went out of business in a matter of months, for on 25 June of that same year William Hervey and Malcolm McMillan, distillers, are recorded as facing bankruptcy and assigning their lease of 'Thistle Distillery' to trustees, who were John Grant, distiller, Peter Stewart, distiller, and William Watson, merchant. The same document identifies as a third partner in Hervey & McMillan one 'Mathew Hervey Feuar in Campbeltown and Keeper of the Mull Lighthouse'.[627] This Mathew was a son of William Hervey (or 'Harvey' or 'Harvie') and Agnes Orr, whose son William, born in 1769, is likely to have been the distiller above. William Sr., who died in 1828, aged 80, was the first light-keeper at the Mull of Kintyre, from its erection in 1788 until Mathew succeeded him c 1803. Mathew died in 1863, aged 91, and his wife, Agnes Giffen, in 1866, aged 79. Harvey, Orr and Giffen are all 17th century Lowland Plantation names.

In December 1834, six months after the dissolution of Hervey & McMillan, the new owners were Peter Watson & Co., and the distillery had become 'Mountain Dew',[628] which *Pigot* of 1837 confirms — see 'Peter Watson'. According to Stirk, p 117, the distillery was built next to Springside in Burnside Street. There is no known record of when it closed. 'Mountain dew', like 'moonshine', was a colloquial name for whisky.

Muir, Hugh, died at the age of 64 on 2 May 1928 at 'Glengyle House',[629] the mashman's residence attached to Glengyle Distillery, which had closed three years previously. He appears — handsome and full-bearded — in a photograph of cask-gauging outside duty-free warehouse No. 1 at Glengyle, c 1915, published in *The Campbeltown Book* (p 146). His parents were Arthur Muir, carter, and Mary Stewart. His Gaelic-speaking wife, Ellen, whom he married in 1883, and who died in 1936, was a daughter of Malcolm Smith, farm worker, and Ellen Shearer. Between 1881 and 1905, Hugh and Ellen had 12 children, most of whom were long-lived, and Annie most of all: she was aged 102 when she died in 2005 at Auchinlee Eventide Home in Campbeltown, outliving her husband, Hugh Smith, by 47 years. Four of the five Muir sons served in the First World War, and all but John, the youngest, survived. He was mobilised with the Argyll Mountain Battery at the outbreak of the war, but was later transferred to the Durham Light Infantry, with which regiment he was killed, aged 19, on 14 April 1917, at Arras. His family had to wait until February 1918 before 'posted missing' became 'killed'.[630]

Murdoch, James. On 12 March 1894, friends and family gathered in the house of James Murdoch, manager of Ardlussa Distillery, to celebrate his 25th wedding anniversary. He and his wife were presented with a marble clock, a set of studs and a gold brooch, by 'Captain Reid', the oldest representative of the owners, James Ferguson & Sons. Murdoch had been manager there for 15 years[631] and was still there when a journalist called at the distillery in 1905.[632] Both he and his wife, Jessie Menzies, were born in Morayshire, and married there, at Inchberry, on 12 March 1869. When their golden wedding anniversary came around in 1919, they were back at Inchberry,[633] in retirement.

Murdoch, John. If Neil Munro Kelly (q.v.) was the best-known native Exciseman, John Murdoch was unquestionably the most distinguished of all those who served in Kintyre. He was born in 1818 at Ardclach, Nairn, in North East Scotland, but brought up on Islay. After his retirement from the Inland Revenue, he founded the *Highlander* newspaper (1873-81) to promote the crofters' cause during the Land Agitation movement, in which he was a 'tireless anti-landlord campaigner of major political significance'.[634]

His service with the Inland Revenue in Kintyre may have been of relatively brief duration, but the Highland historian, James Hunter, says that Murdoch covered his time in Kintyre in his manuscript autobiography, on which Hunter drew heavily for his *For the People's Cause: The Writings of James Murdoch* (1986).[635]

In the 1851 Census of Campbeltown, Murdoch was living on Low Askomil with his 59-year-old mother, Mary, and 15-year-old brother, David, who was attending school and whose birthplace was recorded as Islay.

On 6 March 1851, three weeks and three days before the day of the census, 'Mr Murdoch' addressed the fortnightly meeting of the Campbeltown Temperance Society on the subject of 'Temperance and Money', a report of which, reproduced from the *Campbeltown Journal*, appears as Appendix 5. In the year after, the *Journal* published the following accounts of Murdoch's smuggler-hunting activities in the Largieside:

'A few days ago, we understand that Mr Murdoch, the officer of Inland Revenue, who surveys part of the Largy-side of Kintyre, accompanied by a Cuttersman, found a small quantity of malt on the Kiln attached to the corn mill of Tangy. The quantity found was enough to indicate that the kiln had been used for the illegal purpose of drying illicit malt, and that more of that commodity must be in existence not far away.

'On Friday last, the same party succeeded in discovering the bothy in which they suppose the malt to have been made, choke full of good grain, in the process, and some ready ground for mashing. This was at least six miles farther off than the mill. About a mile and a half away into a remote moor, they came upon a party of men busily employed preparing a house, partly built and partly sunk in the moss, for the purpose of bringing to perfection the pure "peat reek" whiskey ... begun in the establishment previously discovered. These unexpected visitors, of course, put their hand to the work and put a speedy termination to the hopeful labours of the lawless mountaineers.

'On Tuesday the 2d inst., again, the same party destroyed another distillery in a moor somewhere into the middle of the country between the head of Barr glen and the east coast of Kintyre. The owners thereof had just finished their distilling period and left the most of their utensils and a quantity of spirits in the bothy, no doubt concluding that no official would ever find out so perfect a hiding place. Again, destruction was made to mark their progress.'[636]

Murdoch returned to Kintyre as a celebrity in July 1885, at the invitation of the local branch of the Land Restoration League, and stayed for a week, lecturing on 'The Land for the People' in the Town Hall, Campbeltown, followed by outdoor meetings in Southend, Campbeltown again (Kinloch Green), Glenbarr and Tayinloan. His temperance convictions were as strong as ever, and he claimed that, from his own investigations, the amount of money spent on 'drink' between 1842 and 1849 was £11,000,000, 'which was sufficient to buy all the encumbered estates in the land'.[637]

Napier, James, who belonged to Glasgow, was one of the five original partners in Scotia Distillery in 1832. He captained the *Duke of Lancaster*, the first vessel acquired, in 1826, by the Campbeltown & Glasgow Steam Packet Joint-Stock Co. Ltd. (q.v.), and subsequently commanded the *Saint Kiaran* (built in 1836, in which year he became a shareholder in the company), the *Duke of Cornwall* (1842) and the *Celt* (1848), before retiring, through ill-health, in 1856. Napier's date of death has not been established. In 1866, when described as 'one of the most obliging and gentlemanly Captains that sailed on the Frith of Clyde', he was referred to as dead;[638] but a James Napier was reported as a guest at a dinner held after the trial trip of the Steam Packet's *Gael* in April 1867.[639]

Olsén, Gottfrid. Between 26 April and 2 May 1872, the Swedish whisky pioneer, Gottfrid Olsén of Gothenburg, studied whisky-making at Scotia Distillery. His trip to Scotland took him to Pulteney Distillery, Wick, and Millburn Distillery, Inverness, before he arrived in Campbeltown. Regrettably, the local newspaper, the *Argyllshire Herald*, failed to report his presence in town. The fragments of his long-forgotten story have been presented in the short film, researched and produced by Carl Lonndahl, 'Between Yeast and Stills: The Story of Sweden's First Whisky', which was released in 2018. Olsén's investigative trip to Scotland preceded by almost half-a-century that of Masataka Taketsuru (q.v.).[640]

Orr family. When Alfred Barnard visited Glenside Distillery in 1885, he paid his respects to the 'managing partner', J. Orr, and inspected his 'quaint little office over the gateway'. Barnard had probably met John MacIntosh Orr, a son of John Kerr Orr, who was a partner in Glenside Distillery Co. from about 1850 until his death in Glasgow on 4 October 1866,[641] just ten days after he took his brother Daniel into the business (see 'Glenside Distillery'). John K.'s wife, Robina Scott Jarvie, and eldest daughter, Jessie Jarvie, both died in July 1876 at Dalaruan, Campbeltown.[642] Daughter Margaret married John Colville Boyd in 1881. A son of the Rev Dr James Boyd, Longrow Church, and Jeanie Colville, daughter of John Colville Jr. (q.v.#1), he was a grain broker, shipping agent and Lloyd's agent in Campbeltown. He was elected to the Town Council in 1892 and made a Bailie five years later. He died in 1905, a year after Margaret.[643] Another Orr daughter, Robina Marion, married the splendidly named Dr Walker Overend in the Grand Hotel, Glasgow, in 1893.[644] Son Frank died at sea while on passage from Glasgow to New Zealand in 1884.[645]

John K. Orr's fourth son, Robert Louis, was appointed clerk at Glenside in 1877, on the recommendation of the trustees, his siblings, '... for he was unable to live on his salary of £40 a year in Glasgow, and with an equal amount he could manage in Campbeltown by staying in family with his sister, but also he might obtain an insight into the workings of the business'.[646] In Census 1891, he was a 'Distiller', aged 36, living on High Askomil with two unmarried sisters, Robina M. (above) and Mary J., both, like him, born in Glasgow. In Census 1901, he was alone in Tangy Place, High Street, and he died in 1908 in the Cottage Hospital, Campbeltown. He was among the membership of Machrihanish Golf Club photographed in 1884.[647] Thin-faced, black-bearded and bowler-hatted, he somewhat resembled the novelist D. H. Lawrence.

Three Orrs designated distillers were members of the Kintyre Club: John M., in Campbeltown when he joined in 1870; Robert L., in Campbeltown (1879); and James M., in Glasgow (1881). Orr was a Lowland Plantation name in South Kintyre, and the assumption that these distiller Orrs had local connections may not be unwarranted.

Paterson, Duncan, was found unconscious at the bottom of a trap stair in — according to a local newspaper — Burnside Distillery on 14 June 1888, and died the day after.[648] When his widow, Christina Darroch, was admitted to the poor roll the following month, the location of the accident was recorded — probably correctly — as Meadowburn, the neighbouring distillery. She and Duncan had six children, and she was awarded 6s a week for their support.[649] Duncan was born in 1829 on Clochkeil farm, a son of Alexander Paterson, 'labourer', and Flora McLarty. Christina, a daughter of Malcolm Darroch, carter, and Agnes or Ann Stewart, was born in 1843.

Paterson, James, distiller — see 'Meadowburn Distillery'.

Peat. The 'malt' in malt whisky is barley which has been steeped, spread to germinate, and then, as malt, dried in a kiln. That peat was the traditional fuel in the drying process is hardly surprising, since, historically, peat was the only fuel widely available in Ireland and Western Scotland. But peat did not just dry malt, it flavoured it, and the malt in turn infused the liquor with a smoky flavour. Kintyre was unusual in having coal-mining as an industry, but peat, by virtue of its flavouring smoke, remained the preferred malt-kiln fuel.

In 1835, a lease was granted by the Argyll Estate to Lieut Robert MacGregor — father-in-law of Hugh Boyle (q.v.) — Donald MacKay and Kenneth Matheson, granting them the right to extract peat on specified 'mosses' (peat bogs) for selling to distillers, maltsters and other inhabitants of Campbeltown.[650]

When Alfred Barnard visited Campbeltown in 1885, he found that, out of the 21 distilleries, only Scotia, Burnside, Longrow and Kintyre mixed a little anthracite with their peat. Except for one case, sources of peat are not specified. The one exception was Albyn Distillery, which brought its peat in 'large quantities from the Hebrides'. In August 1887, for example, Islay peat arrived in Campbeltown in the *Texa*, for Benmore, and in the *Ina McTavish* for Burnside.[651]

Quantities of peat would have been supplied by local cutters in the Laggan of Kintyre — the flat land between Campbeltown and Machrihanish — but most of the imported peat was brought in from County Donegal in Ireland. In the mid-1880s, the large quantity of imported Irish peat being offered at low prices — 12 to 13 shillings a ton, or around half the price of Kintyre peats — was causing 'suffering' to 'local traders'.[652] In a single day in November 1886, four schooners arrived with peat from Ireland, the largest importation to that date.[653] In December 1899, a Campbeltown smack, on passage to Lough Swilly in County Donegal for peat, was wrecked, a mishap which elicited from a writer in a Glasgow evening newspaper the quip that 'Campbeltown whisky derives something of its reeky flavour from Ireland, and is thus a kind of international spirit'. Kintyre peat, he added, had 'pretty well given out', and 'Irish turf' was now being 'regularly brought to the distilling town'.[654]

John MacKay, a Kintyre cutter and carter of peats, dismissed the Irish product using the same term as above, 'turf'. The peats he cut from Aros Moss were, when dried, big, black and heavy. He was born in 1898 at Darlochan in the Laggan, and, when he died, was the last of his kind. He and a workmate would spend from early May until June cutting peats, and a fortnight in the summer carting the dried peats to distilleries; Benmore, Glengyle and Lochhead were his main customers. In an average season, he would cut about 400 cartloads, or 200 tons. As a young man, he was paid 4s 6d for a cartload of peats, which rose during the First World War, or shortly afterwards, to 25s, but the carts used then were almost twice the size of the earlier ones. Of that sum, Argyll Estate — to which Aros Moss belonged — took 5s, and he received £1.

At about the same time, the farmer at Gortan, Peter Kelly, also cut peats for distilleries, but on a much smaller scale: 30 or 40 cartloads a year. He supplied Springbank regularly and Scotia occasionally, but the income from peat was immaterial to the economy of the farm. He sometimes took on an Irishman — typically, an unemployed drainer — to help with the work, but in some years, when farm work was heavy, his employee, who lived on the farm until the cutting was done, would 'do the lot'.[655]

In February 1913, an 'uncommon sight' was reported — the export of Kintyre peat. Owing to a decrease in demand in Campbeltown for locally-cut peats, two cargoes were shipped to Glenfyne Distillery (Appendix 8) in Ardrishaig.[656]

In 1922, Hazelburn was reported as having 'private supplies of water and peat'. The latter was cut from 'hundreds of acres of rugged moorland rented by the firm, and efficient transport is provided by a light railway and motor lorries'. The Machrihanish & Campbeltown Light

Railway ran through the Laggan, where the peat must have been cut ... but 'hundreds of acres' seems an excessive area of land in which to open a few peat banks! The kiln furnaces at Hazelburn were fuelled by both coke and peat.[657]

The fire-place in the malt-drying kiln of a distillery was known as the 'killogie', or 'kiln-logie', a Scots word which was extended in meaning locally to any confined domestic space, such as a cupboard or a small room underneath a flight of stairs. A 'killogie linnet' described someone loath to leave the warmth of a fireside, from linnets' habit of flying into kiln rooms for heat in winter.[658] The word appeared in a report of an outbreak of fire in the kiln of Benmore Distillery (q.v.) in 1879: 'It is said that there was no fire in the "kilogie" for a couple of days previous to the outbreak ...'[659]

Pibroch, launched for Scottish Malt Distillers Ltd. (q.v.) in December 1956, called at Campbeltown for the first time in mid-July 1957. She would become a familiar sight at Campbeltown Old Quay, but her main function was to carry coal and general cargo to Islay from Glasgow and bring back whisky. She was a 'coaster', one of the new generation of traders which replaced 'puffers', the small, flat-bottomed steam-driven cargo vessels employed along the west coast of Scotland and among the islands, and immortalised in Neil Munro's *Para Handy* tales. Built by Scott & Sons at Bowling on the Clyde, she was 83 feet long, diesel-engined and of improved design. There was 'even a shower-bath in the crew's quarters', which were deemed to be 'the last word in up-to-date coaster accommodation'. She was built to replace the puffer *Texa* — herself originally named *Pibroch* — which for more than 20 years was skippered by a Campbeltown man, George Thomson.[660] The *Pibroch* was scrapped in 2010.

Pot-ale (locally pronounced 'pottle'). Campbeltown distilleries generally discharged their pot-ale, or spent wash, into streams or piped it into Campbeltown Loch. On the question of whether the effluent was a pollutant, opinion was divided, but the distillers were adamant that it was not. In 1894, when the Town Council contacted distilleries on the issue, the responses ranged from moderate to indignant. Reid & Colvilles, Dalintober Distillery, felt 'aggrieved and annoyed' to be addressed as though they were 'criminals'. J. & A. Mitchell, Springbank, explained that 'According to arrangements made with Captain Stewart, all our potale is now discharged into his tank and therefrom pumped by him to his lands at Tomaig, etc'.[661] 'Captain Stewart' was Duncan, whose father, John Lorne Stewart of Coll, was, until his death in 1878, the Duke of Argyll's chamberlain in Kintyre and had the farms of Tomaig and Knockrioch.

Stewart Sr.'s fertilisation scheme, which was operational by August 1854, was ambitious and does appear to have produced higher crop yields. A 'reservoir' for pot-ale was made at the head of Longrow, near Rieclachan Distillery; an engine was acquired from the defunct Drumlemble tile factory; pumps were installed and pipes laid to a second, higher reservoir on Tomaig farm, whence further pipes carried the pot-ale to the fields.[662] In 1895, when an action for interdict was sought against Captain Stewart under Section 16D of the Public Health Act, 1867, the pot-ale settling tank was described as 80 feet long by 30 feet broad. His 'irrigation works' drew on pot-ale from five distilleries and the pumps were kept going for three days a week during whisky production. Stewart admitted that if the effluent was allowed to 'remain too long' in the tank, it would 'emit an unpleasant odour', but denied that the smell was injurious to health.[663] Two years later, in 1897, the 'unmitigated nuisance' of the pot-ale tank was brought to an end. The machinery and the very bricks and stones of the building were sold by public auction and a duty-free warehouse built on the site. The effluent was now 'blended with the town sewage' and piped, for the most part, into Campbeltown Loch below low-water mark.[664]

When Dugald McKendrick took the lease of a Tomaig smallholding in 1929, he found the land to be 'full of' metal pipes and hydrants, by which the pot-ale, pumped up from the town, had been spread over the fields. He got rid of the redundant pipes by digging them up and using them as straining-posts.[665] The pot-ale storage pit at Tomaig is still there, but has been used as a dump and is scarcely recognisable.

Pot-ale held in tanks may or may not have been innocuous, but the unregulated stuff was dangerous and even lethal. In January 1871, a little boy drowned in a pot-ale hole at Millknowe. He was identified only by his surname, 'Killin', which, however, links him to a Killen family of Irish origin in Campbeltown. The hole, which was 'uncovered at the time of the accident', belonged to a merchant named Henderson in Longrow, presumably Archibald Henderson, grocer, who was sued in 1876 for the death of a cockerel by 'the usage it received from his hands',[666] and who died himself in 1884. In May 1876, a child, David Muir, son of a cooper, Alexander Muir, was scalded by a discharge of hot pot-ale from a sewer in the Mussel Ebb at the head of Campbeltown Loch and died the day after.[667]

In 1866, the wife of William McMurchy, carter, had a leg broken in two places when a puncheon rolled off a cart at Burnside and fell on her. The puncheon was full of pot-ale, for which she had been waiting beside the cart. The following year, a lad named William McDonald was 'driving a potale cart from Lady Mary Row' when a cask suddenly burst and scalded the legs of the horse. McDonald 'escaped serious injury by jumping into the burn'.[668]

What was happening with the pot-ale? It contains protein and would have been fed to pigs, which many poor families in town fattened for sale; indeed, in 1919, in the aftermath of the war, Charles J. N. Fleming, in a letter to the local newspaper, advised that, 'in these days of short food supply and high prices', pot-ale, instead of being discharged into Campbeltown Loch, should once again be fed to pigs, more of which could be kept.[669] The late John MacFadyen Campbell, a Kintyre tradition-bearer, was told that free-ranging Dalintober pigs would drink from the 'Pottle Hole', a sandy basin in the Mussel Ebb, opposite Princes Street, in which the effluent welled up from the outfall of a stream.[670] Livestock on farms must also have been fed pot-ale, for in 1878 Robert Ralston, cooper in Saddell Street, offered farmers 'Potale and Water Barrels at very Moderate Prices'.[671]

The issue of effluent pollution from distilleries returned in July 1921, but by then the problem was on the way to being solved by the collapse of the industry. Dr T. Harvey Thomson, the burgh's medical officer of health, submitted, to a meeting of the Town Council, a lengthy report on the 'offensive smell' emanating from the foreshore at the Esplanade. As he pointed out, 'Campbeltown is so peculiarly identified with the distilling industry, that the ratios between domestic sewage and trade effluents are very abnormal ...' His predecessor, Dr William Gibson, had estimated the daily amount of pot-ale discharged into Campbeltown Loch from the 15 distilleries at work in 1920 as 100,000 gallons, but Dr Thomson revised that to 50,000 gallons, plus about 10,000 gallons of 'steep water', which was used in the malting process. Since pot-ale was reckoned to be at least '40 times as strong as ordinary sewage', and steep water '3 to 10 times as strong', Campbeltown, with a population of fewer than 7,000, had to dispose of sewage which 'in polluting properties would be normal in a town of about 50,000 inhabitants'. This, of course, applied only when the distilleries were at work, or for about six months in the year.[672] The final solution to the problem of sewage disposal lay 80 years in the future, with the construction of a processing plant on Baraskomil shore in 2001; and distilling effluent is now spread on farmland.

Pulteney Distillery. In 1888, a 220-ton 'screw steamer', the *Dunbeath Castle*, was launched at Campbeltown

Shipyard, on Trench Point, for James Henderson & Co., Pulteney Distillery. She was to be employed in 'the continental fish trade' — Wick, on the northern coast of Scotland, was a major herring port — and would return with barley from the Baltic ports.[673]

Pursell, Archibald. When Alfred Barnard visited Dalintober Distillery in 1885, the manager, Archibald Pursell, not only gave him a tour of the distillery, but explained 'the whole process of the manufacture of Campbeltown Whisky'. Pursell died in Princes Street, Dalintober, in 1893 at the age of 52, and his wife, Jean McEachran, two years later, aged 56. Four of their children, Robert, Janet, Barbara and Edward, died in infancy; daughter Mary died in 1885, aged 21, and, of those commemorated on the family gravestone, only Margaret, who died in 1942, aged 75, outlived her parents. Son Peter was injured in a fall at Dalintober Distillery in 1886 (Appendix 2). Archibald was a son of Peter Pursell, flesher, and Mary Ramsay. The name 'Pursell' in Kintyre is an Anglicisation of Gaelic *Mac an Sporain*, 'Son of the Purse'. For later notable members of this family refer to my *An Historical and Genealogical Tour of Kilkerran Graveyard*, pp. 52-53.

Ralston family — see 'Glenramskill' and 'Meadowburn' distilleries.

Reid, John, was a founding partner in William Reid Jr. & Co. with his father William (q.v.) and brother William, who built the distillery which was bankrupted before it acquired a name and bought at public auction in 1837 by John and William Mitchell, who named it 'Springbank' (q.v.). When he married a shoemaker's daughter, Isabella Thomson, on 15 August 1836, he was a 'malster'; when daughter Janet was born on 3 July 1837 — at the height of the financial crisis — he was a 'distiller'; and when his next child, Catharine, was baptised almost two years later, on 2 June 1839, he was again a 'malster'. He was born in 1814 on the Southend farm of Chiscan, also known as West Polliwilline, as was his father. Wright (1963) claimed that the Reids were 'in-laws of the Mitchells', but, if there was such a relationship, no evidence of it has emerged.

Reid, Peter, was 30 years old when, in 1832, he became a founding partner in Dalintober Distillery, with the role of agent for the sale of its whisky, at a commission of two pennies and a farthing in the pound.[674] His dealings with the firm were conducted from Glasgow, where, however, he had more lucrative prospects. In 1838 he was one of four Kintyre-born partners in the carpet-making business founded by James Templeton, the other two being Templeton's brothers, Archibald and Nathaniel. By 1881, the year of Reid's death, James Templeton & Co. employed more than 1,100 workers in its factories.

Reid was enrolled in the Kintyre Club in 1827, and in 1834, when elected president, he presented the Club with the Campbeltown 'Herdsman's Horn', which had been passed from one herd to another, in a long succession, and was blown to rouse the townsfolk from their beds to turn out their cows for driving to the common grazing at Whinny Hill. Reid had bought the horn from the town herd, 'Auld MacGregor' — whose right to sell it was debatable — and had it 'transformed and silver-mounted'. It became the Club's snuff 'mull', to be ceremoniously passed around at official dinners.[675] It was loaned to Campbeltown Museum by the Club, which is now defunct, and remains on display there. 'Auld MacGregor' was John, who was 'Town herd' when his daughter Susan married in 1812.

Speaking at a dinner in Campbeltown in 1853, Reid dismissed the cherished notion that setting up spinning and weaving mills in town would generate profit. Such industries, he argued, had to operate 'in the neighbourhood of great seats of population'. Campbeltown, in devoting itself 'chiefly to the spirit trade', had 'adopted the one which was best fitted for it ...'[676] As the century advanced, his commercial judgement in 1853 would be validated.

Reid is now best remembered in the history of piping. Not only was he a piper and respected judge at piping competitions, he was also a collector of *piobaireachd* — the classical music of the Highland bagpipe — and his manuscript of tunes is in the National Library of Scotland. Since his cultural background in Kintyre was Lowland, his interest in Gaelic music remains rather a mystery.

By his own account, Reid, at the age of 21, was one of three pipers who played for King George IV when he arrived in Scotland on 15 August 1822 for his flamboyant visit, which would usher into fashion all things Highland, real and imaginary. Reid and his companion-pipers played at the end of Leith pier when the king landed and continued playing during the procession to Holyrood Palace.[677]

Piping historian Bridget Mackenzie described Reid as 'a crofter's son from Southend', but the Southend connection was not as immediate as that. When his parents — Hugh Reid, cooper, and Janet Langwill — married in 1784, they were in Campbeltown, and Peter was born in the town on 8 December 1801. His great-grandson, Dr Stewart Carslaw, described the family as 'one-time of Kildavie, Southend,[678] which makes perfect sense: Reids were tenant-farmers there during the 18th and for most of the 19th century (see 'David MacDonald').

He died on 26 December 1881 at 33 Kersland Terrace, Hillhead, Glasgow. Although his death notice appeared in the two local newspapers, there was, curiously, no obituary. He left 'just' £894 15s, and his executrix was his widow, Margaret Stewart — she would die in 1884, aged 75 — two of whose sisters married the brothers James and Archibald Templeton, business partners of Reid's.[679]

Reid, William, maltster, was born at West Polliwilline farm, Southend, in 1788, and died there, of dropsy, in 1858. There were Reid tenants in Polliwilline, as also in nearby

Kildavie (above), for the entire 18th and most of the 19th century. William's father was also William, and his mother Janet was a Cordiner, another 17th century Lowland Plantation name. His death certificate described him as a 'pauper, formerly farmer', but his death notice in the local newspaper had him as 'late Malster, Campbeltown',[680] and on his gravestone in Kilkerran he is 'Malster'. His wife, Janet Clark, predeceased him in 1848. See 'Springbank Distillery' for his and his sons' disastrous venture into the distilling business.

Rieclachan Distillery was built in 1825 at the head of Longrow, but had a large malt-kiln and store at 'the foot of Corbett's Close' — at the opposite end of Longrow — which was advertised to let in 1873.[681] The original firm was Wylie, Mitchell & Co., being Archibald Mitchell, distiller; James Ferguson, cooper and maltster; Alexander Wylie, later of Toberanrigh Distillery; and John Harvey or Harvie.[682] In 1850, following Ferguson's death, his share was sold to Mitchell.

There were two James Fergusons, father and son, both identified as maltsters in Longrow in *Pigot* of 1837, but the partner in Rieclachan was the son. Mitchell was a son of Archibald #1 and Isabella Ferguson; Alexander Wylie's wife Isabella was also a Ferguson, as was John Harvey's wife Jean.

By 1869, James Harvey (q.v.), son of John, was managing partner in the distillery.[683] In 1881, after his death, Rieclachan was bought by Archibald Mitchell's son, William, of Glengyle Distillery. The last owner was William's son, Hugh Mitchell — 'managing partner' in 1885, Barnard noted — whose daughter Helen (q.v.) was the last manager, and, in 1934 — the distillery's last productive year — 'probably the only woman in Scotland to hold such a position'. The distillery, at the last, employed 11 men: four maltmen, four stillmen, a brewer, a cooper and a draffman.[684]

In 1878, at the trial of two men accused of stealing whisky from Rieclachan, one of the witnesses was an elderly man, Archibald Wilkinson, who was allowed to sleep in a loft in the distillery 'for charity'.[685]

When Barnard visited the distillery in 1885, he saw it as 'distinctly one of the old "Sma Still" works', but with additions made to it 'as the demand for Whisky increased'. He continued: 'The Establishment is approached by a short lane and entered by an old-fashioned pair of gates, which were evidently made to shut in the secrets of the Distillery from the outside world ... as there is no other possible entrance, without scaling the buildings ...' Seven years earlier, the Rieclachan mashman, Archibald Sillars, testified at the trial of Donald McPhail and George McNaughton (Appendix 3) that the entrance was from Longrow and that there was only one other door in the entire distillery, 'a small one, on the outside wall, used for throwing in peats into the peat-house'.[686]

By May 1936, the distillery was in the ownership of Messrs. Craig Brothers, West Coast Motors Service Ltd. It was converted into a car show-room, and a row of 'individual lock-up garages' was built at the back of the premises. Craig Brothers even made a road from Rieclachan to Glebe Street, for the 'convenience' of customers from Southend and Machrihanish.[687] Part of the premises had already been occupied as a store by Messrs. Macfarlan, Shearer & Co., grain, seed and oil merchants, and in 1936 another part was acquired on behalf of the Campbeltown & District Unemployed Workers' Movement, for conversion into basket-making, rug-making, carpentry and cobbling workshops.[688] In 1943, with the consent of Craig Brothers, the new Air Training Corps headquarters opened at Rieclachan. The last occupant was John Paterson, who had a furniture shop and show-room there, and also undertook funerals.

The site of the demolished distillery is now occupied by a Co-operative supermarket, which uses 'Rieclachan' as its business address. The origin of the name 'Rieclachan' is unknown, but 'rie' may represent Gaelic *ruigh*, 'slope', and *clachan* is translatable as 'a village with a church'.

Ross, George, an Inland Revenue officer, shared several traits with his fellow-Exciseman John Murdoch (q.v.): he was a kilt-wearing Gaelic speaker with roots in Northern Scotland and he espoused Socialism. Ross, however, was born in England while his father, Robert, who was a native of Ross-shire, was stationed there as an I.R. officer. Robert was transferred to Campbeltown when George was still a child and George was educated at Alexander Ross's Free Church Grammar School until about the age of 10, when his father was moved again. When George returned to Campeltown as an Excisemen, in about 1885, 'his boyhood's recollections of the place enabled him to settle down to the peculiar life of the town with almost the facility of a native'.

He served an apprenticeship in Glasgow as an engineer, which occupation he soon exchanged for the Inland Revenue. His earlier service as a 'gauger' was spent in Perthshire and Inverness-shire at a time when whisky smugglers were still active, and he had a fund of tales of his 'exciting adventures on the hills ... searching out the hiding places of users of the wee sma' stills'.

Campbeltown, it seems, was not quite ready for Ross's brand of Socialism. After his retirement in 1901, he was elected to both the Town Council and Parish Council, 'but finding no support for his peculiar views in either of the bodies mentioned, he had generally to be content with the advocacy of his opinions'.[689]

He died in Campbeltown in 1910, aged 71, and was buried in Kilkerran with his parents, Robert M. Ross and Margaret McKenzie, and several of his siblings.

Ross, John. Alfred Barnard, who interviewed Ross at Longrow Distillery the year before he died, noted that he was 'said to be the oldest living Distiller in Scotland'. Ross was undoubtedly the greatest character in the history of Campbeltown distilling, and Barnard testified to having been 'highly amused' by the old man's 'wit and racy anecdotes'. His obituarist, too, observed that 'he possessed a great fund of humour, and many a pleasant story was told, and many a good joke cracked around his hospitable table'.

That same anonymous obituarist described Ross as an 'example of those men, of whom in the past generation the town could boast not a few, who lived, died, and amassed a fortune in their native place'. Ross's father, Alexander, was a ship's captain and merchant in Campbeltown, whose first wife, Rachell Threepland, died in 1794, aged 36. His second wife, and John's mother, was Elizabeth Templeton, a branch of which family had distilling connections (see 'Drumore Distillery'). But Ross began his working life as an apprentice mason, and even tried his hand at monumental sculpture: to visitors and friends he would point out with pride the several tombstones in Kilkerran carved and lettered by his untutored hands.

His apprenticeship, however, lasted merely two years. The story goes that, by working overtime in the building trade, he was able to save his entire weekly basic wage of nine shillings, and that, when he had gathered enough money, he bought enough barley for 'one steeping, and thus commenced the trade of a malster'.

He was 23 years old when, in 1824, he entered into partnership with John Colville and John Beith Jr. The business was Longrow Distillery, which traded as Colville, Beith & Co., and Ross was managing partner. In 1840, Kintyre Distillery was acquired by the firm. The company name, on Colville's death, became Beith, Ross & Co., and ultimately and acrimoniously John Ross & Co.

He was intensely religious and immersed himself in the affairs of the United Presbyterian congregation. Indeed, he contributed £1,000 of the £1,100 cost of building the 150-feet-high bell-tower of Longrow Church, and was given the honour of opening the door of the new church on Sunday 14 July 1872.[690]

A recent historian, Murdo MacDonald, confessed to having difficulty knowing 'what to make of Ross': 'His reported speeches are full of evangelical Christian fervour, which also infuses his little book of poetry, *The Way of Truth*. Opinion of him in the town was not uniformly favourable. In the Sheriff Court Records there is a Petition for Interdict to prevent the publication of a letter ridiculing him in 1877. Again, in the Sheriff Court records, in 1883 we find Ross pursuing John Sommerville, farmer at Belloch, for £1,000 for slandering him. His complaint was that one day, as he stepped outside his Longrow Distillery, Sommerville had assailed him loudly with "You're a damned scoundrel, you are cheating the public", and similar comments.'[691]

In 1876, William McKersie & Co. sued Beith, Ross & Co. for £7, the price of a cylinder and casing, plus £1 interest. Ross told the small debt court in Campbeltown that he had refused to pay the asking price because the articles were 'only worth old metal'. The Sheriff disagreed and awarded McKersie £5. Ross then paid to have a self-exonerating letter published in the *Campbeltown Courier* and ended it with: 'Please ask William McKersie & Co. what good has this prosecution done them. How much has it added to their wealth? How much has it added to their happiness? How much has it added to their respectability?'[692]

When John Beith Jr. (q.v.) was re-elected Provost in 1867, at the customary dinner in the Town Hall for his fellow-magistrates and friends, Ross spoke glowingly of his qualities — 'Mr Beith's heart is as large as your Hall' — and recounted: 'In November 1824, Mr Beith became my partner; we have been together since, and nothing but death will separate us.' He was wrong, because they fell out spectacularly in 1876 (see 'Longrow Distillery').

Ross was in a nostalgic mood that evening as he looked back on the earliest of the distilleries in Campbeltown.

> 'We have found that the more distilleries there are in Campbeltown and the more whisky made in it, we have the better demand for it. The quantity that one

distillery made was very small, but they often found it too much for the demand. So very small was the quantity they made that one of us now makes as much in two weeks as they made in a year, and yet I have often known them stopped for want of sales. When we commenced, the duty was very low; it was only two shillings a gallon and a shilling of drawback, having only one shilling a gallon that we had to pay. Since then they have been from time to time raising it higher and higher on us. When giving the last turn to the screw, that is when raising it from eight to ten shillings a gallon, I met Mr Craufurd, our member [of Parliament]. He said to me, "Are you Campbeltown distillers not going to do anything to try to prevent your trade from being ruined?" I said: "I suppose not; for my part, I feel inclined not to do a thing." — "Why so?" says he. I said: 'Because I think the Campbeltown distillers are like pigs — the more they are kept down, they thrive the better.'"[693]

Ross, late in life, recalled — at much greater length than quoted — an incident at Campbeltown Quay in July 1811, when he was 10 years old. A boat came in to land three 'wifes' who had been gutting herring. Each had a bucket containing the 'guts', or livers, which would be rendered into oil and were the women's only payment for their work. The first two women stepped ashore without mishap, but the third slipped and fell into the water.

'There was a great sensation among the fishers. The air having got under her clothes buoyed her up, and kept her on the surface. She and the boat and all floated out from the quay; she was trying to speak but could not speak distinctly, as her mouth was as low as the surface of the water. The men said one to another, "Try and make out what she is saying, perhaps she is making her will". I at once bawled out, "She says the pail's whammelled". — "If that is all," they said, "never mind it." With that, one man went down into the sea up to his neck, another went down beside him, and another stood on the lowest part of the stair. All three catched hands, the farthest out got hold of the wife's hand, and pulled her in to the stair. A boy in a boat touched the whammelled [emptied] pail with an oar, and pushed it into the stair. With the help of a man, she walked up the stair, and when standing on the quay another man set her empty pail at her feet, at which she gave a melancholy look; another man on the quay came over to her and said, "It is a good thing, Mal, that you are saved." — "What signifies that," she said, "when I have lost a' my guts?" Then two men took hold of an arm each, and commenced walking up the quay, the water pouring from her at a great rate ... In walking along, they met Allan McNaught. He said, "Bless me, Mrs McIllwham, you are all wat." — "Ay, and what is waur [worse] than that, Allan, I've lost my guts." — "That's a great pity," Allan said. "I was never so near heaven in my life, Allan," she said; "they might have let me go, Allan." The man carrying the empty pail said, "We didna like to let her go there without her guts."'[694]

A further flavour of his celebrated story-telling can be tasted in the following anecdotes, which he included in a report he wrote about the supper organised for the 150 tradesmen who built the new Longrow Church in 1872.[695] To each story was attached a moral lesson, which I have removed.

'A farmer once came into a saddler's shop in Campbeltown with a horse's britchen in his hands, which he laid down on the counter and said: "Man, Baldy, this is a bad britchen I got frae you this time." — "What is the matter wi' them, Davie?" Baldy said. Davie said: "They are cracked and gaun tae nonsense." Baldy looked at them and said: "Man, Davie, ye have spoiled them putting oil and grease on them." Davie said: "I never put a morsel o' oil or grease on them in my life." This is the very fact that Baldy wished to establish.

'My dear Christian brethren, there was once a woman in Campbeltown called Jean Corkey. She was a poor mendicant, going about from house to house, taking meat wherever she could get it, and, as she did not get it regularly, taking a belly-full wherever she had an opportunity; and if anyone remonstrated with her when appearing to take too much, and what might injure her, she would say: "It is better to let the belly burst than to let the guid [good] meat go useless."'

Some speakers that evening had praised the building, but Ross admitted that not everyone shared that opinion. On the previous day, he had met in Longrow an old woman whose nick-name was 'Tamar'. She was the 'most economical' person he had ever known, and when he asked her what she thought of the new church, her reply was: "I duvna [don't] like it at a' — it's an ugly kirk.'

In 1881, Ross had three hefty contributions published in successive weeks in the *Argyllshire Herald*. One of them — a rant against the anti-alcohol lobby, containing a fantasy about a visit to Campbeltown by beings from outer space riding a comet — suggests that he was beginning to lose his grip on sanity. It opened as follows:

'Please tell Teetotallers, *alias* Total Abstainers, *alias* Good Templars, to right themselves and give up meddling with their neighbours ... If some stupid people get into the habit of drinking castor oil and injuring themselves by doing so, is that a reason why no more castor oil should be made?'[696]

Ross's favourite maxims were, 'The way to be healthy is not to eat too much; the way to be wealthy is to live within your income; and the way to be wise is to know your own ignorance'; and he never forget his mother's often repeated advice, 'The best way is to be prepared for the worst'.[697]

His wife, Sarah MacMillan, whom he married in 1835, died in 1879, aged 66, at their home, Comely Bank House,

High Askomil.[698] Three years earlier, she had suffered a 'severe head injury' when thrown from a carriage at the foot of High Askomil after the horse had taken fright and bolted. The injured animal was 'killed on the spot' by inserting a tube into one of its veins and 'blowing the blood back to the heart'.[699]

The marriage was childless. When Ross died on 3 March 1886, aged 84, his estate was valued at £12,394 5s 11d, not a lot more than he spent on the aesthetically controversial Longrow Church bell-tower.

Rowatt, Dr Charles (1732-1826), belonged to an old Lowland family in South Kintyre. An ancestor, Alexander Rowatt, factor to the Dowager Duchess of Argyll, was taken prisoner in the aftermath of the Earl of Argyll's abortive rebellion in 1685, questioned by the Scots Privy Council, acquitted and released.

Rowatt was proprietor of the small estate of Kilkivan, near Machrihanish, and also had property at Castlehill, Campbeltown, incorporating Doctor Rowatt's Close (see 'West Highland Distillery'). He was a partner in Campbeltown Distillery, the earliest recorded local distillery, and appears to have established a leather tannery in Dalintober, Charles Rowatt & Co.[700] He set up the first lending library in Campbeltown, which was run by the Relief (Longrow) Church, of which he was a founder-member. By 1861, the library held upwards of 1,500 books and charged an annual membership fee of 1s for patrons connected with the congregation and 2s for others.[701]

An eccentric character, in 1899 he was recalled thus: 'Look at him, shuffling along the street, dressed in slouched beaver [hat], black silk cloak, with tippet, velvet knee breeches, black silk stockings, and shoes with large silver buckles. He was a unique figure. Dr Rowatt's name was a household word, for he claimed acquaintance with very many of the community on their introduction into the world.'[702] This is borne out by the many children named after him, including Charles Rowatt Mactaggart (q.v.), born in 1809, and Charles Rowatt Johnston, born in 1810 (see 'Lochruan Distillery').

His parents were Alexander 'Ruat' — the spelling on Charles's birth registration — and Isobell Campbell, a daughter of Donald Campbell, eighth Campbell laird of Clachan, North Kintyre, who was elected Provost of Campbeltown in 1707.[703]

Rundle, Warwick James, was 84 years old when he died at Witchburn Terrace on 31 July 1940. He was a Customs and Excise officer who came to Campbeltown from England, around 1900, and remained after he retired. For 'fully 20 years he supervised operations in the Bonded Warehouse in Glebe Street'.

'Keenly interested in educational matters', he was appointed to the School Board in 1909, but, aside from that, he took no part in public affairs. He enjoyed an early morning swim, winter and summer, and his hobbies were cricket, cards, feeding small birds and photography. He was 'never seen out in the open country without his camera', but he also photographed interiors, and several fine photographs of his, taken inside Campbeltown distilleries, appeared in Brian Townsend's *Scotch Missed*, published in 1993. Whence came these images, and does Rundle's entire photographic collection survive? The book, which is devoid of sources, does not provide answers to these questions.

Nine years before his death, while participating in a whist drive in the Episcopal Church Hall — he was a member of that congregation — he suffered a 'seizure' from which he never recovered. Rose Ramsay, his first wife, by whom he had a son and a daughter, died in 1924, and his second wife, who was Margaret Ramsay, died in 1942. He was active in the Conservative Club and a member of The Club (q.v.), from which, on the day of his burial, a flag was flown at half-mast.[704]

Scotia Distillery — see 'Glen Scotia Distillery'.

Scottish Malt Distillers Ltd. was a subsidiary of Distillers Company Ltd. (DCL), a trade cartel formed in 1877. Of the eight bonded warehouses in Campbeltown in 1950, S.M.D. owned six, taken over from redundant distilleries — two in Lochend Street, and one in Glebe Street, John Street, Saddell Street and at Hazelburn[705] — and also operated the coaster *Pibroch* (q.v.).

In March 1955, two Campbeltown employees of S.M.D., Archibald Tolmie and Archibald McGougan, were guests at a dinner in the Machrie Hotel, Islay, where each was presented with a silver watch and a long service certificate; the former, manager at Hazelburn, had been 36 years an employee, and the latter, a warehouseman, 31 years. Archie Tolmie — who began his career in 1919 with W. P. Lowrie, Glasgow, was transferred to Oban Distillery in 1924 and to Campbeltown in 1937 — retired in 1963 and was replaced as manager at Hazelburn by Archibald McGougan.[706]

Sherriff, J. B. & Co., entered Campbeltown whisky-distilling history with the purchase in 1895 of Loch-head Distillery. In 1920, the company was taken over by J. & P. O'Brien Ltd., Liverpool, along with two other Scottish distilling concerns, Bulloch, Lade & Co. and Messrs Wright & Greig, Glasgow; but two months later, in April 1920, J. & P. O'Brien was reported to be in liquidation. Several years later, the company name, disposed of with its distilleries, Loch-head and Lochindaal in Islay, was taken up by a new firm of distillers and blenders, J. B. Sherriff & Co. Ltd., which had no connection with the eponymous family. The original firm continued under the name of Sherriff & Co. (Jamaica) Ltd. — directors T. A. B. Sherriff, C. B. Sherriff and J. Neville — which in 1929 owned Bowmore Distillery, Islay, and held the agency for Springbank Distillery.[707] Thomas A. B. Sherriff (above) was enrolled as a member of the Kintyre Club in 1910.

Shipping. Historically — and, indeed, prehistorically — sailing vessels were the main means of travel on the West of Scotland, and, in the case of islands, the only means. Ships were also the main, or only, means of importing and exporting goods of all kinds, including whisky, and until the advent of steam power in the early 19th century, markets for locally made spirits were constrained by geography. That said, the smuggling of illicit whisky to Ayrshire in small boats from creeks along the east coast of Kintyre is well documented.[708] The establishment of the Campbeltown & Glasgow Steam Packet Joint Stock Company (q.v.) in 1826 opened markets in Glasgow and beyond for the legal distilleries and triggered the rapid expansion of the industry in Campbeltown.

Until the introduction of 'packets', or mail boats, sea travel from Campbeltown depended on small smacks, which 'came and went as they pleased and only when they had a full cargo'.[709] A voyage to Glasgow in one of these vessels was recalled in 1866 as 'marine purgatory ... seldom, if ever, taken for pleasure'. The anonymous writer described being confined in a tiny cabin, 'tormented with the smell of bilge water and the smoke of tobacco', so prostrated with sea-sickness that 'you felt as if you cared not though you went to the bottom', and 'thrown off your seat now and again upon a vomit-besmeared floor' as the vessel tacked 'slowly hither and thither against a head wind'.[710]

Travelling by packet was doubtless little better, but these vessels had predictable destinations — the Clyde ports and Ayr — even if the duration of the voyage was entirely unpredictable. James H. Mackenzie maintained that the first packet based in Campbeltown was the *Isabella* in 1811, but this cannot be correct, since Dan Mactaggart is on record, in November of that very year, stating that he and his father had been operating the packet *Caledonia* between Campbeltown and Greenock 'for some years' (Appendix 4). And John Ross (q.v.), in a lengthy account of the genesis of the song 'The Bonnie Green Braes o' Kintyre', which he dated to 1811, stated that his father Alexander was 'master of the "Peggy" packet' in that very year.[711]

Mackenzie preserved a couple of anecdotes about the *Isabella*, on which his maternal great-grandfather was purser and steward. These seem, to modern perception, wildly exaggerated, but probably owe more to truth than not. The *Isabella*'s captain was reputed 'to be able at times to plant his potatoes before he left and dig them when he came back from Glasgow'; and one winter the *Isabella* was 'frozen in somewhere up the Clyde', and before she was able to break out and return to Campbeltown, Nathaniel McNair's *Gleaner* of Campbeltown had crossed the Atlantic to Newfoundland with coal and emigrants and returned to her home port with a cargo of timber and salt fish.[712]

A more credible account survives from 1815, but the voyage was undertaken in summer, not winter. The letter-writer was a schoolmaster employed by the Scottish Society for the Propogation of Christian Knowledge and was travelling from Perthshire with his wife and daughter to take up a new post in Campbeltown. The entire journey took a fortnight. When they arrived in Glasgow, one of the Campbeltown packets was 'just ready to sail', but the wind suddenly shifted and the vessel was stuck at the Broomielaw for five days. When the packet finally sailed, the wind was still contrary and the voyage to Campbeltown took six days and nights, during which a gale blew up: 'My wife and whole family, together with every passenger on board, were like to die with sea-sickness. The sailors could not attend them, for the sea ran very high, but Providence was so favourable as enabled me to attend on my distressed family, being the only passenger on board who was not sick: for I assure you, sir, that I had plenty to do, for sometimes the vessel would be down to the very hatches.' (He was John Stewart, transferred from Spittal of Glenshee to teach poor children in English and Gaelic in Campbeltown. He was superannuated in 1828 and died the following year.)[713]

From John Ross's pen came what appears to be the only description, albeit meagre, of a local packet. When he heard the *Peggy* was coming in, he took two other boys, Matthew Sheddan and Colin Ferguson, with him to the quay. When they jumped aboard the vessel, Ross's father invited them below and gave them each a biscuit. 'She was a very small packet,' Ross recalled. 'She carried both goods and passengers, and, having a hold for goods, the cabin could not be large — I think about six feet square, with two beds on each side, the one above the other; each bed about the size of a coffin.'[714]

When the twin children of William MacMillan and Mary Curlett were baptised in Campbeltown in 1815, he was described as 'Packetmaster'.

Despite the rapid development of steam power, there is no evidence that Campbeltown merchants invested in the new technology. Trading vessels remained, until the end, sail-powered. Many local distillers diversified into shipping, and it would certainly have made economic sense to have the means of shipping in coal, peat and barley and shipping out draff and whisky; but distilling-related trade would not have occupied the vessels all year round and they also engaged in general trading.

In 1862, the brigantine *Helena* — registered at 111 tons and with a carrying capacity of about 180 tons — was built for Archibald McKersie, distiller, and a Campbeltown ship-owner, Lachlan McIsaac.[715]

In December 1863, the sloop *Lewis* sailed from Campbeltown to Irvine, Ayrshire, with a load of whisky and draff, and ran aground on the south side of the harbour. The Irvine life-boat was launched and rescued the crew, and the uninsured cargo, valued at about £500, was salvaged and the vessel refloated.[716] The newspaper report identified the owners as 'Messrs McMurchy and Greenlees', which is unrecognisable, at least as a firm; but, in 1853 the 60-ft. 'gabert' *Lewis* of Port Glasgow was recorded as being sold by her owner, John Miller, Dumbarton, for £240, to the distilling companies Greenlees & Colvill and David Colville & Co.[717]

In June 1866, a 'fine large sloop, upwards of 100 tons burthen', was launched at Rothesay for Archibald McKersie, part-owner of the *Helena*, above. Named the *Albyn*, after the McKersie family distillery of that name, she sank in 1884 when she struck the south pier at Maryport, Cumbria, in 'dark and stormy weather'.[718]

Later in 1866, Alex MacKelvie — since 1864 a partner in Stewart, Galbraith & Co., Scotia Distillery — paid £133 for a quarter share in the schooner *Mary Ann* of Campbeltown.[719]

The schooner *Mary Colville*, built in 1869 at Rothesay for James Greenlees #1 and others, was presumably named after James's paternal grandmother, Mary Colville, who was still alive at the time. On her maiden voyage, she sailed to Liverpool with pig-iron.[720] Donald Smith was known to have captained her before he built the *Finlaggan* (below) with James Greenlees and his brother Alexander. Small local vessels rarely engaged in the Continental barley trade, but in May 1870 the *Mary Colville* discharged 150 tons of grain from St. Malo for Burnside,[721] the Greenlees brothers' distillery. She was later owned by Captain Duncan Martin, Campbeltown, and was wrecked at Sandhaven in the Moray Firth on 29 March 1904.[722]

The 75-ft. schooner *Campbeltown* was evidently named after the distillery. When launched in July 1870, from the Rothesay boat-yard of Robert McLay, she was reported as being 'owned by Duncan McLean of Campbeltown Distillery'; but there is no record of a McLean connected with any local distillery. The Duncan McLean, owner and master of the *Campbeltown* when he died in 1906, had first sailed in her as a boy with his uncle, Robert McCallum. McLean was born in Islay in 1853 and married Mary Vetters, Campbeltown.[723]

In November 1870, the schooner *Benmore* was launched at McLay's yard, Rothesay, for Charles McEachran (q.v.).[724] When sold out of Campbeltown in 1917, she was recalled nostalgically as 'a regular clipper, and in bygone days there were many interesting races across the Firth between her and her rivals in the coasting trade, in which she invariably came out with flying colours'.[725] McEachran and another local businessman, Thomas Brown, had owned the sloop *Scotia*, which in December 1864 ran ashore on the south end of Arran.[726] In 1873 McEachran bought the 117-ton schooner *Wern*, already three years old.[727]

In April 1873, James Greenlees (probably #1) paid £155 for the brigantine *Triad*, which sank off the south side of Davaar Island. She was raised for repair in September by Charles Martin, joiner in Campbeltown.[728]

In April 1877, a 76-ft. schooner, *Bengullion*, was launched at the Rodgers boat-yard in Carrickfergus, Northern Ireland, for Duncan MacCallum — who built Glen Nevis Distillery that same year — Alexander Mitchell and Dugald McCorkindale (her master). Her maiden voyage was modest enough: from Troon to Campbeltown with 130 tons of coal. She was sold for £700 in 1890.[729]

In October 1877, the schooner *Swift*, with a carrying capacity of 160 tons, was also launched at Carrickfergus, for Charles McEachran,[730] above.

The schooner *Finlaggan*, of 190 tons, was launched in 1877 for James W. and Alexander Greenlees, Burnside Distillery,[731] who had the lease of Finlaggan farm on Islay. She was part-owned by Captain Donald Smith, a native of Gigha, whose seafaring reputation was such that in 1889 he was invited to navigate Sir Thomas Lipton's *Shamrock I* to New York for the wealthy merchant's first attempt to 'wrest the America's Cup from the Yankees'. The *Finlaggan* frequently traded to the Baltic, Mediterranean and North America.[732] In March 1888, when she loaded draff at Campbeltown for Belfast, she had been 10 months absent 'in the Newfoundland fish trade'. In May, she took a cargo of pig-iron to Newport, Wales, and loaded coal there for 'Figaro' [Figueira da Foz] in Portugal; from there, she was to proceed with a cargo of salt to Harbour Grace, Newfoundland; from Labrador she would sail to Patria, Greece, with salted fish; and from Patria to Great

Britain or the Continent with fruit.[733] She was sold in 1896 to Alexander Ritchie, Sanda Island.[734] As a ship's name, *Finlaggan* is now well-known as the CalMac ferry, launched in Poland in 2011 for the Kennacraig to Islay run.

The schooner *Moy*, when launched in March 1878, was the first vessel built at Campbeltown Shipyard. She was owned by Samuel Greenlees (q.v.) and Daniel Greenlees (q.v.) and named after the estate, on the outskirts of Campbeltown, which these cousins bought in 1858.[735] In May 1879, she brought a cargo of barley to Campbeltown from the Baltic, prompting the comment in a local newspaper: 'It is a pity we have not more vessels of her class that could do the foreign as well as the home trade.'[736] Her career, however, was brief, for she foundered in a snow storm, within sight of her home port, in January 1884, with the loss of all hands.[737] A little model of the ship — made by Angus McGougan and restored by David McNaughton — has been on display in Campbeltown Museum since 1995.

In a storm in January 1890, the schooner *Kandy*'s sails were carried away while on passage from Irvine to Campbeltown with coal and she was driven ashore near Tarbert. Her crew was rescued by fishermen, but she could not be salvaged and her wreck was sold by auction. She was owned by John McKersie (q.v.).[738]

In 1897, 1,343 coasting and six foreign vessels used Campbeltown harbour. In that same year, 1,933,287 gallons of whisky were shipped from the port, the greatest quantity ever.[739]

As the 20th century progressed, sail increasingly fell from favour. The last sail-powered trader in Campbeltown, the *Glenscott*, was sold in 1931 after the death of her owner, Duncan MacCallum (q.v.). He bought her — as a replacement for his *Star of Doon* — for £368 at Oban in 1922, as the *Ada* of Aalborg, after she had run aground. While based at Campbeltown, she was engaged mainly in coal-carrying from Ayrshire, and, when she left Campbeltown nine years later, she once again flew the Danish flag, having been purchased by Captain Poulsen, Copenhagen.[740]

In December 1924, while the *Glenscott* was on passage from Ayr to her home port with a cargo of coal, a 26-year-old Campbeltown seaman, Duncan McArthur, was lost overboard in a gale while the topsail was being lowered. Early in October 1926, while on passage to Campbeltown from Glasgow with a cargo of whisky for 'warehousing', she was driven ashore at King's Cross, Arran, in a storm. After several attempts to refloat her, the cargo was transferred to the puffer *Skylight*. Towards the end of the month, she was finally pulled off the beach and towed to Irvine.[741]

John MacFadyen Campbell, who was born in 1904 in Dalintober, sailed for two years as deckhand on the *Glenscott*. Her master, Joe Burdon, belonged to Annalong in County Down, Ireland. He had earlier skippered the *Moses Parry*, running coal for Scotia and Albyn distilleries. In 1920, he married Euphemia McMillan, whose father James had been brewer at Hazelburn Distillery, but she died two years later.[742] In order to effect 'a wee bit play in the wages', the crew of the *Glenscott* comprised just Burdon, a mate and John. Being a man short made sail work difficult and at times Burdon would lock the wheel and himself go aloft. The vessel had, as auxiliary power, a 26 h.p. 'Gleniffer' engine.[743]

Sillars, James, distillery manager, who died on 24 October 1933, at 78 Longrow, had a remarkable length of service at Rieclachan — 56 years — and his father, Archibald, was mashman there from at least 1857, when, at Whitehill farm, he married Martha Templeton,[744] 'up to the time of his retirement as an old man'. James began his working life as a draper, but after a couple of years went to Rieclachan as a clerk and was, his obituarist records, 'three years with the original firm before the distillery was acquired by the late Mr William Mitchell'. He was a keen horticulturalist and an enthusiastic member of Argyll Bowling Club. Like his father before him, he was an office-bearer in Lochend United Free Church, but left to join the Longrow congregation — an 'unhappy experience', endured 'for principle's sake' — after the controversial union of the U.F. and the Established Church in 1929.[745] His wife, Catherine McKendrick, died in 1938, aged 71. They had no family.

Sinclair, Daniel. On 27 November 1873, at Lloyd's Hotel, Campbeltown, Daniel Sinclair, mashman at Benmore Distillery, married Ann Brown.[746] He died on 12 July 1899, in the Royal Infirmary, Glasgow, and four years later his widow inserted an 'In Memoriam' notice in a local newspaper, with the following verse:
All is dark within our dwelling.
Lonely is our home today,
For the one who smiled to cheer us
Has forever passed away.[747]
Daniel was a son of Andrew Sinclair, sawyer, and Margaret Stevenson, and Ann a daughter of John Brown, farm servant, and Jean McLarty. They had six children: Jeanie, Peter, John, Mary, Annie and Isabella. Ann was admitted to the Campbeltown poor roll in 1911, aged 60 and suffering from rheumatism, and given 2s 6d support per week.[748]

Smith, Christopher Vetters, started out in the whisky trade in his native Campbeltown just after the First World War, but in 1923 moved to Kilmarnock to work in the blending department of John Walker & Sons. In 1935 he was put in charge of the department and in 1946 was appointed to the board of directors. When he retired in 1961, he was production director and living in Troon, Ayrshire, where he intended to 'spend his retirement with his wife'.[749] She was Preston H. B. C. Grubb, M.A., who died in 1978, aged 76. Christopher returned to Campbeltown and lived at Kilkerran, in a bungalow which he named 'Cardhu', after the Speyside distillery which John Walker & Sons acquired in 1893. He died in 1985, aged 88. His parents were Hugh Smith, joiner, and Montgomery

Vetters. The surname 'Vetters' appears to be an exotic, but is actually a bizarre form of Gaelic *MacGillePheadair*, 'Son of the Servant of [Saint] Peter'.[750] He was named after his grandfather, Christopher Vetters, fisherman and seaman in Campbeltown, who was 'Christie Vitres' when he married Mary MacPhee in 1845.

Smith, Dugald, a 45-year-old distillery workman in Dalaruan, was feeling ill on the morning of 13 June 1864. His wife, Barbara McMillan, bought a small quantity of 'salts and senna' (dried laxative leaves), which she mixed and gave to him before she left to work at potato harvesting. When their children returned from school, they found their father sitting in his chair dead. As 'sinister reports' were circulating that his wife had received 'some other ingredients than Epsom salts', local doctors performed a *post-mortem*, and established heart disease as the cause of death.[751] His parents were Donald Smith, farmer, and Isabella Galbraith.

Smith, Harry James, was appointed manager of Glen Scotia in 1949 after the resignation of Hugh Thomson (q. v.). He was a native of Morayshire and had been 20 years in the distilling business. He began his career in Balmenach Distillery, Cromdale, and came to Campbeltown from Glen Rothes Distillery, where he was brewer. His son Mike (below) replaced him as manager. He died in 1978, aged 76, having been predeceased by his wife, Mary McDonald, in 1964.[752]

Smith, Henry Michael, known as 'Mike', was a son of Harry Smith (above) and came to Campbeltown from Morayshire as a schoolboy. He was born near a distillery and 'played in stills as a child', he recalled in 1977. Despite his background in the industry, he eschewed a 'ready-made career' and initially worked for the Post Office in Campbeltown; but, as he admitted, 'the calling was there', and he started work in Glen Scotia as assistant manager to his father in about 1962 and succeeded him in the post when his father retired. He oversaw the radical modernisation of the distillery in the mid-1970s and later became managing director. He married a local schoolteacher, Nancie Blair, with whom he had two daughters, Alison and Susie, and died in 2003, aged 65.[753]

Smith, John James, who died at Springbank, Low Askomil, on 30 January 1929, was described as 'late manager of Hazelburn Distillery'. His obituary was brief: a member of the Town Council and of 'the old School Board'; in politics, a staunch Unionist; recreationally, he took a keen interest in football, and, by his administrative abilities, 'helped to lift the game locally'.[754] In 1895/6, he successfully defended a legal action brought against him by Charles McKinven, distillery workman, who claimed that Smith had implied or insinuated that he was involved in the theft of coal or other goods from his workplace, Argyll Distillery, and sued for £500 damages.[755] In Census 1901, he was in Kirk Street, Campbeltown, with an older brother and sister, both of whom were born in Ayr; he himself was born in Campbeltown in about 1870. His parents were Robert Smith, Quarter Master Sergeant, Highland Light Infantry, and Margaret McConnell,[756] and he evidently never married.

Smith, Peter, who died on 8 March 1929, was a 'lifelong employee' of Stewart, Galbraith & Co., Scotia Distillery, and 'rose to the position of secretary', as his gravestone in Kilkerran confirms. In 1910, he noted that his 'own people' — his father and brother and, of course, himself — had been with the company for 70 years.[757] He built a villa, Elyside, in Dalintober, but sold it when his health began to fail, and moved to 38 Saddell Street, a tenement demolished in the early 1970s and replaced by the ugly brick warehouse built for Glen Scotia. He was 75 when he died, 'after a long and trying period of invalidity', and was survived by his wife, Mary McMillan.[758]

Smith, William Junior. His *Views of Campbelton and Neighbourhood*, published in 1835, contains the earliest account of the Campbeltown legal whisky industry in its transitional stage from small-scale to larger operations. Smith correctly identified John Beith & Co.'s Campbeltown Distillery, built in 1817, as the first of the 'new' distilleries, and claimed that in 1835 there were 'upwards of twenty-three' distilleries in 'full operation'. The advent of 'steam navigation' had provided a great boost to the industry, enabling distillers to get their whisky to the Glasgow market in a matter of hours, instead of days, and at 'a very moderate expense', though the locally-owned 'steam packet', the *Duke of Lancaster*, captained by James Napier (q.v.), ran only thrice a fortnight between Glasgow and Campbeltown at that time.

In the earlier phase of legal distilling, Smith reported, if 300 gallons were in bond 'the whole work was stopped until a market had been found for this amazing quantity'. By 1835, some of the distillers could have 3,000 gallons 'on hand' when prices were low, yet continue producing, 'feeling confident of a sure market'. The Campbeltown distilleries were each producing an average of 20,000 gallons a year, and in 1834 the *Duke of Lancaster* had shipped nearly 300,000 gallons of local whisky to Glasgow.[759] Such quantities were, of course, small compared with what would come as the century approached its end.

Smith, William, who belonged to Campbeltown and began his career in distillery management at Benmore, was transferred in 1931 from Lochindaal Distillery, Islay, to Convalmore, Dufftown.[760]

Smoke pollution. In 1868, the Deacons' Court of the 'Free English Church' at Lochend complained to Campbeltown Town Council about the 'nuisance' caused by smoke from the distillery chimneys behind the newly opened church. The Dean of Guild was 'instructed to call the attention of the proprietors to the works complained of ...'[761]

In 1921, the issue of smoke pollution from distilleries again came to the attention of the Town Council. At a meeting in December, a letter from R. E. Johnson, Roy Place, complaining of 'excessive emission of smoke from the chimneys of two distilleries in Dalintober', was read out. The complaint was dealt with by Colonel Charles Mactaggart, convenor of the health committee and retired from a distinguished career in the Indian Medical Service. He had spoken with the sanitary inspector, who suggested to the distillery managers that 'by careful stoking, the emission of smoke might be minimised'. Mactaggart added, however, that he himself lived near the two distilleries — in Dalintober House — and had 'never seen much to complain about'. He added that he 'only wished he saw every chimney in Campbeltown from the Trench [Point Shipyard] to the Network putting out a great deal more smoke than they are doing at present'. The response was 'Hear! Hear!' and applause, for at that time joblessness in the town was rife and Provost John Colvill had opened the Campbeltown Unemployment Relief Fund for 'those suffering from want'. (By January 1923, Sam Greenlees, London — see 'Greenlees Brothers' — headed the list of donors with £50).[762]

In 1956 the issue reappeared. 'The black smoke from the distilleries constitutes a nuisance under the Public Health Acts', the Campbeltown sanitary inspector reported to the public health committee of the Town Council in June. He complained that he had been unable to make any progress in the 'discontinuance' of the nuisance, and the committee agreed to notify the distilleries of its concern and to 'ascertain from them whether there was any reason why appropriate action should not be undertaken to have it mitigated'. Six weeks later, Springbank Distillery reported that two engineers from the National Industrial Fuel Efficiency Service had 'examined their fuel arrangements' and that 'it was hoped to carry out tests, when distilling operations were resumed, to eliminate, or at least mitigate, the smoke nuisance'. No response had been received from A. Gillies & Co., Glen Scotia.[763] The number of distilleries operating at that time was precisely two — Glen Scotia and Springbank — which prompts the question of how bad pollution must have been when there were 27 working!

Springbank Distillery. Barnard (1887) gave 1828 as the year the distillery was built and Colville (1923) followed suit, but Glen (p 156) cautioned in 2003: 'Reputed to have been licensed in 1828, but there is no reference in the Excise returns.' Barnard also erroneously stated that Springbank was built by 'the father-in-law of one of the present proprietors': the father-in-law of John Mitchell, to whom he was referring, was Alexander Wylie.

The founding firm was William Reid, Jr. & Co., the partners in which were William Reid Sr., maltster, William Reid Jr., grocer, and John Reid, distiller.[764] In the Argyll Estate archive in Inveraray, there is a memorial from William Jr., dated 7 July 1836, requesting a piece of ground in the Longrow for building a distillery under the firm of William Reid Jr. & Co.[765] A year later, in *Pigot* of 1837, the Reids' distillery was still without a name and is represented merely by 'William Reid, jun., & Co. Longrow st'.

The Reids must have plunged immediately into financial difficulties, for in 1837 their creditors sold the distillery to John and William Mitchell, who would operate as J. & W. Mitchell. The Colville papers, in the Live Argyll archive in Lochgilphead, contain a mass of detail concerning the Reids' failure, including a list of 51 creditors. Most of the sums were small — the smallest was 1s 11d due to Archibald Colville Jr. — but John Colvill Jr. (q.v.) was owed £339 18s, the Commercial Bank £285 19s 3d, and, of 11 Glasgow creditors listed, William Graham & Co. was owed the most: £137 17s 6d. Some local tradesmen, who had presumably been involved in the building of the distillery, were badly hit, particularly Nathaniel McNair, wright (£76 1s 3d), and Robert Armour, coppersmith (£54 5s 3d). Nathaniel

McNair and John Colville Jr., along with Robert Greenlees, distiller, were the Reids' trustees. Debts totalled £1,739 10s and the business was sold by public auction on 5 October 1837.[766] See 'John Reid' and 'William Reid'.

The Argyll Estate archive papers relating to the lease of Springbank begin in 1838 and end in 1878. Wright (1963) records that the first sale of Mitchell whisky was on 14 November 1837 — just 40 days after the distillery was bought — to Isabella Brown, who purchased 24 gallons at 8s 2d a gallon, duty paid. *Pigot's Directory* (p 221) of that same year records Isabella in Back Street, one of 59 'vintners' in the town and Dalintober. She was in Back Street 12 years earlier, when described less fancily as a 'publican'.[767]

According to Wright, the two Mitchell brothers 'quarrelled violently' over sheep and parted company; for their farming partnership, see 'John Mitchell'. On 20 November 1872, Springbank was offered for sale, by public auction, at an 'upset', or reserve, price of £3,500, and was bought for £5,055 by John Mitchell,[768] who took his son Archibald #3 into the business, which then became J. & A. Mitchell, as it remains to this day. Less than a year after the split, the other brother, William, had built Glengyle Distillery.

In the early afternoon of 26 October 1862, six-year-old Duncan McLaren set off from his house to meet his father returning home from work for dinner. The meeting never happened and a search was made for the boy. One of the Springbank workmen saw a bonnet floating in the well at the back of the distillery and the body was recovered. The wooden cover on the well had been removed, but it was 'difficult to imagine' how the boy himself could have dislodged it.[769]

In April 1885, while workmen were unloading Springbank whisky from a wagon, one of the puncheons fell and broke open and a hundred gallons of whisky spilled out. Word quickly spread and people hurried to the scene of the accident, some immediately lapping up the 'flowing and inebriating liquor', while others, 'with more systematic and deliberate ideas', filled small dishes. The free-for-all ended, however, with the arrival of the police.[770]

Towards the end of the First World War, two sons of Donald Sinclair, head maltman at Springbank, were decorated while serving as privates in the Argyll & Sutherland Highlanders: Alex was awarded the Military Medal in 1917 and Norman the Distinguished Conduct Medal in 1918.[771]

In 1905, Springbank was reported to have three stills, one of 4,000 gallons, one of 1,700 and one of 1,300. That same year, a new 'draff drainer' had been built outside the still-house. The grains were pumped from the mash-tun to the drainer with the third water, and from there carted to the draff factory, 'with a minimum of trouble'. By 1923, the annual output of Springbank in 'a good season' was around 100,000 gallons, most of which was shipped to Glasgow.[772]

In December 1935 it was reported that Springbank would 'recommence operations' early in the New Year. The distillery had not worked since 1930, but 'the plant has been kept in perfect repair, with the result that, now that the prospects of the Scottish distilling industry have improved, it is possible for an immediate start to be made'. The manager, C. C. McSporran (q.v.), had purchased barley, and, as soon as enough malt had been prepared, production would begin. Glen Scotia also planned to resume distilling.[773]

In the winter of 1939, Springbank was working to full capacity, unaffected by the outbreak of war. Its whisky, 'produced only for blending', was being bought 'as quickly as it can be produced'; but in the following year the Government cut the output of whisky by two-thirds and soon afterwards requisitioned all barley stocks held by distilleries. Production was resumed in January 1945: malting was then in progress and distilling would begin in March.[774]

In December 1965, an 'entirely modern' bonded warehouse, incorporating the first racking system in

Campbeltown, was opened at the distillery by Provost Duncan McMillan.[775]

In 1967, remarkable as it may now seem, the marketing of Springbank whisky in its own right was negligible. Single malt whisky was 'not readily available', owing to the demand for it in 'the popularly priced blends'; but change was in the air, and 'limited quantities' were 'now being reserved for distribution as a single malt'.[776]

The name 'Springbank' is surely connected to the lane in which the distillery was built, Well Close. Mrs Moira Herd, writing in 1981, remembered when the lane was a corridor of trees, flowers and grass, endowing it with 'sweetness in summer'. As a child, she thought that 'everyone lived next door to a distillery', and she remembered falling sleep to the sounds of the workmen 'rhythmically turning the grain through the night'.[777]

Springbank 50-year-old. In 1963, Hedley G. Wright (q.v.), managing director of J. & A. Mitchell & Co. Ltd., described a hogshead of 1919 Springbank whisky, which lay in a company warehouse, as a 'fine, clean-tasting Spirit without any trace of woodiness', and revealed that it would be kept for seven more years before bottling.

Sure enough, on 25 November 1970, the whisky remaining in the refill sherry hogshead — distilled in December 1919 and filled on the 26th of that month at a strength of 11.2 over-proof — was bottled. Evaporation during the half-century of storage had reportedly reduced the quantity from 59.1 proof gallons (c 266 litres) to 16.4 proof gallons (c 74 litres). The contents yielded 12 cases and one extra bottle, and each bottle was specially labelled and numbered and carried a certificate signed by Wright.[778]

In May 1974, a container-load of whisky which left Springbank, destined for Italy, included, among more than 700 cases, one containing 12 bottles of the 50-year-old malt. The distillery's Italian distributor dealt in 5-, 8-, 10-, 12-, 15- and 21-year-old malts, and this was the first 50-year-old ever exported.[779]

In June of 1974, the Scottish *Daily Mail* declared that its sister newspaper, the *Sunday Mail*, had a bottle of 'the most exclusive whisky in the world' and would be offering it as a prize to the reader who told the 'best whisky story'. There were 'only 36 bottles in existence and it's so unique that no one dares drink it'. Angus Mackenzie, of the Kingsknowes Hotel in Galashiels, had a bottle of that 50-year-old Springbank, which was reckoned to be 'worth about £50 on the market'. He had no intention of opening it, but was charging customers 10 pence just to look at it![780]

In August 1977, at the distillery, Springbank's export manager, Bob Buglass, presented a bottle of the 50-year-old malt to the company's distributor in France, 'Mr Uranken, owner of Messrs Centrachat, Paris', who had exceeded 'the French sales target for Springbank by 100 per cent'. In 1977, the distillery also began exporting its malt whisky to Japan, and by 1981 Springbank was 'the best-selling Scotch whisky' in that country. Bob Buglass even had business cards printed in Japanese for his visits there; and in 1979 two directors of the import company, Kinoshita Shoji, flew from Japan to visit the distillery ... and each left with a bottle of 50-year-old malt. (Buglass left Springbank in 1981, after nine years there, to become sales manager of Tobermory Distillers Ltd.)[781]

In January 1988, Neil Clapperton — then a 'franchise dealer in rare malts' in Edinburgh and now managing director of J. & A. Mitchell — sold a bottle of 50-year-old for the 'staggering' sum of £2,500. The buyer was a Glasgow businessman who walked into the shop in Cowgate to purchase his favourite 10-year-old, at £14 a bottle, saw the bottle with its £2,500 price tag and announced: 'I'll take that as well.' By then, according to the local newspaper, there were just nine bottles of the 50-year-old 'remaining ... in the world'. In 2013, Springbank sold its last remaining bottle to a whisky bar in China for £50,000.[782]

Since then, prices of rare whiskies have soared to absurd heights. A bottle of 1926 Macallan, e.g., sold for £1.2

million in 2018, as noted in the *Daily Mail*, 7 August 2019. The article, by Iona Bain, appeared in the newspaper's financial section, appropriately, because investment is what drives up prices. In September 2019, it was reported that Springbank whisky had claimed 'top spot in the investor rankings for the first time',[783] and a bottle of the 50-year-old Springbank, with an Italian importer's slip, was later sold at Sotheby's for £266,200.

Springside Distillery, in April 1927, was the scene of an auction ... not of distilling equipment, though the plant had closed in the previous year, but of a variety of articles stored there: three small boats, sails, spars and oars, a 'coach roof for a boat', two stoves, a ferret hutch and wood 'suitable for farmers'.[784] Springside, situated in Burnside Street, was the smallest of all the distilleries when Barnard visited Campbeltown in 1885. It was built in 1830 by John Colvill #2, who died in 1883. His nick-name was 'The Saddler', from his original trade as a saddle-maker and leather-cutter in Burnside Street,[785] and the entrance to Springside was popularly known as 'The Saddler's Close'.[786] The distillery traded as John Colvill & Co. for its entire life of almost a century.

In 1899, Springside's bonding storage was increased by the building of a 'handsome' three-storied duty-free warehouse. 'Not many years ago,' a local newspaper remarked, 'the idea of building a distillery warehouse of more than one storey would have been regarded as utter folly, but nowadays ... distillers, in this district at least, seldom think of putting up anything but two- or three-deckers, and thus make [the] most of the ground space at their disposal.'[787]

Mr David Mayo in 2018 donated several artefacts from Springside Distillery to Campbeltown Heritage Centre, including a handsome weighing balance and a wheelbarrow. These were discovered at Bellgrove, where David's grandfather John Colvill #3 died, and which David inherited.[788]

Stalker, Charles. In the whole of Kilkerran cemetery, there is only one headstone which refers to a distillery by name — not even the richest of distillers thought to name their properties — and it was erected by Charles Stalker and his wife Helen Luke in memory of their son Charles, 'accidentally killed at Dalaruan Distillery, 16th March 1931'. Charles was not, however, a distillery worker; he died, aged 22, during the demolition of the distillery, when a wall collapsed on him. He was one of a squad employed by James Carmichael, road contractor, Lochgilphead, some of the men knocking down walls and others 'melling', or hammering, the rubble into material for road-making. Charles Sr. was 'sent for' at the Gas Works and the body removed to Loch-head Distillery.[789]

Stewart, Agnes — see 'Hugh Mitchell #1'.

Stewart, Galbraith & Co., Ltd was set up in 1891 by a consortium, headed by Duncan MacCallum (q.v.), to operate Scotia and Glen Nevis distilleries as a joint-stock company. The first subscribers, all but one of them living in Campbeltown, were: Duncan MacCallum, distiller; John Marshall Horne, merchant, Glasgow; Thomas Lambert Brown, distiller; Daniel Mactaggart, solicitor; John Norman Mactaggart, solicitor; and Alexander Duncan, bank agent.[790] The company was voluntarily liquidated in January 1922,[791] two years after MacCallum established a new consortium, West Highland Malt Distilleries (q.v.).

Stewart, Isabella — see 'Peter Gilkison'.

Stewart, James, one of the founding partners of Scotia Distillery, died at his home, Craigbank, on 15 January 1895 at the age of 87. He had been remarkably prominent both in civic life and in the affairs of the whisky industry.

He served for almost 40 years on the Parochial Board,

with responsibilities in poor relief, housing and burial-grounds, and was for 19 years — 1848 to 1867 — a Town Councillor, occupying, for 16 of those years, the prestigious office of Dean of Guild. He was instrumental in founding the Campbeltown Savings Bank in 1859, and, in his capacity as a director, was in attendance every Saturday night 'to receive the savings of the working classes', for whom the bank was 'specially designed'. In politics he was a 'staunch Liberal' and in religion he was attached to Longrow Church.

Stewart was chairman of the local Distillers' Association from its formation in 1848 until his resignation in 1874, and, to mark his long service, he was given a 'banquet' in the White Hart Hotel and presented with a large portrait of himself, painted by an English artist, James Bright Morris (1844-1912), who attended the event, along with representatives of all the local whisky firms.

The *Argyllshire Herald* report of the presentation, for all its length, contained remarkably little biographical content on Stewart, but, if the testimony of the oldest distiller present, John Ross (q.v.), is to be believed, Stewart dedicated his life to the service of the community and to making people happy. He never married, but appears to have had what might be described as a magnetic personality. Ross had 'heard some very powerful preachers, but he questioned if he had heard anyone more powerful than our own worthy Dean'. Stewart was evidently especially popular with women. Ross: 'After a wedding or party of any kind, the ladies would be talking over the amusing incidents and saying, "Oh! The Dean, the Dean — what fun we had with the Dean!" In those days, the word "Dean" acted like an electric shock. It would send a thrill of delight through a whole legion of young ladies.' It may be conjectured what 'fun' the presumably chaste and devout Dean might have enjoyed in the present social climate of religious decay and moral laxity!

The painting, described as 'a speaking likeness of Mr Stewart', was restored in 2014 by the Friends of

Campbeltown Museum and hangs in the Burnet Building, while a full-scale reproduction is displayed in Glen Scotia Distillery tasting-room and shop. Stewart was said to have prized the portrait very highly 'until the day of his death', and it was left to his brother William's daughter Jeanie, with the stipulation that it 'should be retained in Campbeltown'. Among other items she inherited were a portrait of Stewart's mother, presumably the one which hangs eerily in the background of his own portrait, and a photograph of his friend, John Galbraith (q.v.). She also received the extraordinary sum of £500 for the sole purpose of maintaining his grave and gravestone 'in good order and repair as long as she lives'.[792] He left £350 to four local charities.

He was, an obituary stated, 'highly esteemed by his brother-distillers in the town, as being a very able and accurate businessman, and was on several occasions chosen as a delegate to represent them in London when important questions affecting their trade were at issue and before Parliament'.

At the time of his death, he was the 'oldest surviving ex-director' of the Campbeltown Steam Packet. His first term as chairman came in 1865, and in 1867 he was on the Steam Packet's paddle-steamer *Gael* when, on her trial run, she achieved a speed of 18 knots between the Cloch and Cumbrae light-houses.

He was already retired from business when, in October 1894, he was 'prostrated by a serious illness from which he never recovered'. Between one and two o' clock on the afternoon of his funeral, the Town Hall bell and the bell of Longrow Church were tolled, and throughout the day flags flew at half-mast from vessels in the harbour.[793]

James's death certificate reveals that he had been paralysed for four months and also suffered from apoplexy and aphasia (loss of speech). His parents were recorded as Peter Stewart, 'joiner', and Janet McMurchy. Peter, who died in 1825, is described on the family gravestone in Kilkerran as a 'wright' and in *Pigot's Directory* of 1825 as a 'carpenter' and ship-owner. The great size of the tombstone, which has four panels, suggests that he was a wealthy businessman. Peter's parents were William Stewart and Mary Langwill, which places the Stewart family in the Lowland camp, at least by marriage and association.

Stewart, Peter, was the main partner in Peter Stewart & Co., Caledonian Distillery, which he founded in 1832 with his brothers William and Edward. Eighteen thirty-two was also the year in which his brother James (above) founded Scotia Distillery; but Peter's involvement in distilling was, unlike James's, not marked by success. He was described as 'Distiller' when he married Margaret Langlands in 1836, but his gravestone in Kilkerran has him as 'agent for the Campbeltown Steam Packet Co', his subsequent identity. In fact, in 1841, 10 years before Caledonian was liquidated, when Stewart baptised his daughter Janet on 21 March, he was 'Manager of Steampacket coy'. Margaret's father, William Langlands, land-surveyor, was a brother of Ralph Langlands, Dalaruan Distillery, and her cousin Jackie Langlands married Peter Watson (q.v.). Peter Stewart died, aged 66 — of 'epilepsy, 9 months' — on 4 June 1868, at McLean Place, Main Street. His daughter Sarah, who died in 1915, was 'travelling secretary' for the Young Women's Christian Association, a post which took her all over Scotland addressing meetings, and she was 'deeply interested in temperance work'.[794]

Taketsuru, Masataka, pioneering Japanese malt whisky-distiller, spent part of 1920 in Campbeltown in the final stage of his mission to penetrate the mystique of the Scottish distilling craft. In 1919, a course in organic chemistry at the University of Glasgow was followed by spells at several Scottish distilleries before he arrived in Campbeltown, in May 1920, with his wife, Kirkintilloch-born Rita Cowan, to conclude, at Hazelburn Distillery, his voluntary apprenticeships. Back home, he established Japan's first dedicated whisky distillery on the cold, remote coast of Hokkaido Island, which he reckoned provided the closest natural conditions for replicating Scotch whisky.

In the summer of 1981, a Japanese journalist appeared in Campbeltown looking for 'some facts' about Taketsuru's stay in Kintyre all of 61 years back. He was lucky: Roy Allan, manager of Springbank, took him to Mrs Flora Gillies, who had been secretary and cashier at Hazelburn and remembered Taketsuru's visit to the distillery. The manager, Peter M. Innes (q.v.), 'showed him round, explaining in detail the process involved in making whisky'.[795]

Mrs Gillies was interviewed again in 1986 — for the third time, she said — when Manichi Film Productions from Japan arrived in Campbeltown. The team of photographers and researchers found four persons in town who remembered meeting Taketsuru and his wife: Mrs Gillies, Alex Colville, who was also employed in Hazelburn Distillery at the time, and Mr and Mrs Peter Stuart Armour (p 11). Muriel Armour's father, Thomas Mair, was lessee of the White Hart Hotel, in which the Taketsurus stayed during their time in Campbeltown. She remembered a racist incident, when a couple of other guests in the hotel complained about the Taketsurus' presence. Mair's response, his daughter said, was: 'If you object, you can get out.'[796]

Talisker Distillery. In 1878, Talisker Distillery in Skye advertised in Campbeltown for 'an Energetic Man having a general knowledge of Distillers Work, and who can do a little Coopering'. In 1897, the distillery was seeking a 'Brewer, Tunroom Man, Foreman and two Under Maltmen, Under Cooper and a Carter'. Interested readers were invited to apply to the distillery manager with references and 'wages expected'.[797] Such appeals were not unusual in Campbeltown newspapers, but the extent of the need, in this case, was.

Taylor family. James Taylor, a mason, was one of four partners in Kirkwood, Taylor & Co., which built Meadowburn Distillery in 1824. He later bought Loch-head Distillery with his son William and ran the business as William Taylor & Co. In 1811, Taylor married Ann MacNab, daughter of Archibald MacNab, dyer. (Her sister Anabella married William Johnston, maltster, in 1821.) In 1836, he took the lease of Upper Ranachan, which is now known as 'High Ranachan' and is one of the cluster of farms, in the hills north of Campbeltown, owned by Paul McCartney. He soon afterwards 'built an entirely new steading' on the farm, but there is no evidence that he lived there. In Census 1841 he was at Lochend, Campbeltown, with his sons William and Archibald. He was described as a 'builder', as was Archibald, aged 20; William, 25, was a 'distiller'. In 1842, his daughter Margaret married an Excise officer, Thomas Place.

Several weeks after James's sudden death at the age of 61 in November 1847, his son William applied for a five-year extension of the Ranachan lease. Since only he and his brother Archibald could 'undertake the management of Ranachan' — the rest of the family were 'minors' — and since they were 'fully engrossed' in the business of Loch-head Distillery, he asked to be allowed to sub-let the farm.[798]

William would die in 1851 at West Kilmichael,[799] a farm on the outskirts of Campbeltown, of which he had taken a 19-year lease in 1841. His trustees, who renounced the lease in the year after his death, were his brother Archibald, distiller, William Watson (q.v.), merchant, James Stewart (q.v.), distiller, and Charles Munro, lawyer.[800]

Archibald Taylor put Loch-head on the market in 1854. He died on 4 February 1857 at Lochend. In his death notice he appeared as 'Mr Archibald Taylor, Esquire, Architect'.[801] In 1841 he had described himself as a 'builder', but at that time builders generally also designed the structures they were contracted to erect, and he may later have decided to elevate his status. In a plan of ground held in lease by John Grant (q.v.) and dated 1845, the 'architect' was A. Taylor.[802] He was referred to disparagingly in 1851 as a distiller who is 'moreover a kind of Architect and engineer but in truth knows little about it'. [803]

Temperance Movement — see 'Total Abstinence'.

Templeton family — see 'Drumore Distillery'.

Thistle Distillery — see 'Mountain Dew Distillery'.

Thom, John, was Collector of Inland Revenue in Campbeltown — the top job — for some 20 years until his retirement in 1874, when he returned to his native Rattray, in Perthshire, on a full pension. His retirement was less comfortable than it should have been, for his savings were 'swept away' by the City of Glasgow Bank crash in 1878. He was a 'zealous and devoted Free Churchman', and, during his time in Campbeltown, was a member of Lochend Free Church, in which he was an elder, Sunday school superintendent and treasurer. In 1866, he delivered a lecture on astronomy to the Free Church Young Men's Literary Association. His only son followed him into the Inland Revenue Service, and in 1876 his only daughter, Ellen, who predeceased him, married William McNaughton Love, a Campbeltown-born merchant with interests in London and Melbourne. He died at Rattray, aged 76, in 1887.[804]

Thomson, Hugh, succeeded his father Samuel (below) as manager of Glen Scotia in 1937, but his employment was broken by the Second World War, and in 1949 he resigned to run Robert Armour & Sons (q.v.). He died in 1983, aged 70. For a fuller account of his life and career, see *Glen Scotia Distillery: A History*, pp. 43-44, from which the following account (pp. 35-36) of his wartime experiences is extracted.

In June 1940, Lieutenant Hugh Thomson, 201st (Campbeltown) Anti-Tank Battery, Royal Artillery, was captured at Saint-Valery-en-Caux in France and would endure almost five years' imprisonment in an *Oflag* (officers') camp at Laufen, near Salzburg, Austria. He and his fellow-prisoners were marched there through France, Belgium and Holland. When he returned home in May 1945, his account of his experiences was terse. There were, he said, several attempts to escape from *Oflag* VIIC, but only two succeeded and he 'felt disinclined' to reveal the methods of escape. He did, however, express his gratitude to the Red Cross and other local organisations for packages of food and clothing received, without which 'conditions would have been very hard'. During his incarceration, he engaged in 'educational studies'.

He also spoke of a book which he had sent home from the camp. It was an account of his column's march into captivity, compiled by Lieut. Leslie C. Hunt of the East Surrey Regiment, and illustrated with pictures sketched *en route* by 'artistic members of the party'. On the fly-leaf of the book were two stamps: one designating the camp and the other confirming that the manuscript had been passed for publication, on 7 July 1941, by the Press and Censorship Bureau.

Thomson, Samuel, who died on 21 July 1957, at the age of 76, was born in Dalziel, Ayrshire, the son of a boot-maker who later moved to Campbeltown with his family. Samuel joined Stewart, Galbraith & Co. in January 1897, and remained with that firm, ultimately as a director, until its liquidation in 1919. When West Highland Malt Distilleries (q.v.) was formed, he became the firm's office manager. After the collapse of the distilling industry in Campbeltown in the 1920s, he was retained by Duncan MacCallum and managed the remains of the business: Scotia, as a working distillery, and Ardlussa and Glen Nevis as bonded warehouses. He was a pall-bearer at MacCallum's funeral and an executor of his estate. When Bloch Brothers bought the business in 1933, after MacCallum's death, Samuel was retained yet again, and effectively remained with that company until his retirement in 1956 (but see 'Glen Nevis and Ardlussa Warehouses Ltd.')

He was a member of Campbeltown Town Council from 1931 until his resignation in 1933. Recreationally, he was closely associated with Campbeltown Football Association and was a keen bowler with competitive successes to his credit. After he retired, he and his wife, Elizabeth, a daughter of Alexander McMillan (q.v.), moved to a cottage in Southend. He was survived by Elizabeth, a daughter, and sons Alan and Hugh (above). For a fuller account of his life and career, see my *Glen Scotia Distillery: A History*, pp. 38-39.

Toberanrigh Distillery appears to have existed for fewer than 30 years. It was built in 1834, at 48 Longrow, by Alexander Wylie (q.v.), on land leased in 1819 to James Ferguson, cooper, and assigned by him to Wylie in 1824. Wylie was granted additional ground by the Duke of Argyll in 1837,[805] presumably for expanding the distillery, and was later joined in the business by his son John (q.v.). In 1851, the distillery lease was bought by John Mitchell, distiller, Hugh Ferguson, baker, and Daniel McMurchy, cooper. John Mitchell (q.v.) was a son-in-law of Alexander Wylie — he married Mary Wylie in 1839 — and a brother-in-law of William McKersie #1, whose wife was Jane Mitchell and whose daughter Mary married Alexander Wylie's son John (q.v.). Alexander immediately got a sub-lease of the distillery, which suggests that he resumed its management. He died in 1862, which was about the time the little distillery ceased production. The name represents Gaelic *Tobar an Rìgh*, 'The King's Well', significance unknown.

Total abstinence may be preferred to 'Temperance', which implies moderation. In March 1904, a local newspaper reported that the local lodge of the Good Templars now had

500 members, below which item was noted the export of 13,000 gallons of whisky on the steamer *Kinloch*.[806] The co-existence of an ardently teetotal association and a booming whisky industry found expression in 1876 when the Good Templars' Hall, with bowling-green attached, was built directly across the road from Hazelburn Distillery. (The hall was demolished in 2003 and the distillery became a 'business park'.)

In 1851, while stationed in Kintyre with the Inland Revenue, John Murdoch (q.v.), who would later rise to prominence as a radical land reform campaigner, addressed the Campbeltown Temperance Society on the subject of 'Temperance and Money' — see Appendix 5.

In 1856, an 'Edinburgh Gentleman' reported that there were no fewer than a hundred public houses in Campbeltown and that 'in many of the streets every third shop is a whisky store'.[807]

In 1857, when Patrick Murray, Helensburgh, married Janet McMurchy, milliner in Campbeltown, at Burnside Chapel, 'The festivities [were] celebrated on the Total abstinence principle'.[808]

William Hunter Jr., son and brother of distillers — see 'Lochside Distillery' — but himself an ardent teetotaller, in 1866 delivered an 'interesting and humorous' speech to the local Annual Temperance Festival, in which he ridiculed the 'many dodges practised by parties going to drink together, as if ashamed of it, trying to get into public houses without being seen'.[809] For his like-minded daughter, Isabella, see below.

In 1891, the organising secretary of the British Women's Temperance Association (Scottish Christian Union), Miss Wallace, denounced 'Whiskyopolis' as 'a source of much evil, sin, misery and wretchedness', and claimed that, on a visit to Campbeltown, she 'could see the evil in the town as she entered it'.[810]

A Campbeltown minister, Rev D. F. Mackenzie, in 1889 delivered controversial opinions on the Campbeltown whisky industry to a meeting of the Highlands and Islands

Committee of the Free Church in Edinburgh. There was more whisky made in Campbeltown than in 'any other part of Scotland', but he was glad to say that 'temperance sentiment there was stronger than in any other town in Scotland, or out of it'. While whisky-drinking in Campbeltown was decreasing, he was sorry to say that the making of whisky was not. He regretted that 'last year the revenue of this country was helped from Campbeltown alone by a sum of no less than £675,000'. This might suggest that Campbeltown was very wealthy, but 'the wealth was very much restricted to a certain class of the community, and they were not of the Free Church'.[811]

The president of the local branch of the British Women's Temperance Association during the Great War was Isabella Hunter, wife of Archibald McTaggart (p 119). Both her grandfather, William Hunter, and her uncle, Peter Hunter, were involved in the distilling business, but her father, William, a watch-maker, had been a public advocate of total abstinence and a prominent Good Templar, and Isabella had clearly followed his example. In 1916, at a monthly meeting of the Association, she quoted a statement attributed to David Lloyd George at the start of the Great War, 'We are fighting Germany, Austria, and Drink, and, as far as I can see, the greatest of these deadly foes is Drink', to which she added her own plea: 'Our British Women's Temperance Association and other kindred societies are all continuing to fight the common foe. In this warfare we shed no blood, nor burn down houses, nor destroy property, and we are most anxious to get the young people to join our ranks.'[812]

Train, Thomas, a wholesale wine and spirit merchant in Glasgow, headed Thomas Train & Co. until his death on 7 June 1883. He died at 10 Berkeley Terrace, Glasgow, but his birthplace, Innean Mòr, was an unsanitary thatched steading on the rugged Atlantic coast between Machrihanish and the Mull of Kintyre, and he happened to be the last person born there, on 2 December 1818. The

Kintyre Way hiking trail passes through the ruins of his birthplace, from which may be seen Rathlin Island and the North Antrim coast and Islay and Jura.

Thomas was a grandson of a shepherd from Carmichael in Lanarkshire, Thomas Train, who settled in the Mull of Kintyre *c* 1775, and a son of Thomas Train, shepherd, and Janet Campbell. In Census 1841, he was a 22-year-old 'merchant' lodging in Back Street — later more stylishly renamed 'Union Street' — with one Susan McNair. His future wife, Mary Ann Gilkison, born in Campbeltown in 1820, was living nearby in Longrow with her parents, John Gilkison, merchant, and Martha Langwill. She and Thomas married in 1845 in Gorbals, Glasgow, and they were there, in 2 Apsley Place, when the 1851 census was taken. He was a distiller's agent and they had a four-year-old son, John Gilkison Train, who would become a Presbyterian minister and end his career in Southend, Kintyre, where he died in 1920. Thomas's entry into the whisky business may have been facilitated by his brother-in-law, Peter Gilkison (q.v.), a founding partner in Lochside Distillery.

From 1856 until 1873, Thomas was treasurer of the Kintyre Club, at the annual dinners of which 'The Bonnie Green Braes o' Kintyre' — composed in 1811 by John Wilson, Paisley, whose mother was Agnes Train[813] — was a favourite song. The first verse mentions his grandfather, the earliest Thomas:

Ye low country swains, extol your green plains,
Your towns and your cities admire;
I'll skip o'er the main and I'll spier [ask] for Tam Train
And the bonnie green braes o' Kintyre.

Given his shepherding background on the Mull of Kintyre, Train may have been a Gaelic speaker; certainly, he attended a 'Gaelic lecture' on Highland superstition at the Choral Hall in Glasgow in 1872, delivered by the noted scholar, Rev Robert Blair. James McWilliam, who was certainly a Gaelic speaker — see 'J. & J. McWilliam' — was also in the audience.[814] Thomas was succeeded in the business of Thomas Train & Co. by another native of South Kintyre of mixed Gaelic and Lowland parentage, David MacDonald (q.v.).

Union Distillery adjoined Campbeltown Distillery in Longrow, hence, perhaps, the name. John Mactaggart (q.v.) leased a house and ground at the head of Longrow in 1806, on which he built Campbeltown Distillery in 1817, and he proposed to erect another distillery at that same location in 1826,[815] which may be accepted as approximately the year Union was built. John died in 1832 and by 1834 the distillery was being operated by Mactaggart & Henderson, comprising John's son Charles (q.v.) and Hector Henderson (q.v.), who leased the premises from Charles. On 1 December 1835, the distillery was sold to John Grant & Co., partners Charles Kelly (q.v.) and John Grant (q.v.),[816] who was a brother-in-law of Charles Mactaggart. In 1849, after Grant's death, Kelly and George Melville (q.v.) offered his representatives £1,000, 'exclusive of debts', for his two-thirds share of the business, which was accepted. These representatives, acting on behalf of Isabella Grant and her children, were her brother, Daniel Mactaggart (q.v.) and her brother-in-law, James Grant, ironmonger in Campbeltown,[817] who had married Eliza Hunter, daughter of an Ayr inn-keeper, in 1822; but Glen (p 156) reckoned that Union Distillery ceased production c 1850, the year after Kelly and Melville bought out Isabella Grant.

Wallace, Robert, an Inland Revenue officer, spent the greater part of his life in Campbeltown. Both he and his wife, Agnes Galbraith Macdonald, were born in Ayr. When he died in 1910, aged 72, he had been 37 years in Campbeltown and seven years retired. Remarkably, apart from a brief initial spell at Springbank, he spent his entire career in Campbeltown attached to one distillery, Rieclachan, and was 'Chief Excise Officer' there in 1885 when Barnard called. Two of his daughters married into local whisky families: Christina, known as 'Teenie', married John Colvill #3, and Agnes married James Greenlees #3. His son, Robert Hugh, oil merchant in Glasgow, died in 1907, aged 32, at the family home in Dell Road. Robert Sr. was survived by his wife, who died in 1928, and five daughters. Politically, he was a Unionist and he served on the Town Council for six years.[818]

Water, one of the fundamental ingredients of whisky, was required by the distilling industry in huge quantities. Barnard mentions two wells bored on the site of Scotia Distillery to tap underground springs and to supplement the water from the town reservoir at Crosshill, which, from his descriptions of the 20 other distilleries, was clearly the primary source of water. These two wells at Glen Scotia are still in existence, but unused.[819] Eight other distilleries are noted as having a well or wells on their premises — Argyll, Benmore, Dalaruan, Dalintober, Glenside, Kinloch, Kintyre and Longrow — and, in the case of Benmore, the 'springs inside the work' were the only sources of water. At Lochhead, a stream ran through the premises, and Barnard identified the main supply for Glenside as 'Aucholochie Loch at the back of the Distillery'; but Auchalochy, in the northern hills, was far to the back of the distillery! It would become the town's main domestic water source 65 years later.

In May 1876, a select committee of the House of Commons met to discuss the Campbeltown Harbour and Burgh Bill, one of the main issues in which was water supply. Much of the evidence taken by the committee dealt with the testy relationship between the Duke of Argyll, who owned Crosshill Reservoir, and the Town Council, and the distilling industry was naturally represented.

The first witness was Charles Mactaggart, town clerk and son and grandson of past distillery-owners. He stated that the population of the town in 1871 had been 6,688 and was now about 8,000. There were 20 distilleries. In 1875, the quantity of proof gallons produced was 1,636,484; in

1865, 1,140,946; and in 1855, 1,014,800. If all the whisky made in Campbeltown were charged with duty, he said, it would yield £880,000 to the national revenue; duty was not, however, charged on the whole, because some of the whisky was exported and some sent 'under bond' to London and elsewhere. The amount of duty actually paid in town in the previous year, 1875, was £489,561; in 1865, it was £416,104; in 1855, £213,495; and in 1845, £132,085.

Construction of Crosshill Reservoir began in 1848 (two years after the lease was granted) and was completed in 1852, but in 1866 a six-inch pipe remained the only means of supply from the reservoir, though population and industry had steadily grown. The number of water-taps in town in 1859 was 192 and by 1875 was 1,006. The water was of poor quality and was periodically infested with red insects. The distillers paid the Duke 2d per 1,000 gallons, which earned him, from the 72,000,000 gallons used, an annual income of £600, but they also obtained water from 'private wells', and their annual consumption totalled about 150,000,000 gallons.

Duncan Colville, managing partner of Reid & Colville, Dalintober Distillery, said that it took about 100 gallons of water to produce one gallon of whisky. Dalintober Distillery obtained additional water from a well and, by 'gravitation', from 'a neighbouring hill'. In wet weather, these sources were adequate, but in dry seasons the distillery was wholly dependent on Crosshill water, 'and we do not get so much as we require ... Crosshill water is unsuitable for washing'. Under examination, he admitted: 'The reason we never formally complained to the Duke's chamberlain was because we found from experience that our best interests were secured by simply taking whatever supply was allowed us, and being thankful.' When Charles C. Greenlees, Dalaruan Distillery, was pressed for his reasons for not complaining, his reply, which prompted laughter, was: 'Well, the supply might be cut off altogether!'[820]

In 1877, a year after that enquiry, Crosshill Reservoir was operating with 'improved pressure', and a 'gravitation Water

Works' had been ceremonially opened at Loch Ruan, north of Campbeltown, to supply the population of Dalintober.[821] In 1884, a water-filter was installed at the Crosshill storage-tank, which measured 30 by 7 feet.[822] The Loch Ruan tank, on Auchinbreck farm at the top of High Askomil, was 56 by 25½ feet, with a capacity of 27,126½ gallons. Its roof was wrecked in a gale in November 1880.[823]

Until a new and more capacious reservoir at Auchalochy — which neighbours Loch Ruan — became productive in 1950, Crosshill, bought from the Duke of Argyll in 1945, for £17,000, before the 99-year lease ran out, was the main source of water for Campbeltown. Auchalochy Reservoir, in its turn, was created when Crosshill could no longer supply the water requirements of a rapidly modernising society; but Crosshill remains the source of water for the town's distilleries by reason of its being free from chemical treatment.

From an unknown date, the field on the north side of Crosshill Reservoir was left uncultivated in the interest of protecting its water from agricultural contaminants. In 1917, Campbeltown Town Council dealt with a letter from the Board of Agriculture — which was concerned with increasing wartime food production — enquiring why the field was 'in pasture' and not being cultivated.[824] From 1934, the tenant of Crosshill Farm, John Currie, was paid £4 a year by the Council for 'allowing his field draining into Crosshill Loch to remain uncultivated'.[825] The issue of water purity came up again in 1955, when the Council rejected an application from the Kintyre Fish Protection and Angling Club to add calcium carbonate to the reservoir, 'in the belief that this would improve the stock of trout'. A letter from Springbank Distillery, endorsed by Glen Scotia, argued that 'the proposal would alter the character of the water completely, and, in so doing, would affect their product deleteriously'.[826]

The quantities of water required by the town's whisky industry may be judged by the fact that of three 10-inch diameter pipes ultimately laid to conduct the water from Crosshill Loch, two were for the distilleries and one for the general population.[827] In 1955, when a burst pipe damaged the road surface at the junction of Main Street and Lorne Street, it was identified as 'the older of the two known as the "Distillery Mains"'.[828]

A small circular reservoir north of Crosshill, and now behind the houses on the lower end of Ralston Road, was said to have been formed in 1825 (or 1816, according to another source). Its water came from a nearby hill called Barley Bannocks and was led to the well at the town's market cross in Main Street by a 3-inch pipe.[829] That reservoir, which is now an overgrown swamp known as Taddy Loch, was erroneously described, in a caption in *The Distilleries of Campbeltown*, as 'the main source of water for the town's distilleries'.

In March 1898, an unidentified distiller had casks of water carted from Tangy Loch, in the hills north of Campbeltown. He was anticipating a water shortage later in the year and tried a 'mash, brew and distillation' using the water. The quality of the product was judged to be 'encouraging',[830] but no more was heard of the experiment.

Watson, Peter (1808-64), of Peter Watson & Co., Mountain Dew Distillery, was a merchant and Lloyd's insurance agent in Campbeltown, whose partner in the distilling venture, William Watson,[831] may have been his father, who died in 1846, or his brother. His wife Jackie (1810-67) was a daughter of Ralph Langlands — see 'Dalaruan Distillery' — and Jean Fleming. He was for many years a Town Councillor and in the year before his death was appointed a Bailie.

His obituarist referred to his 'excellent business talents and self-denying energy', but paid particular tribute to his conduct as Lloyd's agent, which involved dealing with shipwrecks: 'In sailors and emigrants he took a special interest, and many widows and orphans and emigrants in far distant climes could tell of his kindnesses to them in the hour of need.'[832] His father was William Watson Jr., merchant, insurance agent and the Provost of Campbeltown from 1833 to 1836. His brother James, a merchant in Havana, Cuba, died in 1848, aged 38. Another brother, William, who died in 1865, was a merchant and agent in Campbeltown for the Commercial Bank of Scotland, whose daughter Annie was the mother of the famous Scottish Colourist S. J. Peploe (1871-1935).[833]

Weir-Loudon, David Nisbet, was the sole surviving son of the Rev Walter Weir, whose family was decimated by diphtheria in 1863 (p 96). When his mother remarried, David's stepfather's surname, Loudon, was added to his birth name. David's sister Jessie Eliza married Samuel Greenlees — see 'Greenlees Brothers' — and David later married Samuel's sister Isabel, in 1898 in Bearsden.[834] They appear in Census 1901 at Muneroy House, Campbeltown, with baby Hamish and two domestic servants. Described as a 41-year-old 'bonded store-keeper', he must have been in the employ of Greenlees Brothers. He died at Glenadale, Campbeltown, on 25 June 1931, aged 73. Curiously, neither his death notice nor his obituary mentions his wife or first son, though they are buried with him in Kilkerran; she died in a Glasgow nursing home in 1934 and Hamish died at Westminster Hospital, London, in 1944.

David Weir-Loudon's obituary states that he went to Canada as a young man and engaged in ranching until compelled, for health reasons, to return home. Thereafter, he was 'for many years ... associated with the management of Argyll Distillery' (owned by Greenlees Brothers). In his youth in Glasgow he was a 'footballer of recognised ability' and a runner 'of note', and in retirement he was an enthusiastic bowler; indeed, he played on Stronvaar bowling-green on the day of his death.[835]

His second son, Norman Greenlees Weir-Loudon, who used the surname Loudon, was born in Campbeltown in 1902. Norman Loudon became a wealthy businessman and film producer, and founded Shepperton Studios in 1931. With his uncle, Samuel Greenlees, he was prominent in the London Argyllshire Association.[836]

West Highland Distillery, built in 1830, stood in Argyll Street, on the site of Ramsay Place (erected in 2008 on the site of a demolished garage). Its malt-kiln was across the street, behind the present Barochan Place, with access from Castlehill, through an entrance known as 'Doctor Rowatt's Close', after a local physician, Charles Rowatt (q.v.). (Rowatt's property was replaced c 1842 by Fleming's Land, built by Captain John Fleming, who, in retirement, after a distinguished career in the Royal Navy, bought Muasdale and Glencreggan estates.)[837] The founding partnership was Andrew & Montgomery, being Archibald Andrew (q.v.) and Andrew Montgomery (q.v.), both born in Southend. For these partners, however, distilling was a passing interest, subordinate to agriculture. In 1853, when Archibald Andrew took a 19-year lease of North and South Killocraw farms, he was identified on the lease as 'Distiller, Campbeltown', but it seems likely that this move signalled the end of West Highland Distillery, which Glen (p 156) reckoned went out of business between 1852 and 1860.

West Highland Malt Distilleries. In November 1919, a new company, West Highland Malt Distilleries Ltd., was formed under the Companies Consolidation Act, with its headquarters at 106 West Nile Street, Glasgow, and capital of £150,000 in £1 shares. Described as a 'private company', it was created to 'acquire the undertakings' of Scotia, Glen Nevis, Glengyle, Kinloch, Dalintober and Ardlussa distilleries, and to 'carry on the business of distillers, etc.'

The subscribers were T. L. Brown, distiller, 38 York Place, Edinburgh, and Alex J. Wightman, merchant, 106 West Nile Street, Glasgow, and the directors:

Thomas W. Dewar, distiller, Harperfield, Lanarkshire;
Duncan MacCallum, distiller, East Cliff, Campbeltown;

Alex C. Robertson, distiller, Sandhills, Monkton, Prestwick;

Thomas L. Brown, merchant, Caledonia Hotel, Edinburgh (as above, subscriber);

Major Alex Wightman, M.C., merchant, Bellevue, Troon (as above, subscriber);

James Duff, merchant, 18 Eglinton Drive, Glasgow.[838]

All, except Duff, were members of the Kintyre Club (Appendix 1).

One of the directors, Duncan MacCallum (q.v.), had been instrumental in setting up the earlier consortium, Stewart, Galbraith & Co., Ltd. (q.v.), which was liquidated in January 1921.

whisky, the word, represents Gaelic *uisge*, which is 'water', but there is, of course, more to whisky than that! The full form is *uisge beatha*, 'water of life', which equates with Latin *aqua vitae*.

Whisky Enquiry (1891), The. Three Campbeltown men gave evidence in 1891 to the parliamentary enquiry into the bonding, blending, sale and use of British and foreign spirits: James Dunlop #2, William McEwing (q.v.) and James Greenlees of Greenlees Brothers (q.v.), a whisky-blender and merchant, and co-owner of three Campbeltown malt distilleries.

The evidence of Greenlees on whisky-blending is of interest for its insights into the theories and practices of the time; and his judgement that 'The taste for milder whisky is increasing enormously' might have sounded a warning to the Campbeltown distillers, whose products — described as 'potent, full-bodied, pungent' by Aeneas MacDonald in his *Whisky* (1930) — would ultimately fall from favour in blending. (But his opinion on the paramount role of water in the character of malt whisky is no longer accepted):

'In Scotland, the manufacture of each particular district has its own peculiar flavour, principally caused by the water used in distillation, and to arrive at a thoroughly palatable and perfect Scotch whisky it is necessary to take the products of the various districts and blend them in certain proportions so as to get the required flavour. The taste for milder whisky is increasing enormously, and it depends on the experience of the blenders, and the nature of the whiskies, and the tastes of their customers, as to the character of the whisky to be produced. The public like an old whisky with less flavour, and a blend is made more palatable by using a little grain spirit. Supposing you make a blend of fine malt whiskies without grain, unless they had been blended for a very long time you could always detect the different whiskies. That is if you had a very expert taste. You make them milder by putting in a very small amount of grain spirit, and you cannot then detect them. Grain spirit is enormously used in blending for the purpose of mellowing it down to suit the taste of the customer, and also as a question of price ...

'I estimate [Greenlees Brothers'] trade for consumption as follows: — 5 per cent under two years old, 10 per cent between two and four years old, 20 per cent between four and five years old, 50 per cent between five and seven years old, 15 per cent between seven and twelve years old. The increase in the consumption of old whisky has been most marked of late, and it is within my own knowledge that there are many licensed victuallers in London who supply Scottish whisky over the counter, the age of which ranges from 6½ to 12 years.'

He also addressed the issue of warehouses, complaining that his company's plans to increase its accommodation in Campbeltown, by building a warehouse on cleared ground, had been rejected by the Commissioners of Inland Revenue, whose own officers complained of 'the difficulty they experience in examining casks at Hazelburn and Argyll distilleries in consequence of the number of casks in the warehouses'. The Greenlees warehouses in Campbeltown were all full and the proposed new warehouse would have relieved the pressure. He concluded: 'I consider it a very great hardship to distillers that they should be denied facilities for building warehouses in districts where ground and labour are cheap, thus compelling them to forward their goods to large cities, such as Glasgow or Edinburgh, where the cost of bonding is infinitely greater. The warehouse which we proposed to erect in Campbeltown would amount, with interest and depreciation of buildings, to an annual rent of £300, whereas our rent in Glasgow is at present £1,255.'[839]

'Whisky Panic, The'. In March 1854, an anticipated rise in the duty on spirits resulted in the sale of 'quantities of spirit greater than we ever witnessed'. In the space of five days, about 60,000 gallons of whisky were shipped from Campbeltown in the *Celt* and *Duke of Cornwall*. The panic, however, was unnecessary: duty remained the same in the budget. In 1855, an 'alteration of the duty on spirits' on 3 October precipitated the export of about 30,000 gallons of whisky to Glasgow, Paisley and Ayr on the following day: 'The lower end of the quay was literally covered with puncheons, there being not fewer than 250. The steamer being unable to take so many at once, a number were left over.'[840]

Whisky, theft of. Histories of the distilling industry tend to concentrate on the manufacture of whisky, the distilleries which produce the stuff and the qualities of the individual products — a blend of factual information coloured with an infusion of romance and mystique. The social history of the distilling industry isn't quite so romantic. Many distillers became very wealthy, built mansions on the shores of Campbeltown Loch — well away from the hub of their prosperity and the squalor which surrounded it — and enjoyed the trappings of that prosperity: a luxurious domestic lifestyle, servants, fancy yachts, foreign holidays, and the rest.

The living conditions of the majority of their fellow-townsfolk were very different. Many families lived in cramped, unsanitary housing, on low wages or no wages; and poverty, hunger and destitution were rife. Alcoholism, the disease of temporary solace and escape, was a social problem — arguably, it still is, albeit with a less visible public face — as court reports in local newspapers demonstrate, week after week, in the late 19th and early 20th centuries.

The abundance of whisky in distilleries and, more especially, in warehouses, was a constant temptation to men with a craving for alcohol. In 1922, for example, a cargo of 2,240 barrels, or about 124,000 gallons, of Speyside whisky, worth nearly a million pounds, was shipped into Campbeltown for Mackie & Co., producers of the *White Horse* blend. Eight special trains were required to carry the consignment from Craigellachie Distillery to Lossiemouth for shipment in the steamers *Avington* and *Royal Firth*. That load of whisky was destined for just one warehouse.[841]

The catalogue of whisky thefts from Campbeltown distilleries and warehouses in Appendix 3 contains relatively few prosecutions of distillery employees caught stealing from their workplace. Pilfering, however, was common, but on such a small scale that management might overlook it.

John McKersie (q.v.), a partner in Lochruan Distillery, was evidently not of that mind, more especially when theft involved damage to equipment. At the trial, in 1871, of John McFadyen, who pled not guilty to boring a hole in a pipe from a still to the spirit-safe, and extracting spirits from it, McKersie testified that, in March, he had 'warned the men against taking away whisky', after a hole was discovered in the pipe and plugged. When a second hole was found, he and his mashman, Archibald MacPherson (q.v.), 'set a watch' on the night of 4 April. They saw McFadyen enter the distillery by the back gate, lie below the pipe and hold a jug to the hole. At that point, the two detectives sprang from cover. When McKersie hailed him with 'Halloa, McFadyen!', his response was, 'It's the first time I was caught stealing whisky,' to which McKersie replied, 'It will be the last here'. He was jailed for three months.[842]

In the matter of theft, there was no latitude from Excise officers, who were tasked with ensuring that no whisky left any distillery without duty being paid on it. Not all distillery employees were thieves, of course, and those who were would probably have objected to being described as such: their reasoning would have been that they were merely removing minuscule amounts of spirit from an immense stock of the stuff, much of which would be lost, anyway, by natural evaporation: the hackneyed 'angels' share'.

In warehouses, whisky was often extracted from casks using a bottle with a string attached to the neck. The bung, or stopper, of the cask was first prised off and the bottle was lowered into the cask and filled. This tool was known both as a 'dooker' (Scots, 'ducker') or 'plunker' (Scots, 'dipper').[843] The next stage in the operation was to get the whisky off the premises without attracting the attention of the ever-vigilant Excise officer attached to the distillery, and many stories were told of the ingenious tactics devised to elude detection.

There were several names for newly made spirit, of which 'maloogrum', of uncertain derivation, is the most memorable.[844] This veritable fire-water was unquestionably consumed more for effect than flavour, but to improve the taste and add colour, sugar could be burnt in a pan and mixed in it. Of 'still whusky', as he termed it, local author, artist and musician Jack McKinven remarked that it would 'burn a hole in a goblet'.[845]

The wash, or fermented wort — known locally as 'pook'[846] — was also in demand, but it was freely available to workers, within the premises, as Archibald MacPherson (above) explained in 1871: 'They could drink wash; it is quite open to them; some men drink it.' Another workman at Lochruan, John McIntyre, agreed that 'some men take wash', but added that it was 'not so intoxicating as whisky' and that, in order to get drunk, 'their bellies would be very fou [full] with it'.[847] For theft of wash from distilleries, refer to 1869 and 1880 in Appendix 3.

'Bunging' or 'mooking' was largely confined to Campbeltown Quay and involved extracting the dregs of whisky — and also beer — from barrels unloaded from ships for uplifting or left for shipping out. This practice was rife and many men were prosecuted for it, some repeatedly. It was a highly dangerous practice, because the nature and strength of the residues were unknown. Several deaths occurred, including that of James McDougall in 1884. He and some other men had been 'tapping barrels' on the Old Quay on a Saturday night and had decanted an unusually large find of 'impure whisky' into a small keg which they had found on the quay. The keg had contained tobacco juice for sheep-dipping and the mixture was toxic. The following morning, all the drinkers 'showed symptoms of a very alarming nature', and McDougall, before he died, was in a 'state of *delirium tremens*'.[848] McDougall's wife, Isabella McLean, was admitted to Campbeltown poor house about a year and half later. Her entry in the register described her husband as a 42-year-old fisherman when he died on 1 November 1884. They had three daughters and a son, who was born 39 days after his father's death. Isabella's mother was dead and her father, a fisherman, was homeless.[849]

whisky tours. The guided tour is now a vital part of the malt whisky business, not least in the opportunities afforded distilleries for direct sales, but public access to distilleries is of relatively recent origin. Perhaps the earliest tour in Campbeltown took place in April 1957, when a party of 25 foreign students spent a week in town on a 'vacation course' organised by the British Council and a visit to Glen Scotia was one of the many organised events. Thirty-three years on, in 1990, the concept of the tour, let alone the visitor centre, as a marketing device and an arm of the tourist industry, had still to emerge in Campbeltown. Even so, the manager of Glen Scotia, Charles Paterson, revealed that he had been asked by many visitors to see the distilling process, and had conducted parties of English, French, German, Canadian and American tourists around the distillery.[850]

Wright, Gordon Mitchell, featured in the *Campbeltown Courier* of 6 May 1916 as 'Private Mitchell Gordon Wright' of the Highland Light Infantry, severely wounded in May 1915 and visiting friends in Campbeltown during his slow recovery. He was a son of John Bennett Wright, a Glasgow merchant who married Martha Mitchell, daughter of John Mitchell (q.v.), in 1881, and was enrolled seven years later in the Kintyre Club. Gordon Mitchell Wright was also a Kintyre Club member; when enrolled in 1904, his address was 100 Huntingdon Road, Cambridge. His marriage in 1924 was reported in the *Campbeltown Courier* under the weak headline 'Interesting Wedding in London'. His bride, Georgina Briggs Constable, belonged to a landed Fife family: her late father was W. Briggs Constable of Benarty. The bridegroom's father, too, was dead, but his mother Martha was described as 'of 18 Royal Terrace, Glasgow, and Ardmore, Campbeltown'. The best man was C. B. Sherriff (see 'J. B. Sherriff & Co.'). When G. M. Wright died in an Edinburgh hospital on 18 August 1960, he was chairman and managing director of J. & A. Mitchell & Co. Ltd. He was survived by his wife and two sons,[851] one of whom, Hedley (below), took charge of the family business.

Wright, Hedley Gordon, tall, kilted and full-bearded, was an unmistakable figure wherever encountered. He was born in Cambridge on 7 March 1931,[852] a son of Gordon Mitchell Wright (above) and a great-grandson of John Mitchell, co-founder of Springbank Distillery. In 1967, as a director of both J. & A. Mitchell & Co. Ltd. and Eaglesome Ltd., he was one of just 10 candidates in the U.K. and Europe awarded the Diploma of the Oenological Research Laboratory. He explained to a local newspaper reporter that there 'was nothing extraordinary in combining interests in whisky and wine, since his family owned the famous Glasgow wine merchants, Bennett & Company, who were large wine importers and bottlers'.[853] Mr Wright, however, has seldom been as publicly forthcoming; self-publicity is assuredly not his style, and all credit to him in this age of rampant media intrusion and instant internet judgement. The whisky writer, Jim Murray, remarked of him obliquely in 1997 that his 'idiosyncratic personality has ensured that his particular operation has always been just a little detached from the rest of the industry'.[854] He set up the Hedley Gordon Wright Trust 'to benefit the people of Campbeltown, specifically those with a musical talent',[855] and has for long been a benefactor of Campbeltown and its people. He is listed as having directorships in five companies, all with charitable status: Kilkerran Developments Ltd., Olivia Bennett Ltd., J. & A. Mitchell & Co. Ltd., William Cadenhead Ltd. and Springbank Distillers Ltd.[856] He has an M.A. degree and has described himself in company documents as a geologist. His essays, 'A Note on Campbeltown and the Distilling Trade' and 'Scotch Whisky Distillers of To-day: Springbank Distillery, Campbeltown', were published together in *The Wine and Spirit Trade Record* of April 1963.

Wylie, Alexander, was a founding partner in Rieclachan Distillery in 1825, and in 1834 built Toberanrigh Distillery, in which his son John (below) became a partner. He was a son of John Wylie, farmer, who died in 1797, and Helen Wilson, at Ranachan, in the hills to the north of Campbeltown, and now owned by Sir Paul McCartney. Alexander's first wife was Isabella Ferguson, whom he married in 1816; when he married Agnes Colville in 1829, he was nearly twice her age. In Census 1841, his age is given as 66 (which was correct) and Agnes's age as 35. They were in Longrow with 10 children, of whom David was the youngest, at a month, and John, 'Distiller' — a son by his first marriage — was the oldest at 20 years. Alexander was still going strong in Longrow when the 1861 census was taken, and described himself as a 'Retired Distiller'. He died the year after. His death certificate recorded his age as 87 and the cause of death as bronchitis. Daughter Mary married John Mitchell (q.v.) in 1839; daughter Isabella married John King, baker in Campbeltown, in 1851; and in 1852, at Harlem, Winnebago County, Illinois, second son James married Jane, eldest daughter of William Greenlees, farmer in Ardnacross, Kintyre.[857]

Wylie, John, son of Alexander (above), died in Dalintober on 5 March 1891, aged 74. He was 'most part of his career in the counting-house department of Rieclachan Distillery', of which he was a partner, and was latterly in the office of the Steam Packet Company.[858] In the Campbeltown Old Parish Registers, John was a 'Distiller' in 1852 and 'Merchant' in 1854. In Census 1871, he was a 'Distillery Manager'. His death certificate described him as a 'clerk' and gave the cause of death as a malignant stomach ulcer. He left a widow, four sons and one daughter. His wife Mary, whom he married in 1842, and who died in 1899, aged 83, was a sister of William McKersie #1.

Appendix 1

Distillers with membership of the Kintyre Club

The Kintyre Club was founded in 1825, 'for social and charitable purposes', by twelve Glasgow merchants of Campbeltown origin: John Anderson, Andrew Campbell, John Campbell, John G. Campbell, James Galbraith, Archibald Harvey, Thomas Harvey, Alexander Johnstone, John Ker, Daniel McLean, Daniel Niven and James Reid. The membership list, as published in 1928, in *The Kintyre Club: Rules and Roll of Members*, more than a century later, reads as a 'who's who' of the Kintyre landed and business elite, but included others whose connection with Kintyre was peripheral or conjectural, such as Calvert Worthington, brewer in Burton-on-Trent (1864). Only members who identified themselves as 'distillers' have been listed below, along with the year of their enrolment. Unless otherwise stated, their addresses were in Campbeltown. Some members with distilling interests, such as John Galbraith (q.v.), were otherwise identified (he was 'ex-Provost'), while members in related businesses and professions, such as grain merchants and agents and collectors of Excise are omitted. In general, however, individuals whose main, or only, business interest was in whisky-distilling appear to have identified themselves as 'distillers', because the designation was not without social status. The largest surname group in the list below is Greenlees, with 10 members, and the Greenlees total in the full list is a staggering 55. The Kintyre Club was dissolved in 1981, by which time its function as a charitable organisation was no longer relevant. An excellent history of the Club by Hugh Ferguson appeared in *Kintyre Magazine* No. 10.

James Armour, 1847; Thomas L. Brown, Edinburgh, 1903; G. Mackie Campbell, Monkton, Ayrshire, 1927; David Colville, 1878; Duncan Colville, 1854; Matthew Colville, 1859; Matthew Colvill, 1888; Thomas W. Dewar, Glasgow, 1909; James Dunlop, 1859; George Ferguson, Glasgow, 1878; James Ferguson, 1845; Arthur H. Gardiner, 1899; Peter Gilkison, 1835; Robert Glen, Glasgow, 1890; W. M. Gordon, Glasgow, 1921; John Grant, 1833; Alexander Greenlees, 1865; Archibald Greenlees, 1848; Charles C. Greenlees, 1851; Daniel Greenlees, 1833; James Watson Greenlees, 1868; Robert Greenlees, 1845; Robert Greenlees, 1848; Samuel Greenlees, 1860; Samuel Greenlees, London, 1878; William Greenlees, 1877; James Harvey, 1860; Robert Hunter, 1860; Robert Johnstone, 1837; Charles Kelly, 1837; Duncan MacCallum, 1878; Archibald McCorkindale, 1835; William McEwing, 1878; Alexander MacKelvie, 1860; Archibald McKersie, 1860; John McKersie, 1866; William McKersie, 1835; William McKersie, 1870; Sir Peter J. Mackie, Glenreasdell, Kintyre, 1921; Duncan McKinnon, 1828; Donald McMurchy, Melbourne, 1861; John McMurchy, 1840; Alexander Mitchell, 1876; Archibald Mitchell, 1878; Hugh Mitchell, 1878; John Mitchell, 1840; William Mitchell, 1848; James M. Orr, Glasgow, 1881; John M. Orr, 1870; Robert L. Orr, 1879; David Ralston, 1833; A. C. Robertson, Monkton, Ayrshire, 1921; John Ross, 1846; Thomas A. B. Sheriff, Glasgow, 1910; James Stewart, 1835; William Taylor, 1833; Alex James Wightman, Glasgow, 1921; Harry A. Wilson, Glasgow, 1909.

Appendix 2

Distilling-related accidents

1854. John McEachran, Glenside: had a leg broken when his horse ran off in Kirk Street and a cart-wheel ran over him. *CJ* 18/5

1856. Henry McCrorie, Hazelburn: his neckerchief caught in moving machinery while he was oiling it, and he required the amputation of two fingers and a thumb. In 1871, 'having his hand disabled', and his wife Isabella Duncan being 'in bad health', he was admitted to the poor roll on 4s a week. *AH* 30/5/56 & 16/3/71

1856. Unnamed workman, Meadowburn: rendered unconscious by fumes when he climbed into a tun before it had been cleaned and ventilated. *AH* 5/12

1857. Gilbert McMillan, Lochruan: a limb 'severely' injured by part of a fly-wheel which disintegrated and struck him as he was passing an engine. *AH* 6/11

1859. 'Mr O'Donoghue', Inland Revenue officer: fell through a 'hatchway' in Longrow and broke an arm. *AH* 23/9

1863. Angus Galbraith, Longrow: struck by a windlass and knocked unconscious while helping hoist bags of grain up to a malt-kiln. *AH* 2/10

1863. Archibald Fullarton (q.v.), foreman mashman, Scotia: his cravat got tangled in machinery which he was oiling, and but for the intervention of a workmate, who stopped the engine, he would have been strangled. *AH* 20/11

1865. Duncan Loynachan (q.v.), Campbeltown: a foot 'severely bruised and mangled' in the fly-wheel of an engine he was oiling. *AH* 9/12

1866. John Colville, Dalaruan: fell 'from a height' and broke a thigh-bone. *AH* 14/4

1866. William McKersie (q.v.), Albyn: a foot and arm scalded when the plank on which he was standing slipped and he fell into hot water. *AH* 12/5

1867. Donald McSporran: right hand 'fractured by machinery'. Admitted to poor roll on 13 August on 4s per week until 20 November. *RP* 453

1869. Duncan Loynachan (above), Campbeltown: 'severe internal injuries' after falling about 19 feet to the stone floor of the mash-house. *AH* 7/8

1870. Gavin Ralston, Kintyre: scalded in an empty tun when a fellow-workman, Donald McPhail, turned on a hot-water cock. He later died and McPhail was jailed for three months for culpable homicide. *AH* 3/8 & 8/10

1870. James Mitchell, Hazelburn: fatally 'suffocated' by gas in the 'jackback', when, despite warnings, he climbed into it to retrieve a fallen bag. *AH* 8/10

1870. Daniel McGrath, Loch-head: head crushed fatally while adjusting a fly-wheel. His widow, Mary McFarlane, 'burdened with three children under six years of age', was admitted to the poor roll on 4s a week. *AH* 10/12/70 & 14/1/71

1873. Lachlan McLachlan (q.v.), Dalaruan: had an ear 'split' and a thumb severed when his cravat caught in a roller, while oiling machinery. He was able to walk home, but died soon afterwards. *AH* 8/2

1874. John McIntosh, carter: had a leg broken when a 220-lb. sack of barley fell on him at Dalaruan Distillery. *AH* 24/10

1876. John Milloy, foreman maltman at Hazelburn: cut and bruised and one leg broken when his shirt caught in the shaft of moving machinery while oiling it. *AH* 27/5

1876. Donald McMillan, distillery carter: injuries to the head and limbs when the horse he was driving bolted and he fell off the cart, which ran over him. *AH* 17/6

1876. William Court, Excise officer, died from scalding injuries after falling into a large 'copper' of boiling water in Kintyre Distillery while avoiding 'cockroaches crawling about'. *AH* 16/9

1876. Edward McGeachy, Dalintober: legs severely scalded when he stepped into a mass of hot mash which he had been 'casting out of the tun'. *AH* 1/12

1878. Hugh Cook, Argyll: severely injured when he fell from a heap of draff and his face struck the iron teeth on the edge of the mash-tun. *CC* 6/4

1885. 'Mr Proctor', Inland Revenue, slightly scalded when the lid of a heater in Springside gave way and a leg slipped into the boiling water. *AH* 28/3

1886. Peter Pursell, Dalintober: fell from a 'trap' (ladder) while painting machinery and suffered head injuries and a broken arm. *AH* 23/10

1887. Hugh Hall, an 'old man', Longrow: died from head injuries after slipping and falling from the bonded warehouse roof he was tarring. *AH* 12/2

1888. A son of Donald McPhail, when sent 'to procure some hot water' at Glenside, took a dizzy turn, couldn't turn off the tap and was scalded. *AH* 21/1

1888. --- Graham, Glenside: missed his footing, fell and broke a leg. *AH* 4/2

1888. Duncan Paterson (q.v.), Meadowburn: found unconscious near a 'trap stair' and presumed to have fallen from an upper storey; he died the next day. *AH* 23/8

1890. --- Kelly, Kinloch: a compound fracture to a leg when he fell in a warehouse. *AH* 13/9

1891. Duncan McSporran, Glengyle: a compound fracture to a leg and 'severe internal injuries' when a wind-swung door knocked him to the ground floor while he was throwing bags out of a window in the third storey of the kiln. *AH* 28/3

1891. George Cook, Burnside: fell 10 feet in still-room and lay unconscious until discovered, when a doctor was summoned. *AH* 26/9

1893. Malcolm Mitchell, carter, Glengyle: fell between a barley steamer and the quay and sustained internal injuries. *AH* 24/12

1894. Dugald Smith, Glen Nevis: 'severely injured' when

an arm was caught between the stirring machinery of the mash-tun and a wall. *AH* 2/2

1896: John Taylor, Springside: fatally injured through the bolting of the horse of which he had charge at the coal depot in Argyll Street. *CC* 11/4

1899. William Rodgers, mashman, Ardlussa: fatally crushed when his clothes became entangled in 'the shaft which drives the rollers in the mill room'. *AH* 23/12

1903. William McAllister, 70-year-old brewer, Kinloch: fell from a ladder after helping lower casks of whisky by winch and chain from a warehouse loft to the ground floor. He died the following day from head injuries. *AH* 17/1.

1903. Daniel McTaggart, carter, Dalintober: bruised and shaken after a bag of grain came down a chute from a barley steamer and knocked him to the ground. *AH* 21/11

1904. Alex O'May, carter, Kinloch: a thigh-bone fractured at the distillery entrance, when he fell from the cart after a pig ran under his horse and it bolted. *AH* 10/12

1905. William Mason (q.v.), Benmore: fell 10 or 12 feet and landed on his head in tun-room. *AH* 20/7

1908. William Mason (above), Benmore: 'hurt at Distillery'. *RP 1965*

1908. Lachlan McCallum, Campbeltown: fell about 15 feet while closing a trap-door and sustained a compound fracture of the ankle. *CC* 17/10

1919. Peter Cook, Scotia: badly scalded when he fell into the worm-tub, the water in which was almost at boiling point. *CC* 20/3

1920. Donald McNiven, carter, Hazelburn: 'severely crushed' and had a thigh bone broken when his horse took fright and bolted as he was yoking it. *CC* 14/2

1920. John McKinlay, Hazelburn: found unconscious, with a serious head injury, on the floor on the still-house, and afterwards died. *CC* 15/5

1923. Malcolm McCallum, Hazelburn: fractured his right wrist and gashed his head when he fell about 20 feet while painting in the still-house. *CC* 25/8

Appendix 3

Whisky thefts

1862. Distillery workman, Malcolm McCallum, jailed for 60 days for having removed a quart of whisky from a spirit-safe in Rieclachan. *AH* 2/5

1869. Robert 'Dusan' McNeill jailed for 60 days after pleading guilty to the theft of half-a-gallon of 'wash' from Argyll Distillery. *AH* 27/3

1871. John McFadyen, Lochruan Distillery, jailed for three months for boring a hole in a pipe from a still to the spirit-safe and stealing whisky. *AH* 10/6

1876. About 35 gallons of whisky ingeniously siphoned from a cask in a Glenside Distillery warehouse, without the building being entered. *AH* 8/7

1876. The door of a bonded warehouse at Meadowburn wrenched from its hinges and a 33¼-gallon cask of whisky stolen. *AH* 16/9 & 11/11

1877. Duncan and Donald Smith, workmen in Burnside, jailed for four months for stealing whisky from the distillery. *AH* 14/7

1878. The door of a Glenside Distillery bonded warehouse 'wrenched open' and 'a small cask of spirits' stolen. The intact cask was later found concealed in a drain leading into the Mill Burn. *CC* 9/2

1878. Donald McPhail and George McNaughton jailed for a year for stealing whisky from Rieclachan. At McNaughton's house, police found a file and 41 keys, including 'skeleton' keys. *AH* 6/7

1880. John McPhee, Peter Loynachan, Donald Sinclair, Donald O'May and Alexander Colville caught by police in the tun-room of Glenside Distillery, after breaking in to steal 'wash'. *CC* 28/2

1892. Some whisky stolen from the bonded warehouse of Glen Nevis. Entry was gained by forcing the iron stanchions of a window with a large plank. *AH* 9/4

1896. Two unidentified workers at Argyll Distillery pleaded guilty to stealing whisky and were jailed for 20 days. *CC* 28/3

1896. A labourer fined £2 for stealing a pint of whisky from an unidentified distillery. *AH* 16/5

1900. William Colville, labourer, jailed for 7 days for being found in Hazelburn Distillery 'with intent to steal'. *AH* 1/9

1901. A bonded warehouse at Burnside Distillery broken into, two casks tampered with and about two gallons of whisky stolen. An attempt was also made to enter Albyn Distillery through one of the barred windows. *CC* 12/1

1901. William Colville, Peter McGill and John Bowie jailed for 14 days for stealing a pint of whisky from four casks in the yard of Hazelburn. *AH* 20 & 27/7

1905. Robert Ralston, caught by police with a can of whisky removed from 'empty' casks stored at the back of Hazelburn, was jailed for 20 days. *AH* 21/10

1916. George and William McAulay, Hugh Stewart and James Greenwood fined 5s, or five days' imprisonment, for the theft of whisky from casks in a field near Glenside Distillery. *CC* 27/5

1926. Three Campbeltown men tried on a charge of having broken into a warehouse in Longrow, belonging to John Ross & Co., and stolen 35 gallons of whisky. One of them, John Anderson, was jailed for two months. *CC* 30/1

1927. John Stalker, labourer, after a lengthy trial, found guilty of having attempted to break into No. 3 Bonded Warehouse, Albyn Distillery, and fined £6, with the alternative of 60 days' imprisonment. *CC* 16/7

1955. Colin McC———, cooper, and Gavin S———, maltman, fined £12, or 60 days' imprisonment, having been caught by an Excise officer with a bottle of 'concealed spirits' taken from a warehouse. *CC* 1/12

Appendix 4

John and Daniel Mactaggart and Customs, 1811

From Letter-books, Custom House, Campbeltown, 18 November 1811

Gentlemen,

I have been proprietor of one of the Greenock and Campbeltown Passage Boats for some years, and have done everything in my power to Suppress the Smuggling of Whisky. I have frequently seized Whisky belonging to passengers and gave it to the Custom house Officers, and when they were not at hand I have thrown it into the sea. I have seized Whisky in almost every possible shape that Whisky in skins could be placed upon a woman's person or concealed in bladders about her. I have seized bladders filled with whisky in the insides of fowls that passengers had for sea stores, in butter dishes, and bags with corn for fowls, and in almost every other case in which Whisky could be concealed. On one occasion a large skin filled with Whisky and dressed out like a child sucking its Mother's breast was seized on board the Vessel, but as I am afraid the ingenuity of the passengers may at times defy the strictest search I shall take it extremely kind that your Honours would allow one of Boatmen or Tidewaiters* to search the Caledonia along with me every time she sails from this Port, and I shall pay any compensation for their trouble that your Honours may think reasonable and proper. I have copies of the enclosed Bill placed up in the Cabin and Forecastle of the Caledonia, but the people who attempt to Smuggle are those who have nothing to lose, and I am therefore alone accountable for the consequences of their shipping Contraband Goods on board the Vessel. I however upon one occasion got a woman imprisoned for 2 days for concealing Whisky on Board the Packet.

I have been for some time indulged with one of the Boatmen of the Port to rummage the Caledonia along with me, but from a trifling difference with some of the Officers of the Customhouse I have been led to understand that if any Whisky be found on board of the Caledonia that she is to be detained, which would hurt me considerably.

From the number of people that always crowd on board at the time of Sailing I find it impossible to search the Luggage and persons of the passengers untill the Vessel be under way, when the hatches are opened and every package examined and thereafter the persons of the passengers as they go below, so that, between the shipping of the passengers and the searching of their Luggage and persons, as much Whisky may be found as would be sufficient to seize the Vessel. But I hope your Honours will be pleased to consider the Case and allow one of your Boatmen or Tidewaiters of this port to search the Caledonia every time she leaves this Harbour that can then be spared.

I smuggle none myself and am pretty certain that the Crew do not, so that it would be extremely hard for me to suffer for the misconduct of passengers who might be perfectly indifferent whether I lost the vessel or not.

I am, &ca, Signd Dan Mactaggart

*Customs officers who board ships to enforce regulations.

Commentary by Rev Fr. James Webb:

The above letter was forwarded to the Board [of Customs] in Edinburgh on Dec 5th by the Collector, Archibald Buchanan, and the Comptroller, Alex Beith. The Board's reply, 16 Dec 1811, signed by H. Osborn, Hen. Veitch, and L.H. Ferrier, instructed the Collector to inform Mr Mactaggart that 'it is his concern as much as it is the Duty of the Officers to prevent frauds against the Revenue', but that 'the Officers in accordance with their duty will concur with him on every proper occasion' in preventing such frauds, meanwhile the Officers are to conduct themselves with caution, temper and firmness.

The 'trifling difference' mentioned in par. 2 of above letter, which is dated 18 Nov 1811, must refer to the fact that proceedings against Daniel Mactaggart and John Mactaggart, father of Daniel Mactaggart, had been ordered by the Board of Customs in Edinburgh for alleged hindering and obstructing the Officers of Customs in the execution of their duty by seizing and throwing overboard a phial of whisky which the Officers had taken from a cask on board the Packet for the purpose of testing its strength. Also, they were under suspicion of misusing Excise Permits for the transfer of whisky from Campbeltown to Glasgow, a matter which many others in the town were also implicated.

The Collector reported to the Board, Dec 4th 1811, that, as the offence had been committed on the deck of the Packet, 'it falls to be brought before the Admiral Depute here who is Duncan Stewart and likewise a Justice of the Peace, whose Conduct in this latter Capacity is so recently before your Honours that it is not for us to decide further than what we have already stated'. The Collector therefore suggests that the case be 'brought before the Judge of the High Court of Admiralty at Edinburgh'.

Meanwhile, notice had been served on the Customs Officers at Campbeltown that 'I Daniel Mactaggart residing in Kirk Street of Campbn for John Mactaggart residing in the Longrow of Campbeltown' had instituted proceedings before the Justices of the Peace for restoration of 3 casks containing 32 gallons whisky seized by the Officers in September last, and for loss and damage sustained by the said Daniel Mactaggart.

The Board subsequently advised the Collector to intimate to the said Daniel Mactaggart that the three casks of whisky claimed by him would be delivered to him on condition that he withdrew his case against the Officers and desisted from all further proceedings. This appears to have been done.

The correspondence, attestations, etc., concerning these cases cover some 30 pages in the letter books. In this correspondence, John Mactaggart is described as a merchant and dealer in spirits, and his son Daniel as a Writer and Notary Public, and both were partners in the business and ownership of the Caledonia Packet.

It is evident from the accounts and figures given in the Customs Letter Books at this period that the traffic in smuggled, i.e. illicitly distilled, whisky was on an enormous scale and nearly everybody in the town and district was implicated in it from the Provost and Magistrates down. There are letters almost beyond number from the Collector to the Board complaining of the difficulty, and sometimes the impossibility, of securing a conviction in these cases from the Justices of the Peace, and nearly every letter from the Board authorising the Collector to institute proceedings for smuggling contains this or a similar phrase, 'provided you are satisfied that the Justices concerned are prepared to carry out their duty according to law'. In a letter from the Collector dated 20 Nov 1811, it is stated that the purpose of the misuse of Excise Permits is to enable merchants here to send illicit whisky to Glasgow 'where it brings from 17/- to 25/- p. Gallon whereas Glasgow Distilled Spirits is sold for about 9/- p Gallon'.

Copy of a document compiled in April 1960 by Rev Fr. James Webb, parish priest in Campbeltown and local historian, for Charles Mactaggart, solicitor in Campbeltown. From John Mactaggart, Campbeltown, 7 February 2019.

Appendix 5

John Murdoch (q.v.) on 'Temperance and Money' (1851)

At the regular fortnightly meeting of the Temperance Society held in the Burnside Chapel, on Tuesday evening, the 6th instant, Mr Murdoch delivered a lecture on 'Total Abstinence in connection with the pecuniary interests of Campbeltown', of which we give the following epitome.

Although he had consented to speak on the monetary bearings of the Temperance question, he held that no moral principle ought to be tried by a standard of money; that, whatsoever was proved to be good and true ought to be embraced, however unprofitable in a commercial point of view, and that the lucrativeness of an error ought to be no argument in its favour.

Every social, political and spiritual movement had been met by the adverse arguments, arising out of the pecuniary losses attending the changes produced by them. Christianity, eighteen hundred years ago, and Teetotalism now, were cases in point.

At the dinner given to the Duke of Argyll, in the Town Hall, on the occasion of his Grace's recent visit to this town, Mr [John] Galbraith had stated that the exchequer of this country derived a revenue of not less than £300,000 a-year from Campbeltown, in the shape of excise duties; a sum, the bare mention of which suggested that the locality must derive a vast amount of benefit therefrom.

The mere circulation of money, however, was not enough to confer a benefit upon the community. It might be circulated for ever in large sums and do next to no good. It must be distributed in the form of wages, ere it could benefit the people, and support the town, giving employment to labourers and custom to traders, the two classes whose prosperity was the life of society. This vast sum was sent off without the great bulk of the people being at liberty to finger it. Assuming that the whole of the duty derived from this article was two thirds of the price, we might add £150,000 to the sum already mentioned and find that the total amount which Campbeltown drew for spirits was £450,000 a-year.

Those acquainted with the town estimated that the average number of men employed at each of the 23 distilleries was 5, making a total of 115. These, at average wages of 12s a-week, received £3,588 a-year, being less than twopence half-penny a pound sterling, out of the £450,000. But, supposing that those establishments gave employment to as many more outside, as porters, carters and lumpers, and distributed among them an equal sum, it would increase the £3,588 to £7,176, and raise the share of the labourers to fivepence a pound, or three-halfpence a gallon. As some might think it but right to do so, the amount which the officers of inland revenue drew as salaries might be added, and thus make the total amount expended as wages, in connection with this branch of the trade of Campbeltown, up to £14,176 a-year, and showing the share of these two or three classes put together to be, at a liberal estimate, tenpence a pound sterling, or threepence for every gallon of spirits produced. In this way, the spirit-making business gave employment to about 230 operatives, and some 60 revenue officers, and the incomes of both went to support the rest of the community, who were engaged as shopkeepers, tradesmen and farmers.

Taking the familiar article of leather, about which there was but little mystery, it appeared that a medium hide, bought for 8 shillings from the tanner and currier, as upper and sole leather, increased in value by labour to 24 shillings, of which labourers received at least 8 shillings. This, made into 8 pairs of shoes of various sizes, leaving out the profits of the leather merchant and several other things, will give operative shoemakers, at the rate of two and sixpence a pair, twenty shillings, and increase the value of the article to 44 shillings, showing the labourer's share of the gross amount thus laid out upon the finished commodity to be above twelve shillings and eightpence half-penny a pound sterling.

The Campbeltown Journal, 15/3/1851.

Appendix 6

The Scottish Dried Grains Company factory in Campbeltown, 1894

On entering the work, which is a large building, two storeys in height, one is confused at first by the whirr of the machinery, which fills the entire structure from roof to floor, and even underneath, also the impossibility of getting a clear view owing to the air being thickly impregnated with the fine dust arising from the draff. But this soon wears away, as the noise, notwithstanding the large amount of machinery constantly in motion, is inconsiderable.

The company have entered into a contract with the Distillers' Association to take half of their weekly output of draff, and this is emptied into a pit at the north-west corner of the building. By means of an ingeniously contrived self-feeding elevator, it is conveyed in small quantities at a time into a channel about ten feet above the floor, along which it flows until it reaches two shoots, whose output is regulated by the man in charge. As it falls from the floor to there, it is wrapped in layers in canvas and put (13 or 14 at a time) into a powerful hydraulic press, where the water is pressed out. The draff is then emptied into a receiver, from which it is fed into an elevator which takes it to nearly the roof of the building. Here, the real process of drying and sifting begins.

As it emerges at the top of the elevator, it enters an open channel running nearly the whole length of the works, and in which is placed a continuous screw, revolving at a high rate of speed, which, while pressing the draff steadily forward, turns it swiftly round and round. In the centre of the works are placed three large drying machines, rising from the floor to a height of over 20 feet, and in connection with the trough or channel, above alluded to, are 'plungers' (one for each) which press a certain amout of draff at a time into the feeders of the machines, the surplus passing on and going down a shoot into bags to be carried back and restarted through the channel again.

In the drying machines lie the chief patents of the company, and of necessity our reference to these must be brief. The top part consists of a series of circular trays, about 9 or 10 feet in diameter, in which the draff rotates with an inward movement, passing successively downwards from tray to tray. It afterwards passes through a series of circular hot-air chambers, rather larger than the trays, and then, repeating the first process in other trays, emerges from an outlet at the bottom of the machine in a very hot and dry state into the trough with continuous screw, as aforementioned, from which the draff is lifted by a self-acting elevator into a sifting machine, screened from observation, which rejects the impure grain and passes on the finished articles into bags, which are carted away for export all over the kingdom.

About 280 tons of wet draff enters the works weekly, and after undergoing the process we have described this represents 70 tons of the prepared article. The motive power used is a large engine of 25 horse power, the boiler of which not only supplies water to drive the engine, but also steam for the grain-drying process, and economy is so far practised that the unutilised steam is condensed into water and used again for the boiler ...

To the east of the manufactury, a large two-storey store, measuring 95 feet long by 60 feet wide, is in course of erection, and the two flats of which, when finished, will be capable of storing 600 tons ... The works and machinery at Campbeltown are valued at over £6000, and the latter has been constructed according to the company's designs by Mr John Cochrane, engineer, Barrhead, while the hydraulic work is by Mr John Binnie, engineer, Glasgow. The entire building is fire-proof, the corrugated iron roof having been provided by Messrs Brown and Murray,

Possilpark, Glasgow. The structure was designed by Mr W. T. McGibbon, architect, 221 West George Street, Glasgow, and built by Messrs Robert Weir & Son, contractors, Campbeltown; Messrs Robert Armour & Son, Longrow, doing the plumber work. The local agent is Mr John C. Boyd, commission agent, Old Quay Head.

Edited from *Campbeltown Courier*, 24/3/1894

Appendix 7

Nineteen-twenties: the collapse

By the winter of 1925, merely eight out of the 22 pre-war Campbeltown distilleries were working, a meeting of the Town Council was informed,[859] and within 10 years that number would be down to two. The factors behind the catastrophic collapse of the Campbeltown whisky industry have been much debated. The main causes may be summarised thus:
1. National and world-wide economic depression.
2. In the USA, from 1920 until 1933, a total — even if ineffectual — prohibition on the production, importation and sale of alcoholic drinks.
3. The failure, by some Campbeltown distillers, to maintain the quality of their products.
4. Over-production.
5. In a market dominated by blended Scotch whisky, Campbeltown malts increasingly fell from favour as components in the blending process.
6. The buying up, by outside interests, of local distilling firms for their bonded stock and warehousing capacity and the closure of the distilleries themselves.

Factor 3. Hedley G. Wright (1963) maintained that some Campbeltown distillers, 'confident of their Glasgow monopoly, became careless and produced inferior spirit which they filled into poor-quality casks'. Their distilleries, he said, 'were the first to fail but ... they dragged almost the whole Campbeltown trade with them'. The late Alex Colville, a distillery workman who experienced the collapse and subsequently helped 'scrap' Argyll, Dalintober, Hazelburn and Lochruan distilleries, alleged that West

Highland Malt Distilleries' reliance on old casks for storing whisky, instead of sourcing new sherry casks, damaged the reputation of Campbeltown malts.[860]

Factor 4. Another Colville, Duncan #2, also experienced the collapse, but from the other side of the fence: he belonged to a prominent Campbeltown whisky family. He was a sound historian, and his assessment is worth quoting:
'... this seeming prosperity in the [1890s] had been fostered to some extent by an insidious evil which had created an artificial demand for whisky in all parts of Scotland. People unconnected with the distilling or blending trades began to speculate by purchasing whisky to hold for future sale. New distilleries were erected in the Highlands and new companies floated to build them. The inevitable result was over-production, followed by a drastic reduction in the output of many distilleries. In Campbeltown the output for 1900 was 668,473 gallons less than that for 1897, and it can readily be understood that a distillery is not likely to yield remunerative results unless working to full capacity.

'Another problem confronted the Campbeltown distiller. Originally [he] sold his whisky before it was made. Latterly, however, he began to find it more and more difficult to sell new whisky, and had to provide warehouses to store it in for several years until he could find a purchaser. This involved a much greater capital outlay, and with falling prices and a falling demand, it eventually made business more and more difficult for the Campbeltown distillers.

'... Artificial conditions arising from the First World War enabled some of the local distilling firms to dispose of their businesses to large firms operating elsewhere, whose natural policy was the closing down of redundant distilleries to enable others to be worked at a higher rate of output.'[861]

The Distillers' and Brewers' Magazine maintained in 1899 that Campbeltown distillers had 'never encouraged the speculative buyer' and that the bulk of their whisky went to 'those who were going to use it'.[862]

Factor 5. In September 1924, White Horse Distillers Ltd., Hazelburn Distillery, appealed to Campbeltown Town Council against a £928 rateable valuation of the distillery, draff factory and coal store.

Evidence was taken from Theo. P. Scott, company secretary. Campbeltown whisky, he said, was in 'very great disfavour with blenders, few of whom would buy it'. Consequently, while the industry was 'experiencing a boom' in the North of Scotland and in Islay, it was 'very seriously depressed' in Campbeltown. His company, with a 'highly trained sales organisation', could not sell Campbeltown whisky, and 'if they could not sell it, it would be difficult for anyone else to sell it. Blenders simply wouldn't have Campbeltown whisky'.

Scott went on to submit tables illustrating the market value of Campbeltown whisky, at various stages of maturity, in comparison with Speyside and Islay malts. No quantity was specified, but Hazelburn whisky distilled in 1922 was quoted at 8s, Craigellachie at 16s and Ardbeg at 18s 6d. At Hazelburn last season, only 10 'mashing periods' were worked, while a full working season was reckoned at 50 periods. His firm had recently attempted to sell Hazelburn, but had received no offers. Had an offer of £7,000 been received, the distillery would have been sold. He concluded: 'Experiments had been tried to remove the cause of objection to Campbeltown whisky, but so far no cure has been discovered.' These comments are significant, whatever the partiality of their source.

J. B. McClement, assessor for the burgh of Campbeltown, stated that in the previous year, 1923-24, Hazelburn had been valued at £1,020, or £92 higher than the rating in dispute. He disagreed that 'the present condition of the local distilling industry was sufficient ground for a reduction in the valuation for rating ...', basing his case on Court of

Session rejections of claims for reductions in valuations from the ship-building and engineering industries, in which 'conditions of trade' were 'admittedly bad'.

The valuation, after private deliberation by the Council's appeal court, was reduced from £928 to £750. The valuations of other distilleries were: Scotia, £388; Kinloch, £335; Glen Nevis, £500; Ardlussa, £212; Kintyre, £220; Rieclachan, £300.[863]

The only case heard by the Burgh Valuation Appeal Court in 1924 was that of Hazelburn Distillery, but, in the course of the hearing, particulars of several other Campbeltown distilleries emerged in the evidence of Glasgow surveyor and valuer, Robert Hendry, who had carried out valuations for the burgh assessor.

Archibald Stewart, solicitor for the appellants, asked Mr Hendry for the figures at which he valued certain distilleries, and received the following: Scotia, £7,733; Kinloch, £7,225; Ardlussa, £4,205; Glen Nevis, £9,721; Glengyle, £6,224. Mr Stewart then pointed out to him that these distilleries had 'recently sold' for: Scotia, £2,500; Kinloch, £1,500; Ardlussa, £1,500; Glen Nevis, £500; Glengyle, £350. 'Does that not in itself indicate a depression?' Mr Stewart asked. 'It does,' Mr Hendry agreed, albeit with reservations.

Earlier in the hearing, Stewart had memorably remarked: 'Campbeltown whisky refuses to blend. It preserves its individuality in any company. Like the Campbeltown people, it always comes to the top.' The comments were doubtless intended as humour, but, unfortunately for the Campbeltown whisky industry, they were not prophetic.[864]

Factor 6. Two years later, in 1926, at another Burgh Valuation Appeal Court, W. P. Lowrie & Co., owners of Lochruan Distillery, appealed for a reduction on their property from £792 to £250. The company, which also owned Dalintober Distillery as an adjunct to Lochruan, was represented by Robert Henry, surveyor and valuer (above), who bemoaned the state of the local distilling industry, which he reckoned had been 'declining for the past twenty years' and was now 'in a dying condition'. When questioned, however, by the burgh assessor, J. B. McClement, a rather different story emerged:

Q — Do you know that Messrs Lowrie bought Dalintober Distillery in 1923?
A — Yes.
Q — For what purpose?
A — I cannot answer that. It has been put to some purpose.
Q — Then presumably it was acquired as a commercial proposition?
A — No doubt.
Q — So there were prospects of commercial prosperity in 1923?
A — I believe it was bought for bonded stores. The firm have imported whisky there. They acquired the premises for the purpose of utilising the warehouses.
Q — So that the warehouses were valuable to them and are still?
A — Admitted.
Q — Can you tell me how many hundreds of thousands of gallons are stored there?
A — I have no information on that point.
Q — You can take it from me that there are round about 600,000 gallons of whisky stored there. Do you know that a rent is charged for the storage of spirits?
A — That is so.

McClement estimated that Lowrie & Co. had an annual revenue of about £2,500 from the storage of whisky, a steady income from 'a big empty shell where nothing had been doing for five years'. The appeal was refused.[865] By 1930, bonded warehouses in Campbeltown held about two million gallons of locally made whisky and about three-quarters of a million of Islay and other West Highland whiskies.[866]

This much may be added: Had the present tourism-driven market in single malt whiskies expanded half-a-century earlier than it did, it is certain that more Campbeltown distilleries would have survived; but in a market dominated by blending interests, Campbeltown whisky was clearly found wanting.

Appendix 8

Glenfyne Distillery

Glenfyne Distillery was the first and also the final of three names by which the distillery at Ardrishaig — the nearest to Campbeltown on the Argyll mainland — was known. It was founded in 1821 as 'Glenfyne' and then became 'Glengilp'.

In 1856, a 10-acre site on the estate of Auchindarroch, which was to be sold by public auction in Edinburgh, included Glengilp Distillery, a dwelling-house and other buildings; but the 'machinery and other moveable property' were excluded from the sale.[867]

The name became 'Glendarroch' in 1870 and remained so until 1887. In 1888, whisky from Glendarroch joined that of 14 other Scottish distilleries in what was described as 'the largest blend of whisky ever made in Scotland — perhaps in the United Kingdom'. There was one Campbeltown malt in the blend, that of Campbeltown Distillery, to which refer for more information on the experiment.

In 1887, when acquired by Scotch Whisky Distillers Ltd., the original name was restored. In December 1900, it was reported that Glenfyne had shipped more than 6,000 gallons of its whisky to Glasgow on the steamer *Minard Castle*, its greatest ever export. A 'scare about poisoned beer' was said to have increased the demand for whisky; in the previous week, the newspaper had reported 'further deaths from beer poisoning' in England.[868]

A fire which broke out at Glenfyne Distillery in December 1902 was brought under control before any serious damage was done. The blaze reportedly 'originated through the igniting of an accumulation of vapour from the whisky'.[869]

The distillery manager in 1905 is known to have been John Campbell, for in June of that year he married Catherine Carmichael in Glasgow.[870]

By 1919, Glenfyne — 'which has been silent for a long time' — had been bought by a new company and was 'now in full activity'. Its water supply came from Loch a' Nighean, at the foot of Cruach nam Breacan, and the new owners were contemplating harnassing the stream for powering machinery and generating electricity.[871] By 1929, the distillery had 'not worked for some time',[872] and it closed in 1937.

References and Notes

1. *The Wine and Spirit Trade Record*, 14/6/1923.
2. *CC* 5/6/1920.
3. *CC* 6/4/1979.
4. *CC* 10/5/1927 & 12/5/1928.
5. *CC* 11/2/1954 & 7/4/1955.
6. DR/4/8/9.
7. KEL, p 148.
8. DR/4/8/9.
9. KEL, p 130C.
10. *AH* 20/4/1867.
11. *AH* 17/1/1880.
12. DR/4/8/19.
13. *AH* 30/11/1867.
14. *CC* 28/12/1929.
15. *CC* 8/12/1877, *AH* 6/4/1878 & *CC* 6/9/1879.
16. *CC* 6/9/1879.
17. *AH* 15/12/1883, 'The Destructive Gale'.
18. *CC* 5/1 & 27/9/1924; Glen, p 153.
19. *AH* 9/1/1897.
20. *AH* 24/12/1887 & 11/8/1888.
21. *AH* 17/12/1892.
22. *AH* 17/10/1896.
23. *The Wine and Spirit Trade Record*, 14/3/1923.
24. *CC* 13/9/1919.
25. *The Wine and Spirit Trade Record*, 14/3/1923.
26. *CC* 10/8/1929.
27. *AH* 9/11/1860 & 20/2/1863.
28. RP 1291.
29. *CC* 24/6/1988.
30. *CC* 8/9/1955.
31. *AH* 6/12/1873.
32. *AH* 7/8/1875.
33. *CC* 6/3/1926.
34. A. Martin, *Kintyre Country Life*, p 44.
35. *AH* 24/10/1874.
36. *AH* 13/5/1859.
37. *AH* 20/2, 10/4, 24/4, 22/5 & 19/6/1863.
38. *AH* 14/5/1870.
39. *AH* 3/1/1874.
40. *CC* 22/3/1879.

41. *AH* 18/4/1885.
42. *AH* 20/1 & 19/5/1894.
43. Copied in *CC* 10/4/1897.
44. *AH* 9/3/1878.
45. *AH* 6/2/1892.
46. *CC* 30/9/1933.
47. *CC* 26/2/1898.
48. *AH* 25/11/1864.
49. *CC* 10/3/1877.
50. *AH* 5/3/1881.
51. *AH* 14 & 21/2/1891.
52. *AH* 27/10/1906.
53. A. Martin, *Fish and Fisherfolk*, 2004, p 169.
54. *CC* 5/2/1916.
55. *CJ* 4/8/1853 & *AH* 9/8/1861.
56. *AH* 5/9/1862, 28/8/1863 & 4/9/1869 & *CC* 26/8/1876.
57. *CC* 23/4/1964 & 7/1 & 18/11/1965.
58. *AH* 4/3/1876.
59. *AH* 22/3/1879, obituary.
60. A. Martin, *Kintyre Families*, p 3.
61. *AH* 22/3/1879.
62. *AH* 4/2/1859.
63. *AH* 25/1/1861.
64. *AH* 30/12/1864.
65. *AH* 5/4/1879.
66. *AH* 26/8/1899.
67. *CC* 18/1/1913.
68. *Ibid.*
69. *AH* 22/8/1868.
70. *CC* 7/2 & 10/4/1920.
71. Glen, p 154.
72. *CC* 2/5/1936.
73. *CC* 5/2/1953.
74. *AH* 14/1/1871.
75. *AH* 19/4/1879.
76. *AH* 21/6 & 28/6/1879.
77. *AH* 17/12/1881.
78. *AH* 4/9/1886.
79. A. Martin, *Glen Scotia Distillery: A History*, pp. 32, 33, 34, 35, 37 & 39.
80. *CC* 13/2/1969 & *CJ* 13/10/1853, 'To the Spirit Trade'.
81. DR/4/8/19.
82. *AH* 18/10/1861.
83. DR/4/8/19.
84. *AH* 29/8/1864.

85. *AH* 5/3/1870.
86. DR/4/8/6.
87. A. Martin, *Glen Scotia Distillery: A History*, p 34.
88. *The Wine and Spirit Trade Record*, 8/5/1905.
89. DR/4/8/26.
90. AP Bundle 1940.
91. Colville 1923.
92. *AH* 13/10, 3/11, 1/12 & 8/12/1888.
93. *AH* 24/9/1881.
94. *AH* 11/8/1866.
95. *CC* 19/5/1989.
96. *AH* 6 & 13/9/1873.
97. *CC* 5/12/1936.
98. Colville 1923.
99. DR/4/8/26.
100. DR/4/8/19.
101. *CJ* 6/4/1851.
102. DR/4/8/19.
103. *AH* 8/10/1870.
104. *CJ* 19/2/1854.
105. D. Colville, *CC* 8/5/1937.
106. *Jim Murray's Complete Book of Whisky*, p 90.
107. *AH* 28/9/1901 & 12/10/1895.
108. A. Martin, *Glen Scotia Distillery: A History*, p 10, and *AH* 18/8/1866, 'Notes of an Excursion from Ayrshire to Kintyre'.
109. *AH* 12/2/1867.
110. *AH* 20/8/1870.
111. *CC* 6/3/1937.
112. *The Wine and Spirit Trade Record*, 8/5/1905.
113. *AH* 4/4/1862.
114. *AH* 27/4/1860.
115. *AH* 31/8/1860.
116. *AH* 18/7/1874.
117. A. Martin, *Glen Scotia Distillery: A History*, p 12.
118. *AH* 4/9/1875.
119. *National Guardian*, 25/9/1908.
120. D. Colville, *CC* 24/2/1923.
121. IMAP.
122. *AH* 20/11/1869.
123. *AH* 18/10/1873.
124. *AH* 24/3/1888.
125. *The Wine and Spirit Trade Record*, 8/5/1905.
126. *CC* 5/1 & 22/3/1924.
127. In *AH* 16/12/1905.
128. *AH* 15/10/1887.

129. *AH* 28/1 & 11/2/1888.
130. *AH* 12/1/1889.
131. *AH* 11/4/1896.
132. *The Wine and Spirit Trade Record*, 8/4/1905 & 8/5/1905.
133. *CC* 22/11/1962.
134. *The Wine and Spirit Trade Record*, 8/5/1905.
135. *AH* 26/11/1858 & a biographical sketch by Duncan Colville, dated 1934, from Alan Colvill.
136. *AH* 7/1/1871 & 22/6/1872, *CC* 22/6/1940, obituary of Margaret Colville, & *AH* 9/8/1861, from the *Fife Herald*.
137. *AH* 11/11/1865.
138. *AH* 4/9/1875.
139. *CC* 11/3/1916.
140. *CC* 18/2/1922.
141. *AH* 3/3/1883.
142. *CC* 8/7/1916.
143. *CC* 19/3/1927.
144. *CC* 15/7/1939 & 22/6/1940.
145. *CC* 24/2/1923.
146. *CJ* 18/12/1851.
147. Duncan Colville, family tree.
148. *AH* 23/4/1881.
149. *AH* 12/10/1860 & 11/4/1862.
150. Duncan Colville, family history, 1942, per D. Mayo.
151. *AH* 25/10/1905.
152. *CC* 27/2/1926.
153. *AH* 24/2/1860 & 22/8/1862.
154. *CC* 19/1/1946.
155. *AH* 28/11/1891.
156. *AH* 29/6/1895.
157. *CC* 8/12/1894.
158. *AH* 11/4/1903.
159. *AH* 18/6/1904.
160. *AH* 31/10/1908.
161. A. Martin, *Kintyre Families*, p 9.
162. DR/4/8/6.
163. J. H. Mackenzie, 'The Early Crafts and Industries of Kintyre', Part 2, *CC* 30/4/1938. James H. Mackenzie, who died in 1943, was a cooper and son of a 'master cooper', John Mackenzie. He retired from the business in 1932 to become librarian and museum curator in Campbeltown. His memoir of the Gallipoli campaign with the Argyll & Bute Mountain Battery was published in 1936 as *Crowded Hours* (*CC* 6/2/1943).
164. Largely from A. Glen, 'Coopers in Campbeltown', *The Campbeltown Book*, pp. 158-60.

165. *AH* 13/12/1873.
166. Copied in *CC* 10/4/1897.
167. DR/4/8/6.
168. DR/4/8/15.
169. E. R. Cregeen & A. Martin, *Kintyre Instructions*, pp. 120-22.
170. *AH* 12/11/1898.
171. *The Wine and Spirit Trade Record*, 8/5/1905, p 490.
172. *AH* 14/10/1864, 20/10/1877 & *CC* 24/4/1875.
173. *AH* 7/8/1880.
174. *AH* 4/7/1896 & *CC* 22/8/1896.
175. *AH* 2/2/1867.
176. *AH* & *CC* 23/12/1899.
177. DR/4/7/15.
178. *CC* 18/9/1926.
179. A. Martin, *Glen Scotia Distillery: A History*, p 5.
180. *CC* 9/3/1984 & B. Townsend, *Scotch Missed*, 1993, p 150.
181. *AH* 26/9/1856, Letter to the Editor.
182. *AH* 2/9/1859.
183. *CC* 17/5/1956.
184. Wm. Smith Jnr., *Views of Campbelton and Neighbourhood*, 1835, p 12.
185. *AH* 16/5/1862 & 21/10/1864.
186. *AH* 4/11/1859.
187. *CC* 23/12/1876 & *AH* 20/1/1894.
188. *CJ* 19/2/1853.
189. *AH* 19/2/1887.
190. *AH* 15/11/1884.
191. *AH* 11/4 & 18/4/1885.
192. *AH* 26/12/1885.
193. *AH* 13/11/1886.
194. *AH* 23/11 & 14/12/1889.
195. *Glasgow Herald*, copied in *AH* 2/9/1899.
196. *AH* 10/6/1871.
197. D. Colville, 'Trade and Industry', in *Campbeltown 1700-1950*, Campbeltown 1950, pp. 23-24.
198. *CC* 24/3/1894.
199. *AH* 20/1/1894.
200. *AH* 28/4/1894.
201. *CC* 8/5/1897.
202. *CC* 19/9/1903.
203. *The Wine and Spirit Trade Record*, 8/5/1905.
204. *CC* 29/3/1924.
205. *The Wine and Spirit Trade Record*, 14/12/1922.
206. *CC* 3/1/1931, 'Death of Mr Duncan MacCallum'.
207. *AH* 26/1/1867.

208. DR/4/8/19.
209. M. Borland, 'Templetons of Kintyre', *KM* 50, p 6.
210. DR/4/8/21 & 4/8/19.
211. *CJ* 23/5/1851.
212. F. Bigwood, *Justices of the Peace in Argyll*, 2001, p 121.
213. D. Colville, *CC* 9/1/1932, 'Burnside Independent Chapel, Campbeltown'.
214. *AH* 22/7/1871.
215. *AH* 21/2/1891.
216. *AH* 9/11/1901.
217. *CC* 15/8/1903.
218. *AH* 2/12/1859 & *CC* 28/7/1894.
219. J. Pacy, *Reminiscences of a Gauger*, the Campbeltown chapter of which appeared in *KM* 38, pp. 9-11.
220. *AH* 27/6/1874.
221. *CC* 22/3/1879.
222. *AH* 15/1/1887.
223. *AH* 16/9/1876.
224. *AH* 8/9/1932, 'Campbeltown Assessments in 1832'.
225. *Pigot & Co.'s Directory*, p 209.
226. *Pigot & Co.'s Directory*, p 222.
227. *AH* 2/9/1859.
228. *CC* 22/9/1923, 'Pages from the Past'.
229. *AH* 12/4/1884, 'Inland Revenue Grievances'.
230. *AH* 13/3/1886.
231. *AH* 24/6 & 12/8/1859 & 7/6/1861.
232. A. McKinven, *Kit and Caboodle: The Story of Football in Campbeltown*, p 15.
233. *AH* 13/11/1869.
234. *AH* 9/5/1891.
235. *AH* 20/1/1894.
236. *AH* 15/6/1867.
237. *AH* 11/11/1876.
238. *CC* 30/5/1903.
239. K. Holland, 'Customs and Excise', *KM* 2, pp. 18-19.
240. *CC* 22/4/1922.
241. *AH* 23/10/1857.
242. *AH* 13/1/1872.
243. *AH* 11/7/1874.
244. *CC* 11/1/1908.
245. *CC* 5/3/1921.
246. A. Martin, *The Place-Names of the Parish of Campbeltown*, 2009, p 52.
247. A. Martin, *An Historical and Genealogical Tour of Kilkerran Graveyard*, 2006, pp. 11-13.

248. *CC* 13/9/1930, 'A Bit of Old Campbeltown'.
249. *CC* 24/1/1920 & 15/6/1927.
250. *AH* 4/5/1901.
251. A. Martin, *An Historical and Genealogical Tour of Kilkerran Graveyard*, p 26.
252. *DR*/4/8/8 & 4/8/28.
253. *AH* 15/6/1878.
254. *CC* 21 & 28/5/1964.
255. *CC* 20/7/1918 & 24/5/1956.
256. *AH* 15/2/1902 & *CC* 22/5/1920.
257. A. Martin, *Glen Scotia Distillery: A History*, pp. 13-14.
258. J. H. Mackenzie, *CC* 12/6/1943, 'Campbeltown in 1811-1837'.
259. *CC* 15/8/1914 & 18/12/1926.
260. *AH* 27/9/1873.
261. A. Martin, *Glen Scotia Distillery: A History*, p 17.
262. *AH* 25/10/1855.
263. *CC* 17/7/1915.
264. *DR*/4/7/15 & *CC* 4/5/1940.
265. I. MacDonald, 'Kintyre Smugglers', *KM* 37, p 4.
266. *AH* 2/10/1875.
267. *AH* 6/4/1901.
268. *AH* 27/1/1906.
269. *AH* 6/1/1906.
270. *AH* 18/1 & 22/11/1873.
271. *AH* 10/1/1874.
272. *AH* 2/8/1873.
273. *AH* 17/6/1876.
274. *CC* 5/1, 29/3 & 27/9/1924.
275. *CC* 8/4/1925.
276. *CC* 11/9/1926 & 10/8/1929.
277. *CC* 6/1/1940.
278. *CC* 11/7, 19/9 & 26/12/1957 & 15/9/1960.
279. *AH* 24/4/1875.
280. *CC* 20/10/1877.
281. *AH* 8/6/1878.
282. *AH* 22/3/1890.
283. A. Martin, *Glen Scotia Distillery: A History*, pp. 21 & 26.
284. *CC* 5/4 & 27/9/1924.
285. *AH* 7/3/1896.
286. *The Wine and Spirit Trade Record*, 8/5/1905.
287. *CC* 3/7/1915.
288. *CC* 8/10/1949.
289. *CC* 12/9/1936.
290. R. Paterson with G. D. Smith, *Goodness Nose*, pp. 30-53.
291. *AH* 8/2/1856.

292. *AH* 26/9/1856, 'Letter to the Editor'.
293. Colville, 1923.
294. *AH* 14/2/1903.
295. *CJ* 18/3/1854.
296. *CJ* 13/10/1853 & 4/4/1854.
297. *AH* 8/5/1857 & 5/3/1858.
298. A. Martin, *Glen Scotia Distillery: A History*.
299. *CC* 28/5/1938.
300. DR/4/8/9.
301. National Records of Scotland catalogue, Campbeltown Sheriff Court, SC50/5/1851/1.
302. Colville 1923.
303. DR/4/8/26.
304. DR/4/8/16.
305. DR/4/8/9.
306. DR/4/8/26.
307. DR/4/8/23.
308. Glen, p 155.
309. *CC* 6/12/1930 & 19/9/1931.
310. *CJ* 18/8/1853.
311. *AH* 1/2/1873.
312. *CC* 10/12 & 24/12/1921 & 14/3, 11/7 & 3/10/1931.
313. *CC* 2/12/1971.
314. *CC* 21/2/1957.
315. *CC* 9/4/1927.
316. W. Crossan, 'Three Hundred Years of Education in Campbeltown', *The Campbeltown Book*, pp. 177-78.
317. *CC* 28/9/1929, 'The Late Miss Mary MacNish: A Link with the Disruption.'
318. *AH* 16/10/1868.
319. *AH* 30/11/1867.
320. DR/4/8/9.
321. *AH* 23/8/1861.
322. *AH* 17/1/1874.
323. *AH* 11/8/1888.
324. *AH* 7/11/1874 & 10/11/1877.
325. *AH* 14/1/1893.
326. *CC* 20/2/1937.
327. *AH* 28/5/1904.
328. *AH* 18/12/1863.
329. A. Martin, *An Historical and Genealogical Tour of Kilkerran Graveyard*, pp. 13-15.
330. *AH* 23/9/1871.
331. *AH* 22/8/1896.
332. *CC* 21/6/1879.

333. *AH* 13/3/1880.
334. *AH* 2/5/1885.
335. *AH* 16/11/1889.
336. *AH* 4/7/1891.
337. *CC* 19/11/1910.
338. *AH* 13/10, 3/11, 1/12 & 8/12/1888.
339. *CC* 19/5/1894.
340. *AH* 9/9/1916, 'Death of Mr James Greenlees'; *CC* 4/2/1939, 'The Late Mr Samuel Greenlees'; A. Martin, 'Notes on Greenlees Families', *KM* 67, pp. 17-18; R. Haydock, 'Argyll's Forgotten Whisky Barons', *KM* 67, pp. 13-17.
341. *AH* 20/5/1905.
342. *CC* 16/5/1908.
343. *The Wine and Spirit Trade Record*, 8/5/1905.
344. *AH* 15/2/1896.
345. *AH* 4/2/1859, 27/3/1863 & 29/8/1864.
346. Rev John Thomson, *AH* 9/7/1892.
347. *AH* 2/7/1892.
348. *AH* 2/11/1867.
349. *AH* 22/1/1870, 27/5/1876 & 31/1/1885.
350. *AH* 27/5/1882 & 1/9/1888.
351. *AH* 20/10/1888.
352. *CC* 7/8/1926.
353. *CC* 4/12/1926.
354. *CC* 23/2/1956.
355. *CJ* 12/11/1855.
356. *AH* 17/3/1858 & 8/8/1868.
357. *AH* 19/8 & 18/11/1864.
358. *AH* 8/4/1899.
359. *AH* 9/1/1897.
360. *AH* 24/8 & 31/8/1901.
361. *AH* 23/5/1862 & 4/4/1874.
362. *AH* 27/4/1878.
363. *AH* 15/5/1886, 'Death of Mr Samuel Greenlees of Moy'.
364. *AH* 16/1 & 6/3/1897.
365. *CC* 13/8/1932, obituary of Colonel George P. Rome.
366. *CC* 11/3/1933.
367. *CC* 26/3/1964.
368. *CC* 11/11/1922.
369. *CC* 12/5/1923.
370. A. Martin, *Glen Scotia Distillery: A History*, pp. 46-47.
371. DR/4/8/5.
372. *AH* 7/12/1867.
373. *CC* 20/1/1900.
374. DR/4/8/9.

375. *CJ* 15/4/1852.
376. *AH* 27/3/1857.
377. *AH* 21/4/1866.
378. *AH* 23/10/1880.
379. *AH* 29/7/1865.
380. *AH* 18/11/1871.
381. *AH* 25/12/1880.
382. *AH* 18/8/1866, 'Notes of an Excursion from Ayrshire to Kintyre'.
383. *AH* 25/9/1863.
384. *CC* 26/3/1937.
385. R. Haydock, 'Argyll's Forgotten Whisky Barons', *KM* 67, pp. 13-17; *AH* 15/5/1886, 'Death of Samuel Greenlees'; & *AH* 7/3/1891, 'The Whisky Enquiry'.
386. *AH* 8/1/1864 & 13/6/1862.
387. *AH* 16/2/1867.
388. *AH* 26/3/1904.
389. *The Wine and Spirit Trade Record*, 8/5/1905.
390. *AH* 11/11/1905.
391. *The Wine and Spirit Trade Record*, 14/12/1922.
392. DR/4/8/26.
393. DR/4/8/24.
394. DR/4/8/26.
395. DR/4/8/24.
396. *AH* 13/5/1859.
397. Live Argyll Archive, BC/19/2.
398. *AH* 17/1/1862.
399. *AH* 23/10/1869.
400. *CC* 19/9/1931.
401. *AH* 19/6/1857.
402. *AH* 15/2/1890.
403. *CJ* 17/6/1854 & *AH* 11/12/1886, obituary of William Hunter Jr.
404. *AH* 17/10/1856.
405. *AH* 30/10/1863 & 6/5/1864.
406. *AH* 3/3/1888.
407. *KM* 85, p 12.
408. *AH* 10/1/1862.
409. A. Martin, *KM* 81, p 4.
410. *AH* 17/1/1903, report of public enquiry under the Fatal Accidents Enquiry (Scotland) Act, 1895, in Campbeltown Sheriff Courthouse.
411. *AH* 16/7/1892.
412. *AH* 16/12/1871.
413. *AH* 25/10/1913.
414. DR/4/7/15.

415. *CC* 18/9/1923.
416. *CC* 29/9/1923.
417. *CC* 27/9/1924.
418. *CC* & *AH* 17/4/1897.
419. *CC* 18/5/1918.
420. *CC* 13/11/1920.
421. *AH* 30/9/1893.
422. *CC* 25/4 & 6/6/1914.
423. DR/4/8/10.
424. *CJ* 4/12/1851.
425. *AH* 28/11/1868.
426. *AH* 21/1/1888.
427. *CC* 2/6/1906, 'Kintyre Worthy Dead'.
428. *The Wine and Spirit Trade Record*, 14/4/1923.
429. AP Bundle 1999.
430. DR/4/8/19.
431. *AH* 20/2/1875.
432. *AH* 29/9/1868.
433. DR/4/8/26.
434. DR/4/8/6 & D. Colville, *CC* 26/5/1945, 'Mystery Man of Buchenwald'.
435. *CC* 15/12/1928.
436. DR/4/8/6.
437. *AH* 1/5/1875.
438. *CC* 21/4/1877.
439. *AH* 19/4/1879.
440. *CC* 17/4/1926.
441. *AH* 8/10/1870.
442. *AH* 3/4/1875.
443. *AH* 4/2/1854.
444. *AH* 25/12/1857.
445. *CC* 29/4/1899 & *AH* 13/5 & 30/12/1899.
446. *The Wine and Spirit Trade Record*, 14/9/1923.
447. *AH* 25/2/1871 & 28/12/1872.
448. *AH* 15/3 & 23/8/1873.
449. *AH* 18/6/1881.
450. R. Colby, personal communication, 16/11/2018.
451. A. Martin, 'The Wm. Low Supermarket', *KM* 34, pp. 18-19.
452. DR/4/8/17.
453. *Pigot & Co.'s Directory*, p 209.
454. DR/4/8/6.
455. DR/4/8/6 & 24.
456. *AH* 26/9/1856, Letter to the Editor.
457. *AH* 20/5 & 27/5/1865.
458. *AH* 22/9/1866.

459. *CC* 12/7/1879.
460. *CC* 15/5/1920.
461. *CC* 12/3/1927.
462. *The Wine and Spirit Trade Record*, 14/7/1923.
463. *CC* 23/1/1971.
464. *AH* 2/12/1876.
465. *AH* 4/3/1876.
466. *AH* 11/8/1888.
467. *CC* 23/12/1971.
468. *AH* 12/4/1861.
469. *CC* 23/6/1917.
470. *CC* 29/7 & 4/11/1916.
471. *AH* 19/9/1874.
472. *AH* 9/12/1865 & 7/8/1869.
473. RP & A. Martin, *Kintyre Families*, p 26.
474. *CC* 19/8/1933.
475. *CC* 19/2/1921.
476. *The Wine and Spirit Trade Record*, 14/6/1923.
477. *CC* 27/12/1930.
478. *CC* 9/4/1932 & 11/3/1933.
479. A. Martin, *Glen Scotia Distillery: A History*, pp. 30-31.
480. *AH* 2/10/1880.
481. A. Martin, *Kintyre: The Hidden Past*, p 75, *and* A. Martin, *An Historical and Genealogical Tour of Kilkerran Graveyard*, pp. 8-9.
482. Eunice MacCallum Crook & Avril McAllister Coffield, by e-mail, 10/4/2019.
483. *AH* 20/1/1894.
484. *CC* 28/11/1936.
485. *CC* 9/9/1933.
486. DR/4/7/20.
487. *CJ* 4/8/1853.
488. *AH* 3/10/1862 & 26/2 & 30/9/1864.
489. *AH* 27/4/1867, 25/2/1871, 17/2 & 13/4/1872 & 19/8/1882.
490. RP 2010.
491. *CC* 27/3/1920.
492. *CC* 10/7/1915.
493. *The Celtic Monthly*, June 1898, No.9, Vol VI.
494. *CC* 16/1/1926.
495. *CC* 22/1/1898.
496. *CC* 26/2/1898.
497. *CC* 19/5/1928.
498. *AH* 19/10/1907.
499. *CC* 30/6/1906 & 1/7/1899.
500. *CC* 24/1/1920.
501. *CC* 30/9/1916.

502. A. Martin, *Glen Scotia Distillery: A History*, pp. 17-18.
503. *AH* 13/1/1860.
504. *AH* 22/12/1866.
505. *AH* 16/5/1874.
506. *AH* 4/7/1862.
507. *CC* 16/1/1932.
508. A. Martin, *An Historical and Genealogical Tour of Kilkerran Graveyard*, pp. 41-42.
509. William Norman McKersie, letter, 2/11/2006.
510. *CC* 7/8/1952.
511. *AH* 12/11/1904.
512. *AH* 18/3/1905.
513. *CC* 22/6/1940.
514. *CC* 14/9/1929.
515. *AH* 7/12/1878.
516. *CC* 5/8/1916.
517. *AH* 12/5/1866.
518. *CC* 21/12/1940.
519. *CC* 12/1/1946.
520. *CC* 24/4/1952 & 11/2 & 23/6/1960.
521. *AH* 29/3/1873.
522. *AH* 28/3/1885.
523. Ballinderry Presbyterian Church Burials website.
524. *AH* 26/4 & 3/5/1890 & *CC* 15/7/1916.
525. *CC* 11/2/1905.
526. *CC* 28/2/1920.
527. *CC* 12/6/1920, 'King's Birthday Honours', 29/1/1921, 'Marriage Rejoicings at Glenreasdell and Stonefield' & 27/9/1924, 'Death of Sir P. J. Mackie, Bart'.
528. *AH* 4/8/1900, *CC* 15/7/1922 & 14/7/1894.
529. *CC* 29/10/1927.
530. *AH* 8/2/1873.
531. RP 1355.
532. *CC* 11/10/1924.
533. *CC* 18/7/1908 & 2/4/1910.
534. *AH* 28/2/1891.
535. KEL, p 133.
536. RP 335.
537. *AH* 15/2/1873.
538. IMAP.
539. *AH* 17/6/1864.
540. *CC* 7/3/1931.
541. *AH* 3/2/1860 & 13/1/1872.
542. A. Martin, *Glen Scotia Distillery: A History*, p 25.
543. *CC* 6/7/1912, death notice of son Archibald.

544. *AH* 14/7/1866.
545. *AH* 27/7/1867.
546. *AH* 20/11/1869.
547. RP 1101.
548. *CC* 29/8/1936.
549. *CC* 5/1/1945.
550. *AH* 1/5/1897 & *CC* 5/3/1921.
551. *CC* 7/9/1946.
552. *AH* 22/5/1857 & *CC* 19/5/1917 & 15/3/1919.
553. C. Mactaggart, *A Ramble Through the Old Kilkerran Graveyard*, 1922, p 6.
554. I. MacDonald, 'Kintyre Smugglers', *KM* 37, p 4.
555. *CJ* 26/2/1852 & *AH* 10/6/1859.
556. D. Colville, *CC* 24/2/1923.
557. KEL 64A.
558. www.oldglasgowpubs.co.uk
559. *CC* 30/3 & 6/4/1901.
560. A. McKerral, *Kintyre in the Seventeenth Century*, 1948, p 145.
561. F. Bigwood, *Justices of the Peace in Argyll*, 2001, p 112.
562. IMAP.
563. *Ibid.*
564. *AH* 29/11/1855 & 21/9/1889.
565. *AH* 10/1/1866.
566. *AH* 9/8/1873 & 10/9/1881.
567. *CC* 6/7/1878.
568. *CC* 16/7/1927.
569. *AH* 20/7/1905.
570. RP 1965.
571. AP Bundle 1966.
572. DR/4/8/19.
573. DR/4/8/26.
574. *AH* 17/3/1853.
575. DR/4/8/26.
576. *AH* 29/4/1865.
577. *AH* 11/8/1866.
578. DR/4/8/26.
579. IMAP.
580. *AH* 4/2 & 4/3/1865.
581. *AH* 27/10 & 10/11/1866.
582. *CJ* 29/4/1854.
583. *AH* 8/8/1891.
584. *CC* 27/8/1913.
585. *CC* 19/1/1929.
586. *CC* 2/12/1944.
587. Mrs J. Brodie, by e-mail 31/3/2019.

588. A Martin, *Kintyre Families*, p 40.
589. *CC* 20/1/1917 & 15/1/1919.
590. DR/4/8/9.
591. *CC* 1/9 & 29/9/1877.
592. *AH* 2/12/1905.
593. *CC* 5/5/1917.
594. *CC* 31/3/1917.
595. A Martin, *Kintyre Families*, p 60.
596. *AH* 10/1/1874.
597. *AH* & *CC* 14/12/1912.
598. F. Bigwood, *The Commissary Court of Argyll*, pp. 31 & 345.
599. *AH* 10/4/1863.
600. *AH* 1/7/1865.
601. *AH* 10/7/1903.
602. *CC* 9/11 & 16/11/1946, 2/8/1954 & 23/4/1959.
603. *AH* 28/10/1859.
604. *CC* 8/5/1952.
605. *CC* 23/2/1935.
606. *CC* 9/11/1946.
607. *CC* 14/5/1892, obituary.
608. *AH* 28/3 & 11/4/1874.
609. *AH* 7/10/1864, 7/10/1865 & 23/5/1874.
610. 'Notes upon Campbeltown', *Scottish Standard*, reproduced in *AH* 20/8/1870.
611. *AH* 27/6/1874 & 9/7/1881.
612. *AH* 9/9/1893.
613. *CC* 15/11/1913.
614. *AH* 21/12/1901 & 23/3/1907.
615. *AH* 13/2/1875.
616. *AH* 27/8/1887.
617. *AH* 23/12/1899.
618. KEL, p 148.
619. *AH* 21/5/1892.
620. *AH* 2/9/1871.
621. A. Martin, *Kintyre Families*, p 61.
622. *Pigot*, p 220.
623. DR/4/8/22.
624. *CC* 10/7/1952, 'Old Kirk Close Demolished'.
625. Rev John Thomson, *AH* 9/7/1892.
626. *AH* 7/5/1870.
627. DR/4/8/6 & 21.
628. A. D. Armour, DR/4/8/6.
629. *CC* 5/5/1928.
630. Sadie Galbraith, Muir family history file, by e-mail, 3/10/2019, & *CC* 26/5/1917 & 2/2/1918.

631. *AH* 17/3/1894.
632. *The Wine and Spirit Trade Record*, 8/5/1905.
633. *CC* 22/3/1919.
634. D. E. Meek, *The Companion to Gaelic Scotland*, ed D. S. Thomson, 1983, p 206.
635. J. Hunter, e-mail to author, 12/12/2011.
636. *CJ* 4/3/1852.
637. *AH* 18 & 25/7 & 1/8/1885.
638. *AH* 13/10/1866, 'Notes of an Excursion from Ayrshire to Kintyre'.
639. A. Martin, *Glen Scotia Distillery: A History*, pp. 10-11.
640. *Ibid.*, pp. 14-15.
641. *AH* 6/10/1866.
642. *AH* 22/7 & 29/7/1876.
643. *AH* 11/6/1881 & *CC* 13/8/1904 & 4/11/1905.
644. *CC* 11/11/1893.
645. *AH* 9/8/1884.
646. DR/4/8/9.
647. Reproduced in *The Old Book of Castlehill*, 1921.
648. *AH* 23/6/1888.
649. RP 1213.
650. AP Bundle 2015.
651. *AH* 6/8/1887.
652. *AH* 12/9 & 7/11/1885 & 16/10/1886.
653. A. Martin, *Kintyre Country Life*, p 93.
654. *AH* 9/12/1899.
655. A. Martin, *Kintyre Country Life*, pp. 92-94.
656. *CC* 22/2/1913.
657. *The Wine and Spirit Trade Record*, 14/12/1922.
658. A. Martin, *South Kintyre Dialect*, 2016, p 39.
659. *CC* 21/6/1879.
660. *CC* 13/12/1956 & 18/7/1957.
661. *AH* 28/7/1894, 'The Potale Nuisance'.
662. *CJ* 3/2/1855.
663. *CC* 28/9/1895, 'The Potale Tank'.
664. *CC* 8/5, 10/7 & 25/9/1897, from the *Distillers' Magazine & Spirit Trade News*.
665. D. McKendrick, in conversation with the author, 27/11/1995.
666. *AH* 28/1/1871 & 18/3/1876.
667. *AH* 3/6/1876.
668. *AH* 3/3/1866 & 13/7/1867.
669. *CC* 13/9/1919.
670. A. Martin, *Kintyre: The Hidden Past*, p 115.
671. *CC* 16/3/1878.
672. *CC* 16/7/1921, 'The Mussel Ebb'.
673. *AH* 28/8/1888.

674. DR/4/7/20.
675. H. Ferguson, 'The Kintyre Club', *KM* 10, p 6.
676. *CJ* 28/4/1853.
677. Dr Stewart Carslaw, Connel, letter to *CC* 28/8/1958.
678. *Ibid.*
679. M. Borland, 'Templetons of Kintyre', *KM* 50, pp. 5-8; B. Mackenzie, 'The Riches of Campbeltown: The Piping Tradition', *KM* 54, p 7; A. Martin, *Kintyre Families*, pp. 66 & 72.
680. *AH* 2/4/1858.
681. *AH* 24/5/1873.
682. Colville 1923.
683. *AH* 27/3/1869.
684. *CC* 20/1/1934.
685. *AH* 6/7/1878.
686. *CC* 6/7/1878.
687. *CC* 2/5/1936.
688. *CC* 28/11/1936.
689. *CC* 10/12/1910.
690. *AH* 20/7/1872.
691. *KM* 75, p 5.
692. *AH* 18/3 & *CC* 25/3/1876.
693. *AH* 30/11/1867.
694. *KM* 8, pp. 13-14.
695. *AH* 10/8/1872.
696. *AH* 26/2/1881.
697. *AH* 6/3/1886, obituary, & *CC* 10/2/1877, 'To the Inhabitants of Campbeltown'.
698. *AH* 12/7/1879.
699. *CC* 23/9/1876.
700. *Pigot's Directory*, 1825-6, p 209.
701. *KM* 14, p 16 & *AH* 3/5/1861.
702. *AH* 22/11/1899.
703. C. Mactaggart, 'Provosts of Campbeltown in 18th Century', *CC* 8/3/1924.
704. *CC* 10/8/1940.
705. DR/4/8/6 & 28.
706. *CC* 17/3/1955 & 1/8/1963.
707. *CC* 10/4/1920 & 7/9/1929. In a copy of H. Stopes's *Malt and Malting* (1885), which belonged to A. S. Miller (q.v.), manager of Loch-head Distillery, the signature on the fly-leaf is 'J. B. Sherriff, Carronvale'. J.B. Sherriff & Co. bought Loch-head in 1895, and John Bell Sherriff died the following year. Carronvale Estate in Stirlingshire was inherited by Sherriff's son, George, and the house is now a conference and training centre. The book now belongs to Mrs Jeanette Brodie, Campbeltown.

708. A. Martin, *Kintyre Country Life*, pp. 105 & 110-12.
709. J. H. Mackenzie, *CC* 5/6/1943, 'Campbeltown in 1811-1837'.
710. *AH* 28/7/1866, 'Notes of an Excursion from Ayrshire to Kintyre'.
711. *KM* 8, p 12.
712. J. H. Mackenzie, *CC* 5/6/1943, 'Campbeltown in 1811-1837'.
713. *CC* 23/5/1936 & *SSPCK Schoolmasters, 1709-1872*, ed A.S. Cowper, Edinburgh 1997, p 98.
714. *KM* 8, p 12.
715. *AH* 14/3 & 21/3/1862.
716. *AH* 18/12/1863.
717. DR/4/8/21.
718. *AH* 12/6/1866 & 4/10/1884.
719. *AH* 13/10/1866.
720. *AH* 8/5/1869.
721. *AH* 14/5/1870.
722. *AH* & *CC* 2/4/1904.
723. *AH* 23/7/1870 & *CC* 5/1/1907.
724. *AH* 26/11/1870.
725. *CC* 4/8/1917.
726. *AH* 6/1/1865.
727. *AH* 30/8/1873.
728. *AH* 26/4 & 13/9/1873.
729. *AH* 21/4 & 28/4/1877 & 12/4/1890.
730. *AH* 27/10/1877.
731. *AH* 9/3/1878.
732. A. Martin, *An Historical and Genealogical Tour of Kilkerran Graveyard*, pp. 5-6.
733. *AH* 31/3 & 12/5/1888.
734. *AH* 28/3/1896.
735. *CC* 23/3/1878.
736. *CC* 17/5/1879.
737. A. Martin, *An Historical and Genealogical Tour of Kilkerran Graveyard*, p 2.
738. *AH* 1/2/1890.
739. *AH* 1/1/1898.
740. *CC* 10/6/1922 & 20/6/1931.
741. *CC* 6/12/1924 & 16, 23 & 30/10/1926.
742. *CC* 31/1/1920 & 30/12/1922.
743. J. Campbell, recorded by the author, 9/2/1982.
744. *AH* 14/8/1857.
745. *CC* 12/10/1929 & 4/11/1933.
746. *AH* 29/11/1873.
747. *CC* 11/7/1903.
748. RP 2073.
749. *CC* 5/10/1961.

750. A. Martin, *An Historical and Genealogical Tour of Kilkerran Graveyard*, pp. 26-27.
751. *AH* 17/6/1864.
752. A. Martin, *Glen Scotia Distillery: A History*, p 37.
753. *Ibid.*, p 48.
754. *CC* 9/2/1929.
755. *CC* 13/4/1895 & *AH* 8/2/1896.
756. Kikerran Cemetery.
757. *CC* 26/3/1910.
758. A. Martin, *Glen Scotia Distillery: A History*, p 30.
759. *Views of Campbelton and Neighbourhood*, pp. 11-13.
760. *CC* 18/7/1931.
761. *AH* 5/9/1868.
762. *CC* 24 & 31/12/1921 & 3/2/1923.
763. *CC* 21/6 & 2/8/1956.
764. Colville 1923.
765. AP Bundle 1941.
766. DR/4/8/23.
767. *Pigot's Directory*, 1825, p 209.
768. *AH* 23/11/1872.
769. *AH* 31/10/1862.
770. *AH* 2/5/1885.
771. *CC* 10/11/1917 & 6/7/1918.
772. *The Wine and Spirit Trade Record*, 8/5/1905 & 14/5/1923.
773. *CC* 28/12/1935.
774. *CC* 2/12/1939, 2/3 & 20/5/1940 & 27/1/1945.
775. *CC* 23/12/1965.
776. *CC* 16/2/1967, from a Springbank brochure, hand-dated October 1966 by Duncan Colville, in DR/4/8/6.
777. *CC* 23/1/1981.
778. *CC* 3/12/1970.
779. *CC* 23/5/1974.
780. *Daily Mail*, 16/6/1974.
781. *CC* 26/8/1977, 27/4/1979 & 23/1/1981.
782. *CC* 29/1/1988 & 28/6/2013.
783. Annie Butterworth, *Scottish Daily Mail*, 14/9/2019.
784. *CC* 16/4/1927.
785. *Pigot* 1837, p 221.
786. D. Colville, *CC* 8/5/1937.
787. *CC* 14/1/1899.
788. D. Mayo, e-mail, 13/12/2018.
789. *CC* 25/4/1931, 'Fatal Accident Enquiry'.
790. A. Martin, *Glen Scotia Distillery: A History*, p 21.
791. *CC* 31/12/1921.
792. Extracts from Stewart's will from Christine Ritchie, by e-mail, 3/9/2019.

793. A. Martin, *Glen Scotia Distillery: A History*, pp. 21-22.
794. *CC* 23/1/1915.
795. *CC* 26/6/1981.
796. *CC* 10/10/1986.
797. *CC* 16/3/1878 & *AH* 9/10/1897.
798. KEL, p 168C.
799. *CJ* 18/7/1851.
800. KEL, p 133.
801. *AH* 6/2/1857.
802. AP Bundle 1941.
803. DR/4/8/22, James D. Ferguson, Bywell Castle, Northumberland, to John G. Houston, writer in Glasgow, 14/10/1851.
804. *AH* 3/2/1866, 19/8/1876 & 13/8/1887.
805. DR/4/8/12.
806. *CC* 5/3/1904.
807. *AH* 19/9/1856, 'Description of Campbeltown'.
808. *AH* 6/11/1857.
809. *AH* 13/1/1866.
810. *AH* 28/11/1891.
811. *AH* 1/6/1889.
812. *CC* 16/12/1916.
813. *KM* 8, p 14 & Sir J. Landale Train, *CC* 27/6/1957.
814. *AH* 16/3/1872.
815. DR/4/8/26.
816. *Ibid.*
817. DR/4/8/10.
818. *CC* 13/4/1907 & 17/9/1910.
819. A. Martin, *Glen Scotia Distillery: A History*, pp. 20-21.
820. *AH* 13/5/1876, 'Campbeltown's Harbour and Burgh Bill'.
821. *CC* 17/11/1877.
822. *AH* 19/4/1884.
823. *AH* 27/11/1880.
824. *CC* 1/12/1917.
825. *CC* 17/2/1934.
826. *CC* 15/12/1955.
827. *CC* 19/6/1952.
828. *CC* 12/5/1955.
829. J. H. Mackenzie, *CC* 12/6/1943, 'Campbeltown in 1811-1837'.
830. *AH* 19/3/1898.
831. DR/4/8/6.
832. *AH* 25/3/1864.
833. A. Martin, 'S. J. Peploe's Campbeltown Mother', *KM* 86, pp. 16-17.
834. *CC* 20/8/1898.
835. *CC* 4/7/1931.

836. *CC* 2/4/1938.
837. A. Martin, *Kintyre Families*, p 14.
838. A. Martin, *Glen Scotia Distillery: A History*, p 26.
839. *AH* 7/3/1891, 'The Whisky Enquiry'.
840. *AH* 11/3/1854 & 4/10/1855.
841. *CC* 23/9/1922.
842. *AH* 10/6/1871.
843. A. Martin, *South Kintyre Dialect*, pp. 21 & 50.
844. *Ibid.*, p 42.
845. *CC* 27/8/1964, in 'Wullie the Maltman'.
846. A. Martin, *South Kintyre Dialect*, p 42.
847. *AH* 10/6/1871.
848. *AH* 8/11/1884.
849. RP 1134.
850. A. Martin, *Glen Scotia Distillery: A History*, pp. 38 & 45.
851. *CC* 20/12/1924 & 25/8/1960.
852. *The Scotsman*, 11/3/1931.
853. *CC* 1/6/1967.
854. *Jim Murray's Complete Book of Whisky*, 1997, p 89.
855. *CC* 24/10 & 7/11/2003.
856. beta.companieshouse.gov.uk
857. *CJ* 5/2/1852.
858. *AH* 7/3/1891.
859. *CC* 13/2/1926.
860. A. Colville, in conversation with the author, 2/1/1996.
861. D. Colville, 'Trade and Industry', in *Campbeltown 1700-1950*, pp. 22-23.
862. *AH* 11/2/1899.
863. *CC* 27/9/1924, 'Burgh Valuation Appeal Court'.
864. *Ibid.*
865. *CC* 18/9/1926.
866. *CC* 8/11/1930.
867. *AH* 2/5/1856.
868. *AH* 15/12 & 22/12/1900.
869. *CC* 13/12/1902.
870. *CC* 10/6/1905.
871. *CC* 4/10/1919.
872. *CC* 8/11/1930.

Index

Since the principal distillers appear alphabetically in the text, and are, moreover, extensively cross-referenced, they do not appear in this index individually, but collectively under family surnames. Appendixes are only loosely indexed.

Aberfeldy Distillery, 37
agriculture, 5, 6, 47, 57, 62, 76-77, 103, 104, 105, 107, 125, 187, 190-91, 205, 235
Ainslie & Heilbron (Distillers) Ltd., 9
Albyn Distillery, 3, 8, 12, 57, 76, 124, 136, 139, 140, 141, 151, 153, 154, 202, 228
Alexander & Macdonald Ltd., Leith, 148
Allan, D. R. 'Roy', manager, Springbank, 39, 244
Amalgamated Distilled Products, 88
Anderson families, 4-5, 89, 193
Andrew families, 5-7, 101, 104, 131, 143, 177, 258
Ardbeg Distillery, 37, 134, 288
Ardlussa Distillery, 7-8, 11, 81, 138, 178, 197, 247, 258, 289
Ardshiel Hotel – see Hazelbank
Argyll & Sutherland Highlanders, 28, 46, 72, 163, 166, 183, 236
Argyll Distillery, 8-10, 29, 48, 78, 99, 101, 102, 105, 107, 161, 168, 231, 253, 257, 286

Argyll, Dukes of, 21, 30, 53, 97, 128, 146, 248, 253, 254, 255, 280
Argyll Group/Foods, 89, 109, 110
Argyll Militia, 25, 92
Argyllshire Herald, 95, 137, 151, 194, 218, 241
Armour families, 4, 10-12, 45, 64, 72, 89, 93, 104, 115, 117, 123, 150, 166, 179, 244
Armour, Robert & Sons, 11-12, 26, 75, 83, 122, 125, 136, 234, 246, 285
Arran, 11, 226, 228
Auchalochy (reservoir), 253, 255
Auchinblae Distillery, 148
Auchnagie Distillery, 37
Auchtermuchty Distillery, 25
Auchtertool Distillery, 36
Australia, 3, 15, 66, 79, 87, 98, 125, 131, 143, 153, 160, 165, 246
Ayrshire, 16, 38, 58, 59, 65, 78, 116, 124, 158, 160, 163, 224, 226, 227, 229, 231, 247, 252

bagpiping & pipers, 33, 72, 123, 145, 140, 210
ballman, 12-13
Balmenach Distillery, 230

315

banks, 18, 19, 28, 41, 44, 65, 78, 86, 100, 105, 109, 113, 153, 189, 234, 241, 257
Banks, Iain, 12
barley & bere, 13-18, 25, 67, 72, 81, 83, 129, 132, 175, 192, 227, 236
Barnard, Alfred, 18, 30, 36, 51, 57, 74, 136, 143, 200, 202, 208, 211, 212, 214, 234, 239, 253
Barr/ Barr Glen/ Glenbarr, 125, 144, 176, 177, 199
Beith families, 18-22, 31, 35, 56, 130, 137, 153, 214, 215
Belfast, 58, 59, 60, 226
Belgium, 190
Ben Gullion, 28, 30, 97
Benmore Distilleries Ltd., 22, 37
Benmore Distillery, 8, 22-23, 37, 54, 74, 80, 123, 178, 179, 203, 204, 229, 232, 253
Benmore Street, 22
Bennett & Co., wine merchants, 103, 104, 265
Ben Nevis Distillery, 37, 84
Benromach Distillery, 142
Ben Wyvis Distillery, 36
Bequet, Stanislas, St. Malo seaman, 15
Bladnoch Distillery, 92
Blair, Mary (*née* McGeachy), 16
blended whisky – see whisky, blending of
Bloch Brothers, 23, 81, 82, 85, 88, 247
Bloch, Joseph, 24
Bloch, Sir Maurice, 23-24, 88
'Bonnie Green Braes o' Kintyre', song, 222, 251
Bonthrone family, Fife, 25

bowling & clubs, 45, 138, 158, 169, 189, 193, 228, 248, 257
Bowmore Distillery, 221
Boyd, Rev Dr James, 44, 200
Boyd, John Colville, commission agent, 200, 285
Boyle, Hugh, distiller, 25-26, 31
Boyle, Jane MacGregor, wife of above Hugh, 26
Boyle, Jane, daughter of above Hugh, 26
Breackenridge families, 104, 163, 164, 176
British India Steam Navigation Company, 151, 161, 180
Brodie, Jeanette, 183
Broombrae Distillery, 26-27
Brown, Isabella, publican, 235
Brown, Dr James P., 27, 141
Brown, Thomas Lambert, distiller, 22, 27-28, 129, 240, 258
Brown, Thomas, businessman, 22, 28, 113, 226
Bruichladdich Distillery, 92
Buchanan, James, & Co., 134
Buchanan, Wilson & Co., Glasgow, 134
Buglass, Bob, Springbank, 238
Bull family, Campbeltown, 151
Bulloch, Lade & Co., 22, 23, 80, 120, 123, 179, 221
Bunnahabhainn Distillery, 37, 103
Burdon, Captain Joseph, Annalong, 228
Burnside Distillery, 28-30, 44, 78, 86, 94, 99, 102, 103, 105, 145, 168, 195, 202, 226
Burns, Robert, 20, 36

Cadenhead, William, 30, 266
Caledonian Distillery, 25, 30-32, 243
Caley Close, 31
Cameron Bridge Distillery, 129
Campbell, Provost Donald, 220
Campbell, Donald, spirit merchant, Campbeltown, 91
Campbell, Dugald of Kildalloig, 64
Campbell, Duncan, Sheriff, 172
Campbell Henderson, wine & spirit merchants, 81
Campbell, James, baker, 186
Campbell, Sir John Eyton of Auchinbreck, 78
Campbell, John of Glensaddell, 56
Campbell, John MacFadyen, tradition-bearer, 207, 228
Campbell, John, nameless distillery in High Street, 117
Campbell, Sheriff J. Macmaster, 141
Campbell, 'Highland Mary', 36
Campbeltown & Glasgow Steam Packet Joint Stock Company, 6, 23, 32-33, 41, 42, 46, 47, 50, 65, 66, 76, 77, 81, 91, 93, 100, 102, 103, 105, 106, 113, 114, 115, 118, 144, 146, 149, 153, 172, 189, 199, 222, 242, 243, 267; company ships: *Celt*, 33, 199, 261; *Dalriada*, 33; *Davaar*, 23, 33, 61; *Druid*, 33, 191; *Duke of Cornwall*, 33, 199, 261; *Duke of Lancaster*, 33, 76, 199, 232; *Gael*, 6, 33, 54, 115, 199, 242; *Kinloch*, 33, 49, 249; *Kintyre*, 33, 80; *Saint Kiaran*, 33, 199

Campbeltown Bonding Co., 33
Campbeltown Building Co., 42, 106, 149
Campbeltown Courier, 17, 169, 189, 264
Campbeltown Creamery, 30
Campbeltown Distillers' Association, 34-35, 42, 59, 60, 61, 62, 75, 103, 116, 121, 145, 149, 159, 184, 189, 241
Campbeltown Distillery, 17, 18, 35-37, 38, 85, 115, 116, 125, 138, 144, 145, 149, 163, 164, 167, 168, 173, 174, 180, 219, 232, 252
Campbeltown Harbour & Burgh Bill, 253
Campbeltown Museum, 209, 227, 242
Campbeltown Shipyard, 208, 227, 233
Campbeltown Town Council, *vii*, 5, 9, 10, 20, 22, 23, 40, 41, 42, 44, 45, 46, 65, 68, 77, 81, 82, 90, 92, 93, 95, 100, 102, 106, 108, 109, 113, 117, 118, 127, 129, 132, 134, 149, 153, 155, 157, 172, 173, 180, 181, 187, 189, 192, 200, 205, 207, 213, 215, 231, 232-33, 241, 248, 253, 255, 256, 286, 289
Campbeltown Unemployed Relief Fund, 233
Campbeltown whisky region, 32
Canada, 72, 95, 143, 194, 223, 226
Cannes, 150, 165
Caol Ila Distillery, 56, 115
Cardhu Distillery, 229
Carmichael, ----, manager, Loch-head, 132

317

Carrick, John, Benmore, 22
carters, 38, 39, 191, 203, 206
China, 238
cholera, 31, 106, 170, 176
churches and religion, 7, 19, 20, 21, 45, 50, 61, 64, 65, 69, 70, 77, 93, 96, 100, 102, 105, 113, 124, 132, 133, 138, 151, 155, 157, 161, 166, 170, 189, 192, 194, 195, 214, 215, 217, 218, 219, 220, 228, 232, 241, 246, 250, 251
City of Glasgow Bank crash, 34, 149, 246
Clapperton, Neil, 238
Clark families, 20, 44, 164, 190, 211
Clarke, Robert, manager, Benmore, 37
Clifford, Henry E., architect, 4, 132, 133, 155
Club, The, Campbeltown, 37-38, 158, 220
coal, 16, 17, 38-40, 149, 226, 227
Colby, Robert, 133
Colman, Olivia, actress, 145
Colvill(e) families, 8, 11, 28, 29, 40-50, 53, 54, 55, 64, 77, 88, 94, 100, 101, 102, 105, 106, 111, 112, 114, 128, 129, 130, 133, 137, 146, 164, 165, 176, 180, 192, 195, 200, 214, 225, 233, 234, 235, 239, 253, 254, 266, 286
Colville, Alex, distillery workman, 286
Colville, Duncan, local whisky historian, 43-44, 60, 111, 161, 234, 287
Conley, Neil, secretary, Dalaruan, 50

Convalmore Distillery, 232
coopering & coopers, 50-52, 128, 151, 166, 207
Cooper's Close, 166
coppersmiths, 6, 11, 12
Corbet families, 65, 77
Corkey, Jean, beggar, 218
Cragganmore Distillery, 37, 122
Craig Brothers, 9-10, 22, 81, 212
Craigellachie Distillery, 115, 262, 288
cricket, 69, 96, 220
Crosshill Reservoir/Loch, 17, 141, 253, 254, 255
Cumbrae, Isle of, 118, 119
Currie, John, Crosshill Farm, 255

Dailuaine Distillery, 148
Dalaruan Distillery, 81, 50, 52-54, 81, 100, 101, 107, 114, 133, 145, 162, 165, 240, 253, 254
Dalintober Distillery, 17, 40, 41, 42, 49, 53, 54-56, 143, 146, 205, 208, 209, 253, 254, 258, 286, 289-90
Davaar Island, 64, 97, 143
'Davaar Scotch Whisky', 97
Dawson & Baird, Glasgow, 116
Dean Distillery, 36
Denmark, 13, 14, 227
'Dew of Begullion', whisky blend, 97
Dewar, John, collector of Gaelic tradition, 174
Dewar, Peter, manager, Dalintober, 56, 78, 121
Dickie, Robert, farmer, Killeonan, 63, 191
Dickson, William & Co., 30, 52
Disruption, The (1843), 19, 93

Distillers Co. Ltd. (DCL), 9, 22, 110, 134, 159, 221
Doctor Rowatt's Close, 219, 258
draff, 57-59, 79, 135, 159, 226
dramming, 59-60
dried grains & factory, 35, 60-62, 74
Drumore Distillery, 62-64, 123
Drury Lane Theatre, 99
Dundee, 24, 58, 155
Dunlop families, 11, 40, 64-66, 77, 86, 87, 101, 128, 163, 176, 259

Eaglesome's, 30, 91
East Cliff, Kilkerran Road, 40, 108, 111, 141, 142
Edinburgh, 27, 71, 158, 210, 238
Edward, Alexander, distiller, 27
Edward, A., & Co., 27
electricity, 9, 115, 293
emigration, 30, 72, 87, 119, 139, 146, 191, 193
Excise, including Inland Revenue & Customs & Excise, 36, 40, 63, 66-72, 76, 80, 86, 112, 119, 120, 122, 125, 126, 135, 151, 161, 172, 184, 197, 213, 220, 245, 246, 252, 260, 262, 276-79

Ferguson, Alexander, rifle marksman, 73
Ferguson, Duncan, Springbank, 72
Ferguson families (Lowland), including Hugh & James, below, 5, 62, 72, 73-74, 104, 113, 114, 176, 177, 185, 211, 248, 266
Ferguson, George, missing person, 74

Ferguson, Hector, Hazelburn, 73
Ferguson, Hugh, Glenside, 73, 89
Ferguson, James, Rieclachan, 73-74
Ferguson, Neil, builder, 73, 80, 83
Ferguson, Peter, distillery manager, 74, 117
Ferguson, William, Benmore, 74
Ferrier, Louis Henry of Belsyde, 78
Fife, 25, 41, 48, 111, 129, 180, 182, 183, 265
Finefare, 110
fire-brigade, Campbeltown, 23, 54, 55
fires in distilleries, 23, 35, 54, 55, 117, 129, 130, 132, 168, 292
fishing (including angling), 5, 42, 51, 78, 138, 139, 142, 153, 169, 182, 216
Fleming, Alexander, ironmaster, 96
Fleming, Archibald, merchant, London, 52
Fleming, James Nicol, merchant, 34, 77
Fleming, John, Captain R.N., 258
Fleming, John, draff agent, 59
Fleming, Matthew, maltster, 194
football, 37, 69, 231, 248, 257
Forbes Mackenzie Act, 56
France, 13, 14, 15, 16, 28, 75, 95, 152, 165, 238, 247
Fraser, George Greig, Dried Grains Factory, 74-75
Freemasonry, 28, 102
Fullarton, Archibald, master of the *Maid* of Campbeltown, 58
Fullarton, Archibald, foreman mashman, Scotia, 75

Fullarton, Archibald, I. R. officer and distillery manager, 3, 76
Fullarton, James, son of Archibald, Scotia, 23, 75
Fullarton, Margaret, wife of William Beith, 21
Fulton, Mary (*née* Mitchell), Drumore, 62, 63, 64, 123
Fulton, Robert, merchant, 62, 63, 64

Gaelic language, 19, 20, 48, 61, 79, 93, 124, 126, 140, 144, 170, 171, 174, 177, 186, 188, 196, 213, 223, 230, 251
Galbraith families, 44, 63, 76-77, 100, 107, 115, 125, 176, 230
Galbraith, Provost John, 19, 34, 76-77, 88, 137, 153, 242, 280
Gardiner, Arthur H., distiller, 29, 77-78
Gardiner, Robert, manager, Lochruan, 78, 135
Gardiner, Robert, illicit distiller, 78
gas works, 10, 130, 240
Germany, 14, 60, 62, 65, 95
Gibson International Ltd., 89
Gibson, Dr William, Campbeltown, 207
Gigha, 11, 118, 226
Gilkison family, 6, 79, 251
Gilkison, Peter, Lochside, 79, 118, 136
Gillies, A., & Co., 85, 88
Gillies, Flora, Hazelburn, 244
Girvan, James Hunter, draff manager, 79

Glasgow, 7, 8, 9, 24, 27, 29, 33, 36, 61, 65, 71, 75, 76, 77, 90, 96, 98, 100, 103, 105, 109, 113, 116, 134, 148, 154, 156, 157, 158, 162, 164, 167, 174, 175, 179, 181, 185, 188, 191, 209, 222, 223, 232, 234, 236, 250, 251, 253, 257, 261, 292
Glasgow, University of, 23, 50, 110, 187, 244
Glenalbyn Distillery, 142
Glen, Ann, historian, 27, 51, 234
Glendarroch Distillery – see Glenfyne Distillery
Glendronach Distillery, 142
Glendullan Distillery, 148
Glenfyne Distillery, 36, 203, 292-93
Glengilp Distillery – see Glenfyne Distillery
Glengyle Distillery, 80-82, 188, 189, 192, 193, 196, 203, 235, 240, 258, 289
Gleniffer Distillery, 36
Glenkinchie Distillery, 185
Glenlivet Distillery, 37
Glenlussa (place-name), 5, 64, 97, 174, 193
'Glenlussa' blended whisky, 97
Glen Nevis & Ardlussa Warehouses Ltd., 84, 248
Glen Nevis Distillery, 11, 27, 81, 82-84, 88, 142, 161, 226, 247, 258, 289
Glenramskill Distillery, 29, 85-87, 107
Glen, Robert, Bulloch, Lade & Co., 80

Glen Rothes Distillery, 37, 230
Glen Scotia Distillery (pre-1935 as 'Scotia'), 15, 16, 24, 27, 31, 32, 36, 55, 76, 82, 83, 85, 88-89, 142, 152, 153, 162, 177, 199, 200, 202, 203, 225, 228, 230, 231, 233, 236, 240, 243, 246, 247, 253, 255, 258, 264, 289
Glenside Distillery, 4, 5, 89-91, 112, 117, 142, 183, 200, 253
Glentauchers Distillery, 138
Glenturret Distillery, 12
golf, 28, 78, 95, 99, 104, 109, 148, 152, 167, 189, 201
Gosson, Charles, Nantes seaman, 15
Grace, W. G., 96
Graham, Donald or Daniel, schoolteacher, 160-61
Grangemouth Bonding Company, 91
Grant, A. B. & Co., 92
Grant, James, ironmonger, 89, 92, 252
Grant, John, distiller, 89, 92-94, 112, 116, 196, 246, 252
Grant, John Mactaggart, son of above, 44, 94
Grant, John, publican, 10
Greenlees families, 8, 9, 28, 29, 30, 35, 40, 42, 44, 48, 50, 53, 73, 89, 94-109, 110, 114, 117, 118, 129, 130, 137, 142, 154, 176, 177, 179, 186, 188, 192, 195, 225, 226, 233, 235, 253, 254, 257, 258, 259, 267
Greenlees Brothers, 9, 29, 73, 95-99, 107, 114, 124, 147, 150, 233, 257, 259

Greenock, 7, 41, 70, 76, 87, 123, 156, 172, 222
Grogan, Jim, Glen Scotia, 135
Gulliver, James G., 88, 109-11

Haig, William, distiller, 41, 111
Hall, The, High Street, 42
Hancock family, 89, 91, 93, 112
Harvey/Harvie families, 65, 73, 106, 112-13, 117, 151, 176, 181, 194-95, 196
Haston, Dugal, mountaineer, 170
Hazelbank, now Ardshiel Hotel, 42, 49, 108
Hazelburn Distillery, 9, 17, 53, 62, 96, 97, 99, 101, 104, 114-15, 122, 123, 145, 150, 159, 168, 203, 221, 228, 231, 243, 249, 286, 288
Henderson, Hector, distiller, 35, 115-16, 171, 252
Hendry, Robert, property valuer, 289
Herd, Moira, 237
herdsman's horn, 209
Highland Distillers Company, 102
Highland Distillery, 74, 90, 92, 93, 116-17, 172
High Street, nameless distillery in, 101, 117-18
Hillcoat, Robert & Sons, 36
Hogg, James, coal-mine manager, 130
Holland, 13, 51, 60, 61
Honeyman, John, Highland Distillery, 116
Houghton, Joe, trades union organiser, 121-22
Huie families, 10, 17, 47, 74, 165

Hunter, Isabella, Temperance campaigner, 119, 250
Hunter, James, Highland historian, 198
Hunter, Peter, Lochside Distillery, 118, 136
Hunter, Robert, Lochruan, 118-19, 134, 181
Hunter, William Sr., owner of distilleries & watch-maker, 119, 136, 194
Hunter, William Jr., watch-maker & Temperance campaigner, 119, 249

illicit whisky & distillers, 11, 57, 69, 78, 126, 127, 140, 160, 172, 175, 176, 198-99, 213, 276-79
Illinois, USA, 73, 118, 193, 266
India, 7, 48, 113, 143, 153, 167, 180, 181, 233
industrial accidents, 39, 68, 75, 79, 120-21, 130, 138, 145, 157, 162, 172, 201, 208, 270-73
industrial unrest, 121-22
Inland Revenue – see Excisemen
Inland Revenue Literary Association, 69
Innes, Alexander, I. R. Supervisor, 69
Innes, Peter M., manager, Hazelburn, 122
insurance companies, 10, 200, 256, 257
Ireland, 25, 58, 59, 68, 80, 154, 158-59, 175, 202, 226, 228
Islay, 12, 22, 32, 40, 56, 61, 62, 74, 85, 92, 93, 103, 115, 123, 134, 135, 148, 152, 159, 162, 163, 197, 198, 202, 204, 221, 225, 290
Italy, 238, 239

Japan, 238, 243-44
Johnston families, 31, 64, 73, 122-24, 133-34, 150, 245
Jura, Island of, 7, 12, 32, 90

Keith, Archibald, manager, Albyn, 3, 124-25
Kelly, Charles, distiller, 35, 125, 252
Kelly, Rev Daniel, 56, 126
Kelly, Neil Munro, I.R. officer, 126-27
Kelly, Peter, farmer and peat-cutter, 203
Keys, John, Caledonian Distillery, 31
'killogie', 204
Kilmichael Farm, 163, 164, 245
Kilmun, 25, 123
Kinloch Distillery, 64, 65, 66, 82, 103, 120, 128-29, 148, 182, 253, 258, 289, 253
Kintyre Agricultural Society, 28, 46
Kintyre Club, 6, 10, 27, 42, 73, 76, 79, 80, 103, 106, 108, 110, 119, 134, 148, 153, 159, 160, 161, 164, 169, 173, 175, 201, 209, 221, 251, 259, 265, 268-69
Kintyre Distillery, 81, 31, 108, 109, 129-30, 168, 214
Kintyre Farmers, 82
Kintyre Fish Protection & Angling Club, 255
Kintyre Literary Association, 167

Kintyre Scientific Association, 70
Kirk Close, 166, 195
Kirkwood, Alexander, merchant, 130, 179

Lagavulin Distillery, 159
Lagnagarach, 21, 73
Lamb, Robert, lawyer, 128, 171
Land Restoration League, 199
Langlands family, 53, 125, 243, 256
Langwill families, 77, 79, 119, 136, 193, 210, 243, 251
Largieside, 41, 126, 140, 144, 151, 153, 162, 169, 176, 187, 198
Linlithgow Distillery, 12, 37
Lintmill village, 4, 53, 109, 167
Littlemill Distillery, 115, 116
Liverpool, 93, 129, 132, 146, 186, 225
Lochgilphead, 18, 184
Loch-head Distillery, 6, 8, 10, 22, 37, 74, 82, 131-33, 162, 170, 177, 182, 191, 203, 221, 240, 245, 253
Lochindaal Distillery, 22, 74, 93, 132, 162, 221, 232
Loch Katrine Distillery, 120, 123
Loch Lomond Distillery Co., 89
Loch Lomond Group, 82, 89
Lochruan Distillery, 3, 55, 56, 62, 78, 118, 133-35, 154, 156, 158, 167, 168, 262, 263, 286
Loch Ruan reservoir, 135, 255
Lochside Distillery, 79, 118, 119, 136
London, 34, 39, 65, 73, 94, 96, 98, 99, 101, 147, 254, 257, 258
Londonderry, 25, 175

Longrow Distillery, 18, 76, 103, 108, 109, 136-37, 145, 168, 202, 214, 253
Longrow (street), 11, 137, 166, 248
Lonndahl, Carl, film-maker, 200
Lorimer, David G., manager, Ardlussa, 8, 138
'Lorne Highland Whisky', 97, 98
Loudon, Norman, film producer, 99, 257
Louise, Princess, 22, 97
Love families, 79, 149, 153, 171, 246
Lowrie, W. P. & Co., 36, 52, 56, 135, 138, 221, 289-90
Lowrie, William Phaup, 138
Loynachan, Duncan, workman, Campbeltown Distillery, 138-39
Lyle, Archibald, Supervisor of Excise, 70
Lynskey Tribunal, 24

Macaffer, 'Madame' Maggie (née MacCallum), singer, 144
McAllister, Margaret, wife of Joseph Hancock, 89, 93, 112
McAllister, William, brewer, killed, 120
McArthur, Duncan, seaman, drowned, 228
MacCallum, Donald, workman, Albyn, 139-141
MacCallum, Donald, Auchinbreck, illicit distiller, 177
MacCallum, Duncan, distiller, 7, 27, 59, 62, 83, 88, 90, 108, 121, 129, 141-43, 167, 182, 227, 240, 247, 258, 259

323

McCallum, Edward 'Iver', brewer, Campbeltown Distillery, 143-44
McCallum, Rev John, Kincardine, 66
McCallum, Neil, distillery workman, 145
MacCallum, Ronald, maltman at Dalaruan & piper, 145-46
McCartney, Sir Paul, 245, 266
McClement, J. B., burgh assessor, 288, 290
McCorkindale, Archibald, distiller, 40, 54, 145-46
MacCorquodale, Rev Donald, 41, 49
McCulloch, Duncan, distiller, 116
McDiarmid, Dugald Stewart, Greenlees Brothers, 147
MacDonald, Aeneas, whisky writer, 259
Macdonald & Muir, Leith, 104
MacDonald, David, whisky-blender, 147-48, 252
Macdonald, Rev Donald John, 48
Macdonald, Greenlees & Williams Ltd., 9, 148
McEachran, Charles, distiller, 35, 149-50, 184, 225
McEachran, David, blacksmith, 127
MacEachran, Hector, Meadowburn, 179
McEachran, J. J., Cardiff, 150
McEwan, Murdo, manager, Hazelburn, 122
McEwing, William, distillery manager, 150-51, 259
Macfarlane, Lieut John, High Street distillery, 117

McGougan, Archibald, Scottish Malt Distillers employee, 221
MacGregor, John, town herd, 209
MacGregor, Captain John, 25
MacGregor, Lieut Robert, 25, 26, 202
MacGregor, Rob Roy, 82
McIntyre, Alexander, mashman, Albyn, 141, 151, 170
MacIntyre, Alex, mountaineer, 170
Macintyre, Dugald Campbell, manager, Glenside, 90
Macintyre gamekeeping family, Kilchenzie, 183
McIntyre, John, & Co., 148
McIntyre, Malcolm, Port Ellen Distillery, 152
MacKay, John, peat-cutter, 203
MacKeith, Agnes, wife of Edward MacCallum, 144
MacKelvie, Alexander, distiller, 70, 88, 152-53, 165, 225
McKendrick, Dugald, farmer, Tomaig, 206
MacKenzie, Bill, whisky-broker, 56
Mackenzie, Bridget, piping historian, 146, 210
MacKenzie, Rev D. F., Campbeltown, 249-50
Mackenzie, James H., local historian, 89, 222, 223, 297 (note 163)
McKerral, Andrew, historian, 174
McKerral, John, workman, Glenside, 90-91
McKerral, Peter, farmer, Brunerican, 18

McKersie family, 3, 17, 34, 58, 87, 89, 105, 108, 112, 124, 134, 136, 139, 153-59, 192, 215, 224, 225, 227, 248, 262, 267

Mackie & Co., Distillers, 114, 115, 159, 262

Mackie, Sir Peter, 159-60

MacKinnon's Distillery, 8, 160-61

MacKinnon, Duncan – see MacKinnon's Distillery

MacKinnon, Sir William, 161, 180

McKinven, Donald, son of John, below, 162

McKinven, Jack, writer, artist and musician, 263

McKinven, John, Glen Nevis, 161

McLachlan, Lachlan, distillery workman, 162

McLaren, Duncan, boy drowned in well, 235

McLean, Donald, seaman, 16

McLean, Captain Duncan, 225

McLean, D., commission agent, 164

MacLellan, Peter, Meadowburn, 179

McLennan, George, distiller, 93, 116

MacLeod, Alick J., editor *Campbeltown Courier*, 189

Macleod, Rev Dr Norman, 172

MacMichael, Rev Neil, 41, 49

McMillan, Alexander, distillery manager, 162-63, 191, 248

McMillan, Daniel, mashman, 163

McMillan, Duncan, distiller, 35, 164, 180

McMillan, James, jailed for assault, 141-42

McMillan, John, Drumore Distillery, 62, 63

McMillan, Malcolm, Mountain Dew, 196

McMurchy families, 28, 29, 41, 45, 53, 86, 128, 131, 152, 165-66, 177, 206, 242, 248, 249

MacNab, Archibald, dyer, 245

McNair families, 29, 63, 65, 86, 113, 176, 179, 186, 251

MacNair, Isabella, Glenside, 89, 93, 112, 184

McNair, Nathaniel, wright, 52, 223, 234

McNaughton, Smollett, seaman, 58

Macneals of Ugadale, 101

McNeill, Amelia, 86

Macnish, Neil, 35, 166-67

McPhee, John, mashman, Albyn, 178

MacPherson, Archibald, 60, 167-68, 262, 263

McSporran, Charles C., Springbank, 168-69, 236

McSporran, Donald, distillery manager, 168-69

McSporran, Morris, mashman, 170, 192

Mactaggart & Henderson, 252

Mactaggart, C. & D., solicitors, Campbeltown, 78, 171

Mactaggart/McTaggart families, 18, 33, 35, 39, 78, 92, 93, 115, 116, 119, 128, 144, 158, 170-74, 176, 222, 233, 240, 250, 252, 253-54, 276-79

McTaggart, William, artist, 119, 160

McWilliam family, 6, 174-75, 251

325

Madeira, 45
maltsters, 25, 175-77, 186
Martin, Charles, joiner, 83, 188, 226
Martin, Captain Duncan, 225
mashmen, 7, 80, 123, 125, 163, 170, 177-78
Mason, William, workman, Benmore, 178-79
Matheson, Murdoch, draff ship fatality, 58
Mathieson, Dugald, Benmore, 22
Mavrocordato, A. H., barley superintendent, 16
Mayo, David, Campbeltown, 239
Meadowburn Distillery, 30, 47, 48, 104, 130, 179-80, 201, 245
Melville, Captain George, distiller, 35, 164, 180-81, 252
Mile-End Distillery, 181
Millburn Distillery, 200
Miller, A. S., manager, Lochhead, 182-83
Miller, D.S., distillery manager, 183
Miller, Jessie, co-founder of Glenside, 89, 93, 183-84
Milloy, Archibald, Campbeltown Distillers' Association, 35, 184
missions, Christian, 48, 64
Mitchell families, 5, 6, 45, 62, 63, 64, 73, 80-82, 94, 102, 109, 134, 155, 156, 169, 176, 185-93, 211, 226, 234, 235, 248, 265, 266
Montgomery, Andrew, distiller, 5, 193-94, 258
Montgomery families, 194
Montgomery, Lucy Maud, novelist, 194

Morrison, Robert, boy trapped in Glen Nevis, 84
Mossfield Distillery, 119, 194-95
Mountain Dew Distillery, 196, 256
Moy farm, 107, 114, 227
Moy schooner, 107, 227
Muir, Alexander, cooper, 206
Muir, Hugh, mashman, Glengyle, 196-97
Mull, 32, 61
Murdoch, James, manager, Ardlussa, 8, 178, 197
Murdoch, John, I.R. officer & land rights activist, 56, 197-99, 249, 280-82
Murray, Jim, whisky writer, 32, 265

Napier, Captain James, 33, 88, 199
Newlands, Hugh, TGWU, 62
New York, 15, 98, 147, 186
New Zealand, 119, 127, 143, 169, 200
Nimrod, HMS, 135
Northampton, HMS, 54
Norway, 51, 143

Oban Distillery, 221
O'Brien, J. &. P. & Co. Ltd., 22, 132, 221
'Old Parr' blended whisky, 97
Olsén, Gottfrid, Swedish distiller, 200
Orr families, 52, 89, 90, 117, 195, 196, 200-1

Pacy, Joseph, Excise officer, 66-67
Paterson, Charles, manager, Glen Scotia, 264

Paterson, Duncan, Meadowburn, 201
Paterson, James, Meadowburn, 179
Paterson, Richard, whisky-blender, 85
Pearson, James, I.R. supervisor, Campbeltown, 28
peat & cutting of, 9, 17, 23, 39, 130, 160, 201-4, 212
Pennant, Thomas, 13
Peploe, S. J., Scottish artist, 257
photographers, 180, 220
Pibroch, whisky coaster, 204, 221
pig-keeping, 57, 207
Poland, 14
poor roll & poorhouse, 10, 11, 147, 162, 164, 168, 179, 201, 229, 264
Port Ellen Distillery, 152
Portugul, 16, 226
pot-ale, 180, 204-7
'puffers', 204, 228
Pulteney Distillery, 200, 207-8
Pursell, Archibald, manager, Dalintober, 208

Ralston families, 27, 28, 29, 86-87, 107, 108, 117, 128, 130, 207
Reid families, 41, 45, 54, 55, 63, 139, 147, 208-11, 234-35
Rennie, J. C., ship broker, 15, 150
Revenue cutters, 67, 176, 181
Rieclachan Distillery, 73, 80, 85, 112, 113, 178, 186, 187, 188, 189, 192, 193, 211-13, 228, 252, 266, 267
Ritchie, Alexander, Sanda, 227
Robertson, Alexander & Co., Liverpool, 93

Robertson & Baxter, 90
Ross, Alexander, headmaster, 93, 213
Ross, George, I. R. officer, 213
Ross, John, distiller, 19, 70, 130, 137, 213-19, 222, 223, 241
Rothesay, 58, 225
Rowatt, Dr Charles, 171, 219, 258
rugby, 44
Russia, 14
Rundle, Warwick James, Customs & Excise officer, 220
Ryburn families, 28, 29, 94, 195

Saddler's Close, 239
schools, 50, 93, 110, 118, 162, 213
Scotch Whisky Association, 32
Scotch Whisky Distillers Ltd., 83, 168, 292
Scotia Distillery – see Glen Scotia Distillery
Scottish Dried Grains Company, 60-61, 283-85
Scottish Licensed Trade Defence Association, 175
Scottish Malt Distillers Ltd., 133, 204, 221
Scottish Society for the Propogation of Christian Knowledge, 223
Seafield House (now Hotel), 95, 102, 103, 188
Seggie Distillery, Fife, 111
Shepperton Studios, 99, 258
Sherriff, J. B. & Co. Ltd., 132, 163, 221
Sherriff family, 221, 265, 310 (note 707)
ships & shipping, 13-16, 32-33, 38, 58-59, 76, 80, 87, 114, 202, 203, 222-28, 276-78

327

shooting, 78, 139, 193
Sillars, Archibald, mashman, Rieclachan, 178, 212, 228
Sillars, James, son of above, manager, Rieclachan, 228
Sinclair, Daniel, mashman, Benmore, 229
Sinclair, Donald, maltman, Springbank, 236
singers, 68, 75, 95-96, 144, 145, 158, 193, 251
Smith, Christopher Vetters, John Walker & Sons, 229
Smith, Captain Donald, 225, 226
Smith, Dugald, distillery workman, 230
Smith, Harry James, manager, Glen Scotia, 230
Smith, Henry Michael, manager, Glen Scotia, 230
Smith, Rev Dr John, Gaelic minister, Campbeltown, 13, 57
Smith, Rev John Burns, Greenock, 102
Smith, John James, manager, Hazelburn, 231
Smith, Peter, secretary, Scotia, 231
Smith, William Jr., author, 85, 232
smoke pollution, 232-34
South Africa, 7, 107, 143
Southend, Kintyre, 139, 148, 149, 193, 199, 209, 210, 248, 251, 258
Springbank Distillery, 8, 16, 17, 25, 32, 39, 72, 80, 88, 104, 115, 124, 136, 137, 169, 177, 185, 187, 190, 192, 203, 205, 208, 221, 233, 234-39, 252, 255, 265, 266

Springbank 50-year-old malt, 237-39
Springside Distillery, 44, 239
Stalker, Charles, 240
Stephen, John, manager, Loch Ruan, 135
Stewart, Agnes, wife of Archibald Mitchell, 188
Stewart, Archibald, solicitor, Campbeltown, 289
Stewart, Dugald, farmer, Tonrioch, 6, 79, 188
Stewart, Captain Duncan, 205
Stewart, Galbraith & Co. Ltd., 27, 83, 88, 142, 167, 173, 240, 259
Stewart, Isabella, wife of Peter Gilkison, 79
Stewart, James, distiller, 31, 34, 35, 70, 75, 83, 88, 119, 240-43, 245
Stewart, Jean, wife of Archibald Andrew, 5, 6
Stewart, Jeanie, 242
Stewart, John, Excise officer, 184
Stewart, John Lorne of Coll, 205
Stewart, John, SSPCK schoolmaster, 223
Stewart, Peter, Caledonian Distillery, 31, 196, 243
Stewart, Sarah, Y.W.C.A., 243
Stirk, David, whisky writer, 27, 43, 83, 85
St. Malo, 15, 16, 225
'Strathduie' blended whisky, 174
Stronachie Distillery, 148
Sweden, 14, 200
Syme sisters, Fife, 41, 42, 112

'Taddy Loch' reservoir, 256
Taketsuru, Masataka, 122, 243-44
Talisker Distillery, 148, 244
Tangy Loch, 256
Taylor family, distillers & builders, 6, 64, 131, 132, 177, 179, 245-46
Taylor, Colonel James, farmer, Machrimore, 17
Taylor, John, workman, Springside, 39
Temperance movement – see Total abstinence
Templeton families, 62-64, 193, 209-10, 214, 228
Thistle Distillery – see Mountain Dew
Thom, John, Collector of Inland Revenue, 246
Thomson, Hugh, manager, Glen Scotia, 12, 246-47
Thomson, Samuel, distillery manager and whisky-blender, 57, 85, 163, 247-48
Thomson, Dr T. Harvey, Campbeltown, 207
Toberanrigh Distillery, 190, 248, 266
Tobermory Distillery, 238
Tolmie, Archibald, Scottish Malt Distillers employee, 221
Total abstinence, 106, 119, 198, 199, 218, 243, 248-50, 280
tours, whisky, 264
trades unions, 62, 121-22
Train & McIntyre Ltd., 148
Train, Thomas, 79, 148, 250-52
Train, Thomas, & Co., 148, 250, 252

tuberculosis, 45, 47, 145, 153
Tullymet Distillery, 36
Tweedie, Andrew, shepherd, 145

Uigle farm, 174
Union Distillery, 92, 93, 115, 116, 125, 171, 252
USA, 30, 72, 73, 98, 110, 118, 125, 139, 143, 146, 151, 158, 163, 182, 188, 191, 193, 266

Volunteers, Artillery, 106, 107, 149, 189
Volunteers, Rifle, 28, 34, 50, 54, 73, 78, 100, 145

Wales, 16, 150, 226
Walker, Hiram & Sons, 88
Walker, John & Sons, 229
Wallace, Robert, I.R. officer, & family, 47, 104, 108, 252-53
warehouses, bonded, 9, 23, 54, 55, 81, 83, 84, 85, 92, 115, 129, 131, 132, 133, 134, 135, 137, 153, 168, 185, 196, 221, 236, 239, 260-1, 262
Warm Water Close, 31
water supplies, 31 (hot), 55, 131, 133, 253-56
Watson (local) families, 61, 152, 165, 171, 196, 245, 256-57
Watson, John B., Scottish Dried Grains Co., 61
Watson, Peter, Mountain Dew, 196, 243, 256-57
Webb, Fr James, 172, 277, 279
Weir-Loudon, David N., 96, 257
Weir, Robert, builder, 9, 115, 285
Weir, Rev Walter, 96, 257
Well Close, 237

329

West Coast Motors – see Craig Brothers
West Highland Distillery, 5, 6, 193, 258
West Highland Malt Distilleries, 8, 27, 56, 81, 83, 85, 88, 90, 129, 142, 240, 247, 258-59, 287
West Indies, 4, 5, 143, 257
Wet Review, 78
whisky, blending of, 36, 65, 85, 96, 97, 174, 229, 236, 237, 259-60
Whisky Enquiry (1891), 65, 259-61
whisky, illicit – see illicit whisky & distillers
'Whisky Panic' (1854), 261
whisky, theft of, 261-64, 274-75
White Horse Distillers Ltd., 114, 159, 288
Wilkie, T., Glenside Distillery, 89, 112
Williams, William, & Sons, 148
Wilson families, 5, 78
World War, First, 28, 37, 72, 74, 75, 84, 95, 108, 138, 140, 141, 150, 152, 156, 158, 159, 160, 163, 183, 185, 189, 197, 236, 250, 265, 287
World War, Second, 24, 81, 135, 169, 183, 236, 246-47
Wright & Greig, 221
Wright family, 191, 265-66
Wright, Hedley G., 17, 82, 235, 237, 265-66, 286
Wylie families, 76, 87, 176, 186, 191, 211, 234, 248, 266-67

yachting & cruising, 46, 99, 143
Yoker Distillery, 27, 145

www.ingramcontent.com/pod-product-compliance
Lightning Source LLC
Chambersburg PA
CBHW050201240426
43671CB00013B/2206